SOUND AND VISION

SOUND AND VISION

SIXTY YEARS OF MOTION PICTURE SOUNDTRACKS

JON BURLINGAME

BILLBOARD BOOKS

AN IMPRINT OF WATSON-GUPTILL PUBLICATIONS/NEW YORK

Senior Acquisitions Editor: Bob Nirkind

Editors: Liz Harvey & Carrie Cantor

Production Manager: Hector Campbell

Book and cover design: Leah Lococo Ltd.

Copyright © 2000 by Jon Burlingame

First published by Billboard Books,
an imprint of Watson-Guptill Publications,
a division of BPI Communications, Inc.
770 Broadway New York, New York 10003

Library of Congress Cataloging-in-Publication Data
for this title can be obtained from the Library of Congress
Library of Congress Card Number: 00-103566
ISBN: 0-8230-8427-2

Manufactured in the United States of America

Typeset in Adobe Garamond

First printing, 2000

1 2 3 4 5 6 7 8 9 / 08 07 06 05 04 03 02 01 00

The cover names only one author, but he had a lot of help in preparing this volume. First, a big thank-you to Bob Nirkind for commissioning this work and for his enormous patience in waiting for the final product; to BMI's Lisa Feldman for suggesting me for this project in the first place; and to Carrie Cantor for her first-rate editing skills.

Thanks also go to my many friends in the music and film industries who helped with my questions along the way: film-music historian Clifford McCarty; composers David Raksin, Bruce Babcock, John W. Morgan, and Alex Shapiro; music supervisor Joel Sill; Miles Kreuger of the Institute of the American Musical; my colleagues at *Daily Variety*, notably Steven Gaydos and Steve Chagollan; Marc Zubatkin at *Billboard*; ace photographer Peter Sherman; and, for various favors and assistance, Lori Barth, Bob Benson, Hanna Bolte, Jeff Bond, Lance Bowling, Dan Carlin, Linda Danly, Lois Dilivio, Vic Ghidalia, Gina Handy, Preston Jones, Lukas Kendall, Nancy Knutsen, Royce Malm, Dave Mitchell, Kevin Mulhall, Mike Murray, Jeannie Pool, Craig Spaulding, John Waxman, and Steve Winogradsky.

At the University of Southern California, special thanks go to Ned Comstock in the cinema-TV library and Dace Taube at the university's Regional History Center; at the University of California at Los Angeles, to the music library's Stephen Fry, Timothy Edwards, and Stephen Davison; at Brigham Young University, archivist James D'Arc; and at the Margaret Herrick Library of the Academy of Motion Picture Arts & Sciences, Stacey Behlmer, Warren Sherk, and Russ Good. *Billboard*, in particular its online member service, has been of enormous help throughout, as was the awards department of the National Academy of Recording Arts & Sciences.

Special thanks to my friends at various record labels, including Chris Kuchler, Lisa Okikawa, Bruce Kimmel, Andrea Sine, and Bob Townson at Varèse Sarabande; Marilyn Egol at RCA/BMG; Gary LeMel and Bob Merlis at Warner Bros.; Olga Makrias at Universal Music; Maria Kleinman at Walt Disney Records; Richard Henderson at Milan; Tom Null at Citadel; Doug Fake and Roger Feigelson at Intrada; Shari Sedlis at Silva Screen; Laurence Vittes and Joshua Cheek at Marco Polo; Susan Jacobs and Amy Kolker at Sony Classical; Christine Bergren at MGM; and Tom Cavanaugh at 20th Century–Fox. Composer representatives and publicists, including Ronni Chasen, Katurah Clarke, Ray Costa, Lynda Dorf, Laura Engel, Michael Gorfaine, Richard Kraft, Maureen O'Connor, and Jamie Richardson, have been supportive as well.

And finally to the cream of the crop: my good and dear friends, writer-producers Nick Redman, Steven Smith, and Rudy Behlmer, who received calls at all hours asking about obscure films and scores that they invariably knew, often owned, and were ready to discuss; and my wife, the warm, generous, and exceedingly patient Marilee Bradford—indefatigable researcher, first-rate copy editor, and award-winning soundtrack-album producer.

J.B.

April 2000

I suppose my taste in movie music could be called eclectic. My favorites range from Max Steiner's *King Kong* to Howard Shore's *Ed Wood*. I've always loved Erich Wolfgang Korngold (especially his classic scores for *The Adventures of Robin Hood* and *Kings Row*), but I'm equally fond of Danny Elfman.

Finally, there is a book that offers practical information and informed opinions on this enormous topic, and covers everyone from Shostakovich to Henry Mancini.

Nearly everyone likes movie music; the hitch is, some people know it and some don't.

The average movie-watcher probably doesn't think much about background music when he or she is enjoying a film. In fact, it used to be said that if someone noticed the music, the composer wasn't doing his job. The score is supposed to be an integral part of a film, not a separate entity that calls attention to itself. That's a nice theory, but let's face it: great movie music does get noticed.

There has always been a small but loyal cadre of soundtrack aficionados. The same people who bought Miklós Rózsa's 78-rpm discs of *The Jungle Book* and *Spellbound* in the 1940s probably purchased LPs of Max Steiner scores in the 1950s. Then, in the late 1970s and early '80s, John Williams's majestic scores for *Star Wars*, *Close Encounters of the Third Kind*, and *Superman* brought the movie soundtrack to a new plateau of public awareness.

Nearly twenty years later, the enormous (and unprecedented) sales of James Horner's soundtrack for *Titanic* caused the record industry to reconsider the impact—and value—of movie scores once again.

Major symphonies around the world now regularly include programs of film music in their repertoires, and, in an industry where ageism is a sad fact of life, such gifted Hollywood veterans as Jerry Goldsmith and Elmer Bernstein are busier than ever plying their trade. Movie scores are indeed America's new classical music.

There are few chroniclers of the film music scene as astute and accurate as Jon Burlingame, and this book is a valuable gift to anyone who's just getting hooked on soundtracks. Because there are so many records and CDs in the marketplace, including original soundtracks, reissues, re-recordings, and knockoffs, it's great to have a guide to help navigate those muddy waters.

Jon's concise history of film music—and its relationship to the record business—will, I hope, pique the interest of young people and perhaps steer them in new directions. If one admires Thomas Newman's score for *American Beauty*, why not try his father Alfred's great music for *All About Eve*, written fifty years earlier but just as exciting to listen to today?

Now if you'll excuse me, I want to finish listening to Ennio Morricone's score for *The Legend of 1900*. . . .

LEONARD MALTIN
Los Angeles, March, 2000

Leonard Maltin is best known for his annual paperback reference, Leonard Maltin's Movie & Video Guide. *He is also a familiar face on television, where he has appeared on* Entertainment Tonight *since 1982, and comments regularly on the Encore and Odyssey cable networks. He serves as film critic and columnist for* Playboy *magazine, and teaches at the University of Southern California.*

Errol Flynn swashbuckles across the silver screen to the fanfares of Erich Wolfgang Korngold. Vivien Leigh swears she'll never be hungry again to the strains of Max Steiner's "Tara" theme. Ex–galley slave Charlton Heston prepares for a Roman chariot race to the martial music of Miklós Rózsa. Clint Eastwood squints across western vistas to a strange, half-screamed, half-whistled tune by Ennio Morricone.

Marshal Gary Cooper waits for killers arriving on the noon train to Tex Ritter's "Do Not Forsake Me, Oh My Darling." A confused Dustin Hoffman returns home from college to Simon & Garfunkel's "The Sounds of Silence." John Travolta struts through the streets of New York to the rhythms of the Bee Gees' "Stayin' Alive." Patrick Swayze and Demi Moore wallow in wet clay to the Righteous Brothers' old classic "Unchained Melody."

You don't even have to identify the movies. The music and the images are an intertwined memory, one element unimaginable without the other.

Movie soundtracks were once an afterthought, both on the part of movie executives (who didn't think anyone listened to the music in their films) and record executives (who didn't think anybody would buy music that no one listened to in the first place). Now, with albums like *City of Angels* and *Titanic* selling by the millions, movie soundtracks are big business. Entire divisions, both in the movie studios and at the major labels, are devoted exclusively to marketing music from movies.

This book is a general, all-around guide to the world of movie soundtracks. It's divided into three parts: a history of the field from its beginnings to the complex international business it has become; an overview of many of the composers who have written music for movies over the years, each with a brief biographical sketch and a discussion of their best work as made available on long-playing records or compact discs; and a look at movie musicals and song-compilation scores that have been issued over the years, many of them still available today.

This is not intended to be an all-encompassing directory of movie soundtracks. Rather, it's a selected guide to the most notable, the award-winning, and the biggest-selling soundtracks from their start in 1938 to the present—a basic repertoire of music composed for motion pictures.

In choosing the discs that adequately and faithfully represented both composers and movies, a handful of basic rules seemed to apply. All of the records chosen had to be legitimate, licensed commercial recordings available for sale to the public in the United States. It should be pointed out that not all of the records cited on the following pages are truly "original soundtrack" recordings—that is, the same recorded music tracks that accompany the film. Few true soundtracks appeared before the 1950s, and through the 1960s and '70s some composers tended to re-record their scores for commercial release on disc. Older scores were recorded en masse beginning in the 1970s, and because they have become such a crucial element of the contemporary soundtrack market, it seemed appropriate to include them.

I have tried to avoid listing foreign discs but have done so in a handful of cases simply because the music is a cornerstone in the canon of a composer (e.g., Michel Legrand, whose film music is woefully underrepresented on CD in the U.S.); in those cases, I have included only discs that can be easily purchased as imports in American record stores. In addition, I have attempted to focus on those records featuring performances conducted, supervised, or authorized by the composer for the truest musical representation of the scores.

The label and number after each title is the compact disc number, unless otherwise indicated (by "LP"). Luckily, of the hundreds of albums listed on the following pages, nearly all are or were recently available on compact disc; those that aren't can still be found in used-vinyl stores and the used-CD bins at many record outlets.

No privately issued records, promotional discs, or bootleg pressings are included (at least to my knowledge). The shocking proliferation of overseas bootleg discs—illegal, unauthorized "soundtracks" sold by the thousands to cater to the whims of fanatic film-score collectors—should be discouraged at every turn. A handful of enterprising labels are now issuing classic soundtracks on a limited basis (often via mail order), and those efforts should be encouraged.

All dates throughout this book refer to the year of release of the film, which is not always the same as the soundtrack.

My intent was to create a single book that could serve as a ready reference to film composers, a handy and noncritical guide to classic and bestselling soundtracks, and an informative historical look at the world of movie music since the advent of talkies. I hope you will find it useful.

Movie Music? Who'd Buy *That*?

Music and movies have been inseparable since the first flickering images crossed a room in Paris in 1895. Of course, in those days the piano was used as much to cover up projector noise as to add any dramatic or aesthetic value to the moment. But before long music became an integral part of the filmgoing experience.

Interestingly, the development of the gramophone and the first commercial recordings paralleled that of the early motion-picture industry, and at similarly rapid pace. In fact, the first 33$\frac{1}{3}$-rpm discs were produced in 1926 by Bell Laboratories for Warner Bros.' soundtrack for John Barrymore's romantic adventure *Don Juan*—the first Vitaphone feature containing synchronized music (by William Axt) and sound effects.

The vast majority of films continued to be silent, although exhibitors were by now accustomed to receiving full musical scores (played by pianists in the smaller houses, sometimes full orchestras in the big-city movie palaces) that occasionally incorporated popular songs. When savvy producers discovered that sheet music was a nifty marketing tool for their pictures—and sometimes produced a hit—they urged composers to incorporate tunes specifically written either for the score or as pure promotion for the picture.

The result was the movie song. Canadian bandleader Guy Lombardo's first big hit was "Charmaine," written for Dolores Del Rio's character in *What Price Glory?* (1926). "Charmaine" composer Erno Rapée followed that with "(I'm in

Heaven When I See You Smile) Diane," for Janet Gaynor in *Seventh Heaven* (1927), which generated a trio of top-20 hits in early 1928.

Perhaps the most successful exploitation of an early movie song came with "*Ramona*," written for the United Artists film and, like "Charmaine"—also written for Dolores Del Rio—a memorable waltz. Shrewd UA executives had Del Rio herself sing the song on a coast-to-coast radio broadcast six weeks before its May 1928 premiere as well as at several openings of the film. "Ramona" was inescapable on radio during the first half of the year, with four different versions in the top 20 (including best-selling versions by Gene Austin with Nat Shilkret's orchestra and Paul Whiteman & His Orchestra featuring Austin Young).

When Ramon Novarro strummed his ukelele and sang "The Pagan Love Song" (another waltz, this one by Arthur Freed and Nacio Herb Brown) in MGM's part-talkie *The Pagan* (1929), moviegoers—mostly swooning women, one guesses—rushed out to buy not only the sheet music but any available phonograph recording of the song. Within three months after the film's release, no fewer than three recordings had jumped into the nation's top 10.

Warner Bros.' colossal success with the Vitaphone sound in *The Jazz Singer* (1927), coupled with the public fascination for movie tunes, led to the inevitable explosion of "all talking, all singing, all dancing" movie musicals. The biggest beneficiaries were MGM (for whom songwriters Arthur Freed and Nacio Herb Brown wrote hits like

"Singin' in the Rain" and "Temptation") and Warner Bros. (whose Busby Berkeley films revitalized the already burned-out genre, with such now-classic Harry Warren–Al Dubin songs as "We're in the Money," "I Only Have Eyes for You," and "Lullaby of Broadway").

Still, no one considered releasing the film performances of these songs on phonograph records—the "original soundtrack," as they would come to be known. In the early 1930s, many song-and-dance performances were filmed live on the set, with all their attendant stage noise, multiple takes, and various angles, and were deemed unsuitable for release as phonograph records. Fresh (and often shorter) versions were arranged and performed by bands and vocalists the public knew and liked. Moviegoers who might have preferred the original artists and arrangements were regularly frustrated in their search at music stores.

The first exception to this rule came in January 1938, when Victor Records released "Songs From Walt Disney's *Snow White and the Seven Dwarfs*" (Victor J-8), an album of three 78-rpm discs offering eight Frank Churchill–Larry Morey songs from the animated feature. This was the first American original soundtrack album from a feature film—that is, movie music drawn directly from the film's soundtrack for a commercially released phonograph record—and it was a smash. All three discs charted, with the original renditions of "Whistle While You Work" and "Heigh Ho" becoming fixtures on radio's popular *Your Hit Parade* for four months and Adriana Caselotti (the voice of Snow White) reaching *Billboard*'s top 10 with "Some-day My Prince Will Come."

Despite the active extra-celluloid lives of movie tunes in the 1930s, the so-called "background music" that made so many films such compelling entertainment remained unrecorded and unavail-

able. In retrospect, it seems shocking that such classically styled scores as those of Viennese composer Erich Wolfgang Korngold (for such films as *The Sea Hawk,* 1940, or *Kings Row*, 1942) or the tremendously popular music of Max Steiner for *Gone With the Wind* (1939) would not find commercial release. (As late as 1951, not a single Korngold film theme was available on phonograph records.)

The craft of movie scoring, which began in somewhat tentative fashion in the early 1930s, had grown by leaps and bounds as composers discovered the secrets of marrying music and image. Steiner had gone from his 1933 triumph with RKO's *King Kong*, which combined romantic themes with dark, primitive rhythms, to the multithematic, Southern-flavored masterpiece of David O. Selznick's *Gone With the Wind* just six years later. 20th Century–Fox music director Alfred Newman had progressed from the Gershwinesque *Street Scene* (1931) to the romantic *Wuthering Heights* (1939). Korngold, perhaps the most respected composer in Hollywood by virtue of his background as a composer of "serious" concert music, had won Oscars for his rich symphonic tapestries for *Anthony Adverse* (1936) and *The Adventures of Robin Hood* (1938).

But film music fell through the cracks. It was not taken seriously by most critics. It was rarely noticed by the average filmgoer. And it was considered a poor commercial risk by the record companies. Despite its 19th-century classical roots and frequently memorable melodic themes, it was deemed neither classical nor popular. No one seriously believed movie music would sell.

Even *Gone With the Wind* couldn't break into the marketplace. Steiner's grand, sweeping "Tara" theme was inseparable from memories of Selznick's four-hour epic, winner of nine 1939 Oscars including Best Picture and for many years the biggest-grossing movie ever. Selznick asked his friend William S. Paley, chairman of the board of the Columbia Broadcasting System, to consider releasing the music. "I know that under ordinary circumstances the musical score of a picture couldn't be expected to sell records," he wrote, "but everything in connection with *Gone With the Wind* is apparently attracting such unprecedented attention that this may be the exception. And incidentally, the score is quite beautiful."

It didn't happen. Fifteen years later, Steiner was finally offered the opportunity to re-record and release a suite of his magnum opus (on a 10-inch RCA album totaling about 30 minutes). The soundtrack music itself wasn't released by MGM Records until 1967.

Another 1939 movie had a little more success: *The Wizard of Oz*, whose "Over the Rainbow" topped radio's *Your Hit Parade* for seven weeks in September and October. But again, it wasn't a true soundtrack album: Judy Garland performed two songs (one of them, "Over the Rainbow") with Victor Young's orchestra, and the Ken Darby Singers sang new versions of "We're Off to See the

Wizard," "Munchkinland," and others on a four-disc 78-rpm Decca set (A-74).

Songs from such family films, often perceived as children's fare, were apparently deemed marketable. Young re-recorded songs from the animated 1939 feature *Gulliver's Travels* (Decca A-100), and it was on a Disney package that the term "original sound track" first appeared. The February 1940 release of three discs from *Pinocchio* (Victor P-18) bore the description "Recorded from the original sound track of the Walt Disney Production."

The perception of film soundtracks as commercial risks began to change in mid-1942 with the release of the first album of dramatic underscore. It was a tentative step: a symphonic suite based on a classic book, containing narration and styled like Prokofiev's familiar *Peter and the Wolf*, suitable for children. RCA Victor commissioned Hungarian-born composer Miklós Rózsa to refashion his colorfully exotic score for *The Jungle Book* into a 28-minute work with narration (based on Rudyard Kipling's original writings) by Sabu, in character as Mowgli, on three 12-inch, 78-rpm

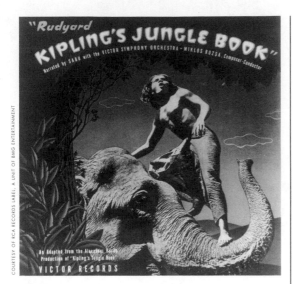

discs (Victor M-905). "We recorded the *Jungle Book* suite in New York," Rózsa recalled in his memoirs, "and I was thrilled to be conducting Toscanini's great orchestra, the NBC. . . . *The Jungle Book* was the first American film score to be commercially recorded by a major company."

Despite healthy sales—42,000, the composer estimated some years later—RCA Victor didn't cash in on the commercial potential of movie music. It was Decca, whose popular recording artist Victor Young was not only under contract but was also a busy Paramount film composer. In October 1943, following the box-office success of the Ernest Hemingway novel *For Whom the Bell Tolls*, Young recorded three 10-inch discs of his score (Decca A-360). In December, Fox's Alfred Newman recorded four discs of his inspirational music for *The Song of Bernadette* (Decca DA-365), which would shortly win the Oscar for Original Dramatic Score over Young's music.

These, and their immediate successors, were re-recorded for commercial release. Still, the 78-rpm discs were the exception, and only a handful of other film scores made it into the marketplace:

Rózsa's *Spellbound* (four discs, ARA A-2, 1945) and *The Red House* (two discs, Capitol CB-48, 1947); Dimitri Tiomkin's *Duel in the Sun* (four discs, RCA Victor DM-1083, 1947); Young's *Golden Earrings* (three discs, Decca DA-644, 1947); David Raksin's *Forever Amber* (three discs, RCA Victor P-197, 1947); Newman's *Captain From Castile* (three discs, Mercury A-69, 1947); and Franz Waxman's *The Paradine Case* (two discs, ALCO A-10, 1948).

Movie songs, however, continued to do well. On the strength of big box-office returns for *Casablanca*, RCA Victor re-released Rudy Vallee's 1931 recording of "As Time Goes By" (which Dooley Wilson sang so memorably in the Humphrey Bogart–Ingrid Bergman classic) and it shot to the number 1 spot; the song itself was a *Hit Parade* fixture for six months during mid-1943.

Even more notable was the remarkable success of Irving Berlin's "White Christmas," which Bing Crosby sang (backed by the Ken Darby Singers) into recording history. Written for the Paramount film *Holiday Inn*, it topped the *Hit Parade* for 10 weeks in 1942 and sold an estimated 30 million copies to become the biggest-selling record of all time. Two years later, another movie song, "Swinging on a Star" from *Going My Way*, generated another number-1 hit for Der Bingle. Both "White Christmas" and "Swinging on a Star" won Best Song Oscars.

David Raksin's *Laura* was an instance where the composer, with no thought about future commercial recordings, came up with a haunting theme for a compelling film and watched as it took on a life of its own. Inspired by the Dana Andrews–Gene Tierney romantic drama about a detective who falls for a murder suspect, Raksin interwove the tune throughout his score for Otto Preminger's 1944 film. Thousands of letters poured in to the studio (20ᵗʰ Century–Fox) about the music: Who wrote that theme? How can I get a recording? Will there be a song?

It took months for the studio and its music publisher to commission a lyric. Raksin convinced them to ask Johnny Mercer, the great lyricist ("Blues in the Night," "Ac-cent-tchu-ate the Positive"), to put words to the tune. Five records of "Laura" were in the nation's top 10 by April 15, and the song was on the *Hit Parade* for 14 consecutive weeks, reaching number 1 the week of June 2, 1945.

The first non-Disney film albums to actually employ the original soundtrack recordings were on the new MGM label. Producer Jesse Kaye, who ran the label's West Coast operation, initiated the concept with MGM's 1946 musical *Till the Clouds Roll By.* An all-star movie built around the songs of Broadway great Jerome Kern, it translated into a successful album featuring vocal highlights by Judy Garland, Lena Horne, Kathryn Grayson, Tony Martin, Virginia O'Brien, and June Allyson, all "Recorded Directly from the Sound Track of the M-G-M Production" according to the cover art (MGM-1). Frank Sinatra's and Dinah Shore's

Columbia contracts precluded the studio from including their numbers; Caleb Peterson substituted for Sinatra. Other song scores quickly followed, including June Allyson and Peter Lawford in *Good News* (1947, MGM-17), Garland and Gene Kelly singing Cole Porter in *The Pirate* (1948, MGM-21) and Garland, Horne, and Mickey Rooney performing Rodgers & Hart in *Words and Music* (1948, MGM-37), all "Recorded Directly from the Sound Track of the M-G-M Technicolor Musical."

On the dramatic-score side, Rózsa's music for *Madame Bovary* was the groundbreaker. Jennifer Jones starred in the 1949 adaptation of Gustave Flaubert's classic, and Rózsa had written a richly lyrical score whose centerpiece was an elaborately choreographed, ever-accelerating waltz. Released on two 10-inch discs (MGM-43) with cover art announcing "Recorded Directly from the Sound Track," this album marked the beginning of "original soundtrack" music for dramatic composers.

About this time, Columbia introduced the 33 1/3-rpm, 10- and 12-inch "long-playing" (LP) records, and RCA Victor launched the 45-rpm, seven-inch disc (whose running time would later be expanded into EP, or extended play, mode). In a matter of a few years the fragile 78-rpm discs were outmoded; long orchestral selections, such as classical music and the occasional movie soundtrack, would be released in the LP format and popular songs on the 45.

Give Us a Hit Song!

In 1952, the unlikeliest of songs—a cowboy ditty—became the catalyst for an entire shift in thinking about music for movies. The film was *High Noon*, and what changed things was the commercial sensibility of its composer, Russian-born Dimitri Tiomkin.

Tiomkin, a Hollywood veteran who scored several Frank Capra films and such westerns as Selznick's *Duel in the Sun* and Howard Hawks's *Red River*, was signed to provide the music for Stanley Kramer's production. Gary Cooper and Grace Kelly starred in this suspenseful tale of a town marshal who stood alone against a vengeful killer.

Kramer asked for a folk-style tune, and Tiomkin and lyricist Ned Washington complied with a simple ballad they called "Do Not Forsake Me, Oh My Darling," sung by former B-movie star Tex Ritter. Kramer confessed in his autobiography that he "became so enamored of the song" that he used it throughout the picture, causing preview audiences to laugh and sing along derisively after the first few occasions. Colleagues begged Kramer to dump "that damned song."

But Kramer was determined to keep the tune—just use it a little less frequently to bridge scenes here and there. Meanwhile Tiomkin, aware of the negative response and fearing that the movie might even be shelved, decided to "salvage something," in his words. He asked for, and received, publication rights to the song. "Now I would see if

I could make anything on the song on phonograph records. A flop song from a film fiasco didn't look very promising, but there was no harm trying," he wrote years later in his autobiography.

Ritter's label, Capitol, initially said no to a record, so Tiomkin went to Columbia's arranger-producer Mitch Miller and vocalist Frankie Laine (who had enjoyed a 1949 hit with "Mule Train"). As for the film, it was finished and screened for critics in April 1952 but not released by United Artists until July 25 in New York and August 13 in Los Angeles.

In the meantime, Laine recorded the song; once word was out that Columbia was releasing a version, Capitol relented and Ritter recorded his own. Both records—significantly, called "High Noon" and not "Do Not Forsake Me"—were released in June. Laine's impassioned rendition, backed by a ghostly chorus and a strong drumbeat, was the more successful of the two. It reached the *Billboard* charts on July 12 and climbed to number 5. Ritter's less compelling version didn't hit the charts until late September but reached number 12 (and effectively rejuvenated Ritter's singing career).

By mid-September, according to *Time* magazine, the song had sold nearly 2 million copies and Tiomkin had "already earned more in royalties than he got for supplying the movie score." More to the point, the industry looked at Tiomkin's song hit as perfect promotion for a movie whose box-office prospects were gauged as iffy at best. As Tiomkin boasted: "The record was an immediate success. They couldn't turn out copies fast enough. . . . The picture was released after the record and packed the theaters, a box-office gold mine. The success of the record promoted it."

Hollywood listened, and, practically overnight, producers were asking their composers for "a hit song," seemingly unaware that hits were completely unpredictable and that songs were not appropriate for every dramatic film.

Then on March 19, 1953, Tiomkin accepted Best Song (with Washington) and Best Original Score Oscars for *High Noon*, with Ritter performing the song on the first nationwide Oscar telecast. Tiomkin's victory was complete. He became Hollywood's favorite western composer for the next several years, scoring—and writing songs for—*Gunfight at the O.K. Corral*, *Rio Bravo*, *The Alamo*, and others.

The idea was solidly implanted in every marketing executive from that time on: Put a song in the movie, get the song on the radio, and voilà! Immediate and inexpensive promotion that could add millions to the box-office tally.

Two years later, another movie song would alter fortunes, this time in a different realm: "(We're Gonna) Rock Around the Clock," which director Richard Brooks featured over the opening credits of *The Blackboard Jungle* to establish the rebellious attitudes of the students in Glenn Ford's inner-city school class. Bill Haley and The Comets had recorded the song in 1954, and it made no special splash. But its use in the film, released in the spring of 1955, caused a sensation (and even riots in some theaters) and sent the song to number 1 on the *Billboard* charts, where it stayed for eight weeks. Popular culture historians today cite "Rock Around the Clock"—its popularity, the direct result of use in a movie—as the enormously influential beginning of rock 'n' roll as a force in American culture. Haley even made a movie by the same title the next year, the first of an entire subgenre of rock pictures.

Still, the big movie-soundtrack successes of the '50s were, for the most part, based on more traditional popular songs, often from screen adaptations of major Broadway musicals (especially anything written by Richard Rodgers and Oscar Hammerstein II). By far the most successful album of 1955, for example, was Doris Day's *Love Me or Leave Me*, which lasted 17 weeks at number 1. Out of three 1956 albums to hit number 1, two were Rodgers & Hammerstein movie musicals: *Oklahoma!* for four weeks and *The King & I* for one. Two of 1958's most popular albums were the soundtracks from *South Pacific* (Rodgers & Hammerstein, 31 weeks at number 1) and *Gigi* (Lerner & Loewe's original screen musical, 10 weeks at number 1).

If movie or record executives had any doubt about the staying power of rock 'n' roll in movies, it was wiped out by the coming of Elvis Presley—and his manager Col. Tom Parker's insistence on using movies as a springboard for launching more hit records. One of the most successful albums of 1957 was Presley's *Loving You* album, half of which consisted of tunes made popular in his early films. In fact, most of The King's top-selling albums for the next few years were his movie soundtracks, notably 1960's *G.I. Blues* (10 weeks at number 1); 1961's *Blue Hawaii* (20 weeks at number 1); 1962's *Girls!*

Girls! Girls!; 1963's *Fun in Acapulco*; and 1964's *Roustabout* (his last number 1 album until 1973).

The soundtrack success of its time was *West Side Story*, the Oscar-winning film adaptation of Leonard Bernstein and Stephen Sondheim's Broadway smash, which spent an astounding 54 weeks at number 1 in 1962 and 1963. (By comparison, the Beatles' *Sgt. Pepper* LP spent just 15 weeks in the top spot, Simon & Garfunkel's *Bridge Over Troubled Water* was there for 10, and even Michael Jackson's *Thriller* was displaced after 37 weeks.)

Songs, for the most part, continued to drive movie albums. Henry Mancini and Johnny Mercer's Oscar-winning "Moon River" sold millions of albums—first for Mancini, sending the 1961 soundtrack for the Audrey Hepburn movie, called *Breakfast at Tiffany's*, to the number-1 spot for 12 weeks; then for Andy Williams, whose *Moon River and Other Movie Themes* lasted on the charts for a remarkable 176 weeks and gave Williams his own signature tune. Williams's *Days of Wine and Roses* album, led by the next Mancini-Mercer tune to win the Oscar, did even better, enjoying a long stretch at number 1.

Shirley Bassey's rendition of the James Bond theme "Goldfinger" powered John Barry's soundtrack album to the number 1 spot in early 1965, and Frank Sinatra's rendition of "Strangers in the Night" (from a turkey nobody remembers called *A Man Could Get Killed*) not only became a best seller for Ol' Blue Eyes in 1966 but a standard that he sang for the rest of his career.

The success of instrumental themes and orchestral scores continued to depend largely on the box-office success of the films they were written for. Occasionally one crossed over into the mega-sales category, like Mancini's *Breakfast at Tiffany's* or Barry's *Goldfinger*, but both of those hinged on the success of their famous songs. That

was not the case with Victor Young's *Around the World in 80 Days* (10 weeks at number 1 in 1957) or Ernest Gold's *Exodus* (14 weeks at number 1 in 1961). With the former, the lyrical and sometimes exotic nature of the score delighted record-buyers; with the latter, the powerful, unforgettable theme sold massive numbers.

Sometimes an instrumental theme was enough. Seventy-seven-year-old Max Steiner—20 years after his big success with *Gone With the Wind*—proved that he could sell records with the best of the youngsters when his instrumental theme from *A Summer Place* (1959) landed at number 1 on the singles charts (Percy Faith's arrangement) and number 1 on the album charts (Billy Vaughn's version) in early 1960.

For the next few years, the middle-of-the-road artists staged a tug-of-war with the rockers for dominance of the charts, and more often than not it was the movie songs that fought their way through the increasingly dense rock 'n' roll jungle. Consumers were particularly susceptible to romantic themes from big popular movies. *Born Free* was a top-10 hit for pianist Roger Williams in 1966; Henry Mancini's piano-and-orchestra version of the "Love Theme From *Romeo & Juliet*" went all the way to number 1 in 1969.

The big winner from that era was *Doctor Zhivago*, the David Lean epic (starring Omar Sharif and Julie Christie) whose orchestral score by Maurice Jarre, incorporating the romantic "Lara's Theme," hit the top of the charts in early 1966, around the time it won the Academy Award. A song would have been inappropriate in the film, but after the score was recorded, lyricist Paul Francis Webster was asked to add a lyric to "Lara's theme."

The result, a song called "Somewhere My Love," was a bonanza for all involved. The Ray Conniff singers had a top-10 hit with the vocal

version, which was recorded by dozens of other artists; Roger Williams, Percy Faith, Paul Mauriat, Henry Mancini, and still others recorded instrumental versions. The song was inescapable, even at the 1966 Grammy Awards, where its five nominations included Record of the Year and Song of the Year; it ultimately won a choral-performance award for Conniff and the original-score award for Jarre. At 157 weeks on the *Billboard* album chart, MGM's *Doctor Zhivago* LP became one of the biggest-selling orchestral-score albums of all time.

Rodgers & Hammerstein again proved their viability in the marketplace, despite the onset of rock 'n' roll, both in movies and on the radio. The enormously popular 1965 film version of *The Sound of Music* spent just two weeks at number 1 but managed an astounding total of 233 weeks on the *Billboard* album chart all told, making it one of the bestselling movie albums ever.

The Beatles, meantime, were breaking records of their own. Their contributions to soundtrack history, of course, were their 1964 album of songs for *A Hard Day's Night* (number 1 for 14 weeks), the 1965 *Help!* (number 1 for nine weeks), and the 1969 album of songs from the animated *Yellow Submarine* (number 2 for two weeks). American pressings of the Beatles albums also included instrumental versions of the songs (on *A Hard Day's Night* and *Yellow Submarine*, by Beatles producer George Martin; on *Help!*, by score composer Ken Thorne).

Television, incidentally, was not to be left out. From the time Henry Mancini turned *Music from Peter Gunn* (1958) into a top-selling, Grammy-winning stereo LP until NBC created the wacky rock-wannabe group The Monkees in 1966 (generating four successive number 1 albums in a single year), music that originated on television was a subgenre of its own. By and large, these albums did not sell as well as the movie scores, but produced plenty of listening pleasure for consumers interested in often jazzy orchestral music from their favorite shows. Richard Rodgers's classically oriented *Victory at Sea* albums were enormously popular, as were the soundtracks to the series *77 Sunset Strip* (1959), *Mission: Impossible* (1967), *Dark Shadows* (1969), and others.

The Graduate, 2001, and Easy Rider

Three individuals permanently changed the way that films utilized music, particularly in connection with marketing and promotion—and none of them were musicians: Mike Nichols, director of *The Graduate* (1967); Stanley Kubrick, director of *2001: A Space Odyssey* (1968); and Peter Fonda, producer and star of *Easy Rider* (1969).

As writer Buck Henry and producer Lawrence Turman recalled in the 25th-anniversary video reissue of *The Graduate*, the idea of "scoring" the film with popular songs originated with Nichols.

Said Henry: "Nichols always wanted Simon & Garfunkel; he always wanted Paul [Simon]'s songs in there. 'Sounds of Silence' is clearly the perfect selection for that time and place."

In fact, most of Simon's songs were simply lifted wholesale out of previously successful Simon & Garfunkel albums: "Sounds of Silence," a number-1 single in 1966, and "April Come She Will," both off the *Sounds of Silence* album; "Scarborough Fair/Canticle" and "The Big Bright Green Pleasure Machine" from the *Parsley, Sage, Rosemary and Thyme* album. Only "Mrs. Robinson" was new; named after Anne Bancroft's seductress character in the movie, it consisted largely of the famed vocal duo harmonizing on "dee-dee-dees" and singing a brief, two-line song ("Here's to you, Mrs. Robinson . . .").

Simon later said that, while he was working on an entire score for the film, Nichols preferred the old songs and chose to license them instead, so that the only new material in the film was "Mrs. Robinson"—and that song apparently had to be fleshed out for later release as a single. Recalled Turman: "I asked [Simon], directly and/or through his manager, to write the full song so that we would have a merchandising tool, records, out there. He was sort of reluctant about doing it, for whatever reason. The picture came out, [it was a] big success, he quickly wrote the rest of it, recorded it [and it too] became a big success."

The Graduate was released in late 1967 to qualify for the Academy Awards, but because most of the score was not original to the film (and "Mrs. Robinson" was incomplete at best), it received no Academy attention in the score or song categories.

The full version of "Mrs. Robinson" actually appeared on Simon & Garfunkel's *Bookends* album, released on the heels of the *Graduate* LP. Everything went to number 1: the single (for three weeks in June 1968), the soundtrack album (nine weeks), and *Bookends* (seven weeks). The duo nabbed five Grammy nominations, winning three for Record of the Year, for their vocals on "Mrs. Robinson," and for Original Score (enabling composer Dave Grusin to win his first Grammy, too, despite the fact that his sole contributions were Muzak-style source tunes).

Opinions vary about the effectiveness of Simon's songs in the context of Henry and Nichols' satirical look at youthful alienation and empty middle-class values. Some find Simon's songs poignant and relevant; others find them wholly inappropriate, dealing with subjects that have no bearing on the characters played by Dustin Hoffman, Anne Bancroft, and Katharine Ross.

That didn't much matter to film executives. Box-office receipts, and record-store sales, added up to "success" in their eyes. *The Graduate* made a fortune, and so did its soundtrack (on Columbia, which released all of Simon & Garfunkel's work). What more need be said?

Half a world away from Mike Nichols and Paul Simon, secretive American filmmaker Stanley

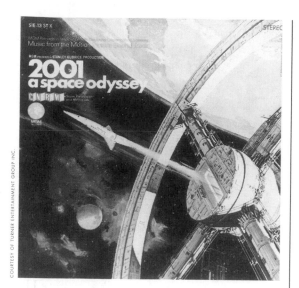

Kubrick was finishing post-production on his long-awaited science-fiction epic *2001: A Space Odyssey*, based in part on a story by Arthur C. Clarke. Kubrick had commissioned an original score by Alex North, the composer of such classics as *A Streetcar Named Desire* and *Spartacus*, but was already enamored of his "temp track"—various classical pieces that he had chosen as a temporary score during editing.

For the opening, Kubrick had chosen the introduction to Richard Strauss's 1894 tone poem *Also Sprach Zarathustra*. To demonstrate the grace and beauty of weightlessness and space travel, there was Johann Strauss's "Blue Danube" waltz; for the numbing boredom of life aboard a long space mission, the melancholy Adagio from Khachaturian's *Gayane* ballet suite. Dominating the film was the music of contemporary Hungarian composer Gyorgi Ligeti (hardly a household name): for the monolith that links the three time periods of the film (the "dawn of man," 2001, and the Jupiter mission 18 months later), his 1965 *Requiem for Soprano, Mezzo-Soprano, Two Mixed Choirs and Orchestra*; for the moonbus sequences, his 1966

choral work *Lux Aeterna*; for the kaleidoscopic Stargate sequences, the 1961 *Atmospheres*, based on changing orchestral clusters; and for Keir Dullea's transformation into a Starchild of the future, a work for vocal soloists and ensemble, also from 1966, called *Adventures*.

North's music was jettisoned and buried (remaining a subject of much speculation until a 1993 recording by conductor Jerry Goldsmith finally unveiled the mystery). Kubrick's film—a visual and aural experience unlike anything ever created for American film audiences—became, despite initial mixed critical reviews, a classic.

MGM Records producer Jesse Kaye saw an early screening of the film and managed to create a "soundtrack album" for *2001* by virtue of its corporate relationship with Deutsche Grammophon —even though the key music of the movie, the opening minute and a half of *Zarathustra*, was a performance by Herbert von Karajan and the Vienna Philharmonic that was markedly different from the "soundtrack" version by Karl Bohm and the Berlin Philharmonic.

The record was a colossal hit, not only on the pop charts (120 weeks, into the top 25 in 1968) but on the classical charts, where it was a staple for years to come. The *2001* theme, as the opening of *Zarathustra* came to be popularly known, even cracked the top-100 singles chart. The album's success begat the first major "inspired by" record—a term that would bedevil films and composers into the '90s.

In 1970, Kaye capitalized on the movie and album by releasing *2001: A Space Odyssey*, Volume Two (in smaller type, "music inspired by MGM's presentation of the Stanley Kubrick Production"). With a stunning cover of the Starchild as he appeared in the film's final frames, and an essay by MGM Records President Mike Curb that referenced "classical compositions that possess the power and grandeur of the selections present in the *2001* score," the LP duped thousands of fans into buying a record that contained absolutely nothing from the film score: More Ligeti, more Strauss, more Khachaturian, some Delibes, Webern, Gounod, all licensed from MGM's partner Deutsche Grammophon.

In a different realm altogether was *Easy Rider*, the Peter Fonda–Dennis Hopper movie about a pair of free-spirited motorcyclists traveling cross-country in search of the "real America." Their low-budget effort (with Fonda producing, Hopper directing, and both starring) earned one 1969 Oscar nomination for Best Screenplay (Fonda, Hopper, and Terry Southern) and another for Jack Nicholson as Best Supporting Actor. It also became one of the year's most successful films and set the tone for an entire era of disenchanted-youth movies with drop-out, turn-on philosophies expressed or implied.

Apparently there was no thought given to creating a traditional score. Instead, the filmmakers sought to build a "score" out of their favorite rock 'n' roll tunes. "It was basically Dennis's record collection," Fonda said in 1999. "Dennis likes to cut to music, and this particular film needed to have that." According to Patrick McGilligan's Nicholson biography *Jack's Life*, they even offered to screen the film for every band whose songs they wanted to license. Steppenwolf's "The Pusher" and "Born to Be Wild" were used for the drug deal that opens the film and the open-road main-title sequence. Songs by The Byrds, The Band, Jimi Hendrix, and other contemporary groups were used to either counterpoint or reinforce the images.

When Bob Dylan reportedly objected to the placement of his "It's Alright Ma, I'm Only Bleeding" (sung by Roger McGuinn of The Byrds) over

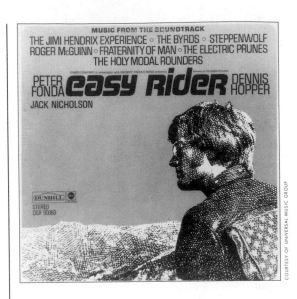

the final scenes of carnage, McGuinn penned a new song, "The Ballad of Easy Rider," to accompany the famous last scene and end credits. It was the only tune specifically written for the film; most of the lyrics, though uncredited, are Dylan's.

Joel Sill, now a top music supervisor but then an executive at Dunhill Records, saw an early cut of the film and made a deal for the soundtrack. Years later, Sill recalled, the cost to license each song was only about $750, and he was able to obtain all but one of the tunes (because of contractual complications, "The Weight" by The Band, was replaced by a cover version). It jumped to number 6 on the album charts. "The Ballad of Easy Rider" even headlined The Byrds' next album and made the hot-100 chart as a single.

Movies prior to *Easy Rider* had littered their soundtracks with rock songs, but none more successfully. Fonda and Hopper's apt song choices, coupled with the tremendous success of the film—which connected with young moviegoers more than any other film of its time—made *Easy Rider*'s soundtrack a trend-setter. Coming less than two years after *The Graduate*, the path for many producers seemed clear: attract younger audiences to movies with their favorite rock songs on the soundtrack.

In many ways, the industry-wide decision to move in this direction changed film music for all time. The ramifications are still felt today, and the corporate impact is greater than ever. Contemporary music—whether pop, rock, soul, country, or rap—can and sometimes does make a legitimate and telling contribution to a film; what's different between then and now is the degree of thought that is applied toward the inclusion of a song. In *Easy Rider*, the lyrics were carefully weighed against the scenes they accompanied. Were they appropriate? Did they comment on the moment? Was something added to the scene that wasn't there before?

By January 1970, the *Easy Rider* album (out just four months) had been awarded gold-record status by the Recording Industry Association of America. In short order, movies like *Performance*, *The Strawberry Statement*, and *Zabriskie Point* (all 1970) were released with wall-to-wall rock scores, and the unprecedented commercial success of such documentaries as *Woodstock* and the Beatles' *Let It Be*, which won 1970 Oscars as Best Documentary and Best Song Score, sent an even stronger message.

One other 1969 film served as a transitional work in terms of its combination of traditional score and fresh sounds out of the rock world: *Midnight Cowboy*, which went on to win the Academy Award as Best Picture. Director John Schlesinger was shooting the film on location in New York City, where composer John Barry happened to be working on another project. Barry (already a three-time Oscar winner for the song and score of *Born Free* and the score of *The Lion in Winter*) was hired as "musical supervisor" on the strength of his background in the British rock 'n'

roll world of the 1950s and early '60s as well as his knowledge of films and film scoring, as demonstrated by his hugely successful James Bond scores. Schlesinger had already found "Everybody's Talkin'," Fred Neil's tune which Harry Nilsson was going to re-record for the main title, but Barry sought out other bands from the New York club scene and chose songs that had the right tempo, lyric, or feel for other scenes in the movie. Then, at the end of the process, Barry wrote the underscore that included legendary harmonica player Toots Thielemans on Barry's own original theme. Both Nilsson's "Everybody's Talkin'" and Barry's "Midnight Cowboy" instrumental became top-10 hits, sending the soundtrack into the top 20 and eventually going gold.

The rock invasion of Hollywood had begun. In addition to licensing pre-existing songs, the more daring producers began to hire rock, soul, and jazz artists, usually with no previous experience in the dramatic and emotional requirements of music for film. Results varied, of course, but even in the strangest of cases the artists came up with music that was refreshingly different from the late 19th-century romanticism that had dominated movie scores for decades. Whether it was dramatically right was a different issue; certainly they sold a lot of records.

This period lasted roughly four years, beginning in 1971. The most successful of these writer-performers was soul singer-songwriter Isaac Hayes, who parlayed an assignment for a black private-detective film set in Harlem—Gordon Parks's film *Shaft*—into a brand-new career. Hayes won the Best Song Oscar and two Grammys (for composing and arranging), and created a number 1–selling double LP.

Shaft also set the style for an entire subgenre of film music: the blaxploitation score, as realized by soul artists Curtis Mayfield (*Superfly*, 1972), Bobby Womack (*Across 110th Street*, 1972), Marvin Gaye (*Trouble Man*, 1972), and Willie Hutch (*The Mack*, 1973, and *Foxy Brown*, 1974).

Other pop, rock, and jazz names to whom producers turned included pop performer Elton John (*Friends*, 1971), blues player Taj Mahal (*Sounder*, 1972), ex-Beatle Paul McCartney (*Live & Let Die*, 1972, with former Beatle producer George Martin writing most of the score), folk-rock legend Bob Dylan (*Pat Garrett and Billy the Kid*, 1973), Argentinian jazz saxophonist Gato Barbieri (*Last Tango in Paris*, 1973), pop singer-songwriter Neil Diamond (*Jonathan Livingston Seagull*, 1973), and jazz composer–keyboardist Herbie Hancock (*Death Wish*, 1974).

In most cases, the soundtrack albums charted, and often quite high. *Shaft* and *Superfly* went to number 1, and *Jonathan Livingston Seagull*, at number 2, became Diamond's highest-charting album ever. The 1973 Grammy nominees for Original Score Written for a Motion Picture or TV Special—once a category reserved for classically trained, full-time film composers like Miklós Rózsa, Henry Mancini, or Jerry Goldsmith—were Diamond, Barbieri, Dylan, Taj Mahal, and McCartney-Martin.

Later efforts at hiring pop and rock artists met with mixed results: Chuck Mangione's 2-LP set for *Children of Sanchez* (1978) reached number 14, and Queen's score for *Flash Gordon* (1980) jumped into the top 25; Toto's album for David Lynch's science-fiction epic *Dune* (1984) was its worst selling album ever.

RCA's Classic Film Scores Series

In November 1972, RCA released an album on its classical Red Seal label that, to the surprise of even those involved with the recording, altered the way people thought about movie music and eventually launched a mini-industry devoted to the field.

Called "*The Sea Hawk*: The Classic Film Scores of Erich Wolfgang Korngold," it debuted without fanfare and quietly leaped onto the best-selling classical album charts in just a few weeks. Starting at number 37 in December 1972, it built momentum slowly until early November 1973, when it was the best-selling classical album in the nation.

The idea belonged to R. Peter Munves, director of classical music at RCA Victor. One day, he casually approached conductor Charles A. Gerhardt about doing an album of Korngold film music. Gerhardt was also a producer who, during a long association with *Reader's Digest* in the 1960s, recorded several movie themes and suites with an ensemble of top London studio musicians he had founded as the National Philharmonic Orchestra.

Munves felt strongly about broadening the appeal of classical music. "In this business, you are an elitist at your peril," he told *Billboard* in April 1973. The *Sea Hawk* album was part of that concept, and Korngold was the ideal choice because, as a well-known concert-hall composer of the '20s and '30s in Europe, he had a classical pedigree that no other "Hollywood" composer could match. Yet his music, written in grandly romantic style, had accompanied some of the most famous Errol Flynn, Bette Davis and Claude Rains movies ever made.

Gerhardt immediately involved a longtime colleague: the composer's son George Korngold, also a producer at RCA. A veteran movie music editor at the Disney and 20th Century–Fox studios, the younger Korngold would serve as producer and annotator of the album, to be recorded by distinguished engineer Kenneth Wilkinson at London's Kingsway Hall. Together, they chose excerpts

COURTESY OF BMG CLASSICS/RCA VICTOR

(ranging from a minute and a half to eight minutes each) from 12 Korngold scores, including bits from all of his classics: *The Sea Hawk, The Adventures of Robin Hood, Captain Blood, Kings Row,* and others. Korngold's great film music, long revered by buffs but never appreciated by the classical crowd, had only been available on a long-out-of-print Warner Bros. LP (recorded in 1961, four years after the elder Korngold's death, by Fox conductor Lionel Newman).

Surprisingly, critics—traditionally disdainful of music written for movies—approved. Royal S. Brown, writing for *High Fidelity*, was among the first to extol its virtues, hailing "the warm, often sumptuous romanticism of Korngold's writing," the "flawless, perfectly executed performances," and "the recorded sound [which] simply dazzles in its realism and its richness."

Even Peter G. Davis, writing for the notoriously picky *New York Times*, cited "the spectacularly rich and full-bodied sound" and the composer's "blazing fanfares, throbbing melodies to fit every mood, all of it served up with extraordinary compositional skill and panache, bathed in the lushest

purple hues of late German romanticism."

Today Korngold is considered one of the century's greatest composers, though he died believing his music had been forgotten. In fact, the Gerhardt recording of Korngold's film music was single-handedly responsible for the resurgence of interest in the composer's concert music. Within a year, the New York City Opera revived his greatest opera, the 1920 *Die tote Stadt*, and a renaissance of Korngold recordings began (many produced by George Korngold).

In one year, *The Sea Hawk* sold 38,000 copies and was the fifth biggest selling classical album of 1973. Early sales were so impressive that Munves immediately commissioned more, and "Classic Film Scores" became a series. In the first year, volumes devoted to Max Steiner (*Now, Voyager*) and Alfred Newman (*Captain From Castile*), an album of music for Bette Davis films (mostly Steiner) and a second Korngold volume (*Elizabeth and Essex*) were also released. In the week that *The Sea Hawk* hit number 1, the Steiner and Davis albums were numbers 5 and 7 respectively. By year's end the five albums had sold more than 100,000 copies.

Other labels rushed to jump on the film-music bandwagon. Angel re-released previously recorded music by Miklós Rózsa (from epics *Ben-Hur, Quo Vadis, El Cid, King of Kings*) and Alfred Newman (*The Robe, Captain From Castile, The Hurricane,* etc.). Angel's budget label, Seraphim, re-released William Walton's scores for Laurence Olivier's Shakespeare films (*Henry V, Hamlet, Richard III*). All three made the best-seller charts within weeks. By late October 1973, five of the nation's top 25 classical albums were collections of movie music.

MGM Records went with their strong suit. Home to some of the screen's greatest movie musicals, the studio issued nine 2-LP sets under the umbrella title "Those Glorious MGM Musicals,"

A BRIEF HISTORY OF MOVIE SOUNDTRACK RECORDINGS

15

reissuing the song scores of such long-deleted classics as *Singin' in the Rain* with *Easter Parade*, *Show Boat* with *Annie Get Your Gun*, *Till the Clouds Roll By* with *Three Little Words*, *Seven Brides for Seven Brothers* with *Rose Marie*, and *The Pirate* with *Pagan Love Song* and *Hit the Deck*. Meanwhile, Warner Bros. received rave reviews for its two lavishly packaged boxed sets *50 Years of Film* (containing classic dialogue excerpts) and *50 Years of Film Music* (original soundtrack music and songs), released in 1973.

Over six years, RCA released a total of 14 albums in the Classic Film Scores series. LPs celebrated the music of Bernard Herrmann (*Citizen Kane*), Franz Waxman (*Sunset Boulevard*), Miklós Rózsa (*Spellbound*) and Dimitri Tiomkin (*Lost Horizon*), with "star" albums focusing on music from the films of Humphrey Bogart (*Casablanca*) and Errol Flynn (*Captain Blood*) and an entire album devoted to Steiner's magnum opus, *Gone With the Wind*. One "current" LP contained Gerhardt's re-recordings of John Williams's then- popular *Star Wars* and *Close Encounters of the Third Kind*, and a final record, *The Spectacular World of Classic Film Scores* (1978), combined a "best of" with previously unreleased material by several composers.

Declining sales probably led RCA to cancel the series. By 1978, Rózsa had recorded several collections of his own for Deutsche Grammophon, London, and Polydor; Herrmann had done a series of recordings for London Phase 4 and Unicorn; and smaller labels, like author-producer Tony Thomas's Citadel Records, were regularly and quietly issuing classic film music, often from the personal tapes of the composers themselves.

Of enormous interest to buffs was a mail-order series called the Elmer Bernstein Film Music Collection. Bernstein, who had taken an industry

COURTESY OF ELMER BERNSTEIN'S FILM MUSIC COLLECTION

leadership role as president of the Composers & Lyricists Guild of America in the 1970s, launched a quarterly publication (*Filmmusic Notebook*) that featured composer interviews and scholarly articles. In conjunction with the latter, subscribers could purchase new recordings of classic film music as re-recorded by Bernstein, often with London's Royal Philharmonic Orchestra and Chorus. Unlike Gerhardt's albums, which consisted mostly of short suites that rarely exceeded 10 minutes each, Bernstein's records often consisted of a single score. He was the first to record such neglected classics as Newman's *Wuthering Heights*, Herrmann's rejected score for Hitchcock's *Torn Curtain*, and his own, long-out-of-print *To Kill a Mockingbird*.

Unfortunately, the relatively small audience of film-music fanatics was insufficient to sustain the enterprise. After 14 LPs (most of which have never been reissued on CD), Bernstein's Film Music Collection ceased operations in 1979.

George Korngold continued to produce, on a freelance basis for several labels, albums of film music by his father (notably complete albums devoted to *The Sea Hawk* and *The Adventures of*

SOUND AND VISION

16

Robin Hood) and others. For the short-lived Chalfont label, he and Gerhardt recorded a complete *Kings Row* and a symphonic suite from Williams's *The Empire Strikes Back*. Korngold died in 1987, Gerhardt in 1999.

John Williams and *Star Wars*

There are a handful of landmark scores in the history of Hollywood music. One could cite Steiner's *King Kong* (1933), Alex North's *A Streetcar Named Desire* (1951), Leonard Rosenman's *The Cobweb* (1955), Bernard Herrmann's *Psycho* (1960)—and John Williams's *Star Wars* (1977).

In the early 1970s, Williams was one of Hollywood's up-and-coming composing talents. As "Johnny" Williams, he had written several memorable television themes, receiving a Grammy nomination for TV's *Checkmate*, working with Robert Altman on several *Kraft Suspense Theatre*s, and winning Emmys for the prestigious TV movies *Heidi* and *Jane Eyre*. Having paid his dues in TV, he was gradually infiltrating the movie world with light comedies like *How to Steal a Million* (1966) and more dramatic fare like *The Reivers* (1969).

Williams's thoughtful approach, craftsmanship, and occasionally inspired writing made him a valued collaborator among filmmakers. By the time he scored *Jaws* (1975) for Steven Spielberg, he had already racked up nine Oscar nominations and won one statue, for adapting and conducting the film version of Broadway's *Fiddler on the Roof* (1971).

Jaws was Williams's breakthrough movie; Spielberg has said on several occasions that the composer's brilliant (and later, Oscar-winning) score was a major contributor to the film's phenomenal success. By the mid-'70s, orchestral film scores had virtually disappeared from the *Bill-board* charts; rock 'n' roll collections like *American Graffiti*—made by Spielberg's friend George Lucas—were more the order of the day. But unlike, say, Williams's *The Towering Inferno*, which got all the way to number 158 on the *Billboard* top-200 chart (primarily because Maureen McGovern's song "We May Never Love Like This Again" was on it), the popularity of the movie sent the *Jaws* album, and even a single of the theme, sailing into the top 40.

Spielberg introduced Lucas to Williams, and two years later, film-music history was made with *Star Wars*.

The film opened on May 25, 1977. Less than two months later, on July 18, a two-LP set of the score was certified gold; a month later, on August 17, it was certified platinum, indicating sales exceeding a million units. No orchestral film score in history had sold so many so fast—and this was a two-record set, a rarity for an original soundtrack, with an above-average list price of $9.98. Twentieth Century Records, which was more accustomed to selling a few thousand copies of scores like Williams's *Cinderella Liberty*, had a massive hit on its hands. By the time the dust had cleared, Williams's score had sold an estimated four million copies, the largest selling non-pop album in history up to that time.

Lucas, who had created a temporary soundtrack of classical selections from Holst, Dvorak, Walton, Rózsa, and more, convinced Williams that his film about events "a long time ago in a galaxy far, far away," demanded a score firmly rooted in 19th-century romantic tradition; that is, similar in style to the old-fashioned Korngold scores of the '30s and '40s. Essentially a distillation of *Amazing Stories*–style space opera, Saturday-afternoon cliffhangers, and grandiose mythological invention, Lucas's film struck a chord with moviegoers everywhere, especially younger ones, and became a cultural phenomenon.

It was Williams's good fortune to have collaborated with the most successful filmmakers of their time. The success of *Star Wars* (and its sequels, *The Empire Strikes Back* in 1980 and *Return of the Jedi* in 1983) altered the course of contemporary film music. After several years of scores dominated by pop and rock songs, filmmakers were suddenly demanding orchestral music in their films. "If it worked for *Star Wars* . . ."

Some critics decried this reversal of recent trends, arguing that *Star Wars* marked a move backwards, toward the moribund tradition of Steiner and Korngold; that it was hardly original, drawing its inspiration from several classical sources; and that a futuristic film demanded a cutting-edge, futuristic sound.

As a practical matter, however, *Star Wars* brought back symphonic music to movies. (It had never really left, of course. Veteran composers like Elmer Bernstein and Jerry Goldsmith had been maintaining the symphonic tradition all along. But they weren't selling albums, and they often fought an uphill battle to convince directors that the orchestral score wasn't dead.)

And *Star Wars* sold albums. Producer Meco Monardo's disco-style medley of the movie theme and its wacky "Cantina Band" number hit the top of the singles charts, while Williams's own soundtrack version of the main title made the top 10 in late summer 1977. Both were nominated for Best Pop Instrumental Performance at the Grammys; Williams won, and also collected Grammys for Best Instrumental Composition (for the main title) and Best Album of an Original Score. The record was even nominated for Album of the Year (competing against more typical Grammy fare in Fleetwood Mac, Steely Dan, the Eagles, and James

COURTESY OF LUCASFILM LTD.

Taylor records), the first time an orchestral score had been nominated since *Doctor Zhivago* more than a decade earlier.

Williams accepted his third Oscar for the *Star Wars* music in March 1978 and was already on his way to fame via public appearances as conductor of pops concerts. With two more blockbusters—Spielberg's *Close Encounters of the Third Kind* and Warner Bros.' *Superman*—behind him, he succeeded the venerable Arthur Fiedler as conductor of the Boston Pops Orchestra in January 1980.

It was the shrewdest possible career move for the otherwise shy and private composer. The orchestra's popular public television series, *Evening at Pops*, offered a visibility for Williams and his music that no other film composer had ever enjoyed. The result was almost instant fame, greater leverage in the Hollywood community, and a growing level of respect for the movie music that became a staple of the Pops repertoire. Millions of viewers (and potential record-buyers) became aware of movie music outside of its cinematic context for the first time.

Williams's new job forced him to scale back

his film scores (he wrote just 15 over the next decade) but his fame afforded him more freedom than ever before. He became the most famous composer in movie history, probably more recognizable to the average American than even Henry Mancini (whose own pops concerts, 20-year RCA recording contract, and syndicated TV series had made him a household name in the '60s and '70s).

Saturday Night Fever and the Influence of MTV

By the early 1970s, the music-in-film lessons of *The Graduate, Easy Rider,* and *Shaft* were becoming clear to studio executives. As a *New York Times* writer put it in 1974: "Producers know that the disc jockey provides a connection between teen-age record buyers and youthful moviegoers that yields pure Hollywood gold." (The same story quoted an anonymous film publicist complaining that the new studio thinking was, "Let's get whoever sold 17 million records last year.")

In a retrospective for *Daily Variety* in 1985, Gary LeMel, then senior vice president of music for Columbia Pictures, traced the high-profile music movie back to three trend-setting record-executives-turned-movie-producers: Motown's Berry Gordy, RSO's Robert Stigwood, and Casablanca's Neil Bogart.

Gordy produced *Lady Sings the Blues* (1972), which cast singer Diana Ross in a major acting role as legendary jazz singer Billie Holiday and involved Motown as a key partner with Paramount in the development of both the soundtrack (which went to number 1 on the *Billboard* album chart in early 1973) and the film's marketing campaign.

Stigwood, manager of the Bee Gees, produced *Saturday Night Fever* (1977), *Grease* (1978), and *Sgt. Pepper's Lonely Hearts Club Band*

(1978), redefining not only the contemporary film musical but also movie-music marketing in the process. Bogart turned Casablanca into a film-and-record company with *Midnight Express* (1978) and partnered with Motown to produce Donna Summer's disco movie *Thank God It's Friday* (1978), which in turn produced the Oscar-winning song "Last Dance."

Saturday Night Fever was the big prize. Within five months of its release, the two-LP soundtrack was the biggest selling album of all time at more than 10 million sold (at $12.98); it ended up at 25 million internationally. More significantly, the carefully orchestrated September release of a theatrical trailer (featuring the Bee Gees singing "Stayin' Alive"), a single in late September ("How Deep Is Your Love"), and the album in November, all preceded the December 1977 release of the movie.

The Bee Gees had been a major band throughout the decade but hit it especially big with the disco craze in '75 ("Jive Talkin'") and '76 ("You Should Be Dancing"). When the 30-second teaser spot was expanded to a three-minute trailer around Thanksgiving, it concluded with a plug for the deluxe fold-out album. By the time the movie opened December 16, RSO had already sold a million albums and 1.7 million singles.

The movie—starring ex-TV star John Travolta as a Brooklyn youth who lives for weekends and dancing at the disco—was a blockbuster, and the album sent a record four singles to number 1 between December 1977 and May 1978: the Bee Gees' "How Deep Is Your Love," "Stayin' Alive," and "Night Fever," and Yvonne Elliman's "If I Can't Have You." Tavares's "More Than a Woman" and the Trammps' "Disco Inferno" also made the top 40.

All of this commercial success left Stigwood scratching his head when the Academy of Motion

Picture Arts & Sciences failed to nominate any of the songs, or the song score, for 1977 Oscars. "For it to be overlooked is just insanity," he told the *Los Angeles Times* in January 1978. "The music branch is so out of touch with the movie audience."

At that time, the Academy was in the habit of releasing a list of "preliminary selections," essentially a pre-nominations list from which the final nominees would be selected. *Saturday Night Fever* failed to make the cut on a "qualitative" basis, and because the decision was made by music-branch members (and not just a committee), the governors felt they could not overrule the choice. The song score and "How Deep Is Your Love" were, however, nominated for Golden Globe awards.

Stigwood followed *Saturday Night Fever* with *Grease*, pairing Travolta with Olivia Newton-John in an adaptation of the Broadway musical about high-school life in the '50s. It was the hit of the summer of 1978, and once again RSO released the album well in advance of the film's June opening; by early April the label already had orders for 1.25 million two-record sets. Four singles hit the top 10, and two of them went to number 1: the

Travolta–Newton-John duet "You're the One That I Want" and Frankie Valli's "Grease," both written for the film; later came Newton-John's "Hopelessly Devoted to You" and the duet "Summer Nights," the former a movie original and the latter from the original show.

Stigwood's one movie misstep was casting Peter Frampton and the Bee Gees in *Sgt. Pepper's Lonely Hearts Club Band*, which interwove two dozen classic Beatles tunes into a loose storyline. Critics scoffed at the film, but the two-record set was a hit, reaching number 5 on the *Billboard* album charts in the summer of 1978.

Travolta's next musical was on the country side: 1980's *Urban Cowboy*, set in Houston and revolving around the nightlife at a sprawling honky-tonk where drinking, dancing, and riding a mechanical bull constituted nightly entertainment. Again, a music executive was one of the film's producers: Irving Azoff, manager of some of rock's top acts including the Eagles and Boz Scaggs. Again, a two-record set went gold a month before the movie opened and generated a half-dozen top-40 singles for artists including Johnny Lee ("Lookin' for Love"), Kenny Rogers ("Love the World Away"), and Anne Murray ("Could I Have This Dance").

In the aftermath of the pop-rock Travolta movies came a new cable television channel that soon began to influence not only the way that movie soundtracks were marketed but the way that movies themselves were made. Launched on August 1, 1981, Music Television (MTV) was a 24-hour channel devoted entirely to "music videos": usually three- to five-minute mini-movies starring popular recording artists singing their current hits.

With their origins in Richard Lester's work on such Beatles films as *A Hard Day's Night* and *Help!*, and later simple promotional films made by record companies, the music video was from its inception a case of style over substance. Flash and excitement were more important than storytelling, and today's quick-cut, slam-bang action films are the direct result of techniques honed by commercial directors and video directors.

Adrian Lyne came out of commercials to make *Flashdance* (1983), produced by Jerry Bruckheimer and Don Simpson and financed by Poly-Gram Records (which had purchased Casablanca Records, the maker of Lyne's earlier film *Foxes*). Critics denounced it as a long rock video, and it was undeniably music-driven, with legendary producer Phil Ramone as music supervisor and Oscar-winning disco pioneer Giorgio Moroder as songwriter and underscore composer.

Jennifer Beals, as the welder-by-day, dancer-by-night focus of the film, danced to a series of contemporary tunes, notably the title song "Flashdance . . . What a Feeling," sung by Irene Cara, and "Maniac," performed by Michael Sembello, both of which went to number 1 and drove the soundtrack album (on Casablanca) to the top spot as well. "Flashdance" won the Best Song Oscar for Moroder, Cara, and their cowriter Keith Forsey.

For Bruckheimer (who had used the commercially savvy Moroder on his *American Gigolo* and *Cat People*) and new partner Simpson, *Flashdance* marked the first of a series of films that utilized MTV-style filmmaking techniques, brought pop and rock to the forefront, and generated best-selling albums.

"We're both rock 'n' roll heads," Bruckheimer told *Rolling Stone* in 1985. "There's music on in our offices all day long, and it's not Mantovani."

Simpson-Bruckheimer films would be increasingly criticized for incoherent or inane plots, loud and often pointless music on the soundtrack, and high-energy direction and editing designed to

appeal to moviegoers with the shortest possible attention span.

But their movies sold millions of records, and labels were happy to comply with their song requests. Their Eddie Murphy action-comedy *Beverly Hills Cop* (1985) generated three top-10 hits including Glenn Frey's "Heat Is On," the Pointer Sisters' "Neutron Dance," and Moroder protegé Harold Faltermeyer's instrumental "Axel F." The album went to number 1 and won a Grammy as Best Album of a Motion Picture Score.

Their Tom Cruise naval-aviator film *Top Gun* (1986), another number 1 album, generated a number 1 single in the love theme "Take My Breath Away" by Berlin—which won the Best Song Oscar, again for Moroder—and a number-2 hit in Kenny Loggins's "Danger Zone." Their Michelle Pfeiffer inner-city drama, *Dangerous Minds* (1995), went to number 1, too, largely on the strength of rapper Coolio's top-selling "Gangsta's Paradise."

And *Armageddon*, Bruckheimer's summer '98 hit about an asteroid on a collision course with Earth, generated yet another number-1 album and a number-1 single in Aerosmith's "I Don't Want to Miss a Thing," written by contemporary film's hottest songwriter, Diane Warren.

Rock Soundtracks Gain a Foothold

Nineteen eighty-four turned out to be a watershed year for the increasingly complex, increasingly lucrative relationship between movie studios and record companies. No fewer than seven films featured pop or rock songs that had an impact at the box office, on the record charts, or both.

Columbia's LeMel told *Variety* in 1985: "What music executives at the studios had long been predicting, and marketing men had long been dreaming of, finally came true: an intensely symbiotic relationship between pop music and film became a Hollywood reality."

Traditionalists moaned about the continuing erosion of the once-valued film composer, but the industry was changing in ways that would tear apart old notions of commercial moviemaking. The era of "Moon River" and "The Days of Wine and Roses" was long gone. The name of the game was now Get a Movie Song on MTV and Top-40 Radio—and if possible, two or three from the same film.

The year actually began with two big holdovers from '83: the soundtracks for *The Big Chill* and *Eddie & the Cruisers*, both of which stunned observers with their tenacious hold on record-buyers. Labeled by *Variety* "one of the most surprising LP success stories of 1983," the Motown soundtrack for Lawrence Kasdan's ensemble drama *The Big Chill* turned out to be one of the biggest movie albums ever, going double platinum and lasting 161 weeks on the *Billboard* album chart overall.

The movie contained no original music, just a collection of old '60s and '70s tunes that the cast (Kevin Kline, Glenn Close, and others, as a reunited group of college chums) used to listen to during their university days; several Motown classics, notably Marvin Gaye's "I Heard It Through the Grapevine" and The Temptations' "Ain't Too Proud to Beg," figured prominently. The film struck such a chord with baby boomers that they rushed out to buy the soundtrack and hear these old favorites again. Radio play was not a significant factor.

Eddie & the Cruisers, about a fictional '60s rock 'n' roll group, was a box-office bomb in '83. But the song score by John Cafferty and the Beaver Brown Band was such a hit—particularly when the film surfaced on cable in '84—that the soundtrack made it all the way to the top 10 in 1984 and ultimately went triple platinum.

The era of the powerful music supervisor had begun. The term "music supervisor" has signified several different job descriptions over the years. It was gradually coming to refer to the individual who coordinated the songs (original or licensed) and interfaced with the filmmakers, studio executives, and record-company officials. Phil Ramone was among the first music supervisors to attain main-title credit, on *Flashdance*.

Becky Shargo, who had assembled the soundtrack for Irving Azoff on *Urban Cowboy* and received main-title credit as "music coordinator," did the same thing for *Footloose* (1984), another Paramount film, and received even more attention (including her name on movie posters) as "music supervisor." *Footloose* perfectly integrated songs into its framework (primarily because lyricist Dean Pitchford also wrote the script). The Columbia soundtrack—because title-song performer Kenny Loggins had a Columbia contract—yielded six top-40 singles, including two number-1 hits: Loggins's "Footloose" and Deniece Williams's "Let's Hear It for the Boy." The album itself spent 10 weeks at number 1.

Columbia's LeMel was also at the forefront of the movement. As head of music for Columbia, he had helped to oversee the soundtrack for *The Big Chill* and was instrumental in two number-1 hits that added significantly to the box-office take of two films: Phil Collins's "Against All Odds (Take a Look at Me Now)," whose domination of the singles chart in April-May 1984 may have added $5 to $6 million to the film's gross; and Ray Parker Jr.'s title tune from *Ghostbusters*, which LeMel suggested to *Rolling Stone* may have "added another $20 million to the box office" during the crucial summer months.

In the case of *Against All Odds*, director Taylor Hackford was directly involved in the choice of Collins—but only after Atlantic had been signed to do the film soundtrack; Collins was chosen as one of the label's leading artists. Hackford flew to Chicago, where Collins was performing, to show him the film and convince him to write and per-

form the song. The music video—believed to be one of the first movie videos to hit MTV—was also a key factor.

Stevie Wonder's song score for *The Woman in Red* (1984) far outperformed the movie it was written for, Gene Wilder's remake of the French farce *Pardon Mon Affaire*. Wonder's song, "I Just Called to Say I Love You," hit number 1 in October, propelled the album (which featured duets with Dionne Warwick) to platinum status, and eventually won the Oscar. In another indicator that the link between film studios and the record business was now complete, all five 1984 Best Song nominees had been number-1 hits: two from *Footloose*, the title songs from *Against All Odds* and *Ghostbusters*, and Wonder's tune from *The Woman in Red*.

The phenomenon of the year, however, was Prince, the bad boy of rock whose semi-autobiographical film, *Purple Rain*—about a self-centered Minneapolis rocker—generated a soundtrack that spent a remarkable 24 weeks at number 1 and generated four top-10 hits, including two at number 1: "When Doves Cry" and "Let's Go Crazy" ("Purple Rain" and "I Would Die 4 U" were the others). A little too cutting edge for Academy voters, Prince may have been denied a Best Song berth, but he won the Original Song Score Oscar (the last, incidentally; the category was abolished the next year). The album is now high on the all-time list of best-selling soundtracks.

Of the hot directors in Hollywood at that time, Taylor Hackford may have demonstrated the keenest interest in the effective utilization of pop music. His movies had included *The Idolmaker* (1980) and *An Officer and a Gentleman* (which included 1982's Best Song, "Up Where We Belong"). His next film, *White Nights*—about two dancers (Mikhail Baryshnikov and Gregory Hines) mixed up in international politics—generated not one but two number-1 singles in late 1985: "Separate Lives," performed by Phil Collins and Marilyn Martin, and "Say You, Say Me," written and sung by Lionel Richie.

When the original ad campaign for *White Nights* failed to ignite the box office, Columbia tried a new one that was headlined "Two Hit Songs. Two Hit Stars. One Hit Movie." And in another wrinkle that demonstrated the increasingly complicated coalition of movies and records, "Say You, Say Me" didn't appear on the Atlantic soundtrack; at the time, Richie owed an album to Motown, which wouldn't grant permission but did issue the single.

The decade's biggest surprise may have been the movie and album of *Dirty Dancing* in 1987. The innocuous little movie about a dancer and a spoiled teen (Patrick Swayze, Jennifer Grey) at a Catskills resort in the '60s caught the popular fancy. It became the sleeper of the year, sending the song "(I've Had) The Time of My Life" to number 1 in November. The album—which featured a mix of new tunes and '60s hits like "Be My Baby" and "Stay"—remained at number 1 for a remarkable 18 weeks, joining *Saturday Night Fever* and *Purple Rain* as the biggest selling soundtracks of their time.

The introduction of the compact disc in 1983 once again altered fortunes in the record business. In fact, among PolyGram's first announced releases in the new format were the soundtracks of *Star Wars, Chariots of Fire,* and *Fame.* As with the initial overlap of the 78-rpm disc and the LP, there was an initial period of production of LPs and CDs, but by 1990 the LP was pretty much phased out. The hardy cassette continued as a viable format, however.

The Soundtrack Specialty Label

Why do people buy soundtracks? The reasons are essentially the same now as in the '60s: In many cases, they saw and liked the movie and want a souvenir of the experience. The packaging usually includes the poster art, color and black-and-white stills, some liner notes discussing the movie, and, of course, the music, all of which help the buyer relive that pleasurable two or three hours in a movie theater.

More discriminating listeners appreciate the music, whether songs or score. Some like the music of specific artists, either singers or score composers. Others appreciate the genre as a whole: the songs specifically geared to a subject or a concept, the orchestral scores which, after decades of atonal, often dissonant concert-hall compositions, seem to be the last bastion of tonal, romantic symphonic music in this century.

The 1970s resurgence of interest in symphonic film music led to the founding of small labels devoted specifically to this music. The label that led the way, and continues to be the leader in recording both original and classic film music, is Los Angeles–based Varèse Sarabande. Founded in 1978, it actually began life as an esoteric classical label (the name being drawn from modernist composer Edgar Varèse and the term for a traditional Spanish dance form) but quickly shifted into film music after licensing out-of-print soundtracks and finding that a collectors' market was waiting to be tapped.

Early, inexpensive releases like *Phantasm, Dawn of the Dead,* and *Escape from New York* eventually gave way to more mainstream fare, like Jerry Goldsmith's *Rambo,* Maurice Jarre's *Witness,* and Angelo Badalamenti's *Blue Velvet.* By 1988, Varèse made a deal with distribution giant MCA, effectively expanding its sales potential by increasing market penetration.

While it was rare for a Varèse soundtrack to crack *Billboard*'s top-200 album chart, the label achieved its greatest success with the album for *Ghost* (1990), which consisted mostly of Jarre's orchestral-and-electronic score but had one special element that record-buyers wanted: the Righteous Brothers' 1965 version of Alex North's "Unchained Melody," used as the love theme for Patrick Swayze and Demi Moore. The movie was a hit, and so was the soundtrack: it became Varèse's first platinum album, reaching number 8 and remaining on the charts for 64 weeks.

The label now releases about 100 discs a year with a back catalog of about 500 older soundtracks. While soundtrack production is unquestionably a niche market, Varèse proudly proclaims that it is "the largest producer of soundtracks in the world."

It has also been a leader in the very specialized field of re-recording classic scores that are not (and, in some cases, have never been) commercially available. This serves an even more specific collector's market, often just several thousand devoted followers of a particular composer or two. Varèse has enjoyed particular success with Bernard Herrmann, one of the most popular film composers: its re-recording of the complete score to the Hitchcock classic *Vertigo* (1958) won the British record publication *Gramophone*'s 1997 award for Best Film Music Recording. It has also re-recorded Herrmann's previously unavailable *The Trouble With Harry* (1955) and his rejected score for *Torn Curtain* (1966). Varèse Sarabande's ongoing relationship with composer Jerry Goldsmith has led to re-recordings of several classic Goldsmith scores (*The Sand Pebbles, Tora! Tora! Tora!,* and others) as well as those of his close friend Alex North (*Viva Zapata!, The Agony and the Ecstasy,* and others).

ORIGINAL MOTION PICTURE SOUNDTRACK

GHOST

MUSIC COMPOSED AND CONDUCTED BY
MAURICE JARRE

London-based Silva Screen Records has an active re-recording program but focuses more on albums that consist of main themes and short suites of music by leading composers, often by movie genre (disaster films, science-fiction epics, etc.). Its 1997 *Cinema Choral Classics* album, consisting of dramatic choral excerpts from scores ranging from *King of Kings* to *The Mission*, sold an estimated 50,000 units worldwide—so far above average for movie music that it spawned a sequel album.

The Hong Kong–based Marco Polo label has perhaps the most ambitious re-recording program: several releases per year of great but previously unreleased scores by Korngold (*Another Dawn*, 1937), Newman (*The Hunchback of Notre Dame*, 1939), Steiner (*They Died With Their Boots On*, 1941), Young (*The Uninvited*, 1944), Waxman (*Mr. Skeffington*, 1944), and others, all meticulously reconstructed from original composer sketches and any remaining documentation (usually from the composer estates, since most of the studios long ago discarded orchestrations and parts for the players).

San Francisco–based Intrada has re-recorded works by Rózsa (*Ivanhoe, Julius Caesar*) and

COURTESY OF TWENTIETH CENTURY FOX

Herrmann (*Jason and the Argonauts*) and has championed several composers, ranging from Goldsmith to Bruce Broughton and Christopher Young. Classical label Nonesuch—which has profited handsomely with the film work of Philip Glass, from *Koyaanisqatsi* to *Kundun*—jumped further into the fray in 1997 with elaborately packaged albums of movie music by Toru Takemitsu, Leonard Rosenman, Alex North, and Georges Delerue.

Somewhat rarer are the unearthing and restoration of truly original soundtrack recordings. In the early '90s, Fox released such classics as *Laura*, *The Robe*, *The Day the Earth Stood Still*, and *Stormy Weather*, while Turner/Rhino produced elaborate presentations of *Ben-Hur*, *The Wizard of Oz*, *Gigi*, and a six-CD anthology of numbers from MGM musicals called *That's Entertainment!*

A Resurgence in Animation Scores

From "Someday My Prince Will Come" and "When You Wish Upon a Star" to "Zip-A-Dee-Doo-Dah" and "The Bare Necessities," songs in animated movies from the Walt Disney Studios have become some of our most beloved tunes.

With *The Little Mermaid* (1989), however, Disney's musical legacy took a giant step forward, and the studio's fortunes at the record rack took an equivalent leap. Composer Alan Menken and lyricist Howard Ashman, the duo who had written the off-Broadway hit *Little Shop of Horrors*, brought a musical-theater sensibility to the animated film. As in the theater, they were involved from the inception of the project (along with scriptwriters and animators), and their songs became an integral part of the storytelling—always moving the story forward and rarely stopping the action for a little song and dance.

The result was Disney's most successful animated feature to date, a musical about a mermaid that won Oscars for Best Song ("Under the Sea") and Best Score and, despite the lack of serious radio airplay, an album that went triple platinum—unheard-of for a Disney soundtrack.

Menken and Ashman went on to create *Beauty and the Beast* (1991), the first animated film to receive a Best Picture Oscar nomination. This time there was not only an exquisite score (that again won Score and Song Oscars) but also a top-10 hit in the title song, done as a duet by Celine Dion and Peabo Bryson. This time a Disney album cracked the top 20.

The stakes rose with the next two Disney animated features. Ashman, sadly, passed away from AIDS-related complications before he and Menken could complete work on *Aladdin* (1992), so lyricist Tim Rice stepped in. With Robin Williams around to add his voice to the Arabian Nights shenanigans, the team again won Oscars, and this time the key theme went all the way to number 1: "A Whole New World," sung in the pop version by Bryson and Regina Belle, sent the album to number 6 and another triple-platinum certification.

The biggest hit of all was Disney's 1994 African epic *The Lion King*. This time the composer was out of the pop world: Elton John, teaming with lyricist Rice, generated two top-20 hits in "Can You Feel the Love Tonight" (number 4) and "Circle of Life" (number 18), sending the album to number 1 for a surprising 10 weeks. The album was on the charts for 88 weeks and went multi-platinum, becoming Disney's most commercially successful soundtrack to date. It too won Oscars for Best Song (John and Rice) and Score (composer Hans Zimmer).

Orchestral Film Music Surges in Popularity

The success of John Williams as a composer and (especially during his tenure with the Boston Pops) a conductor of symphonic film music, paved the way for other conductors to present and record film music. People like the Cincinnati Pops' Erich Kunzel and the Hollywood Bowl Orchestra's John Mauceri championed the cause of movie music in their concerts and television appearances. Not only were film scores selling on disc, they were drawing new audiences to pops concerts all over the country. It became as common to see the march from *Raiders of the Lost Ark* or the "Tara" theme from *Gone With the Wind* on a program as a Strauss waltz or other light-classical selections.

The growing status of film and other media-related compositions became a factor in the 1986 creation of a new *Billboard* chart titled "classical crossover" (generally orchestral but not strictly concert-hall music). When *The Sea Hawk* was re-released on compact disc in 1989, it graced not the classical chart where it had started but rather the classical-crossover chart (where it remained for a year). And Williams's re-released *Star Wars* trilogy,

as a further example, occupied three of the top 5 positions on the crossover charts in 1997.

Soundtracks continue to be placed, for the most part, on the magazine's top-200 album charts, but depending on their "classical" origins, they often grace the classical crossover listing. *Shine*, for example, the 1996 film about the life of Australian virtuoso pianist David Helfgott, made the chart because of its hybrid nature: partly classical excerpts, partly David Hirschfelder's original music and some Hirschfelder arrangements of classical selections.

The rules are quirky. Most film composers tend not to be eligible if they are not perceived as "classical" artists and if their scores are not performed by such familiar ensembles as the London Symphony Orchestra or the Los Angeles Philharmonic. But re-recordings of old film music, such as Kunzel's regular Cincinnati Pops collections of movie themes, are eligible. Williams's *Cinema Serenade* album, featuring violinist Itzhak Perlman soloing on favorite movie themes, topped the classical crossover chart for several weeks in 1997.

Back in the '60s and '70s, Henry Mancini paved the way for film composers to make concert appearances and play their famous movie music to cheering crowds. Michel Legrand, Marvin Hamlisch, John Williams, and now Jerry Goldsmith and John Barry, have followed. Fans create websites by the dozens devoted to their favorite film composers just as pop stars once enjoyed mail-order fan-club attention.

Orchestral film music continues to enjoy popularity in the studios and on records. Directors often "temp" their films—that is, lay in temporary music soundtracks for editing and preview purposes—with favorite scores, then ask their composers to use similar styles or rhythms in their own work. That has turned out to be a mixed blessing, encouraging the tradition of fully orchestral movie scores while tending to stifle originality and creativity by new writers. Practically every major studio release now enjoys a score played by a 100-piece orchestra (regardless of whether the movie really calls for it) and a soundtrack release (regardless of its merits as a listening experience).

The Era of the Compilation Score

As the '90s dawned, the importance of the soundtrack as part of a movie's overall promotion and marketing plan grew so great that deals would commonly be put together without regard to the relevance of music to movie.

The term "movie soundtrack" used to mean music (songs or dramatic underscore) that was specifically designed to augment or complement a scene, used in the film, and then included on an album for moviegoers who had enjoyed the music and wanted to hear it again.

By contrast, today's "movie soundtrack" often has little to do with the movie. The classic example is *Batman* (1989), whose "original soundtrack" was the work of Prince. A Warner Bros. recording artist whose involvement was sought by Warner Bros. Pictures to help sell their expensive, high-profile movie, Prince agreed to write several songs. He had also made five top-10 albums for the label, so it was his album that would be released as the movie's soundtrack—despite the fact that snippets of a few songs, barely heard under the dialogue of a couple of party scenes in the movie, was all that existed of the Prince "score" for *Batman*. The number 1 single "Batdance" wasn't in the movie at all.

The album shipped platinum and spent six week at number 1. Danny Elfman, composer of the 75-minute orchestral score, had to wait a month

BATMAN ORIGINAL MOTION PICTURE SCORE COMPOSED BY DANNY ELFMAN

COURTESY OF WARNER BROS. WORLDWIDE MUSIC

before his album was released; Warner didn't want to confuse consumers. His music—the real score—managed to reach number 30 and sold an estimated 200,000 units but didn't even go gold. *Newsweek*'s headline succinctly captured the concept: "How to Sell a Soundtrack: First, Ignore the Movie."

It happened again to Elfman on *Dick Tracy* (1990), when Madonna's album *I'm Breathless* (containing three Stephen Sondheim songs from the film and nine tunes having nothing to do with it) was released first on Warner's Sire label. Next was *Music From the Motion Picture "Dick Tracy,"* nearly half of whose songs weren't in the picture, also released in advance of the film's opening. Elfman's orchestral score came out about three weeks after the movie. Madonna's album went double platinum; the pseudo-soundtrack reached number 108 and Elfman's score sneaked onto the chart for one week at number 194.

The subtitle of Madonna's album, "Music From and Inspired by the Film," became commonplace on soundtracks in the '90s. At best disingenuous, at worst deceptive, it was a practice that consumers found misleading but to which they didn't strenuously object. The result was acceptance of an industry practice: assembly of a "soundtrack" that may not accurately reflect the music of a movie but that includes some music from the film, some music that may have been written for the film but didn't make it into the final cut, and some music that has nothing to do with the film but was forced into the album as a result of some studio-label handshake.

The *Dick Tracy* trilogy was believed to be the first trio of "soundtrack" albums designed to cash in on the hullabaloo surrounding a high-profile, big-budget Hollywood movie. Eight years later, DreamWorks' animated *Prince of Egypt* would try a similar tactic by releasing a legitimate soundtrack (although it too contained songs that weren't in the film) along with a country album and a gospel album of the same name—neither of which had anything whatsoever to do with the film.

One of the most egregious cases of misleading soundtracks was Fox's album from the action hit *Speed* (1994), whose "music from and inspired by" collection included 12 tunes, only four of which actually appeared in the film, in considerably abbreviated form. Mark Mancina's energetic score (the true "soundtrack") was released quietly and separately and sold few copies by comparison.

These occur regularly now that the movie-soundtrack business has become so complicated. Veteran music supervisor Joel Sill—whose resumé starts with the album deal for the landmark *Easy Rider* back in 1969—explains it via this typical scenario: "The picture company has what they think is a tentpole picture. They instruct the music department to go out and make a big deal, and instruct the filmmakers that this is one of the vehicles they're going to market the movie with: 10 or 12 recordings, two or three videos. . . . They sell this to a record company for $1 million or $1.5

million, whatever the advance is. The record company says, 'That's fine, I'll be happy to pay that, provided that I've got a guarantee of 10 or 12 or 14 recordings that are audible in the film.'

"The film company, as they're marching toward completion, finds that they can only shoe-horn so many pieces in, and they go back and negotiate down the deal with the record company. The record company says, 'If we've only got four or five pieces in the film, that's not enough to sell [records], take it to somebody else.' The film company's too far down the road, and they say, 'What if we just put Music From and Inspired By on the album?' The record company says, 'Fine. We'll pay you $300,000 and we'll put in 10 other artists that we like, and we won't have to worry about the director or anybody [else from the production] approving them.' It happens quite often."

Even on the simpler films, the issues can be complex. The music supervisor, in particular, often acts as a kind of central clearing house for music on a contemporary film. He or she deals with the director, who usually has ideas about the kinds of songs, artists, and appropriate placement within the film; with studio music executives, who are concerned with both financial and artistic issues; with record label executives, who are often interested in placing their own artists on a potential hit soundtrack; with artists and artists' management, particularly when new songs are to be written and recorded for a film; and with other studio and production people ranging from music publishers to marketing and promotion people. The concerns of all can affect the content of a movie soundtrack.

One of the most complicated of such projects in recent years was the song score for director Robert Zemeckis's Oscar-winning *Forrest Gump* (1994), which Sill coordinated. It ultimately involved 57 pieces of music, 44 of which were master recordings of original hits ranging from "California Dreamin'" by the Mamas and the Papas and "Love Her Madly" by the Doors to "Turn! Turn! Turn!" by the Byrds and "Go Your Own Way" by Fleetwood Mac. It was such an eclectic stew of '50s, '60s, and '70s tunes that Sill recalled being initially disappointed by the album, a two-CD set containing 31 of those tracks. "What does Joni Mitchell have to do with The Doors?" he thought. In fact, the Epic set spent five weeks at number 2, sold an estimated nine million units, and spent 94 weeks on the *Billboard* album chart. Beyond its value as a reminder of the music from the film, the album turned out to be a musical time capsule with wide popular appeal.

The *Forrest Gump* album was an aberration among hit soundtracks in the '90s. The vast majority of soundtrack albums that crashed the *Billboard* top 20 were urban-oriented collections, reflecting the musical interests of record buyers in the era of industrial rock, grunge, rap, and hip-hop.

Soundtracks like 1991's *Boyz N the Hood* (which reached number 12) and *New Jack City* (number 2), 1993's *Menace II Society* (number 11), 1994's *The Crow* (number 1), 1995's *Dangerous Minds* (number 1) and *Mortal Kombat* (number 10), and 1996's *Sunset Park* (number 4) and *The Nutty Professor* (number 8) demonstrated the marketability of this music regardless of its use in the films (usually minimal and barely audible). Soundtracks had become less a souvenir of the film and more of a radio- and MTV-driven audio enticement to potential filmgoers.

Hit singles were still a factor, of course, but were often an oddity. Composer Michael Kamen initially objected to the inclusion of a contemporary pop tune over the end titles of Kevin Costner's *Robin Hood: Prince of Thieves* as completely out of place in a medieval tale. He relented, and "(Every-thing I Do) I Do It for You," sung by Bryan Adams and based on Kamen's love theme for Maid Marian, not only reached number 1 as a single, it propelled Kamen's otherwise completely orchestral soundtrack to number 5 and platinum status in 1991.

Eric Clapton's moving song "Tears in Heaven" made its debut on the *Rush* soundtrack the following year, reaching number 2 as a single; and Wayne and Garth's "performance" of Queen's "Bohemian Rhapsody" in *Wayne's World* sent the 1975 tune back into the top 10 and the album to number 1 for two weeks in early 1992.

Warner Bros.' fantasy and animation franchises seemed to generate more record hits than movie smashes. From *Batman Forever* (1995), U2's "Hold Me, Thrill Me, Kiss Me, Kill Me" made the top 20 and Seal's "Kiss From a Rose" went straight to number 1. Warners' *Space Jam* album (1996) was on the charts for 82 weeks, the best-selling album of the first half of '97, launching four top-40 hits (R. Kelly's "I Believe I Can Fly," Monica's "For You I Will," Seal's "Fly Like an Eagle," and Quad City DJ's "Space Jam").

As Gary LeMel, now president of music at Warner Bros., says, "The studio, the director, the producers, everybody wants to help market the film with music, because it's a great free advertising tool that incorporates MTV or VH1 or both." The schedule now often involves planning the first single and video to break six to eight weeks before the film.

LeMel cites Warners' *The Bodyguard* (1992) as the best example of film-and-record synergy in recent times. "The record not only promoted the movie, which did over $250 million all over the world, but also sold 30 million albums worldwide," he points out. Whitney Houston starred in the movie as a singer-turned-actress who falls for her security man (Kevin Costner). The album

Titanic and Beyond

The surprise of the '90s was the success of the score for *Titanic*, the movie phenomenon that made $1 billion worldwide and whose soundtrack far outdistanced all other movie-score albums.

The story is now famous. Composer James Horner and director James Cameron, who had had a falling-out on *Aliens*, patched up their differences, and Horner spent most of a year on Cameron's expensive sea-disaster epic. Horner felt a song could be included, quietly engaged lyricist Will Jennings, and demo'd a song for his friends and past collaborators Celine Dion and her husband, Rene Angelil. Recorded in secret, the demo wowed Cameron and wound up as the final vocal version of "My Heart Will Go On" at the end of the Oscar-winning movie.

"My Heart Will Go On" entered *Billboard*'s singles chart at number 1 in February 1998, at the height of the nation's *Titanic* fever. But the album, containing both the Dion vocal and the Horner score, leaped onto the charts upon release in December 1997, was at number 1 within weeks, and remained there for 16 weeks, longer than any album in the previous five years. It far surpassed Vangelis's *Chariots of Fire* as the top-selling instrumental film score of all time, selling more than 25 million units worldwide.

Horner's *Titanic*, with its orchestral sweep and New Age–style synthesized choral touches, brought about a new appreciation of film music—and renewed the old controversy about whether film music, so often derivative of other sources, is worthy of such attention. Composers groused about Horner's savvy commercial sense, and critics complained that it wasn't very original, but consumers bought the disc at an estimated half-million copies a week. The movie, it should be noted, went on to become the most successful film of all time.

turned out to be one of the biggest successes of the '90s, lasting 20 weeks at number 1 (141 weeks on the chart in all) and generating four top-40 hits, including "I Will Always Love You" (number 1), "I Have Nothing," "I'm Every Woman," and "Run to You."

Houston went on to make *Waiting to Exhale* (1995) with songs by Babyface that once again made the charts if not the Oscar nominations: Houston with "Exhale (Shoop Shoop)" at number 1, Mary J. Blige with "Not Gon' Cry" at number 2, Brandy with "Sittin' Up in My Room" at number 2, and the Houston–CeCe Winans duet "Count on Me" at number 8. The album spent five weeks at number 1.

These, however, are the exceptions to the rule. More often, as Anne Thompson pointed out in an *L.A. Weekly* column in 1987, "what results is a lousy, intrusive assortment of pop singles on a soundtrack that winds up pleasing no one. Record buyers respond only when the music works organically within the movie . . . For the movie companies, the challenge is to find more soundtracks that actually serve the movies *and* their marketing."

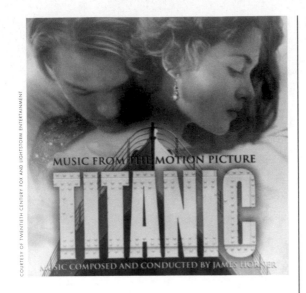

Label executives have begun to broaden the definition of "classical" music to include music written by the best practitioners of the film-scoring craft. Sony Classical, London/Decca, and others have signed composers traditionally associated with films (Williams, Barry, Horner,

Kamen, and others) to deals enabling them to record film collections, and even nonfilm projects, knowing that the market for this music is waiting to be tapped.

Purists scoff at movie music being considered "classical" in any sense, but the failure of most new concert-hall works in the commercial marketplace has led executives to seek out fresh voices. Aware of public response to movie music, both in the success of a handful of soundtracks and in the growing awareness of film composers as concert artists, a new generation of artist-and-repertoire executives have shifted alliances to ensure the survival of their labels.

As Sony Classical president Peter Gelb put it in a *Daily Variety* story in early 1998: "It is essential for the survival and future well-being of the classical record business, and classical music in general, to open up the doors to accessible, melodic classical music. And composers of that music are, more often than not, found in Hollywood."

Addinsell, Richard (1904–1977)

London-born Addinsell studied briefly at the Royal College of Music but spent most of his life as a working composer, writing songs and scores for the theater, radio, and movies. Some of his collaborators were among England's leading artists: Gertrude Lawrence, Noel Coward, Joyce Grenfell, and David Lean. Douglas Fairbanks, Jr., introduced Addinsell to films with *The Amateur Gentleman* in 1936. Just four years later he would write his most famous piece: the Rachmaninoff-styled "Warsaw Concerto," for the 1941 film *Dangerous Moonlight* (known in the U.S. as *Suicide Squadron*), about a Polish concert pianist who becomes a member of a British fighter squadron. The music became far better known than the film it was written for.

Addinsell wrote nearly 50 film scores, including the music for at least half a dozen classics: MGM's *Goodbye, Mr. Chips* (1939), the original *Gaslight* (1940), *Tom Brown's Schooldays* (1951), the Alastair Sim *A Christmas Carol* (1951), and the Tennessee Williams adaptation *The Roman Spring of Mrs. Stone* (1961). He also scored MGM's *Beau Brummell* (1954), and Marilyn Monroe sang a song of his in *The Prince and the Showgirl* (1957).

WARSAW CONCERTO

ASV CD WHL 2108

Led by the nine-minute "Warsaw Concerto" from *Dangerous Moonlight*, this nearly 70-minute disc contains themes and suites from nine of his other films. A 20-minute suite from *The Greengage Summer* (1961), better known as *Loss of Innocence*, starring Susannah York, suggests the film's Continental locale via guitars and accordion. Also included: music for Rock Hudson's period adventure *Sea Devils* (1953), a waltz from Noel Coward's *Blithe Spirit* (1945), an Irish-flavored suite from Hitchcock's *Under Capricorn* (1949), and a romantic piece from David Lean's *The Passionate Friends* (1949). Kenneth Alwyn conducts the Royal Ballet Sinfonia.

RICHARD ADDINSELL: FILM MUSIC

ASV CD WHL 2115

This second volume of Addinsell's movie work contains music from several of his most famous films: the alternately romantic and dramatic prelude from the original 1940 version of *Gaslight*; a 13-minute suite from *Scrooge* (1951), the classic Alistair Sims version that was retitled *A Christmas Carol* for U.S. release; a prelude and waltz from the Noel Coward fantasy *Blithe Spirit* (1945); Elizabethan pomp for *Fire Over England* (1937); a suite from *The Passionate Friends* (1949); and a march and waltz from the Peter Sellers comedy *Waltz of the Toreadors* (1962). Kenneth Alwyn conducts the Royal Ballet Sinfonia.

BRITISH LIGHT MUSIC: RICHARD ADDINSELL

Marco Polo 8.223732

This collection showcases Addinsell's versatility over two decades in British film. Included are a suite from his 1937 Laurence Olivier–Vivien Leigh swashbuckler *Fire Over England*; his stirring theme for schoolmaster Robert Donat in 1939's *Goodbye, Mr. Chips*; an overture from his light-hearted *Tom*

Brown's Schooldays (1940); highly theatrical music for Laurence Olivier and Marilyn Monroe in *The Prince and the Showgirl* (1957); and his grandly dramatic, piano-dominated theme for Dirk Bogarde in the 1958 version of *A Tale of Two Cities*. Kenneth Alwyn conducts the BBC Concert Orchestra.

FROM THE AUTHOR'S COLLECTION

Addison, John (1920–1998)

British-born John Addison studied at the Royal College of Music and happened to meet filmmaker Roy Boulting while both were serving in the military during World War II. Later, Boulting invited him to compose the music for his 1950 suspense thriller *Seven Days to Noon* and Addison's film-scoring career began. A long professional relationship with director Tony Richardson began with Richardson's 1957 staging of John Osborne's *The Entertainer* with Laurence Olivier and continued over the next 30 years, including both stage (three other Olivier-Richardson collaborations in the London theater) and screen (including Addison's Oscar-winning music for *Tom Jones*, now considered a textbook example of comedy scoring).

Charm and wit were the hallmarks of Addison's musical style, from *Tom Jones* to his later Oscar-nominated *Sleuth* (1972), the delightful Sherlock Holmes mystery *The Seven Per-Cent Solution* (1976), and the pirate film *Swashbuckler* (1976).

One of Addison's most interesting assignments was director Richard Attenborough's all-star war film *A Bridge Too Far* (1977), which dramatized the disastrous 1944 Allied airdrop behind German lines in Holland. Addison was, as a soldier in Britain's XXX Corps, a part of the operation. He won an Emmy for the theme and pilot score for TV's long-running *Murder, She Wrote*.

TOM JONES
MCA MCAD-6178

Addison's whimsical, rollicking, and lusty score for 1963's Best Picture winner also won the Academy Award for original score and a Grammy to boot. Tony Richardson directed this delightful John Osborne adaptation of the Henry Fielding novel about the bawdy adventures of an 18th-century rogue (Albert Finney). Addison conducts the Sinfonia of London with lots of fun, period-sounding solo harpsichord.

TORN CURTAIN
Varèse Sarabande VSD-5296

Addison was the composer called in as a replacement after Alfred Hitchcock fired the temperamental Bernard Herrmann, who gave *Torn Curtain* a grim-sounding, brass-heavy dramatic score—exactly what Hitchcock, responding to pressure from Universal executives for a pop score, didn't want. Addison's lighter approach for the Paul Newman–Julie Andrews Cold War thriller didn't help the 1966 picture but features a lyrical love theme.

A BRIDGE TOO FAR

Rykodisc RCD 10746

Addison's connection with Richard Attenborough's 1977 epic, based on Cornelius Ryan's book about the Allies' disastrous 1944 operation behind enemy lines in Holland, was unusually personal. As a British soldier, he was wounded in Normandy just after D-Day and later served in XXX Corps, which was involved in the operation chronicled in this three-hour film. His cheery march for the troops contrasts sharply with his music for the Dutch people. The all-star cast included Michael Caine, Sean Connery, Gene Hackman, Anthony Hopkins, Laurence Olivier, and Robert Redford. It's one of Addison's finest and most compelling scores.

Alwyn, William (1905–1985)

Although his name is rarely mentioned in the same breath as those of Arnold, Walton, and Vaughan Williams—all of whom were distinguished English concert-hall composers who also wrote for film—William Alwyn was an equally talented and seriously underrated composer who wrote five symphonies, six concertos, two operas, and considerable chamber music.

He wrote many documentary scores and music for approximately 60 feature films, including several for Carol Reed, including *Kipps* (1941), *Odd Man Out* (1947), *The Fallen Idol* (1948), *The Running Man* (1963), and Reed's Oscar-winning World War II documentary *The True Glory* (1945).

Alwyn's music played a key role in *The Rocking-Horse Winner* (1950), aided the swashbuckling antics of Burt Lancaster and Errol Flynn in *The Crimson Pirate* (1952) and *The Master of Ballantrae* (1953) respectively, and was widely

heard in America in the Disney live-action films *The Swiss Family Robinson* (1960) and *In Search of the Castaways* (1962). He composed a brief but dramatic score for the classic sinking-of-the-Titanic movie *A Night to Remember* (1958).

WILLIAM ALWYN: FILM MUSIC

Chandos CHAN 9243

This 1993 recording includes lengthy suites from three Alwyn classics and a single theme from a fourth. Two are Carol Reed films: the intense and dramatic music for 1947's *Odd Man Out*, with James Mason's unforgettable performance as a wounded Irish rebel hunted by police; and the Graham Greene–scripted *The Fallen Idol*, made the following year and told almost entirely from a child's point of view. The light and amusing score for John Mills in *The History of Mr. Polly* (1949) and a calypso for Rex Harrison in *The Rake's Progress* (1945, also known as *Notorious Gentleman*), are also included. Richard Hickox conducts the London Symphony Orchestra.

Arnold, David (1962–)

Despite winning a Grammy for *Independence Day* and achieving a high international profile for two James Bond films, the British Arnold is still a film-scoring novice, having only worked in the field since 1993. A clarinet player as a youth, he graduated to guitar and keyboards and toured with rock bands before teaming up with a producer in his hometown of Luton to create music for short films. Arnold's big break came when Bjork's rendition of "Play Dead," a song he wrote for Danny Cannon's low-budget thriller *The Young Americans*, became a hit single. Then came an offer to score the sci-fi epic *Stargate* (1994), directed by Roland Emmerich, who followed it with the even bigger

Independence Day (1996) and the widely reviled *Godzilla* (1998). On the orchestral scores, Arnold, who is without formal training in a classical sense, works closely with orchestrator-conductor Nicholas Dodd.

His most successful score, artistically, has been the music for the James Bond movie *Tomorrow Never Dies* (1997)—probably because he reveres the original John Barry style and spent two years producing "Shaken and Stirred," a new collection of Bond tunes (mostly by Barry) performed by artists ranging from Aimee Mann and Chryssie Hynde to Iggy Pop and the Propellerheads. In 1999 he followed these with music for the next Bond film, *The World Is Not Enough*.

INDEPENDENCE DAY
RCA 09026-6856-2

The most idiotic movie of 1996 was also its biggest hit, and Arnold's score was not only along for the ride—in many cases it was the ride. Arnold's fanfares, military cadences, wordless choir, and portentous battle music for Devlin and Emmerich's jingoistic let's-get-the-aliens adventure—cranked up to ridiculously loud levels in theaters—met all expectations and made Will Smith, Bill Pullman, and Jeff Goldblum look like heroes. It won a Grammy for original music for a film or TV special.

TOMORROW NEVER DIES
A&M 31454 0830 2

Arnold's best work to date, this score for the Pierce Brosnan 007 film was composed over a six-month period in 1997 and, Arnold said, was designed "with one foot in the '60s and one foot in the '90s"—both emulating and updating John Barry's classic style for James Bond. The theme that Arnold and lyricist Don Black wrote (titled "Surrender" and sung by k.d. lang) is the best Bond song in years, far outshining the Sheryl Crow title song which is also on the album.

Arnold, Sir Malcolm (1921–)

Formerly first trumpet for the London Philharmonic Orchestra, the English-born Arnold became a full-time composer in the late 1940s. Since then he has written nine symphonies, concerti for many instruments, operas, ballets, dozens of chamber works—and, amazingly, more than a hundred film scores before he retired from movies in 1970.

He scored three films for the estimable director David Lean: *Breaking the Sound Barrier* (1952), *Hobson's Choice* (1954), and his Oscar winner, *The Bridge on the River Kwai* (1957), although the latter is unfortunately better remembered for its use of Kenneth Alford's "Colonel Bogey" march as whistled by the men under Alec Guinness's command.

Arnold was a master at creating musical atmosphere for exotic locales—Africa in *The Roots of Heaven* (1958) and *The Lion* (1962), China in *The Inn of the Sixth Happiness* (1958), Scotland in *Tunes of Glory* (1960), Norway in *The Heroes of Telemark* (1965), India in *Nine Hours to Rama* (1963)—as well as being a fine tunesmith when the moment called for one. His *Inn of the Sixth Happiness* score won Britain's Ivor Novello Award for outstanding film music of the year.

In the wake of his success with *Kwai*, Arnold was much in demand for films with World War II backgrounds, among them *Dunkirk* (1958) and the original version of *The Thin Red Line* (1964). His final score was a magical one for an all-star television adaptation of *David Copperfield* (1970). He was knighted in 1993.

MALCOLM ARNOLD: FILM MUSIC

Chandos CHAN 9100

Suites from five classic Arnold scores are collected on this 1992 disc. Christopher Palmer arranged four of them: the grim but atmospheric *The Bridge on the River Kwai*, which won the composer a 1957 Oscar; *Whistle Down the Wind* (1962), a charming chamber score for winds, string quartet, guitar, and percussion; *Hobson's Choice* (1954), an alternately droll and romantic piece for Charles Laughton as an overbearing bootshop owner; and *The Inn of the Sixth Happiness* (1958), which combined themes of determination and lyricism for English missionary Ingrid Bergman in China. Arnold's exciting "Rhapsody for Orchestra" from *Breaking the Sound Barrier* (1952), his op. 38, is his own arrangement. Richard Hickox conducts the London Symphony Orchestra.

THE BRIDGE ON THE RIVER KWAI

Columbia CK 66131

Arnold's score was one of seven 1957 Academy Awards (including Best Picture) won by this David Lean film about Allied prisoners of war who are forced by their Japanese captors to build a bridge over a Burmese river. The British officer who wants to comply, played by Alec Guinness, and the American determined to blow it up, played by William Holden, match wits in this intelligent epic. Arnold's jungle atmosphere and heroic theme are memorable, although moviegoers tended to leave the theater humming the "Colonel Bogey" march (by Kenneth Alford) that the soldiers were whistling throughout the movie.

THE INN OF THE SIXTH HAPPINESS

20th Fox 3011 (LP)

Arnold's alternately passionate and thrilling score for Ingrid Bergman's portrayal of the real-life English missionary Gladys Aylward and her harrowing adventures in China was captured in this now-rare 1958 album (which also contains dialogue). Arnold conducts the Royal Philharmonic Orchestra, augmented by a group of Chinese musicians who provided some of the score's musical flavor. The composer—who cleverly intertwined the traditional children's tune "This Old Man," which the Chinese youngsters sing in the film—won England's Ivor Novello Award for this score.

Auric, Georges (1899–1983)

French composer Georges Auric was a member of Les Six (along with Milhaud, Honegger, Poulenc, and others) but gained fame writing ballet music for legendary impresario Serge Diaghilev in Paris. He also wrote more than 100 film scores, beginning in 1930, including six for famed French director Jean Cocteau—notably the classic *La Belle et la Bête* (*Beauty and the Beast*, 1946). Auric's neo-Romantic style was ideal for many films, and he found himself in demand with filmmakers in Britain and America as well as his native France. His classic comedies for the British Ealing studio included *Passport to Pimlico* (1949), *The Lavender Hill Mob* (1951), and *The Titfield Thunderbolt* (1953).

Several others gained wide exposure in the United States, notably the British horror classic *Dead of Night* (1945); *Caesar and Cleopatra*, (1946) with Claude Rains and Vivien Leigh; John Huston's Oscar-winning Toulouse-Lautrec film, *Moulin Rouge* (1952); Henri-Georges Clouzot's suspense thriller *The Wages of Fear* (1952); Audrey Hepburn's Oscar-winning turn in *Roman Holiday* (1953); Otto Preminger's *Bonjour Tristesse* (1958); and Jack Clayton's "Turn of the Screw" adaptation

The Innocents (1961). Auric's waltz theme from *Moulin Rouge* became a popular hit, but the composer himself was never Oscar-nominated.

LA BELLE ET LA BÊTE
Marco Polo 8.223765

Jean Cocteau's stunning 1946 adaptation of the classic fairy tale "Beauty and the Beast" benefited from an impressionistic score that employs orchestra and chorus, providing both atmosphere and emotional content. Jean Marais and Josette Day played the title roles, with Auric's beguiling score playing a more important role than usual (because Auric's music, written while the picture was still being edited, was not designed to synchronize precisely). Adriano conducts the Moscow Symphony Orchestra and Axios chorus in this 1994 re-recording.

FILM MUSIC OF GEORGES AURIC
Chandos CHAN 9774

Ten of Auric's best scores are included in this 1999 collection, with Rumon Gamba conducting the BBC Philharmonic. Suites include Auric's dramatic music for Bernard Shaw's *Caesar and Cleopatra* (1946), the nightmarish score for the horror classic *Dead of Night* (1945), and a chilling score for *The Innocents* (1961). Music for the Ealing comedies is lighter in tone: *Hue and Cry* (1947), *Passport to Pimlico* (1949), *The Lavender Hill Mob* (1951), *The Titfield Thunderbolt* (1953), and *Father Brown* (1954). The lush *Moulin Rouge* (1952), for John Huston's film with Jose Ferrer as artist Toulouse-Lautrec, and the dramatic *It Always Rains on Sunday* (1947), round out the recording.

Bacalov, Luis (1933–)

Argentina-born Bacalov studied with pianist Artur Schnabel and moved to Italy in 1959, where he soon began scoring movies, notably spaghetti westerns and revenge melodramas with titles like *A Bullet for the General* and *We Still Kill the Old Way* (both 1967)—although an early work for acclaimed director Pier Paolo Pasolini, *The Gospel According to St. Matthew*, received a 1966 Oscar nomination for his adaptation of classical works by Bach, Mozart, and Prokofiev.

Later he worked with Fellini on *City of Women* (1980) and on such art-house fare as *Entre Nous* (1983) before finding fame as the composer of *Il Postino*, Michael Radford's moving 1994 film about the Chilean poet Pablo Neruda and the simple Italian fellow who delivers his mail. Bacalov won the 1995 British and American Academy Awards for his music.

IL POSTINO
Miramax/Hollywood MH-62029-2

Bacalov's Oscar-winning music for British director Michael Radford's 1995 charmer about a good-hearted Italian postman (Massimo Troisi) who befriends expatriate Chilean poet Pablo Neruda (Philippe Noiret) is as simple and charming as the postman himself. Bacalov's theme appears in various instrumental combinations including harpsichord and strings, and guitar and bandoneon. The album contains not only Bacalov's complete score but also many readings of Neruda poetry set to Bacalov music.

Bacharach, Burt (1928–)

One of the premier pop songwriters of the '60s, Bacharach studied with Darius Milhaud and, by the late '50s, was both conducting for Marlene Dietrich and writing songs with a young lyricist named Hal David. Together they created such tunes as "Walk on By," "What the World Needs Now Is Love," "Do You Know the Way to San Jose?," and about a hundred other great ones.

Inevitably, Hollywood called. They wrote title songs for films like *The Man Who Shot Liberty Valence* (1962) and exploitation songs (written not for, but after, successful movies) for pictures like *Wives and Lovers* (1963). They received their first Oscar nominations for the title songs to 1965's *What's New Pussycat?* and 1966's *Alfie*.

As a film composer, Bacharach's trademark style was lively, bouncy, and melodic material, often with offbeat or quirky orchestration. He always wrote with an eye on the commercial side, usually including a memorable title song (and often a second or third tune as source music).

Case in point: his score for the immensely popular Dudley Moore–Liza Minnelli comedy *Arthur*, which won a 1981 Best Song Oscar (with

lyricists Carole Bayer Sager, Peter Allen, and Christopher Cross) and went to number 1. His equally famous AIDS-research anthem "That's What Friends Are For" was actually written as part of his *Night Shift* score (1982).

WHAT'S NEW PUSSYCAT?
Rykodisc RCD 10740
AFTER THE FOX
Rykodisc RCD 10716

These albums of Bacharach's first two scores, both for United Artists comedies, are similar in style and tone. The Woody Allen–scripted *What's New Pussycat?*, from 1965, features the Oscar-nominated title song (and two other tunes, Dionne Warwick's "Here I Am" and Manfred Mann's "My Little Red Book"). *After the Fox*, from 1966, has The Hollies' title tune. Both are filled with light, upbeat material containing Bacharach's complex rhythm schemes, warm melodies, and surprising chord changes. Both also sport amusing cover paintings by the renowned fantasy artist Frank Frazetta.

CASINO ROYALE
Varèse Sarabande VSD-5265

Legendary and much sought after on vinyl—the aural equivalent of the Holy Grail for its brilliant, stunningly present sound—this 1967 score for the David Niven–Woody Allen–Peter Sellers James Bond spoof is vintage Bacharach. The title tune is an instrumental played by Herb Alpert & the Tijuana Brass, and the Oscar-nominated love theme ("The Look of Love," with Hal David lyrics) is sung by a sexy, breathy Dusty Springfield. The rest of the score, brimming with Burt's wonderful '60s sound, is a good deal more lively and fun than the movie.

BUTCH CASSIDY AND THE SUNDANCE KID
A&M CD 3159

The memorable first teaming of Paul Newman and Robert Redford as turn-of-the-century western outlaws also won Bacharach two 1969 Oscars, for his score and (with Hal David) the song "Raindrops Keep Fallin' on My Head" (which became a number 1 hit for B.J. Thomas). Much of Bacharach's score is based largely on a melancholy tune (heard in the cuts "Not Goin' Home Anymore" and "Come Touch the Sun"), but two memorable sequences are standalone: the brilliant choral piece "South American Getaway" and the bright New York sequence "The Old Fun City." Although an Oscar winner, the score was widely criticized by film-music insiders as anachronistic and inappropriate. The album, however, went to number 16 on the *Billboard* charts.

PHOTO BY E.J. CAMP, FROM THE AUTHOR'S COLLECTION

Barry, John (1933–)

From the time he was a teenager, John Barry's sole ambition was to write music for movies. His father ran a chain of theaters in the north of England, so Barry's musical ambitions naturally followed cine-matic lines. In the late 1950s, he fronted a popular jazz combo, the John Barry Seven, which backed British pop singer Adam Faith on several hit records. He was asked to rework the original music for the first James Bond film, *Dr. No* (1962), which led to composing 11 more 007 adventures over the next 25 years.

Barry's fresh, pop-orchestral excitement and memorable title songs for the globetrotting British spy—particularly in such '60s outings as *Goldfinger*, *Thunderball*, *You Only Live Twice*, and *On Her Majesty's Secret Service*—not only charted, they created a new sound for action-adventure that few composers successfully imitated.

Although he is equally conversant with jazz-based scores (including 1965's *The Knack*, 1981's *Body Heat*, and 1984's *The Cotton Club*) and choral writing (notably in 1968's *The Lion in Winter* and 1971's *Mary, Queen of Scots*), his most popular theme is probably *Born Free*, which won 1966 Academy Awards for Best Song and Best Original Score; almost as well known may be his harmonica tune for 1969's *Midnight Cowboy*, which won a Grammy. He has three more Oscars, for *The Lion in Winter*, *Out of Africa* (1985), and *Dances With Wolves* (1990).

Once typecast as an action-movie composer based on his success with the Bond scores, Barry in recent years has shifted to a more romantic sensibility as demonstrated in his later Oscar-winning scores and the enormously popular *Somewhere in Time* (1980). In the late '90s he also began composing such concept albums as "The Beyondness of Things."

MOVIOLA
Epic EK 52985

The perfect John Barry sampler, this 1992 collection contains many of the composer's most memorable themes. Of particular interest are his grandly romantic arrangements of the otherwise commercially unavailable scores for *Born Free* (1966), *Mary, Queen of Scots* (1971), *Walkabout* (1971), *Frances* (1982), and the beautiful title track (originally written for, but not used in, *The Prince of Tides*). Also included: *Out of Africa, Midnight Cowboy, Body Heat, Somewhere in Time, Dances With Wolves, Chaplin, The Cotton Club*, and "We Have All the Time in the World" from *On Her Majesty's Secret Service*. Barry conducts the Royal Philharmonic Orchestra.

THE MUSIC OF JOHN BARRY
Columbia 476750 2

Twenty-four tracks culled from Barry's three 1960s movie-theme collections offer a glimpse into his arranging style of that era. Nine are from the Bond films, including his classic twangy-guitar-with-big-band arrangement of the "James Bond Theme." Several others showcase his versatility: dramatic use of the cymbalum in *The Ipcress File* and *King Rat* (both 1965), the delicate raindrop-piano of *Seance on a Wet Afternoon* (1964), jazz organ in *The Knack* (1965), brittle harpsichord for the elderly woman of *The Whisperers* (1967), a grand waltz with balalaikas for "The Girl With the Sun in Her Hair" (a British shampoo commercial from 1967), mandolins for *The Appointment* (1969).

GOLDFINGER
EMI CDP-7-95345-2

Barry's now-classic soundtrack for the 1964 James Bond movie spent 70 weeks on the *Billboard* charts, including three weeks at number 1. This was Sean Connery's third outing as 007, with Honor Blackman and Gert Frobe. Arguably the greatest Bond score ever (and Barry's personal favorite), it features Shirley

Bassey's title-track vocal and the blend of jazzy sophistication, melodic sense, and orchestral suspense-and-action music that would mark all of the best Bond scores.

BORN FREE
Varèse Sarabande 302 066 084 2

Barry's indelible music for this family film based on Joy Adamson's best-selling memoir won two 1966 Oscars, for Best Song and Best Original Score, and became an international hit recorded many times over. The film cast Virginia McKenna and Bill Travers as game wardens in Kenya who adopted a lion cub they named Elsa; Barry's score, with its lyrical and dramatic passages, received three Grammy nominations including Song of the Year. Barry's original soundtrack is unavailable on CD, but Frederic Talgorn re-recorded it in 1999 with the Royal Scottish National Orchestra.

THE LION IN WINTER
Columbia/Legacy CK 66133

Barry's alternately elegant and grim score for James Goldman's 12th-century drama about an English monarch (Peter O'Toole), his jailed queen (Katharine Hepburn), and their conniving to anoint a successor, won a 1968 Academy Award. Adding to the period colors are Latin texts sung by the Accademia Monteverdiana; wordless choir adds power to the most dramatic scenes. Barry's later scores featuring equally effective uses of choir (*Mary, Queen of Scots* and *The Last Valley*, both 1971) are, unfortunately, not available on CD.

SOMEWHERE IN TIME
MCA MCAD-31164

The box-office failure of this romantic fantasy was followed by an enormous success on cable, and the result was a platinum soundtrack for Barry many years after its 1980 release. Christopher Reeve starred as a playwright who wills himself back in time to meet and woo legendary actress Jane Seymour. Rachmaninoff's "Rhapsody on a Theme of Paganini" figures prominently in the score, but it's Barry's unfailing melodic sense, with a tinge of sadness, that carries the day.

BODY HEAT
Varèse Sarabande VSD-5951

Lawrence Kasdan's steamy 1981 thriller with William Hurt and Kathleen Turner got just what it needed for music: ironically, a cool-jazz score courtesy of John Barry. Ronnie Lang's bluesy alto sax solos and Barry's moody colors, ranging from synthesizer and piano ostinatos to sultry, string-dominated passages, heighten the mystery and drama. The original is now hard to find; Joel McNeely re-recorded the score in 1998 with the London Symphony Orchestra.

OUT OF AFRICA
MCA MCAD-6158

Barry's quietly powerful and memorably romantic score for director Sydney Pollack's 1985 Oscar winner as Best Picture won its own Academy Award, for Best Original Score. His music for this Robert Redford–Meryl Streep drama (based on the African experiences of Danish writer Isak Dinesen) lends an occasional melancholy touch, as in Karen's theme and the wordless choir in the flying sequences. The adagio from Mozart's Clarinet Concerto in A figures briefly. Rich, lyrical, and expressive, it is perhaps Barry's best work.

DANCES WITH WOLVES
Epic ZK 46982

"I'm a big symphony guy," said Kevin Costner about his decision to hire John Barry to score his three-hour western epic, which won seven 1990 Oscars including Best Picture and Best Original Score. Barry's symphonic tapestry includes several recurring themes, primarily one of strength and dignity for protagonist John Dunbar (Costner), an Army soldier who eventually joins a Sioux Indian tribe. Lush, powerful, and—although criticized by some critics for its lack of authentic Indian sounds—reflective of a white man's viewpoint in the wild West. Barry also won a 1991 Grammy for this score.

Bennett, Sir Richard Rodney (1936–)

A contemporary British composer who moves effortlessly from music for the stage to films to television to the concert hall, Sir Richard Rodney Bennett is perhaps best known for his scores for such popular movies as *Murder on the Orient Express* (1974) and *Four Weddings and a Funeral* (1994). Born in Kent, he studied at the Royal Academy of Music and, later in Paris, became the first pupil of Pierre Boulez.

He has toured extensively as a jazz pianist and

singer and has written nearly three dozen concert works including concerti for saxophone, guitar, trumpet, harpsichord, and percussion; choral works including "Sermons and Devotions" and "Calico Pie"; and others.

Bennett's best-known work, however, is for movies and British television. His scores range in nature from the austere *Equus* (1977) to the broadly romantic *Murder on the Orient Express*, from the folk-influenced *Far From the Madding Crowd* (1967) to the epic and melancholy *Nicholas and Alexandra* (1971). His TV-movies include the American *Sherlock Holmes in New York*, the British miniseries *Tender Is the Night*, and the cable-TV film *The Tale of Sweeney Todd*. He was knighted in 1998.

FAR FROM THE MADDING CROWD
Sony AK 47023

Bennett received his first Oscar nomination for this lyrical 1967 adaptation of the Thomas Hardy novel (scripted by Frederic Raphael, directed by John Schlesinger, photographed by Nicolas Roeg) with Julie Christie, Alan Bates, Terence Stamp, and Peter Finch. With folk-music expert Isla Cameron consulting on the traditional tunes of Dorset, Bennett constructed a sophisticated score that both incorporated the local musical flavor and imbued the film with feelings of loneliness and passion. The flute solos are by James Galway.

MURDER ON THE ORIENT EXPRESS
Cloud Nine CNS 5007 (U.K.)

Bennett's lush, romantic, and delightfully '30s-style music for the all-star Agatha Christie thriller earned a 1974 Oscar nomination for Original Dramatic Score and a 1975 Grammy nomination. Albert Finney played Hercule Poirot in this lavish whodunit; the suspects included Lauren Bacall,

Ingrid Bergman, Sean Connery, John Gielgud, Vanessa Redgrave, and Richard Widmark. Bennett's grand waltz for the train crossing the European frontier is a highlight.

EQUUS
Rykodisc RCD 10726

One of his most remarkable scores, sadly unappreciated by the Motion Picture Academy, Bennett's music for Sidney Lumet's 1977 film of Peter Shaffer's complex and difficult play (starring the Oscar-nominated Richard Burton and Peter Firth) was written for a unique ensemble of 10 violas, eight cellos, and six basses. As Ross Care points out in the notes, Bennett offers "a quietly tragic elegy for the sacrifice of passion" that is the play's central theme. Monologues by Burton accompany the music.

ENCHANTED APRIL
Bay Cities BCD 3035

Twenty-two minutes of Bennett's lovely score for *Enchanted April*, the British TV-movie that was released theatrically in America in 1991, offer one reason to search out this rare disc. It is accompanied by lengthy excerpts from two Bennett classics: his 1974 Oscar-nominated *Murder on the Orient Express* and the "Elegy for Caroline Lamb" based on his exquisite 1972 score for the forgettable Sarah Miles film *Lady Caroline Lamb*. The *Orient Express* music couples Bennett's grand waltz for the train with his '20s salon sound and dark, dramatic atmosphere for the all-star Agatha Christie adaptation.

Bernard, James (1925–)

For fans of the Hammer films—whether those growing up in Britain during the '60s or those Americans who frequented drive-in horror fare—no music says "frightened" more than that of James Bernard, architect of the sound of Hammer horror.

A graduate of the Royal College of Music, an assistant to Benjamin Britten, and a composition student of Herbert Howells, Bernard actually won a writing Oscar for the 1951 thriller *Seven Days to Noon*. He began scoring BBC radio dramas and, through his friendship with conductor John Hollingsworth, began scoring Hammer films in 1955.

Although dozens of other composers wrote music for Hammer, none wrote more than Bernard: 23 features over 19 years, including several in its *Dracula* and *Frankenstein* series that often starred Christopher Lee and Peter Cushing.

As Randall Larson points out in his book *Music from the House of Hammer*, Hammer music was "as richly Gothic as the moody visuals and as sensual as the flowing, white-robed ladies who floated with evil intent through the echoing catacombs of ancient castles." Bernard's work was often the best of this Gothic tradition.

MUSIC FROM THE HAMMER FILMS
Silva Screen FILMCD 066

Bernard's 13-minute "Dracula Suite" is drawn from the 1958 *Horror of Dracula* and the 1966 *Dracula, Prince of Darkness*. His five-minute finale from *Dracula Has Risen From the Grave* (1968) climaxes in a major-mode triumph over evil, and his 17-minute suite from *Taste the Blood of Dracula* (1970) looms as the most romantic of all. While Bernard's music dominates the album, also featured are a compelling 11-minute suite from Christopher Gunning's *Hands of the Ripper* (1971) and nine minutes from David Whitaker's dramatic *Vampire Circus* (1971). Neil Richardson conducts the Philharmonia Orchestra.

THE DEVIL RIDES OUT:
THE FILM MUSIC OF JAMES BERNARD
Silva America SSD 1059

This second collection of Hammer music is all Bernard. It opens with the "Vampire Rhapsody" from 1964's *Kiss of the Vampire*, a Lisztian-flavored piece for piano and orchestra ("yearning yet decadent," reports the composer in his liner-note reminiscences). A suite from *She*, the 1965 remake with Ursula Andress, filled with awe and mystery; poignant moments from *Frankenstein Created Woman* (1967) and *Scars of Dracula* (1970); dark and horrific music from the 1968 classic *The Devil Rides Out*; and a suite from his strings-and-percussion music for the Quatermass films (*The Quatermass Experiment, X–The Unknown, Quatermass II*, 1955–1957), round out the collection. Kenneth Alwyn conducts the Westminster Philharmonic in three suites; Paul Bateman and Nic Raine conduct the Prague Philharmonic in the others.

PHOTO COURTESY OF CHASEN & COMPANY

Bernstein, Elmer (1922–)

Elmer Bernstein seems to reinvent himself nearly every decade. His landmark score for *The Man*

With the Golden Arm set the standard for jazz-based dramatic music in films during the late 1950s. His score for *The Magnificent Seven* made him the outstanding western composer of the 1960s. He composed a series of comedy scores in the '70s and '80s (including *Ghostbusters*), and in the '90s, he wrote a number of smaller-scale scores that harken back to his gentle, touching music for the classic *To Kill a Mockingbird* (1962) —which is now universally cited as a film-scoring masterpiece.

Bernstein's diverse background and musical training proved to be a firm foundation for scoring films. Encouraged by Aaron Copland, he studied with Roger Sessions, arranged for Glenn Miller while in the Army Air Corps, wrote dozens of radio scores, and was widely heard as a concert pianist in New York City before embarking on his film career in 1950.

Rising rapidly to the top, particularly after his epic score for Cecil B. DeMille's *The Ten Commandments* (1956), he undertook a leadership role in the film-music community, becoming president of the Composers & Lyricists Guild of America in the '70s and acting as an articulate, thoughtful spokesman for the increasingly abused composers in film.

Still active after half a century in the field, Bernstein has written more than 150 film scores and hundreds more for television (including a series of documentaries for David L. Wolper). He won an Oscar for 1967's *Thoroughly Modern Millie* and has become a favorite of Martin Scorsese, who hired him to adapt Bernard Herrmann's score for the 1991 remake of *Cape Fear* and allowed him the necessary time and creative freedom on *The Age of Innocence* that resulted in a 1993 Oscar nomination for best score.

ELMER BERNSTEIN BY ELMER BERNSTEIN
Denon CO-75288

This collection of timeless themes forms an ideal introduction to four decades of Bernstein scores, including long suites from *The Ten Commandments* (1956), *To Kill a Mockingbird* (1962), and the more recent *My Left Foot* (1989) and *The Grifters* (1990). All of the classic themes are here: *The Magnificent Seven* (1960), *The Man With the Golden Arm* (1955), *Walk on the Wild Side* (1962), *Hawaii* (1966), *The Great Escape* (1963), even more recent ones like *Ghostbusters* (1984), *Rambling Rose* (1991), and *Heavy Metal* (1981). Bernstein conducts the Royal Philharmonic Pops Orchestra. The composer's own thoughts on each selection are included in the booklet notes.

THE MAN WITH THE GOLDEN ARM
Decca DL-8257 (LP)

Otto Preminger's 1955 film with Frank Sinatra as a junkie and Eleanor Parker as his wheelchair-bound wife was significant for its unflinching portrayal of drug addiction—and for Bernstein's groundbreaking use of exciting jazz elements in an overall dramatic, orchestral context. The theme has reached classic status, and the jazz segments (featuring Shorty Rogers, Pete Candoli, Milt Bernhart, and Shelly Manne) are vintage '50s. The album spent four weeks at the number-2 spot on *Billboard*'s album chart.

THE TEN COMMANDMENTS
MCA MCAD-42320

Bernstein's rich and inspiring music for Cecil B. DeMille's last great epic, the story of Moses (Charlton Heston) and the Exodus from Egypt of the Jewish people, took a year and a half to write and record in 1955–56. Filled with themes for characters and situations, from the pomp and majesty of the main title to the exuberant, joyful music of the Exodus sequence and the various dances, this is classic film music. Bernstein re-recorded it in 1960 and 1966 for new LP configurations.

SWEET SMELL OF SUCCESS
Decca DL-8610 (LP)
WALK ON THE WILD SIDE
Choreo AS-4-ST (LP)

In the wake of *The Man With the Golden Arm*, Bernstein was asked to write jazz-oriented scores for a number of films including *Sweet Smell of Success* (1957), with its contemporary New York setting and Burt Lancaster as a ruthless columnist, and *Walk on the Wild Side* (1962), set in New Orleans in the 1930s among the bars and bordellos. The latter features a memorable Saul Bass title sequence featuring prowling cats; it reached the top 40 on *Billboard*'s album charts.

THE MAGNIFICENT SEVEN
Rykodisc RCD 10741

Sure, it's in mono, but after 38 years, Bernstein's seminal score for this 1960 western classic finally became available in its original form. Lusty, broad, and rich in every sense, this score bursts with energy and became the prototype for practically every western to follow. Bernstein himself became typecast with a whole series of western scores including such '60s films as *The Sons of Katie Elder* and *The Hallelujah Trail* (both 1965). Had this popular music been released on records at the time of the film, it would have been one of the most successful soundtracks of its era.

TO KILL A MOCKINGBIRD
Varèse Sarabande VSD-5754

This score is universally acknowledged as among the greatest in cinema history. Bernstein—after much agonizing, he confesses in the liner notes—found the key: "To deal in the magic of a child's world." Robert Mulligan's 1962 film of the Harper Lee novel about a small-town Southern lawyer (Gregory Peck) who defends a black man wrongly accused of raping a white woman is a classic, and Bernstein's Oscar-nominated score reflects the drama through the eyes of the lawyer's children Scout and Jem. Chamber-sized ensembles emphasize its Americana sound and its innate lyricism. Bernstein conducts the Royal Scottish National Orchestra in the Varèse re-recording of 1996.

THE GREAT ESCAPE
Rykodisc RCD 10711

Bernstein's jaunty march for this 1963 war classic is almost as recognizable as his music for *The Magnificent Seven* and *To Kill a Mockingbird*. Steve McQueen—reunited with his *Seven* pals Charles Bronson and James Coburn—and James Garner starred in John Sturges's fact-based tale about American and British soldiers building a tunnel beneath a supposedly escape-proof German prisoner-of-war camp. Bernstein's surprisingly lyrical approach suggests the humanity beneath the tough exteriors of the gallant POWs, their resilience and humor in the face of impossible odds.

HAWAII
United Artists UAS-5143 (LP)

Bernstein discovered in researching the music of 19th-century Hawaii that most of its indigenous music involved a flute, some native percussion, and chants. On that meager information he built an entire score for the James A. Michener–inspired epic starring Julie Andrews, Max Von Sydow, and Richard Harris. It received 1966 Oscar nominations for Original Score and its song "The Wishing Doll"; Bernstein confesses it's one of his personal favorites.

THE FILMS OF JOHN WAYNE, VOLUME ONE
THE FILMS OF JOHN WAYNE, VOLUME TWO
Varèse Sarabande VCD-47236, 47264

Few composers in movies have understood the essential American rhythms and colors required by westerns as well as Bernstein. These discs demonstrate Bernstein's power to communicate the era and the settings in rousing and often affecting music. The first contains music from *The Comancheros* (1961) and *True Grit* (1969), the latter of which helped Wayne win his Oscar (the title song was a nominee that year). The second contains suites from three subsequent films: *Big Jake* (1971); *Cahill, United States Marshal* (1973); and the elegiac *The Shootist* (1976). Bernstein conducts the Utah Symphony Orchestra in 1985 and 1986 re-recordings.

MY LEFT FOOT
Varèse Sarabande VSD-5244

Bernstein's chamber score (string quartet, woodwinds, piano, harp, and Ondes Martenot) was a haunting and quietly moving complement to the remarkable performances of Daniel Day-Lewis, Brenda Fricker, and Ray McAnally in this fine 1989 film shot and scored in Ireland. Day-Lewis, who won an Oscar, plays Irish artist-writer Christy Brown, whose cerebral palsy made him less a victim than a courageous man who triumphed over an extremely limiting disability. The score is coupled with that of *Da* (1988), which starred Barnard Hughes and was also filmed in Ireland.

THE AGE OF INNOCENCE
Epic EK 57451

Martin Scorsese's elegant film based on the Edith Wharton novel starred Daniel Day-Lewis, Michelle Pfeiffer, and Winona Ryder. As Scorsese points out in his liner notes, he needed music "that was

absolutely unsentimental and without nostalgia," a sound that offered both detachment and passion. Bernstein accomplished this with a classically oriented score, by turns powerful and memorable; Bernstein received a 1993 Oscar nomination.

Bernstein, Leonard (1918–1990)

The renowned American conductor, composer, and pianist wrote only one original film score, for director Elia Kazan's powerful union-corruption drama *On the Waterfront* in 1954. His Broadway musicals *On the Town* and *West Side Story* were successfully adapted for the screen (in 1949 and 1961, respectively), the latter winning 10 Oscars including Best Picture. In addition to his three symphonies and various chamber pieces, he wrote such dramatic works as the ballet *Fancy Free* (1944), the theater piece *Mass* (1971), and an opera for television, *Trouble in Tahiti* (1952).

On the Waterfront was nominated for 12 Academy Awards and won eight, including Best Picture, Best Actor (Marlon Brando), Best Director (Elia Kazan), and Best Original Screenplay (Budd Schulberg). Curiously, although he was nominated, Bernstein did not win for his dramatic and passionate music, which Kazan featured prominently throughout the film. (Hollywood lore has it that Dimitri Tiomkin's far more forgettable *High and the Mighty* score was the victor that year because of his relentless campaigning and because Bernstein was a New Yorker and not one of the Hollywood "in" crowd.)

Nonetheless, *On the Waterfront* is a classic film and Bernstein's score an indelible part of the experience. As Joan Peyser wrote in her 1987 *Bernstein: A Biography*: "The vivid emotional shifts, the striking alternations of pace and color, the episodes of violence where driving rhythms generate terror are pure Bernstein, sound like only him, and could have been composed by no one else."

BERNSTEIN: CANDIDE / WEST SIDE STORY / ON THE WATERFRONT
Sony Classical SMK 63085

The composer adapted his *On the Waterfront* score into a symphonic suite that he first performed with the Boston Symphony at Tanglewood in August 1955. In six movements, lasting just under 20 minutes, it encapsulates all of the dramatic material: the quiet, dignified theme associated with Marlon Brando's longshoreman character; the explosive, percussion-driven music linked with the violence of the racketeers; the lyrical theme for Brando's growing love for Eva Marie Saint; and the scherzo-like climactic fight between Brando and corrupt union boss Lee J. Cobb. Bernstein conducts the New York Philharmonic in this definitive 1960 recording.

Bliss, Sir Arthur (1891–1975)

The composer who many thought was Sir Edward Elgar's successor in British music spent most of his time writing for the concert hall: orchestral works including *A Colour Symphony*, three ballets, an opera (*The Olympians*), choral works (notably *Morning Heroes*), concerti, songs, and chamber music. He wrote music for only eight films, most of them forgotten today.

One is a certified classic: the music for the H.G. Wells–penned, William Cameron Menzies –designed and –directed science-fiction epic *Things to Come* (1936) starring Raymond Massey. Bliss's contributions were deemed so vital that he and conductor Muir Mathieson were brought in during shooting to contribute ideas.

He also scored the Alexander Korda docu-

mentary-drama *Conquest of the Air* (1940), which lost much of its memorable music in the cutting room; the 1946 drama *Men of Two Worlds*, about an African composer-pianist; the adventure epic *Christopher Columbus* (1949); and the tense 1957 lifeboat drama *Seven Waves Away* with Tyrone Power. He apparently wrote a complete score for the Claude Rains–Vivien Leigh *Caesar and Cleopatra* which was thrown out by the director before its 1946 release.

GREAT BRITISH FILM MUSIC
London 448 954-2

This collection of suites and themes from seven movies produced in the United Kingdom concludes with a 15-minute suite from *Things to Come*. Its somber prologue, relentless wartime march, dramatic "attack on the moon gun" sequence, and optimistic finale demonstrate Bliss's early mastery of film writing. Also notable: suites from Constant Lambert's *Anna Karenina* (1948), Arnold Bax's *Oliver Twist* (1948), Arthur Benjamin's *An Ideal Husband* (1948), William Walton's ballet from *Escape Me Never* (1935), and what is probably the finest recording of Ralph Vaughan Williams's theme for *49th Parallel* (1941). Bernard Herrmann conducts London's National Philharmonic Orchestra.

ARTHUR BLISS: FILM MUSIC
Marco Polo 8.223315

Suites from three of Bliss's more obscure scores are featured in this 1990 re-recording. Twenty-four minutes from the 1949 *Christopher Columbus*, starring Fredric March as the 15th-century explorer, have an appropriately Spanish feel and a sense of heroism and accomplishment. *Seven Waves Away* (known in the U.S. as *Abandon Ship*, 1957) is exciting, and *Men of Two Worlds* (1946) features a seven-minute "concert piece for piano and orchestra with men's voices." Adriano conducts the Czecho-Slovak Radio Symphony Orchestra of Bratislava.

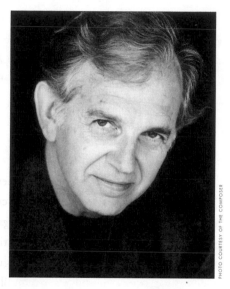

PHOTO COURTESY OF THE COMPOSER

Broughton, Bruce (1945–)

The compleat contemporary film composer, Los Angeles–born Bruce Broughton has Oscar and Grammy nominations for western and period movies, seven Emmys for the finest music in television, and a reputation for creating some of the cleverest music for animation since Carl Stalling.

His parents were Salvation Army officers and band members, so he picked up music fairly quickly. While he originally planned to be an animator, he found himself working in the music department at CBS in the late '60s and early '70s. Scoring shows like *Gunsmoke*, *How the West Was Won*, and later *Dallas* and *Quincy*, he graduated to some of TV's most prestigious TV-movies and miniseries, including *The Blue and the Gray*, *O Pioneers!*, *The Master of Ballantrae*, and *The First Olympics: Athens 1896*.

On the feature side, his music has included classic Americana for the westerns *Silverado* (1985)

and *Tombstone* (1993), a lyrical touch for the family drama *The Boy Who Could Fly* (1986), suspenseful chase music for *Narrow Margin* (1990), a contemporary romantic sound for *For Love or Money* (1993), a beautiful Christmas score for the remake of *Miracle on 34th Street* (1994), and more. Among his notable animation scores are a soaring one for Disney's *The Rescuers Down Under* (1990) and many episodes of the Warner Bros. cartoon series *Tiny Toon Adventures*.

Broughton is artistic director and principal conductor of the Sinfonia of London, which has performed a number of the composer's concert works. They include concertos for tuba and piccolo, works for wind ensemble, and several chamber pieces.

SILVERADO

Intrada MAF 7035D

Lawrence Kasdan's 1985 western starring Kevin Costner, Kevin Kline, Scott Glenn, Danny Glover, and Rosanna Arquette was the first successful oater in some time, and benefited enormously from Broughton's classic Americana score, an Oscar nominee. Kasdan's notes describe it as "stirring, lyrical, exhilarating [and] most importantly, a very emotional score: clear, brave, and unrestrained." And, as Broughton points out, "the orchestration was geared towards power, strength and energy."

YOUNG SHERLOCK HOLMES

MCA 6159 (LP)

One of the great unsung scores of the '80s—but one recognized with a Grammy nomination for its soundtrack album—Broughton's classically styled music for Barry Levinson's Victorian London adventure resounds with period touches and exciting orchestral flourishes. As the youthful Holmes and Watson battle master criminals, the mood runs the gamut from joyous to melancholic to manic.

THE RESCUERS DOWN UNDER
Walt Disney 60613-2

This disc from Disney's 1990 animated adventure is quite rare and therefore a favorite among soundtrack collectors. Written by a composer who is as experienced in animation music as anyone currently working, it's alternately heroic, busy, colorful, and thrilling. The film is a sequel to *The Rescuers* (1977), which reunites voice artists Bob Newhart and Eva Gabor in the roles of two nice mice traveling to Australia to help a boy in trouble.

TOMBSTONE
Intrada MAF 3078D

From television's *Blue and the Gray* to his Oscar-nominated *Silverado*, nobody knows how to score a western like Broughton. He brought an innate sense of musical Americana, a dark dramatic sensibility but none of the usual western clichés to this 1993 retelling of the tale of the Earps, the Clantons, and the legend of the O.K. Corral. Contrasting with the powerful and foreboding nature of much of the score is his melodic motif for Wyatt's love interest, eventually transformed into a grand symphonic waltz in the finale. Kurt Russell and Val Kilmer played Earp and Doc Holliday.

LOST IN SPACE
Intrada MAF 7086

Broughton's exciting score for the 1998 big-screen version of the TV classic—scored with 100 London musicians, a far cry from the small ensemble that Johnny Williams had for the TV show 33 years earlier—was not heard to full advantage in the movie mix. Filled with moments of heroics, high adventure, and dark musical doings for far-off worlds, this score far surpassed the movie it was written for (starring William Hurt, Mimi Rogers, and Gary Oldman).

Burwell, Carter (1955–)

Carter Burwell seemingly came out of nowhere to become one of the leading composers for independent films. Filmmaking brothers Joel and Ethan Coen asked him to score their 1984 film noir *Blood Simple*; its success led them to continue the collaboration, which to date has encompassed six more movies, all with a very different musical style: yodeling and banjos for *Raising Arizona* (1987), an Irish inflection for *Miller's Crossing* (1990), soprano and choir in *The Hudsucker Proxy* (1994), Scandinavian melodies for the hugely popular *Fargo* (1996), and more.

He studied fine arts and architecture at Harvard but played piano on the side while pursuing post-college jobs in such disparate fields as animation and biology. An admirer of Iggy Pop, Brian Eno, and Roxy Music, his unconventional style attracted not just the Coen brothers but more mainstream directors. His credits since then have encompassed horror (*Buffy the Vampire Slayer*, 1992), comedy (*Wayne's World 2*, 1993), adventure (*Rob Roy*, 1995), drama (*The Spanish Prisoner*, 1997), and action (*Conspiracy Theory*, 1997; *Three Kings*, 1999).

Even when he uses an orchestra—and, as he admitted at the time of *Miller's Crossing*, he knew "nothing" about orchestral music—it is in unusual and often surprising ways. His scores for the award-winning *Gods and Monsters* (1998) and *Being John Malkovich* (1999) brought him further acclaim.

FARGO / BARTON FINK

TVT 8010-2

Burwell's music for two of the Coen brothers' most popular films, the 1991 Hollywood satire *Barton Fink* and their Oscar-winning 1996 *Fargo* (for their screenplay and for Frances McDormand's performance), are on a single disc. Burwell's *Fargo* theme is derived from a Norwegian folk melody and is often played by a solo violin, entirely fitting for the snowbound Northern Plains locale where so many of the residents are of Scandinavian descent.

ROB ROY

Virgin 40351-2

For Liam Neeson's 1995 portrayal of 18th-century Scottish hero Rob Roy MacGregor, Burwell created a colorful and authentic-sounding musical backdrop filled with the sounds of the highlands: uilleann pipes, bodhran drums, fiddle, pennywhistle, and voice, all recorded in London and Dublin and augmented by traditional Scottish reels (performed by Capercaillie).

GODS AND MONSTERS

RCA Victor 63356-2

One of Burwell's most haunting works, understated and elegant, this 1998 score for Bill Condon's acclaimed fictionalized biography of Universal director James Whale (played by Ian McKellen) was acknowledged as one of the year's best by the Los Angeles Film Critics Association. Written for a small string ensemble, woodwinds, harp, piano, and percussion, it focused on character more than setting, including a melancholy waltz for Whale's memories of the past.

PHOTO COURTESY OF THE COMPOSER

Conti, Bill (1942–)

Rhode Island native and Juilliard graduate Bill Conti spent seven years studying and composing in Italy before he got his movie break. Paul Mazursky was in Venice shooting *Blume in Love* (1973) and asked Conti to supervise the music for that film; Conti soon returned to America, where Mazursky employed him as composer on subsequent films, including the winning *Harry & Tonto* (1974) and the heartbreaking *An Unmarried Woman* (1978).

Conti's claim to fame is having written the theme for *Rocky* (1976), which became a number 1 single in 1977 and received a Best Song Oscar nomination for Conti and his lyricists. To this day it's instantly recognizable as an anthem for the underdog everywhere. Conti scored three of the *Rocky* sequels and several other films for director John Avildsen (including *The Karate Kid*, 1984, and its sequels) and star Sylvester Stallone (including *Paradise Alley*, 1978, and *F.I.S.T.*, 1978).

The composer scored another major hit with his Oscar-nominated theme for the 1981 James Bond film *For Your Eyes Only*, sung by Sheena Easton to a number-4 spot on the *Billboard* charts (and in one of the most spectacular Oscar-show production numbers ever). He has also become a fixture as music director for the annual Academy Awards telecast, a role he has filled a record 14 times.

In recent years, Conti has been better known for his television themes, which include the popular and long-running soaps *Dynasty* and *Falcon Crest*, the cop show *Cagney & Lacey*, and the 24-hour Civil War miniseries *North & South*. He concertizes regularly around the country, playing his film and TV music—and is always introduced on stage with the theme from *Rocky*.

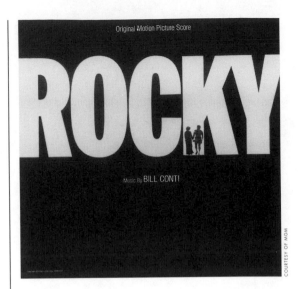

Original Motion Picture Score

Music By BILL CONTI

COURTESY OF MGM

ROCKY

EMI Manhattan CDP 7 46081 2

Few fanfares are as well known as the one Conti wrote for Sylvester Stallone to race up those Philadelphia steps in *Rocky*. Driving, relentless, with both a choir ("flying high now . . . feeling strong now") and a rock guitar solo, it embodied the scrappy-underdog spirit of the boxer in this sentimental 1976 Best Picture Oscar winner. A Best Song nominee, it also received three Grammy nominations and reached number 1 as a single on the *Billboard* charts. Conti scored three of the sequels (*II*, *III*, and *V*).

AN UNMARRIED WOMAN

20ᵗʰ Century–Fox Records T-557 (LP)

Conti's music for Jill Clayburgh's sensational, Oscar-nominated performance—as a woman who learns to cope after her husband decides he wants a divorce—shifts moods effortlessly from bouncy, jazzy cues to dark and emotionally moving ones. His versatile theme can seem optimistic at one moment and tragic the next. This very contemporary score, featuring lots of tenor sax solos, is probably the composer's best work for director Paul Mazursky; it was a 1978 Golden Globe nominee.

FOR YOUR EYES ONLY

Rykodisc RCD 10751

Conti scored what may be Roger Moore's best James Bond film, a 1981 entry that had 007 seeing action all over the Mediterranean. In a departure from the usual credits sequence, title-song singer Sheena Easton is seen on-camera performing the Conti–Michael Leeson tune that received a Best Song Oscar nomination. Conti's score is a good deal more contemporary than usual, with some exotic orchestration touches and liberal use of synthesizers and screaming brass.

THE RIGHT STUFF

Varèse Sarabande VCD-47250

Philip Kaufman's 1983 epic was based on Tom Wolfe's chronicle of the early years of the American space program. Conti's Oscar-winning score is expansive, heroic, and infused with a sense of Americana. His music for Chuck Yeager (Sam Shepard) breaking the sound barrier and for the orbital flight of John Glenn (Ed Harris) are dramatic highlights, both clearly inspired by classical works. An 18-minute symphonic suite from the

SOUND AND VISION

score is coupled with Conti's Emmy-nominated music for the miniseries *North & South* in this 1985 re-recording with the London Symphony Orchestra.

Cooder, Ry (1947–)

Thought by many observers to be the finest blues guitarist of his generation, Ry Cooder stumbled into film scoring when director Walter Hill called him to supply the music for his 1980 western *The Long Riders*. Cooder won the Los Angeles Film Critics Association Award for best music for that first film.

More than half his credits are for Hill films, from the rock sounds of *Streets of Fire* (1984) to the rap-influenced *Trespass* (1992). His evocative score for Wim Wenders's *Paris, Texas* (1984) brought him more acclaim—particularly after the film's triumphant showing at Cannes—and a British Film Academy nomination.

A largely self-taught musician, Cooder played on the soundtracks of such seminal rock scores as *Performance* (1971). Cooder's interests in world music were reflected in the Asian sounds (biwa, koto, shakuhachi) of Louis Malle's *Alamo Bay* (1985), about Vietnamese immigrants on the Texas Gulf Coast; in the Mexican music of Tony Richardson's *The Border* (1982); and in the use of Russian, African, and Native American players on Hill's biographical *Geronimo: An American Legend* (1993).

THE LONG RIDERS
Warner Bros. 7599-23448-2
Ry Cooder's first film score was for Walter Hill's 1980 film of the James-Younger Gang starring the brothers Carradine (David, Keith, Robert), Keach (Stacey, James), Quaid (Randy, Dennis), and Guest (Nicholas, Christopher), and it was an instant hit. A fascinating mixture of contemporary

acoustic and traditional folk tunes ("I'm a Good Old Rebel," "Rally Round the Flag," "Jesse James"), it is both unconventional and just right for the film, featuring dulcimer, harmonium, mandolin, fiddle, guitars, and other period-appropriate sounds for the West of the 1870s.

PARIS, TEXAS
Warner Bros. 25270-2
Wim Wenders's 1984 road movie, based on a Sam Shepard script about a drifter (Harry Dean Stanton) and his search for his estranged wife (Nastassja Kinski), found a perfect musical complement in Cooder's slow, haunting, and occasionally Mexican-flavored score. Cooder's slide guitar has probably never been more effective; much of the score involves the quiet, sensitive solo performance of Cooder.

GERONIMO: AN AMERICAN LEGEND
Columbia 57760
Cooder's most ambitious score to date, the music for Walter Hill's 1993 film about the legendary Apache warrior (Wes Studi) featured an eclectic mix of ethnic musicians, including Tuvan throat singers, a Navajo flutist, unusual percussion, and chanting from other Native American vocalists (in addition to Cooder's own band playing guitar, banjo, mandolin, even bouzouki). Cooder's collaborator was composer George S. Clinton, who also conducted and orchestrated with Van Dyke Parks.

Copeland, Stewart (1952–)

The founder and drummer of The Police, one of the most successful rock bands of the '80s, Stewart Copeland got started in film scoring by accident. Francis Ford Coppola was making his teen angst picture *Rumble Fish* (1983) and, according to

Copeland, "wanted advice on rhythm." Copeland scored the film (playing not just drums but guitar, electric and acoustic bass, keyboard and rhythm synths, tuned percussion, typewriter, and kazoo), then spent two years doing weekly music chores on TV's *The Equalizer*.

His father was a jazz-playing CIA agent, his mother a classical music–loving archaeologist, and Copeland grew up in Egypt, Syria, Lebanon, and the U.S. appreciating all kinds of music. Film music has enabled him to return to his classical and jazz roots while indulging more recent passions for rock, reggae, and various elements of world music.

He has written scores for major directors, including Oliver Stone (1987's *Wall Street*, 1988's *Talk Radio*), John Hughes (*She's Having a Baby*, 1988), and Kevin Reynolds (*Rapa Nui*, 1994) as well as a number of independent directors and projects ranging from *The Wide Sargasso Sea* (1993) to the Discovery Channel's *The Leopard Son* (1996). For the concert hall, he has tackled ballet (*King Lear*, for the San Francisco Ballet), opera (*Holy Blood* and *Crescent Moon*, for the Cleveland Opera), and other orchestral works.

WALL STREET / TALK RADIO
Varèse Sarabande VSD-5459
Copeland's scores for two consecutive Oliver Stone films—*Wall Street* (1987), *Talk Radio* (1988)—reflect the composer's sound of the time: heavy on percussion and synthesizers, with a propulsive rock beat. *Wall Street* contains Michael Douglas's Oscar-winning performance as a financial wizard who manipulates up-and-coming stock trader Charlie Sheen; Copeland even interpolates sampled dog barks. *Talk Radio* starred playright-performer Eric Bogosian as an abrasive Dallas talk-show host and features something of a lighter touch including acoustic piano (as well as dialogue excerpts).

RAPA NUI
Milan 73138 35681-2
Perhaps Copeland's most ambitious work, this score for orchestra and choirs accompanied the Kevin Costner–produced saga of Easter Island circa 1680. Jason Scott Lee and Esai Morales played rivals in this 1994 film. Copeland utilizes native choral chants, a large battery of percussion, ethnic flutes, synthesizers, and orchestra to create an otherworldly soundscape appropriate to the strange and long unexplained mysteries of the Pacific island.

Copland, Aaron (1900–1990)

One of the century's most important composers was, unlike many of his colleagues, no snob about film music. American composer Aaron Copland admired the work of Alex North, Bernard Herrmann, Miklós Rózsa, Leonard Rosenman, and others; and composed several film scores himself, winning an Oscar for one and extracting excerpts from several others for concert performance.

Two of Copland's film scores were for adaptations of novels by John Steinbeck—*Of Mice and Men* (1939) and *The Red Pony* (1949)—and as such possess pastoral and folk-like qualities familiar to fans of the composer's distinctive Americana style.

Not even the great composer of *Appalachian Spring* and *Billy the Kid* was immune to studio meddling, however. After Copland had completed his score for *The Heiress*, director William Wyler discarded the composer's main-title music and replaced it with an arrangement of the song "Plaisir d'Amour" (which figures in the film). Despite the indignity, Copland won the 1949 Academy Award for his music.

Copland scored only eight films, including two documentaries (*The City*, 1939; and *The Cummington Story*, 1945), all retaining his unique musical signature while demonstrating his mastery of the medium. *Of Mice and Men*, *Our Town*, and *The Red Pony*, in particular, are classics of the Americana idiom.

COPLAND: MUSIC FOR FILMS
RCA Victor 61699-2-RC

Leonard Slatkin conducts the St. Louis Symphony Orchestra in this first-rate collection of most of Copland's film music. The familiar seven-movement suite from *The Red Pony* (1949), for a Republic Pictures adaptation that John Steinbeck himself wrote (for Robert Mitchum and Myrna Loy), is as delightful in its folk-like sincerity as the film itself. The nine-minute suite from Copland's Oscar-nominated *Our Town* (1940) quietly and memorably suggests the quaint Middle American life of Thornton Wilder's film adaptation starring William Holden and Martha Scott.

Copland's five-movement "Music for Movies" suite includes two excerpts from *The City* (1939) containing musical depictions of New England

countryside and city traffic, two from *Of Mice and Men* (1939) based on the barley-wagon and threshing sequences, and one from *Our Town* based on the theme for Grovers Corners. Burgess Meredith and Lon Chaney Jr. had the key roles in *Of Mice and Men*, which netted Copland his first Oscar nomination.

A new eight-minute suite drawn from Copland's previously unavailable music for his Oscar-winning score for *The Heiress* (1949) returns the composer's dropped "prelude" music to its rightful place (but briefly alludes, later on, to the song "Plaisir d'Amour" which replaced it). Olivia deHavilland also won an Oscar as the heroine of Henry James's novel *Washington Square*.

COPLAND: SYMPHONY NO. 3 / MUSIC FOR A GREAT CITY
RCA Victor 60149-2-RC

"Music for a Great City," which the composer premiered with the London Symphony Orchestra in 1964, is based in large part on the score he composed for the rarely screened 1961 film *Something Wild*, which starred Carroll Baker as a rape victim and Ralph Meeker as the lonely garage mechanic who befriends her. At nearly 25 minutes, it's Copland's longest suite derived from a film; as Copland wrote in his original liner notes, the music alternates between "evocations of big-city life, with its external stimuli, and the personal reactions of any sensitive nature in the varied experiences associated with urban living." Leonard Slatkin conducts the St. Louis Symphony Orchestra.

Corigliano, John (1938–)

One of America's most respected contemporary composers, John Corigliano has written such acclaimed works as his Symphony No. 1 (a response to the AIDS crisis) and his opera *The Ghosts of Versailles*—but only three film scores: *Altered States* (1980), *Revolution* (1985), and *The Red Violin* (1998).

Director Ken Russell happened to be attending a Los Angeles Philharmonic performance where Corigliano's clarinet concerto was being played; stunned by its "magic and grandeur," as he later said, Russell went straight backstage and asked Corigliano to score his next movie.

The result was a highly original score for a very "out there" movie and an Academy Award nomination. An equally impressive score, for Hugh Hudson's 18th-century epic *Revolution*, followed, and resulted in the British film academy's prestigious Anthony Asquith Award for the year's best film music. Unfortunately, the Al Pacino film's failure at the American box office led to cancellation of a proposed soundtrack album, and Corigliano swore off movies.

Canadian filmmaker François Girard (*Thirty-two Short Films About Glenn Gould*), however, convinced Corigliano to return to movies with *The Red Violin*, which swept the 1998 Canadian Genies including awards for Best Picture and, for Corigliano, Best Original Score. In March 2000, Corigliano added an Academy Award for *The Red Violin* to his many honors.

ALTERED STATES
RCA Victor 3983-2-RG
Written for Ken Russell's 1980 film based on Paddy Chayefsky's novel, Corigliano's score was nominated for an Academy Award and a Grammy. It may have been the most daring score written for a Hollywood film in many years. Corigliano told *The New York Times* that his music was "terribly difficult, eclectic, far out, abstract, wild, and with tremendous energy," all of which was true and per-

fectly in keeping with the film's premise (William Hurt's experimentation that allowed him to regress back into primitive early man). But there was also a love theme (for Hurt's ultimate salvation, his relationship with Blair Brown) of tonality and charm and a distorted use of "Rock of Ages" to evoke religious memories.

THE RED VIOLIN
Sony Classical SK 63010
Corigliano's Oscar-winning score for François Girard's ambitious and remarkable 1998 film was a rare reminder that great works of art can still emerge from film music. The film follows the destiny of a single, unique instrument from its creation in 17th-century Italy to imperial Vienna in the 1790s to Victorian England to the Cultural Revolution in mid-'60s China to an auction of rare instruments in contemporary Toronto. Corigliano composed all of the etudes that are played by the various owners of the violin in the film as well as the underscore (written entirely for string orchestra, with a bit of percussion for a chase near the end) and a 17-minute *Chaconne for Violin and Orchestra* based on the score. Joshua Bell is the soloist; Esa-Pekka Salonen conducts the Philharmonia Orchestra.

Danna, Mychael (1958–)
Mychael Danna, widely considered Canada's leading film composer, was educated at the University of Toronto and received the 1985 Glenn Gould Composition Award. For five years, he was composer-in-residence at Toronto's McLaughlin Planetarium.

His long relationship with director Atom Egoyan began in 1987 with *Family Viewing* and continued with *Speaking Parts* (1989) and *The Adjuster* (1991), *Exotica* (1994), and the widely acclaimed, Oscar-nominated *The Sweet Hereafter* (1997). By 1997, he had branched out further with scores for Mira Nair's *Kama Sutra: A Tale of Love* and Ang Lee's *The Ice Storm*.

What sets Danna apart from many of his contemporaries is his thoughtful, innovative use of unusual sonorities: Indian flute and Indonesian gamelan for *The Ice Storm*, Iranian ney flute for *The Sweet Hereafter*, Indian instruments for *Kama Sutra*, Latin Mass and Gregorian chant for *Lilies* (1996), Indian gat-toras and ghazals for *Exotica*.

Joel Schumacher's controversial *8MM* (1999) marked Danna's debut in a major American film.

THE ICE STORM
Velvel VDL-79713

Most of this soundtrack consists of pop tunes evoking the '70s, the period in which Ang Lee's acclaimed 1997 film about the dysfunctional-family legacy of the free-love '60s (with actors Kevin Kline, Sigourney Weaver, Joan Allen, Christina Ricci, and others) is set. There are, however, nearly 12 minutes of excerpts from Danna's surprising and effective score, which featured Indian flute and Indonesian gamelan music as a means of subtly suggesting the sounds of nature.

THE SWEET HEREAFTER
Virgin 7243 8 44955 2 7

Atom Egoyan's 1997 film concerned the aftermath of a small-town school-bus accident that kills several children and spurs a lawyer (Ian Holm) to try to convince their parents to sue; he imposes a "Pied Piper" theme on the story that suggested an early-music sound to Danna. The composer uses the Toronto Consort (lute, recorder, sackbut, krumhorn, etc.) but also wrote several folk-rock songs (three co-written with actress Sarah Polley) and utilizes an Iranian ney

flute (representing the Piper), This was one of Danna's most impressive scores.

Daring, Mason (1949–)

Mason Daring is best known as the composer on nearly all of independent filmmaker John Sayles's movies. A fresh voice in a sea of often sound-alike orchestral Hollywood scores, Daring endeavors to provide each of Sayles's movies with a sound that appears to generate naturally from the time and place, often rooted in the folk music of the region.

His acclaimed, Celtic-themed score for *The Secret of Roan Inish* (1994); the authentic-sounding union songs of '20s West Virginia in *Matewan* (1987); the Tex-Mex mixture of *Lone Star* (1996); and the diverse sounds of Latin America, from guitars and marimbas to brass bands, of *Men With Guns* (1997), are among the best examples of Daring's work for Sayles. Based in Marblehead, Massachusetts, Daring has worked with a number of other directors, both in the mainstream and independent worlds, notably Disney's *Wild Hearts Can't Be Broken* (1991) and Don Roos's riotous indie *The Opposite of Sex* (1998), with its unconventional jazz score. He has also supplied a number of themes for public television, from the long-running science series *Nova* to the acclaimed documentary *The Great War*. In 1999, he scored *Music of the Heart*, about a dedicated violin teacher (Meryl Streep) working in Harlem.

MATEWAN
Daring CD 1011

For John Sayles's 1987 film about the bloody labor-union wars in the coal mines of West Virginia in the '20s, Daring delved into the sounds of the era. He and Sayles even concocted an original "union anthem" that sounds exactly as if it belonged in that time. Using fiddle, guitar, dobro, mandolin, and mouth harp, and interpolating traditional songs of the period, Daring achieves an authentic musical backdrop. The film, one of Sayles's most powerful, starred Chris Cooper and Mary McDonnell.

THE SECRET OF ROAN INISH
Daring CD 3015

This 1994 work is perhaps the most popular of all of Daring's scores for John Sayles films. One of the best family films in recent years, it weaves a magical spell in its depiction of life for a little girl caught up in the myths and legends of coastal Ireland, where she is living with her grandparents. Daring adapted several traditional Irish folk tunes and recorded in Ireland with an ensemble of musicians who know their field: fiddles, Uillean pipes, Celtic harp, Bodhran drums, flutes, and whistles, for a delightfully authentic sound.

Debney, John (1957–)

One of the most talented of the younger crop of symphonic composers, Debney is a Southern California native and son of a former Walt Disney producer (which enabled him to work summers in the music library on the Disney lot in Burbank as a youth).

He studied both acting and music in college and apprenticed in the Disney music library as a copyist, orchestrator, and arranger. In television, he won Emmys for his music for the western *The Young Riders* and his themes for Steven Spielberg's futuristic adventure series *seaQuest DSV* and the later syndicated series *The Cape*.

His early feature scores, including the football comedy *Little Giants* (1994) and the whimsical witch picture *Hocus Pocus* (1993), led to such later assignments as the animated big-screen *Jetsons: The Movie*, the Jean-Claude Van Damme action film

Sudden Death, and the sci-fi thriller *Relic*. His score for the $100-million Renny Harlin film *Cutthroat Island* landed him such subsequent assignments as the giant Jim Carrey hit *Liar, Liar* (1997), the teen-horror smash *I Know What You Did Last Summer* (1997), and the 1999 Arnold Schwarzenegger thriller *End of Days*.

CUTTHROAT ISLAND
Silva 178

Debney's pull-out-all-the-stops score for Renny Harlin's critically lambasted 1995 pirate movie starring Geena Davis and Matthew Modine is a tribute to, in the composer's words, "Messrs. Rózsa, Korngold, Steiner, and Newman." Deliberately designed to be in the spirit of the Errol Flynn swashbucklers, this is a sonic spectacular of fanfares, lush romantic themes, and exciting chase music. David Snell conducts the London Symphony Orchestra with the London Voices.

PHOTO BY ALAIN MAROUANI. COURTESY OF NONESUCH

Delerue, Georges (1925–1992)

Best known, perhaps, as François Truffaut's longtime musical collaborator, Georges Delerue was one of the screen's greatest melodists. Classically trained, prolific, sensitive, and unpretentious, Delerue wrote music for every medium that will endure well beyond the work of many of his colleagues.

Born to working-class parents in northern France, he overcame class discrimination and won entry to the Paris Conservatory, where Darius Milhaud became his teacher and mentor. Childhood injuries and illnesses left him small of stature and in great pain but determined to succeed at music.

Work in the Paris theater and French television occupied him throughout the '50s. He wrote "La valse" for Alain Renais's now-classic *Hiroshima, Mon Amour* (1959) and, the next year, collaborated with Truffaut on *Shoot the Piano Player*—the first of their 10 films together, a professional relationship that parallels those of Fellini and Rota or Hitchcock and Herrmann.

Delerue's alternately buoyant and melancholy music for the love triangle of *Jules et Jim* (1961), his piccolo-trumpet-and-strings chorale for the joys of filmmaking in *Day for Night* (1973), and the glorious waltz that ends *The Last Metro* (1980) are memorable moments in the Truffaut-Delerue canon. His period English music for *A Man for All Seasons* (1966) and *Anne of the Thousand Days* (1969), his ballet for the sea creatures in *Day of the Dolphin* (1973), his Oscar-winning Renaissance-styled music for *A Little Romance* (1979), and his choral music for *Agnes of God* (1985) are just a hint of the range of this remarkable composer. He also wrote opera, ballet, and chamber music but will be best remembered for his 200-plus film scores (most of which he orchestrated himself).

GEORGES DELERUE: MUSIC FROM THE FILMS OF FRANÇOIS TRUFFAUT
Nonesuch 79405-2

Excerpts from nine of the Delerue-Truffaut films are featured in this collection, the most generous samplings being the nine minutes devoted to the French New Wave classic *Shoot the Piano Player* (1960) and over 15 minutes to the alternately exuberant and melancholy *Jules et Jim* (1961). His stunning chorale for the filmmaking montage of the Oscar-winning *Day for Night* (1973) and his Cesar-winning music for *The Last Metro* (1980) are included, along with bits and pieces from *Love at 20: Antoine and Colette* (1962), *The Soft Skin* (1964), *Two English Girls* (1971), *Such a Gorgeous Kid Like Me* (1972), and *The Woman Next Door* (1981). Hugo Wolff conducts the London Sinfonietta.

THE DAY OF THE DOLPHIN
SLC SLCS-7036 (Japan)

One of the finest scores of the 1970s, yet sadly unavailable on CD in the U.S., Delerue's music for Mike Nichols's 1973 thriller about highly advanced dolphins (trained by scientist George C. Scott) being manipulated into an assassination plot is far better than the film itself. Written largely for strings, woodwinds, and harp, and often classically structured, this beautiful score was Oscar-nominated and helped to establish Delerue in the U.S. prior to his move here.

GEORGES DELERUE: THE LONDON SESSIONS, VOLUME ONE
Varèse Sarabande VSD-5241

This series of three albums recorded by Delerue at London's Abbey Road in May 1989 contains virtually all of the highlights of his work in America during the '70s and '80s. This first disc contains the haunting adagio that Delerue wrote for, but wasn't used in, Oliver Stone's *Platoon* (1986); and suites from his Oscar-winning music for *A Little*

Romance (1979) and very popular *Crimes of the Heart* (1986). Also included: music from *Rich and Famous* (1981), *Her Alibi* (1989), *Beaches* (1988), *Exposed* (1983), and *Biloxi Blues* (1988).

GEORGES DELERUE:
THE LONDON SESSIONS, VOLUME TWO
Varèse Sarabande VSD-5245

A highlight of this second Delerue-conducted disc is his 12-minute "Hommage à François Truffaut," containing themes from 10 of his scores for the French director (the nine on the Nonesuch album plus 1983's *Confidentally Yours*) with piano solos by the composer. Long suites from such popular films as *Steel Magnolias* (1989) and *Salvador* (1986); a theme from *Interlude* (1968); and such lesser-known films as *The Escape Artist* (1982), *The Pick-Up Artist* (1987), *Maxie* (1985), and *An Almost Perfect Affair* (1979) are included.

GEORGES DELERUE:
THE LONDON SESSIONS, VOLUME THREE
Varèse Sarabande VSD-5256

One of the legendary "rejected" scores (that is, written, recorded, then dropped by producers) of Hollywood history is Delerue's music for the Disney film of Ray Bradbury's *Something Wicked This Way Comes* (1983). A 12-minute suite preserves this dark and brooding work. Long suites from his Oscar-nominated choral score for *Agnes of God* (1985) and the popular *True Confessions* (1981) are also featured, along with music from *The House on Carrol Street* (1988), *A Little Sex* (1982), *Maid to Order* (1987), *Man, Woman and Child* (1983), and *Memories of Me* (1988).

Deutsch, Adolph (1897–1980)

London-born Adolph Deutsch came to America in

1910 and spent his formative years working in dance bands as an arranger and bandleader, and on Broadway as an arranger and musical director. Arriving in Hollywood, he joined Warner Bros. in 1937 and toiled for several years scoring "B" pictures of all genres.

Many of his '40s Warner films are now classics, led by John Huston's timeless adaptation of the Dashiell Hammett detective story *The Maltese Falcon* (1941). Deutsch's other Warner films starring Bogart included *They Drive by Night* (1940), *High Sierra* (1941), *All Through the Night* (1942), *Across the Pacific* (1942), and *Action in the North Atlantic* (1943).

He moved in 1945 to MGM, where he switched gears completely and became known as a top arranger and orchestrator for the studio's great musicals. He won Oscars for his work on *Annie Get Your Gun* (1950), *Seven Brides for Seven Brothers* (1954), and the independently released *Oklahoma!* (1955). He was also nominated for MGM's *Show Boat* (1951) and *The Band Wagon* (1953).

Legendary director Billy Wilder hired Deutsch for two of his finest comedies: *Some Like It Hot* (1959) and *The Apartment* (1960).

FILM NOIR
BMG/RCA 09026 68145 2 (Germany)

This collection of music from classic films noirs contains two lengthy suites from the underrated Deutsch: nearly nine minutes of the alternately dark-hued and quizzical *The Maltese Falcon* (1941) and the warm and sprightly *All Through the Night* (1942). Also featured: generous suites from Frederick Hollander's *The Verdict* (1946), Franz Waxman's *Dark Passage* (1947), and Max Steiner's *White Heat* (1949). This sumptuously recorded disc, part of BMG's "100 Years of Film Music" series available primarily in Europe, was recorded in 1995 by the Brandenburg Philharmonic Orchestra conducted by William T. Stromberg. John W. Morgan reconstructed the music.

SOME LIKE IT HOT
Rykodisc RCD 10715

Billy Wilder's wild, hilarious, and still-classic 1959 comedy starred Jack Lemmon, Tony Curtis, and Marilyn Monroe. Monroe's songs ("Runnin' Wild," "I Wanna Be Loved By You," "I'm Thru With Love") are of abiding interest to her fans, of course, but Deutsch's jazzy backdrops and clever period arrangements are also of note.

FROM THE AUTHOR'S COLLECTION

DeVol, Frank (1911–1999)

Veteran arranger-conductor Frank DeVol enjoyed success in every field of media music, dating back to his first arranging job in 1927. A self-taught musician, he played the saxophone, sang, and arranged for big bands (including those of Horace Heidt and Alvino Rey) throughout the '30s and '40s. Equally talented as a humorist and actor, he made Mutual Radio listeners laugh at his "Music Depreciation" programs in the mid-'40s.

He began scoring films in 1954 and was best known for his music for the often dark and gritty films of director Robert Aldrich. Their 16 films together included *Kiss Me Deadly* (1955), *Attack* (1956), *What Ever Happened to Baby Jane?* (1962), *Hush . . . Hush, Sweet Charlotte* (1964, Oscar-nominated for Best Song and Original Score), *Flight of the Phoenix* (1965), *The Dirty Dozen* (1967), and *The Longest Yard* (1974). Paradoxically, his light romantic music was featured in several Doris Day movies, notably *Pillow Talk* (a 1959 Oscar nominee), *The Thrill of It All* (1963), *Send Me No Flowers* (1964), and others.

DeVol's other Oscar nominations came for a pair of comedic classics: the western *Cat Ballou* (1965) and Stanley Kramer's poignant *Guess Who's Coming to Dinner* (1967). He found lasting fame in television, however, as composer of the enduring themes for *My Three Sons* and *The Brady Bunch*, and as bandleader Happy Kyne on the '70s cult favorite *Fernwood 2-Night*.

THE DIRTY DOZEN
Chapter III CHA 0132

DeVol struck just the right balance between the deadly serious and the darkly amusing with his music for Robert Aldrich's World War II adventure. This 1967 film starred Lee Marvin as a tough-as-nails soldier who attempts to make a batch of court-martialed murderers, rapists, and thieves into a crack undercover unit; John Cassavetes, Robert Ryan, Charles Bronson, Ernest Borgnine, and Donald Sutherland were also in the cast. DeVol's military cadences alternate with lighter material (such as his variations on "You're in the Army Now"). The newly issued disc is paired with Jeff Alexander's score for the Frank Sinatra western *Dirty Dingus Magee* (1970).

Disney, Walt—Music Department

A handful of composers never achieved prominence in the film-music world simply because they were exclusive to, or did most of their best work at, the Walt Disney Studios. Nonetheless, their music has resonated with three generations of filmgoers and record-buyers.

Songwriter Frank Churchill (1901–1942) helped to lift Depression-era spirits with his "Who's Afraid of the Big Bad Wolf" from *The Three Little Pigs* (1933) and created the familiar melodies of *Snow White and the Seven Dwarfs* (1937): "Heigh-Ho," "Whistle While You Work," and "Some Day My Prince Will Come." He shared the 1941 scoring Oscar with Oliver Wallace for *Dumbo* (which featured his tender "Baby Mine").

London-born Oliver Wallace (1887–1963), in addition to his Oscar for *Dumbo* (which included his song "Pink Elephants on Parade"), received nominations for *Cinderella* (1950) and *Alice in Wonderland* (1951) and scored the live-action classic *Old Yeller* (1957).

Paul J. Smith (1906–1985) collaborated on several scores, sharing an Oscar with Leigh Harline for *Pinocchio* (1940) and also contributing to *Snow White*, *Cinderella*, and *Song of the South* (1946). He wrote the music for Disney's Jules Verne classic *20,000 Leagues Under the Sea* (1954) and nearly all of the studio's *True-Life Adventure* nature documentaries.

Leigh Harline (1907–1969) won two 1940 Oscars, for Best Song ("When You Wish Upon a Star") and Best Score for *Pinocchio*, collaborated on *Snow White* with Churchill and Smith, then went on to score dozens of films at other studios including *The Pride of the Yankees* (1942) and *The Wonderful World of the Brothers Grimm* (1962).

George Bruns (1914–1983) received an Oscar nomination for adapting the Tchaikovsky ballet for *Sleeping Beauty* (1959), scored such later Disney features as *The Sword in the Stone* (1963) and *The Jungle Book* (1967), and wrote two of Disney's most famous TV songs: "The Ballad of Davy Crockett" and "Zorro."

Buddy Baker (1918–) joined the Disney studios in 1954, served as musical director for TV's *Mickey Mouse Club*, and received an Oscar nomination for *Napoleon and Samantha* (1972). He scored such '60s Disney favorites as *Toby Tyler* (1960) and *That Darn Cat* (1965) and the animated feature *The Fox and the Hound* (1981).

COURTESY OF THE COMPOSERS

Richard M. Sherman (1928–) and Robert B. Sherman (1925–) are perhaps the studio's best-known songwriters, brothers who won 1964 Oscars for the score of *Mary Poppins* and its song "Chim Chim Cher-ee" (the score also included the familiar "A Spoonful of Sugar" and "Supercalifragilisticexpialidocious"). Their other Disney efforts included several hits for Annette Funicello, songs for animated features including *The Jungle Book* (1967), Disneyland's "It's a Small World (After All)," and "Winnie the Pooh."

Alan Menken (1949–) is the exception in this list. Far better known than his Disney predecessors, he revitalized the animated musical with a theatrical sensibility and has won eight Oscars, for Best Song and Best Score for *The Little Mermaid* (1989, "Under the Sea" with Howard Ashman), *Beauty and the Beast* (1991, title song with Ashman), *Aladdin* (1992, "Whole New World" with Tim Rice) and *Pocahontas* (1995, "Colors of the Wind" with Stephen Schwartz).

THE MUSIC OF DISNEY:
A LEGACY IN SONG
Walt Disney 60957-2

This three-CD box, issued in 1992, is a "Disney greatest hits" collection containing 78 songs, from "Turkey in the Straw" (from 1928's *Steamboat Willie* cartoon) to the hits from *The Little Mermaid* and *Beauty and the Beast* (1989, 1991) along with classic tunes from Disney TV shows ("The Ballad of Davy Crockett") and theme parks ("It's a Small World"). The set is accompanied by a lavishly illustrated 60-page book chronicling the history of Disney music.

Donaggio, Pino (1941–)

Italian composer Pino Donaggio studied classical music at conservatories in Venice and Milan before becoming a rock 'n' roll songwriter in the '60s. His "Io che non vivo" was a colossal hit in Europe, later covered by artists including Dusty Springfield and Elvis Presley as "You Don't Have to Say You Love Me" and eventually selling some 60 million records internationally.

This melodic sense—the ability to write a "tune"—has served Donaggio well throughout his film career, which began by accident: an associate producer working on Nicolas Roeg's Donald Sutherland–Julie Christie thriller *Don't Look Now* (1973) claimed to have a psychic vision about Donaggio; he wound up scoring the film.

Brian DePalma, searching for a new composer after the death of his *Sisters* and *Obsession* collaborator Bernard Herrmann, hired Donaggio for *Carrie* (1976) and five subsequent films including the popular thrillers *Dressed to Kill* (1980), *Blow Out* (1981), and *Body Double* (1984).

He was somewhat typecast in the horror and fantasy genre, working on films from *Tourist Trap* (1979) to *The Howling* (1981) and B-movie fare like *Hercules* (1983) and *The Barbarians* (1987). Disney's low-key, likable *Tex* (1982) was a rare exception in that era. Most of his recent work has been on Italian films.

CARRIE
Rykodisc RCD 10701

Donaggio's score for Brian DePalma's 1976 film of Stephen King's best seller launched a long collaborative relationship between the two. Donaggio's lush melodic approach, occasionally interrupted by sharper sounds, seemed both sympathetic to the tormented teenager (Sissy Spacek) and appropriate to the violence she perpetrates in response to her treatment. Two pop songs, heard during the infamous prom-night sequence, are also included.

BRIAN DE PALMA / PINO DONAGGIO
Milan 73138 35660-2

This 1994 collection contains music from six of the director-composer team's collaborations, beginning with the lyrical *Carrie* (1976) and his classically styled *Home Movies* (1980). His string-drenched treatment of the shower scene in the Michael Caine thriller *Dressed to Kill* (1980) contrasts with his dramatically charged theme for John Travolta in *Blow Out* (1981), his catchy pop-synthesizer-with-vocal sound for *Body Double* (1984), and his eerie, jazz-inflected touch with the John Lithgow film *Raising Cain* (1992).

Doyle, Patrick (1953–)

Scotsman Patrick Doyle has been writing music for the theater, radio, and television since the late '70s. Only in the last decade has he gained notoriety as a composer for films, largely due to his association with actor-director Kenneth Branagh.

Ex-actor, pianist, and singer Doyle met Branagh at the Renaissance Theatre Company, where he had composed music for various Shakespearean productions. Branagh commissioned Doyle to compose the score for his *Henry V* (1989) and, later, the music for his *Dead Again* (1991), *Much Ado About Nothing* (1993), *Mary Shelley's Frankenstein* (1994), and *Hamlet* (1996). Branagh has cast Doyle in small roles in nearly all his films (including singing parts in *Henry V* and *Much Ado*).

Doyle's classical training, melodic sense, and probably his sly sense of humor led other notable directors to seek him out: French director Regis Wargnier, for *Indochine* (1992) and *East-West* (1999); Brian DePalma, for *Carlito's Way* (1993);

Ang Lee, for *Sense and Sensibility* (1995); Alfonso Cuarón, for *A Little Princess* (1995) and *Great Expectations* (1998); and Richard Benjamin, for *Mrs. Winterbourne* (1996).

Doyle has received two Oscar nominations, for *Sense and Sensibility* and *Hamlet*, and several Cesar, British Film Academy, and Golden Globe nominations.

HENRY V
EMI CDC 7 49919 2

Doyle's first score for Kenneth Branagh was this 1989 adaptation of the Shakespeare play. Just as Branagh's is a very different production than Olivier's 1945 classic, so this score is vastly different from Walton music. For many the highlight of the score is "Non nobis, Domine," which is sung by Doyle (who appears in the film as Court) with choir after the Battle of Agincourt; it won Britain's Ivor Novello Award as best film theme.

INDOCHINE
Varèse Sarabande VSD-5397

The Oscar winner as Best Foreign Language Film of 1992, Regis Warnier's film tells the epic story of a powerful Frenchwoman (Catherine Deneuve), her adopted Vietnamese daughter, and the young sailor who falls in love with both women. Not well known, it's one of Doyle's most powerful scores, with an arresting main title (a capella voices), a tango that's crucial to the plot, and strong themes for the three key characters.

A LITTLE PRINCESS
Varèse Sarabande VSD-5628

Alfonso Cuaron's charming 1995 film of Frances Hodgson Burnett's children's classic never found a big audience in theaters (unlike the Shirley Temple version, made in a very different era). Rich in melody and color, Doyle's score contains authentic Indian ragas, delightful harp interludes, three memorable songs (two with words by William Blake, one by Doyle), and a grand waltz.

HAMLET
Sony Classical SK *62857*
A 1996 Oscar nominee for Best Original Score, Doyle's stirring music perfectly complements Kenneth Branagh's complete version of Shakespeare's tale of the melancholy Dane. Regardless of one's opinion of the venture's success (too long, too many star cameos, an over-the-top Branagh), Doyle's score offers many rewarding moments including the court fanfare, a string quartet during the Confessional scene, Ophelia's childlike motif, the powerful climax of "My thoughts be bloody" at the intermission, and the choral finale. Placido Domingo performs "In Pace" at film's end.

COURTESY OF THE COMPOSER

Dudley, Anne (1956–)
This British-born arranger and composer had actually been writing competent, well-crafted movie and television scores for years when she seemingly

burst upon the scene in the '90s with scores like *The Crying Game* and her Oscar-winning music for *The Full Monty.*

Anne Dudley studied at the Royal College of Music and Kings College and made her mark in the pop world as a keyboard player and arranger for leading record producer Trevor Horn, writing charts for such groups as Frankie Goes to Hollywood; she also arranged and played for George Michael, Paul McCartney, and other artists.

Dudley was a founding member of the experimental, high-tech pop group Art of Noise, which helped to pioneer the sampling techniques that are so much a part of today's hip-hop musical scene. Beginning in the late '80s she extended her range to films such as Phil Collins's *Buster* (1988) and Neil Jordan's *The Miracle* (1991).

In the States, fans of public television's *Masterpiece Theatre* have been enjoying Dudley's music for years: She wrote the delightful '20s-style theme and underscore for the Hugh Laurie–Stephen Fry series *Jeeves and Wooster,* which began in 1990.

THE CRYING GAME
SBK CDP-*589024*
Neil Jordan's Oscar-winning 1992 film concerned an Irish Republican Army volunteer (Stephen Rea) whose life takes bizarre twists: first guarding a kidnapped British soldier (Forest Whitaker), then becoming involved with the soldier's lover (Jaye Davidson) back in London. This orchestral score, with its military flourishes and rich string sound, put Dudley on the map in a big way. The album contains several songs, including the title tune sung in two versions by Boy George and Dave Berry.

THE FULL MONTY
RCA 09026-68904-2, 09026-63357-2
Dudley's score was a surprise Oscar winner in the

now-defunct category of "original musical or comedy score" at the ceremonies for 1997 films—as much, most observers agreed, for its clever use of songs as for Dudley's minimal score. It's light and jazzy, featuring harmonica and saxophone ("a sort of hybrid ska/reggae," Dudley calls it) that was nicely complementary to the wildly popular British comedy about unemployed British steel workers who become male strippers. Both albums consist largely of the songs to which the boys danced (by such '70s artists as Irene Cara, Donna Summer, Hot Chocolate, and Tom Jones); snippets of Dudley's score fill them out.

AMERICAN HISTORY X
Angel 7243 5 5678 2 6

Tony Kaye's controversial skinhead movie—a 1998 Oscar nominee for Edward Norton's lead-actor performance—inspired a symphonic score from Dudley, one that may be her strongest effort to date. Highly dramatic, featuring full orchestra and occasionally boys' choir singing the Latin "Benedictus," its tone ranges from triumphal to dark to elegiac. That this ambitious score was not Oscar-nominated seemed as surprising as her win for *The Full Monty* the year before.

Duning, George (1908–2000)

Under contract to Columbia Pictures for 17 years, from 1946 to 1963, George Duning created some of that studio's most memorable scores, including five Oscar nominees: *Jolson Sings Again* (1949) and *The Eddy Duchin Story* (1956) in the musical category, and *No Sad Songs for Me* (1950), *From Here to Eternity* (1953), and *Picnic* (1955) in the dramatic-score category.

Later came *Houseboat* (for Paramount), and *Bell, Book and Candle* (both 1958) and *The World of Suzie Wong* (1960, for Paramount). Born in Indiana, he was a jazz trumpet player and became an arranger for bands and radio, notably spending eight years on "Kay Kyser's Kollege of Musical Knowledge" before moving into movies.

From the '60s on, Duning turned his talents largely to the small screen, composing memorable themes for such shows as *Tightrope*, *Naked City*, and especially the Barbara Stanwyck western *The Big Valley*. He also wrote memorable romantic music for the original *Star Trek* and a number of made-for-TV movies.

PICNIC

MCA MCAD-31357

Based on a William Inge play, this 1955 romantic drama starred William Holden, Kim Novak, Rosalind Russell, and (in his screen debut) Cliff Robertson; Joshua Logan (who had produced the Broadway version) was the director. This is probably the best known of Duning's 100-plus film scores, and it won a *Down Beat* award as the year's best score for a non-musical film. Its masterful intertwining of a dance-band arrangement of the popular standard "Moonglow" with his own love theme, against a steamy dance scene between Holden and Novak, is a classic and went to number 1 on radio's "Hit Parade" in 1956.

Edelman, Randy (1947–)

Prolific and in demand, New Jersey–born Randy Edelman was writing songs by the age of 14, arranging horn charts for James Brown while in college, and playing keyboards on Broadway by the early 1970s.

Embarking on a career as a singer-songwriter, he opened for The Carpenters, recorded more than a dozen albums, appeared at the London Palladium, and saw his "Weekend in New England" become a big hit for Barry Manilow. Everybody from Olivia Newton-John to Blood, Sweat & Tears recorded his tunes, and he arranged and conducted for many artists including Bobbie Gentry and Jackie DeShannon (who became his wife).

Edelman scored a few films in the early '70s (notably the early Kennedy-assassination conspiracy film *Executive Action*) but made it his career in the '80s, hitting it big in the comedy arena with hits like *Twins* (1988), *Kindergarten Cop* (1990), *Beethoven* (1992), *My Cousin Vinny* (1992), and *The Mask* (1994). His more dramatic work has

been showcased in such films as *Gettysburg* (1993), Alan Parker's *Come See the Paradise* (1990), and two Rob Cohen movies, *Dragon: The Bruce Lee Story* (1993) and *Dragonheart* (1996). His work on *The Last of the Mohicans* (1992)—he wrote about half the score—won a platinum record and a British Academy Award nomination.

His start as a songwriter has served him well; the result is that several of his movies—notably *Gettysburg* and *Dragonheart*—are now better remembered for Edelman's themes than for anything in the films themselves. He's also known for two TV themes: *MacGyver* and NBC Sports' pro football signature.

COME SEE THE PARADISE

Varèse Sarabande VSD-5306

Alan Parker's 1990 film about an American soldier (Dennis Quaid) and the Japanese girl (Tamlyn Tomita) he falls in love with, as World War II dawns, became one of Edelman's best known scores. Partly orchestral, partly electronic, it was successfully intertwined with a number of period tunes and Japanese songs to evoke the era, but it's Edelman's piano-and-strings love theme that listeners remember.

BEETHOVEN

MCA MCAD-10593

Edelman's playful sensibilities came to the fore in this 1992 family comedy that starred Charles Grodin and Bonnie Hunt as the hapless owners of a big, slobbering St. Bernard. A charming theme, bouncy tempo, classical-sounding piano and silly-sounding electronics, heroes-to-the-rescue parody, and, yes, a bit of a takeoff on Ludwig von, all contribute to this fun score. Edelman also scored the 1993 sequel.

GETTYSBURG

Milan 73138 35654-2

Conceived as a six-hour miniseries for TNT, this 1993 Ted Turner production wound up receiving a four-hour theatrical release as well as multiple showings on cable. Tom Berenger, Jeff Daniels, Richard Jordan, and Sam Elliott starred in this elaborately staged chronicle of the 1863 battle that became a turning point in the Civil War. Heroic and often powerful, Edelman's score resounds with the strength of the tale being told and has become enormously popular with record-buyers. Budgetary limitations made synthesizers a necessity for such a long score, and they are a liability in a period piece like this. Happily, the theme has become a staple at July 4 concerts, where it is performed by full symphony orchestras.

DRAGONHEART

MCA MCAD-11449

Dragon teams up with dragonslayer to battle cruel king: That unlikely premise inspired one of Edelman's most popular scores, a grand orchestral-with-synthesizers-and-voices fantasy sporting a heroic theme that has been used over and over again in trailers and TV spots for other movies. Sean Connery was the voice of the dragon, Dennis Quaid the knight who befriends his former enemy in this ancient-times adventure from 1996.

Eidelman, Cliff (1964–)

Among the youngest of today's crop of talented orchestral composers, Los Angeles–born Cliff Eidelman studied jazz guitar, wrote a ballet at Santa Monica City College, and penned a symphony while studying at the University of Southern California. Before graduation, he had landed his first film-scoring assignment.

For a forgotten Nastassja Kinski film called *Magdalene*, the 22-year-old composer created a massive work for orchestra, choir, and children's choir. Other assignments soon followed, including the Holocaust film *Triumph of the Spirit* (1989) and the epic *Christopher Columbus: The Discovery* (1992).

His best-known work is probably the dark, often primitive music he composed for *Star Trek VI: The Undiscovered Country* (1991), but his career has actually moved in the direction of more introspective dramas like his warm and lyrical *Untamed Heart* (1993), the nostalgic *Now and Then* (1995), and the moving *One True Thing* (1998).

Eidelman continues to compose concert works, most recently a tone poem based on *The Tempest* for inclusion on a Varèse Sarabande collection of music from Shakespearean films and plays.

TRIUMPH OF THE SPIRIT

Varèse Sarabande VSD-5254

Eidelman's ambitious score for this 1989 drama combines orchestra, chorus, vocal soloists, and ethnic instruments in a massive musical statement about the Nazi horrors of the Holocaust. Willem Dafoe starred in the fact-based story of a Greek-Jewish boxer who is forced to fight in Auschwitz (where the film was actually shot). Eidelman asked a cantor to write original poetry in Ladino, a dialect spoken by Sephardic Jews earlier in this century, then set the texts to music as part of the score.

STAR TREK VI:
THE UNDISCOVERED COUNTRY

MCA MCAD-10512

Paramount's final entry (1991) in the canon of original-*Enterprise*-cast films boasts what director Nicholas Meyer called "an operatic score," inspired by moments of Holst and Stravinsky but wholly original Eidelman. Dark, sometimes primitive, and rarely as heroic as its predecessors (fitting the subject matter, which ranges from traitorous Federation politicians to gulag imprisonment), this is probably the most forbidding music in the long history of *Star Trek* scores.

CHRISTOPHER COLUMBUS: THE DISCOVERY
Varèse Sarabande VSD-5389

The two Columbus movies released during 1992, the quincentennial of the explorer's voyage to the New World, contained vastly different scores. Vangelis created the music for *1492: Conquest of Paradise*; Eidelman, the music for the critically lambasted Alexander Salkind production starring Marlon Brando, Tom Selleck, and Rachel Ward. Eidelman's orchestral score was a good deal more compelling than the film, incorporating choir at strategic points, ethnic elements for Spain and the West Indies, and a heroic theme for George Corraface as the title character.

Elfman, Danny (1953–)

The founder of the rock group Oingo Boingo was surprised at first to be called to write the music for *Pee-wee's Big Adventure* (1985). Just a few years later, Danny Elfman was catapulted into the front ranks of film composers with his Grammy-winning score for the late '80s incarnation of *Batman*.

The contrast—from the bouncy, carnival-flavored score for Paul Reubens's alter ego to the Gothic grandeur of the music for the Caped Crusader—is all the more intriguing considering the two were for the same director, Tim Burton. Their collaboration has also produced the clever, quirky score for *Beetlejuice* (1988); music of great charm and sadness for *Edward Scissorhands* (1990); the funhouse-from-hell score for *Batman Returns* (1992); the widely praised song score for *The Nightmare Before Christmas* (1993); and the large-scale, madcap music for *Mars Attacks!* (1996).

The Hollywood musical community's initial skepticism of the self-taught ex-rocker has gradually subsided over the years, as demonstrated by his pair of 1997 Oscar nominations, for the subtle, atmospheric music for *Good Will Hunting* and the tongue-in-cheek score for *Men in Black* (the latter of which also earned him two Grammy nominations).

Another factor may have been Elfman's growing range as demonstrated by the pastoral qualities of his score for *Black Beauty* (1994), the urban funk of his music for *Dead Presidents* (1995), the high-energy tension of his score for *Mission: Impossible* (1996) and other work.

DANNY ELFMAN:
MUSIC FOR A DARKENED THEATRE
MCA MCAD-10065

This 1990 collection provides an introduction to Elfman's early film work, from the Nino Rota–inspired *Pee-wee's Big Adventure* (1985) to a suite from *Batman* (1989). Themes from *Dick Tracy* (1990), *Beetlejuice* (1988), *Nightbreed* (1990),

Darkman (1990), *Midnight Run* (1988), *Big Top Pee-wee* (1988), and *Scrooged* (1988) are included, along with more forgettable films like *Back to School* and *Wisdom* (both 1986), and such TV classics as his themes for *The Simpsons* and *Tales From the Crypt*.

DANNY ELFMAN:
MUSIC FOR A DARKENED THEATRE
VOLUME TWO
MCA MCAD 2-11550

The 1996 sequel is a two-CD set that contains far more generous suites (averaging 10 to 16 minutes in length) from his film and television work. Here are the charming *Edward Scissorhands* (1990), the suspenseful *Dolores Claiborne* (1994), the strange *To Die For* (1995), the sentimental *Black Beauty* (1994), and the extremely dark *Batman Returns* (1992). Disc 2 includes the energetic *Mission: Impossible* (1996), the romantic *Sommersby* (1993), the percussion-based *Dead Presidents* (1995), and *The Nightmare Before Christmas* (1993).

BATMAN
Warner Bros. 9 25977-2

Elfman's massive, brooding score for Warners' 1989 film with Michael Keaton as the Caped Crusader and Jack Nicholson as the Joker was the talk of the Hollywood musical community for months—partly because of unfounded rumors that Elfman's orchestrators were actually writing the music and partly because Prince's hugely popular first *Batman* album (most of which wasn't in the film) had misled many into believing that the reclusive rock star had written the score. This score won a Grammy.

EDWARD SCISSORHANDS
MCA MCAD-10133

Possibly Elfman's finest work, an underappreciated

and touching score that provides the heart in Tim Burton's 1990 fable about a scientist (Vincent Price) whose creation—an unfinished boy (Johnny Depp) left with scissors instead of hands—teaches a town, particularly a girl (Winona Ryder), lessons about love and being different. Elfman's use of choir (adult and boys) is especially effective.

MISSION: IMPOSSIBLE
Point Music 454 525-2

After Alan Silvestri's score was unceremoniously dumped halfway through recording, Elfman came in with just a few weeks to score Tom Cruise's 1996 big-screen version of the TV spy series. His great accomplishment was not only in retaining Lalo Schifrin's classic theme (updated in a high-energy, fully orchestral arrangement) but in adapting Schifrin's original musical ideas: the offbeat time signatures, the extensive use of (particularly military-style) percussion including bongos and cymbalum, and the careful heightening of suspense throughout dialogueless scenes.

A SIMPLE PLAN
Compass III COM 0105

One of Elfman's most interesting scores yet, his music for *A Simple Plan* provided a consistently unsettling tone via the use of detuned instruments, particularly pianos and banjos. Sam Raimi's dark film—a variation on the *Treasure of the Sierra Madre* theme of greed destroying friendship—netted 1998 Oscar nominations for writer Scott B. Smith and actor Billy Bob Thornton. Elfman's eerie tonalities—mostly achieved with an ensemble of strings and nine flutes—made the film seem even more disturbing and ultimately tragic.

Ellington, Duke (1899–1974)

The jazz composer, bandleader, and pianist wrote just four film scores, only two of which have been made available on records: the music from Otto Preminger's *Anatomy of a Murder* (1959) and the Paul Newman–Sidney Poitier film *Paris Blues* (1961). Despite rave reviews for the scores, the music of *Assault on a Queen* (1966), a thriller starring Frank Sinatra and Virna Lisi, and *Change of Mind* (1969), a strange sci-fi film about a white man's mind being transplanted into a black man's body, were never released.

Still, the first two scores are genuine classics, even if they weren't written in the language of traditional film music (that is, symphonic, romantic music). This is American jazz at its best, applied to the medium of film in ways that no one else had tried. *Anatomy of a Murder* has remained in print from the time of its release with the movie, and *Paris Blues* has found new life on CD after being a sought-after LP.

ANATOMY OF A MURDER
Columbia/Legacy CK 6569

Jazz critic Stanley Crouch called this score "one of Ellington's grandest accomplishments. . . . [it] showed just how far Ellington and [Billy] Strayhorn had stretched the language of jazz." Writer Tom Piazza called it "the closest thing we have to a vernacular American symphony." Otto Preminger, always a maverick when it came to music, hired the great jazz composer to create an original score for his 1959 drama about a Southern lawyer (James Stewart) who defends a soldier (Ben Gazzara) against charges that he murdered a bartender who may have raped the soldier's wife (Lee Remick). The 1999 reissue contains far more music than the original Columbia LP, including a contemporary interview with Ellington (who appears briefly in the film) and a 36-page booklet filled with historical detail and a Wynton Marsalis essay.

PARIS BLUES
Rykodisc RCD 10713

Paul Newman played a trombonist, Sidney Poitier a saxophonist and arranger, in Martin Ritt's 1961 drama about expatriate American musicians who prefer the Left Bank to America; Joanne Woodward and Diahann Carroll played tourists in the inevitable romantic tangle. Ellington's score, written and recorded in Paris, was nominated for an Oscar; considerably more sophisticated than *Anatomy of a Murder*, it features the evocative title theme, poignant numbers like "Nite" and "Guitar Amour," and Louis Armstrong blowing up a storm on "Wild Man Moore."

Farnon, Robert (1917–)

Canadian-born composer and arranger Robert Farnon is one of the world's best-known writers and conductors of light classical music. He was educated at the Toronto Conservatory and spent the early years of his musical career as an arranger, conductor, and composer for the Canadian Broadcasting Corporation.

Sent to Britain as a Canadian Army musical director during World War II, he remained there after the war and became established as a light-music specialist; his "Jumping Bean," "Westminster Waltz," and "State Occasion" became standard radio fare, and he became a much sought after arranger for vocalists ranging from Frank Sinatra and Sarah Vaughan to Tony Bennett and Peggy Lee.

Farnon's film scores number fewer than a dozen but include several familiar titles. By far his best, and most famous, work was for Gregory Peck's *Captain Horatio Hornblower* (1951). Others were the Bob Hope–Bing Crosby *Road to Hong Kong* (1962), the Hayley Mills love story *The Truth About Spring* (1965), and the Sean Connery–Brigitte Bardot western *Shalako* (1968).

CAPTAIN HORATIO HORNBLOWER
Reference RR-47CD

Farnon's best-known film score was written for Warner Bros.' 1951 nautical adventure that starred Gregory Peck as Britain's Royal Navy hero during the Napoleonic Wars. Farnon's score is the perfect accompaniment to a seagoing epic: fanfares played with gusto, furious battle music, and a gorgeous love theme for Peck and Virginia Mayo (as the intended wife of an admiral for whom Hornblower falls). Farnon conducts the Royal Philharmonic Orchestra in a five-movement, 21-minute suite in this 1991 re-recording.

Fenton, George (1949–)

Britisher George Fenton became a composer by accident. Born in Kent, he left school to become an actor; in 1974 he was summoned to an audition for a Peter Gill production of Shakespeare's *Twelfth Night* and wound up commissioned to write the score. Several other stage and television projects, for Gill and others, followed.

One of Fenton's earliest films earned him Oscar and Grammy nominations: Richard Attenborough's *Gandhi*, which won the 1982 Best Picture Oscar. Fenton's score was a collaboration with famed Indian composer Ravi Shankar.

As a composer for the small screen in Great Britain, Fenton won three British Academy of Film and Television Arts honors for his music for such '80s films as *An Englishman Abroad* and the internationally successful 14-hour miniseries *The Jewel in the Crown*.

Attenborough, who once pronounced Fenton as "the most brilliant movie composer of his generation," hired him again for the anti-apartheid film *Cry Freedom* (1987, this one a collaboration with African composer Jonas Gwanga), the C.S. Lewis story *Shadowlands* (1993), and the World War I Hemingway piece *In Love and War* (1996). His work on period films has made him something of a specialist in the field, including such assignments as *The Madness of King George* (1994), Arthur Miller's *The Crucible* (1996), the Jekyll-Hyde story *Mary Reilly* (1996), and *Anna and the King* (1999). He also won an Oscar nomination for his colorful score for Robin Williams in *The Fisher King* (1991).

GANDHI
RCA ABL 1-4557 (LP)

For his 1982 epic of the life of Mohandas Gandhi, director Richard Attenborough brought together India's leading composer, sitar specialist Ravi Shankar, and Fenton as orchestral score composer and contributor of the British music of the period. The collaboration produced a unique score, one that was Oscar-nominated, with over half the album attributed to the two of them together. Shankar, and a group of major Indian musicians, joined Fenton's Wren Orchestra. The film won eight Oscars, including Best Picture and, for Ben Kingsley, Best Actor.

CRY FREEDOM
MCA MCAD-6224

Richard Attenborough's fact-based movie about South African activist Steve Biko and newspaper editor Donald Woods received three Oscar nominations, and two of them went to composer George Fenton and his African collaborator Jonas Gwanga for Best Original Song, for the title tune, and for Original Score. (The other went to Denzel Washington as the doomed Biko.) Gwanga acted as vocal director, leading a battery of African singers through choral work ranging from whispers to chants to anthems (often atop Fenton's orchestral tracks), lending the film an authentic-sounding African sound.

DANGEROUS LIAISONS

Virgin 7 91057-2

Glenn Close, John Malkovich, and Michelle Pfeiffer starred in Christopher Hampton's own adaptation of his play *Les Liaisons Dangereuses* (based on an 18th-century novel of sexual manipulation and deceit), a 1988 Best Picture nominee directed by Stephen Frears. Fenton's task was to arrange and conduct a number of classical pieces—by composers including Vivaldi, Handel, Bach, and Gluck—as well as to write new music of a more dramatic nature that nevertheless fit the period and the style of the great masters. Fenton received a Best Original Score Oscar nomination.

DANGEROUS BEAUTY

Restless 01877-72958-2

Catherine McCormack starred in Marshall Herskovitz's 1998 tale of a courtesan in 16th-century Venice, which required Fenton to create music that suggested the time and place—lute and mandolin, strings, and woodwinds including recorder, often in dance-like rhythms—while also underscoring the inevitable romantic and dramatic moments of the screenplay. Lyrical and tender, this ranks among Fenton's best work.

EVER AFTER: A CINDERELLA STORY

London 289 460 581-2

Director Andy Tennant's 1998 retelling of the fairy tale, with Drew Barrymore as a feminist Cinderella, elicited one of Fenton's most beautiful scores. Alternating between the purely romantic and the delightfully period (harpsichord, pipes, lute), Fenton's music proved such a winning element of the story that moviegoers rushed out to buy the album. Its gold-record status is unusual for a record of dramatic underscore in this era.

Fiedel, Brad (1951–)

Brad Fiedel came to prominence in the film-scoring world with his electronic scores for James Cameron's two *Terminator* movies, although his background is actually in more traditional acoustic music.

A New Yorker from a musical family, he played the piano at age six and was composing by seven and pursued a career as a singer-songwriter, signing with Paul Simon's DeShufflin' Music and working as resident composer for the City University of New York's dance department. He also toured with Hall & Oates as keyboard player and backup singer before movies beckoned in the '70s.

Fiedel's electronic music for James Cameron's science-fiction film *The Terminator* (1984) was just one of a diverse collection of movies for which he provided music: a sexy New Orleans score for *The Big Easy* (1987), moody orchestral accompaniment for Jodie Foster's Oscar-winning performance in *The Accused* (1988), Haitian voodoo rhythms for *The Serpent and the Rainbow* (1988), and a lighthearted orchestral romp for Cameron's action-comedy starring Arnold Schwarzenegger *True Lies* (1994).

Fiedel's television credits are even more stellar, including such acclaimed and Emmy-winning TV-movies as *Playing for Time, The Bunker,* and *Rasputin,* and the weekly series *Midnight Caller* and *Reasonable Doubts.*

TERMINATOR 2: JUDGMENT DAY

Varèse Sarabande VSD-5335

Fiedel's all-synthesizer score for James Cameron's 1991 blockbuster, the high-octane sequel to the 1984 Arnold Schwarzenegger adventure, is as high-tech as the look and feel of the movie. Sparing in terms of melody, it was entirely appropriate for the film's grisly futuristic settings. Pounding percussion, eerie synthesized voices, and repeating mechanical sounds create a cold, foreboding atmosphere. While not a blockbuster in terms of album sales, it reached the number-70 position on the *Billboard* charts, making it one of Varèse's biggest sellers.

PHOTO COURTESY OF CAMILLE FIELDING

Fielding, Jerry (1922–1980)

Jerry Fielding might have had a far longer career in films had he not run afoul of the Hollywood blacklist. A veteran big-band leader and arranger with extensive radio and early-TV experience, he took the Fifth Amendment during a 1953 appearance before the House Un-American Activities Committee. The direct and immediate result was unemployment in Hollywood for the next six years.

Two events broke the blacklist: actress Betty Hutton's insistence on Fielding as her musical director for a television series; and the selection of Fielding by maverick director Otto Preminger—who had hired fellow blacklist victim Dalton Trumbo to adapt *Advise and Consent* for the screen—as his composer on the film. Fielding spent much of the '60s and '70s toiling in TV on such shows as *Hogan's Heroes* and *McMillan & Wife*.

In the late 1960s, Fielding began a stormy but productive relationship with director Sam Peckinpah, for whom he scored five films including the classic western *The Wild Bunch* and the controversial *Straw Dogs* (which brought Fielding the first two of his three Oscar nominations, in 1969 and 1971).

His other primary collaborators were the British director Michael Winner, on such diverse films as the western *Lawman* (1970), the Marlon Brando film *The Nightcomers* (1971), and the Charles Bronson hit-man thriller *The Mechanic* (1972); and Clint Eastwood, with an Oscar-nominated score for the revenge western *The Outlaw Josey Wales* (1976) and jazz scores for *The Enforcer* (1975) and *The Gauntlet* (1977). Fielding's music—like the character of the man—was frequently dark, complex, and uncompromising.

THE WILD BUNCH

Warner Bros. WHV-1987

Peckinpah's 1969 masterpiece about a turn-of-the-century outlaw gang led by William Holden, with Robert Ryan in hot pursuit, was wildly controversial for its slow-motion violence. For Fielding, it provided a remarkable canvas and inspired his magnum opus. He received a 1969 Oscar nomination for the score, which skillfully interweaves martial rhythms, traditional Mexican melodies, and complex action material. Few western scores are as colorful, atmospheric, or as inextricably a part of the fabric of the film as this one. The album briefly charted, but it was a re-recording with a smaller orchestra than the film recording. The original stereo movie tracks were restored for a limited-edition CD that accompanied the 1997 laserdisc edition of the film.

JERRY FIELDING: FILM MUSIC
Bay Cities BCD-LE 4001/02

Three of these scores, which Fielding composed over a three-year period, represent some of his best work. *Straw Dogs* (the controversial Sam Peckinpah film with Dustin Hoffman and Susan George), nominated for a 1971 Oscar, opens with a brass chorale and descends into a hell of serialism and strange, electronically altered music befitting the paroxysm of violence that occurs in the film's climax. *Lawman* (1970), for a Burt Lancaster western, is expansive but dark and far from imitation Copland. *The Mechanic* (1972), which cast Charles Bronson as a hit man, is an atonal study in colors—as Fielding once said, "blocks of sound filling the spectrum, all painted in shades of black." Also included: *Chato's Land* (1971), *The Nightcomers* (1972), and *The Big Sleep* (1978).

THE OUTLAW JOSEY WALES
Warner Bros. BS-2956 (LP)

Fielding received his third Oscar nomination for this 1976 western directed by, and starring, Clint Eastwood. The film is an epic post–Civil War revenge tale that is unstinting in its depiction of hatred and savagery in a lawless era. Fielding's music echoes this concept with complex, often melancholy, and downright grim colors, sharply dissonant figures, and rare flights of melody. It's unusually effective in the film and fascinating listening apart from the film.

THE GAUNTLET
Warner Bros. BSK 3144 (LP)

Eastwood, again as star and director, asked Fielding for a jazzy background for his 1977 film about a washed-up, alcoholic cop protecting an endangered organized-crime witness (Sondra Locke). He used a bluesy version of "Just a Closer Walk With Thee" and employed soloists Jon Faddis (trumpet) and Art Pepper (saxophone) throughout, often in interesting duets. As he had done on Eastwood's Dirty Harry movie *The Enforcer* (1976), Fielding employed jazz figures against chase and suspense sequences that worked superbly.

Fox, Charles (1940–)

Although better known for his popular TV themes than his film scores, Charles Fox was among the most sought after composers of the 1970s and '80s and continues to score both movies and television.

A graduate of New York's High School of Music and Art, he studied with Nadia Boulanger in Paris and, upon returning to New York, entered the commercial-music field. He wrote songs and underscore for Jane Fonda's infamous *Barbarella* (1968) and came to Hollywood to score *Goodbye, Columbus* (1969).

He had a string of hits with lyricist Norman Gimbel, including "I Got a Name" for Jim Croce in *The Last American Hero* (1971), "Killing Me Softly" for Roberta Flack, and "Ready to Take a Chance Again" for Barry Manilow from *Foul Play* (1978). The latter tune, and "Richard's Window," sung by Olivia Newton-John in *The Other Side of the Mountain* (1975), were Oscar nominees for Best Song.

Fox scored several successful comedies including *9 to 5* (1980) and *National Lampoon's European Vacation* (1985) but in recent years has concentrated on dramatic music for television films. Fox's TV-series themes are among the most popular ever written: *Love American Style*, *Happy Days*, "Making Our Dreams Come True" from *Laverne & Shirley*, *The Love Boat*, and "Different Worlds" from *Angie*. They are easier to find on CD than his film music.

ONE ON ONE

Warner Bros. BS 3076 (LP)

The film—about a basketball player (Robby Benson, who co-wrote the script) battling a corrupt college-athletics system—is largely forgotten today, but Fox's score was one of his most lively and successful. Fox collaborated with lyricist Paul Williams on several songs for pop duo Jim Seals and Dash Crofts, one of which ("My Fair Share") was a top-30 hit in the fall of 1977. Fox's score is typical of his pleasant, melodic, frequently upbeat style.

PHOTO COURTESY OF BRIGHAM YOUNG UNIVERSITY

Friedhofer, Hugo W. (1902–1981)

Known within the Hollywood music fraternity as a consummate composer and orchestrator, Hugo Friedhofer was also justly famed for his near-pho-

tographic memory when it came to recalling scores throughout the classical repertoire and for his dry wit. (Once praised as one of the greats in his profession, he responded, "Yes, I'm a false giant in a community of genuine pygmies.")

Born in San Francisco, Friedhofer came to Hollywood in 1929. He orchestrated 15 of Erich Wolfgang Korngold's film scores and more than 50 of Max Steiner's. Alfred Newman, as music director first for Samuel Goldwyn and later for 20th Century–Fox, was largely responsible for upgrading Friedhofer's reputation from orchestrator to composer with such films as *The Adventures of Marco Polo* (1938) and *The Lodger* (1944). Friedhofer was highly respected within the fraternity of composers: He could write a swashbuckler based on medieval English music (*The Bandit of Sherwood Forest*, 1946), a vigorous score based on Mexican folk themes (*Vera Cruz*, 1954), an epic western (Marlon Brando's *One-Eyed Jacks*, 1960), or a World War I aerial-battle adventure (*Von Richtofen and Brown*, 1971). He was infamous for composing very slowly and meticulously, however—in part because he knew the vast classical repertoire so well that he feared repeating, even in only a few notes, what some more famous predecessor had written centuries earlier.

Friedhofer's greatest achievement, and his sole Oscar winner out of nine nominations, was his Americana score for the 1946 post-war epic *The Best Years of Our Lives*. Some of his other nominees were equally worthy, though, including *The Bishop's Wife* (1947), *Joan of Arc* (1948), and *Boy on a Dolphin* (1957). In later years, Friedhofer wrote for television (*Outlaws, I Spy*) and tutored younger composers.

HUGO FRIEDHOFER:
THE ADVENTURES OF MARCO POLO
Marco Polo 8.223857

Classic film-music experts John W. Morgan and William Stromberg reconstructed four major Friedhofer scores for this 1996 collection. Included: a rousing 13-minute suite from Gary Cooper's *The Adventures of Marco Polo* (1938), with its authentic-sounding Oriental touches; the dark and sinister score for the turn-of-the-century London chiller *The Lodger* (1944); the sumptuous, romantic, and Indian-flavored music of *The Rains of Ranchipur* (1955); and the exotic, Spanish-flavored sounds of the adventure *Seven Cities of Gold* (1955), which was set in 18th-century California. Stromberg conducts the Moscow Symphony Orchestra.

THE BEST YEARS OF OUR LIVES
Preamble PRCD 1779

Widely considered Friedhofer's masterpiece, this warm and nostalgic music brimming with Americana touches won the 1946 dramatic-score Oscar (one of eight it received, including Best Picture and, for William Wyler, Best Director). Fredric March, Dana Andrews, and Harold Russell starred as three battle-scarred veterans returning from the war and finding difficulty readjusting. It struck a chord with millions of Americans—in part because Friedhofer's music was so moving and so right, from its optimistic opening to the nightmare episodes suffered by its protagonists. Franco Collura conducted the London Philharmonic Orchestra in this 1978 re-recording.

BROKEN ARROW
BYU Film Archives FMA-HF105

One of Friedhofer's best-loved scores (and, interestingly, his first western), the music for this 1950 classic shifts away from the already-clichéd "cow-boys and Indians" approach, reflecting both the nature of the film—a move toward reconciliation between whites and Native Americans in the 1870s—and the composer's more mature approach to the drama. James Stewart and Jeff Chandler starred in the film; Chandler, the screenplay, and the cinematography were all recognized with Oscar nominations.

AN AFFAIR TO REMEMBER
Epic EK 57568

Friedhofer was Oscar-nominated for his score for this amusing and sentimental 1957 film starring Cary Grant and Deborah Kerr, as was the Harry Warren–Harold Adamson–Leo McCarey title song. The movie got a new lease on life when it was featured prominently in the Tom Hanks–Meg Ryan comedy *Sleepless in Seattle* 36 years later. Although several songs are featured on this disc, Friedhofer's romantic and ultimately quite dramatic score remains prominent. Lionel Newman conducted.

THE YOUNG LIONS / THIS EARTH IS MINE
Varèse Sarabande VSD 2-5403

This 2-CD set includes the scores from two late 1950s films that were originally issued on LP. His Oscar-nominated music for *The Young Lions* (1958) accompanied Marlon Brando and Montgomery Clift in a World War II drama; Friedhofer's exciting and powerful main theme is one of the finest ever written for a war story. *This Earth Is Mine* (1959) was a Rock Hudson–Jean Simmons melodrama set in California's wine country, a melodic Friedhofer score (with a Sammy Cahn–Jimmy Van Heusen title song) for an essentially forgotten film.

Frontiere, Dominic (1931–)

Born in New Haven, Connecticut, Dominic Frontiere was well known as one of the country's finest accordion players before he shifted to the role of composer for movies and TV under the aegis of 20th Century–Fox music director Alfred Newman (another New Haven native) and writer-director Leslie Stevens.

Frontiere spent the 1960s and '70s moving back and forth between the big screen and small. For television, he created such classic '60s soundscapes as *The Outer Limits*, *The Invaders*, *The Rat Patrol*, *The Flying Nun*, and *12 O'Clock High*; in films, his music accompanied Clint Eastwood in *Hang 'Em High* (1968), Alan Arkin in *Popi* (1969), and John Wayne in three of his final films: *Chisum* (1970), *The Train Robbers* (1973), and *Brannigan* (1975).

Motorcycle riding occupied him in the documentary *On Any Sunday* (1971), and he became a comedy specialist as a result of such box-office hits as *Freebie and the Bean* (1974), *The Gumball Rally* (1976) and *Modern Problems* (1981). He also arranged for such pop stars as Gladys Knight, Dan Fogelberg, Chicago, and The Tubes. His musical career was temporarily derailed when, in 1986, he was sentenced to a year in federal prison on income tax return charges in connection with a Super Bowl ticket-scalping scheme.

Frontiere's two films for director Richard Rush have been award-winners: *The Stunt Man* (1980) won a Golden Globe, and his title song from Bruce Willis's *The Color of Night* (1994) was a Globe nominee.

HANG 'EM HIGH

Sony AK 47705

This 1991 disc contains the scores for two 1968 westerns: one popular and still a cable-TV staple, one forgotten and rarely seen. Frontiere's music for the Clint Eastwood oater *Hang 'Em High*—an American attempt at a spaghetti western à la Sergio Leone—became enormously popular, especially in a cover version by Booker T. & the MGs that was a top-10 hit. Frontiere's theme, with its harmonica and twangy guitar, bears a resemblance to the Ennio Morricone music of the Leone movies; Morricone's typically colorful score for the Anthony Quinn–Charles Bronson *Guns for San Sebastian* actually occupies more than half the disc.

THE STUNT MAN

20th Century–Fox T-626 (LP)

Frontiere's music for Richard Rush's 1980 film— "kind of a snicker at everything that's going on in the movie," he said at the time—won a Golden Globe Award. Steve Railsback stars as the title character, Peter O'Toole a mad director, in this black comedy about the film business. Frontiere's score, particularly his lighthearted theme, is consistently effective and often amusing; Dusty Springfield sings a Frontiere–Norman Gimbel song called "Bits and Pieces."

Glass, Philip (1937–)

The music community remains divided about Philip Glass: Half seem to find him imaginative and original, the other half boring and repetitive. Baltimore-born, Juilliard-educated, Glass began applying Eastern techniques to his music and became one of the leading exponents of the minimalist school.

Glass's syncopated rhythms, rapid arpeggios, and penchant for musical repetition have found expression in several films, especially in the documentary field. Godfrey Reggio's widely acclaimed *Koyaanisqatsi* (1983) helped to propel Glass—

then best known for his operas *Einstein on the Beach* and *Satyagraha*—to prominence and led to further collaborations with Reggio on *Powaqqatsi* (1988) and *Anima Mundi* (1991).

Glass's other significant documentaries include Errol Morris's *The Thin Blue Line* (1988) and *A Brief History of Time* (1992). He has occasionally chosen to work in fictional film, notably for Paul Schrader (*Mishima*, 1985) and Martin Scorsese (*Kundun*, 1997). For his contributions to *The Truman Show* (1998, mostly scored by Australia-based Burkhard Dallwitz), Glass earned a Golden Globe Award.

KOYAANISQATSI

Nonesuch 79506-2

Perhaps Glass's most popular work for film, his music for Godfrey Reggio's cinematic indictment of 20th-century life is hypnotic, alternately bright and dark, often maddening—and the one element that makes Reggio's non-narrative, dialogueless imagery of America a compelling work. The title is Hopi Indian for "life out of balance." Michael Riesman conducts this 1998 re-recording.

KUNDUN

Nonesuch 79460-2

Martin Scorsese commissioned Glass to score his 1997 film about the Dalai Lama, and the result was Glass's first Oscar nomination. Scorsese speaks in his liner notes of Glass's "Buddhist faith and deep understanding of Tibetan culture" as significant contributions to the film. Tibetan horns and cymbals and the voices of the Gyuto Monks and Monks of the Drukpa Order add authenticity to this score which, while containing all of Glass's usual trademarks, also contains more sheer musical drama than many of his other film scores.

Gold, Ernest (1921–1999)

One of the key voices in the film music of the 1960s, Ernest Gold is best known for his popular theme for *Exodus* (1960), but he also provided the music for such important films as *On the Beach* (1959), *Inherit the Wind* (1960), *Judgment at Nuremberg* (1961), *Ship of Fools* (1965), and *It's a Mad Mad Mad Mad World* (1963), all the work of producer-director Stanley Kramer.

Born in Vienna, Gold's musical studies as a teenager were interrupted by Hitler's invasion of Austria in 1938. Moving to New York, he became a songwriter (with such *Hit Parade* favorites as "Practice Makes Perfect," "Accidentally on Purpose," and "They Started Something") while continuing his serious-music studies and composing for the concert hall. When a critic dismissed his piano concerto (premiered at Carnegie Hall in 1945) as "movie music," he moved to Hollywood and immediately found work.

He befriended composer George Antheil, orchestrating and conducting such scores as *The Pride and the Passion* (1957), which led to his long and productive association with Kramer. Gold later received Oscar nominations for his variations on

"Waltzing Matilda" for the post–nuclear-holocaust drama *On the Beach* (1959); for both the song and score of Kramer's outrageous, over-the-top comedy *It's a Mad Mad Mad Mad World* (1963); and for the score of Kramer's wartime comedy *The Secret of Santa Vittoria* (1969). Subsequent film work included Sam Peckinpah's *Cross of Iron* (1977) and Kramer's *The Runner Stumbles* (1979).

EXODUS
RCA 1058-2-R

Gold's stirring theme for Otto Preminger's 1960 epic (based on Leon Uris's novel about Israel's struggle for independence in 1947) quickly became one of the most famous movie tunes in history and drove this soundtrack to the top of *Billboard*'s charts, where it remained for 14 weeks. It also won the original-score Oscar and two Grammys (as the year's best song and soundtrack album). Preminger hired Gold before shooting, enabling the composer to do extensive research into Israeli and Arabic music, which figured prominently in the score.

JUDGMENT AT NUREMBERG
Rykodisc RCD 10723

Stanley Kramer's powerful 1961 chronicle of the Nazi war-crimes trials that followed World War II received 11 Oscar nominations including Best Picture (winning two, for actor Maxmilian Schell and writer Abby Mann); Spencer Tracy, Montgomery Clift, and Judy Garland were also nominated. Gold's score interpolates German folk songs, military marches, and heraldic brass-choir figures designed for maximum dramatic impact.

IT'S A MAD MAD MAD MAD WORLD
Rykodisc RCD 10704

Stanley Kramer's all-star comedic romp won Gold 1963 Academy Award nominations for Best Song

and Best Original Score. His grand and amusing waltz-time theme (with lyrics by Mack David) sets the stage for dozens of legendary comedians to cavort around for three hours in search of a small fortune. Gold's score (on which he labored for six months) incorporates everything from carousel sounds to mad chase music—rollicking, tongue-in-cheek, a classic comedy score, as over-the-top as the film it was written for.

FILM THEMES OF ERNEST GOLD
Artemis ART-F001

Gold's pre-1964 output was nicely summarized on this beautifully recorded collection with the composer conducting the London Symphony Orchestra. Most of the themes are for Stanley Kramer productions, including a six-minute concert arrangement of *Exodus* (1960), plus *On the Beach* (1959, featuring "Waltzing Matilda"), *Inherit the Wind* (1960), *Judgment at Nuremberg* (1961) and *It's a Mad Mad Mad Mad World* (1963). Also included: the yearning theme for *The Young Philadelphians* (1959), an evocative western landscape for *The Last Sunset* (1961), the jazzy *Pressure Point* (1962), and the dramatic *Too Much, Too Soon* (1958).

Goldenthal, Elliot (1954–)

One of few composers to successfully, and regularly, shift from the classical world to films to stage pieces, Brooklyn-born Elliot Goldenthal was headed toward a career as an academic composer. He studied with John Corigliano in the 1970s and, on an informal basis, with Aaron Copland in the '80s.

His breakthrough film was Gus Van Sant's 1989 *Drugstore Cowboy*. Since then, he has worked regularly in Hollywood—although he continues to make his home in New York with longtime companion Julie Taymor, the acclaimed stage designer and Tony-winning director of Broadway's *The Lion King*.

Goldenthal's ability to write in an advanced musical language has served him well in such science-fiction films as *Alien 3* (1992), and *Sphere* (1998), but he has also written such commercial successes as *Batman Forever* and *Batman & Robin* (1995, 1997). His most consistent professional relationship in films has been with director Neil Jordan, starting with *Interview With the Vampire* (1994).

His most significant nonfilm works have been his Tony-nominated *Juan Darien: A Carnival Mass* (1988), his Vietnam War oratorio *Fire Water Paper* (1996), and his ballet *Othello* (1998). But his thoughtful, challenging, occasionally brilliant work in movies has made him indispensable to films in the '90s.

ALIEN 3
MCA MCAD-10629

The 1992 installment of 20th Century–Fox's popular science-fiction franchise featured the most way out, and in some ways brilliant, score of all. Goldenthal's complex music begins with a choral "Agnus Dei" and descends into a netherworld of strange but purposeful orchestral and synthesized effects; from the use of boy sopranos to the sheer brutality of the brass and percussion writing and the passion-filled finale, this is a score of drama and great power.

INTERVIEW WITH THE VAMPIRE
Geffen GEFD-24719

Goldenthal's first Oscar-nominated score was written in three and a half weeks after another score was discarded. It marked the first of several collaborations with director Neil Jordan and still resonates with anyone who saw the 1994 film version (starring a controversial Tom Cruise) of Anne Rice's novel. Grand, gothic, and wildly romantic, its many astute touches include boys' choir, harpsichord, quotations from the text of the Mass, and musical forms ranging from waltz to tarantella.

BATMAN FOREVER
Atlantic 82776-2

Danny Elfman may have established a style with his first two *Batman* scores, but Elliot Goldenthal took the series in a fresh direction with the third episode of the Warner Bros. comic-book franchise (1995, with Val Kilmer). Massive, dark, and far more varied than its predecessors, this score includes everything from urban jazz to a grim march for the Caped Crusader and a witty, theremin-driven weird-science motif for Jim Carrey's mad Riddler.

MICHAEL COLLINS

Atlantic 82960-2

Goldenthal's Oscar-nominated music for Neil Jordan's 1996 biography of the Irish revolutionary (played by Liam Neeson) is admirable for its refusal (unlike so many of its contemporaries) to beat its listeners over the head with Irish sounds. Yes, there is low whistle and uilleann pipes, but equally colorful and evocative in Goldenthal's hands are hammer dulcimer and plain ol' piano, none overused. Vocalist Sinead O'Connor is featured on three tracks that are stunning musical moments in the film narrative.

TITUS

Sony Classical SK 89171

Perhaps the most ambitious score of 1999, Goldenthal's music for Julie Taymor's film of Shakespeare's *Titus Andronicus* encompassed massive choral forces singing in Latin; dark, primitive percussive sounds for ancient Rome; big-band and industrial rock for the more outlandish sequences; and a stunning orchestral elegy for the finale. Goldenthal abetted the work of actors Anthony Hopkins, Jessica Lange, Alan Cumming, Harry Lennix, and others in this colorful and underrated film.

PHOTO BY MELODIE GIMPLE, COURTESY OF THE COMPOSER

Goldsmith, Jerry (1929–)

Jerry Goldsmith is responsible for some of the most significant scores of the past 40 years. His many Oscar nominations attest to a remarkable versatility and ability to deliver a wide range of musical styles and sounds, from the romance of *Chinatown* (1974) to the otherworldly ambiance of *Planet of the Apes* (1968); from the echoing trumpets of *Patton* (1970) to the grand-scale heroics of *Star Trek: The Motion Picture* (1979).

He won an Academy Award for his unsettling score for the 1976 horror film *The Omen*. His unerring dramatic sense has heightened the power of movies from *Basic Instinct* (1992) to *L.A. Confidential* (1997), and his comedic timing has enlivened lighter movies such as *Gremlins* (1984). In those and other recent films, he has remained in touch with contemporary audiences via the addition of electronic elements to the traditional symphonic array employed on many scores.

One of the few top film composers who was actually born and educated in Los Angeles, Goldsmith began writing for radio and television in the 1950s, including highly original work for *The Twilight Zone* and *Thriller* and great themes for such classic series as *Dr. Kildare*, *The Man from U.N.C.L.E.*, and *Room 222*. Over the years he has won five Emmys for his television scores, mostly for such high-profile miniseries as *QB VII* and *Masada*.

While under contract to 20th Century–Fox in the mid-'60s, he honed his craft to become one of the industry's most respected and sought after composers. And although he continues to be first choice among many filmmakers (with such recent commercial hits as 1997's *Air Force One* and 1999's *The Mummy* on his resumé), he has recently broadened his career to include concert appearances and nonfilm commissions (including the Academy Award fanfare, which debuted in 1998).

A PATCH OF BLUE

Intrada MAF 7076

This sensitive score brought Goldsmith his second Oscar nomination. The 1965 film, about a blind white girl (Elizabeth Hartman) who befriends a black man (Sidney Poitier), won an Oscar for Shelley Winters as the girl's mother. Goldsmith's music, written for an unusual ensemble that prominently features piano and harmonica, lends warmth, joy, and humor to the film.

PLANET OF THE APES

Varèse Sarabande VSD-5848

One of only a handful of truly original movie scores from the past 30 years, Goldsmith's avant-garde music for the first of the popular *Apes* films created such a sensation that, years later, colleagues were still asking him how he created certain effects (all achieved acoustically, not electronically). This impressionistic soundscape was a 1968 Oscar nominee; the 1997 album marks the first time the complete score was made available.

Also included: a 16-minute suite from Goldsmith's score for the second sequel, *Escape From the Planet of the Apes* (1971).

PATTON

FSM Vol. 2, No. 2

Although there is less than half an hour's music in this three-hour epic about legendary World War II general George S. Patton, Goldsmith's Oscar-nominated score has become a textbook example of the subtle use of music to illuminate character in film: the echoing trumpets (hinting at Patton's strong connection with battles throughout history), the organ chorale (his religious convictions), the march (the military man). George C. Scott refused to accept his Oscar for Franklin Schnaffer's 1970 film.

PAPILLON

Silva Screen FILMCD 029

Goldsmith scored seven pictures for director Franklin J. Schaffner, and this, his fourth, is by any standard an unqualified masterpiece. Written for the adaptation of Henri Charrière's book about an escape from a French penal colony (that starred Steve McQueen and Dustin Hoffman), it reflects the moods of the film from anguish to triumph. Goldsmith received a 1973 Oscar nomination for this alternately lyrical and powerful symphonic tapestry.

CHINATOWN

Varèse Sarabande VSD-5677

A modern-day noir classic, this Jack Nicholson–Faye Dunaway film benefited enormously from this score—composed in just 10 days when producer Robert Evans discarded an earlier one by another composer. Goldsmith's romantic trumpet and warm strings echoes the '30s period nicely while remaining modern in musical context. The unorthodox orchestration—four pianos, four harps, two percussion, strings, and solo trumpet—has long been a topic for discussion in film-scoring classes. It was a 1974 Oscar nominee.

THE WIND AND THE LION

Intrada MAF 7005D

Goldsmith's colorful music drives John Milius's 1975 adventure saga, with Sean Connery as the last of the Barbary pirates, Candice Bergen as his American captive, and Brian Keith as an outraged President Teddy Roosevelt. Authentic-sounding Moroccan rhythms, a grandly scored love theme ("I Remember," one of the composer's most passionate), and exciting action material made this one of the great scores of the '70s; it was also an Oscar nominee.

THE OMEN

Varèse Sarabande VSD-5281

Goldsmith's only Oscar-winning score accompanies a truly frightening horror film about the coming of the Antichrist. Gregory Peck and Lee Remick starred in the movie, which opens with a mixed choir chanting pro-Satan verses in Latin ("Ave Satani," a curious Oscar nominee for Best Original Song). The film owes much of its fright content to Goldsmith's alternately beautiful and horrific orchestral-and-choral score. Lionel Newman conducts London's National Philharmonic Orchestra; Goldsmith's wife, Carol, sings the love theme, "The Piper Dreams." Goldsmith scored both sequels, *Damien: Omen II* (1978) and *The Final Conflict* (1981).

STAR TREK: THE MOTION PICTURE

Columbia/Legacy C2K 66134

Recutting and the late arrival of special effects for this first big-screen adventure of Kirk, Spock, and company caused Goldsmith to work on this epic score until just days before its premiere. But from his heroic *Enterprise* theme to Klingon battle music, from the mysterious sounds of Vejur to his gentle theme for the bald navigator Ilia, this is one of the all-time-great sci-fi scores, a 1979 Oscar nominee. The 1999 release adds 25 more minutes of music. *Star Trek* creator Gene Roddenberry insisted on adopting the main theme for his next TV series, *Star Trek: The Next Generation*, and Goldsmith has scored three of the movie sequels (*Star Trek V: The Final Frontier*, 1989; *First Contact*, 1996; and *Insurrection*, 1998).

POLTERGEIST

Rhino R2 72725

"They're heeeere," reminds the cover of this complete version of the Oscar-nominated Goldsmith score—the words of little Carol Anne, the child abducted by spirits from another dimension in this 1982 Steven Spielberg–produced ghost story. Craig T. Nelson and Jobeth Williams were top-billed, but it was the special effects and music that made audiences tremble. Goldsmith's heartfelt lullaby for the little girl and his music for suburbia were the perfect setup for his far more sophisticated and often harsh textures in the most intense scenes.

LEGEND

Silva Screen FILMCD 045

The rejection of Goldsmith's impressionistic, orchestral-and-choral tapestry for Ridley Scott's sumptuously photographed 1985 fantasy—on which he worked for six months, creating both songs and score—in favor of one by German techno-pop group Tangerine Dream, became infamous in the movie-music community. Goldsmith's score remains in European prints of the Tom Cruise film, and 71 minutes of it were released on this 1992 CD. Goldsmith conducts the National Philharmonic; lyrics were by John Bettis.

BASIC INSTINCT
Varèse Sarabande VSD-5360

Director Paul Verhoeven called Goldsmith's music for his 1992 erotic thriller "original, evocative, and audacious in its very simplicity." As sensual and seductive as Sharon Stone is to Michael Douglas in the film, the music is subtle and effective in ways that most slasher-movie scores never are. It earned the composer another Oscar nomination.

FIRST KNIGHT
Epic EK 67270
THE MUMMY
Decca 289 466 458-2

Some of Goldsmith's best work in recent years has been for historical epics. For 1995's *First Knight*, a retelling of the legend of King Arthur (with Sean Connery as Arthur, Julia Ormond as Guinevere, and Richard Gere as Lancelot), the composer wrote a majestic score for orchestra and chorus, rich with the colors of medieval England. For 1999's *The Mummy* (with Brendan Fraser as an adventurer battling an ancient Egyptian monster), Goldsmith's alternately mysterious and powerful music propelled the action and provided the requisite period atmosphere.

Goodwin, Ron (1925–)

Ron Goodwin, long one of Britain's top instrumental recording artists and concert conductors, wrote more than five dozen film scores, including two of the 1960s' great war-movie themes: *633 Squadron* (1964) and *Where Eagles Dare* (1968).

Goodwin worked as an arranger for such popular bandleaders as Ted Heath and Stanley Black before forming his own orchestra for radio broadcasts in the early '50s. He started scoring films in 1958 and became much in demand, scoring four of the Miss Marple films with Margaret Rutherford, beginning with 1961's *Murder, She Said*.

His stirring march for *633 Squadron* was a popular hit in England, just as his thrilling martial score for the Richard Burton–Clint Eastwood war flick *Where Eagles Dare* caught on in the states. Goodwin was then called on to replace two high-profile scores: the music of Sir William Walton for *The Battle of Britain* (1969) and that of Henry Mancini for Alfred Hitchcock's *Frenzy* (1972). Goodwin's anthem for the city of London is still the most memorable aspect of the latter.

Along the way there have been such popular films as *Those Magnificent Men in Their Flying Machines* (1965) and *The Trap* (1966), several Disney movies, and one more war theme: the jaunty march for *Force 10 From Navarone* (1978). Goodwin's concert pieces, including "Drake 400" (1979) and "New Zealand Suite" (1983), are equally effective musical landscapes.

633 SQUADRON / WHERE EAGLES DARE
EMI CDP 794094 2

Goodwin's two classic war scores are perhaps his best-known works. His exciting, uptempo theme for *633 Squadron* (1964), a World War II adventure starring Cliff Robertson, was a bigger hit in the U.K. than in the U.S. *Where Eagles Dare* (1968), based on an Alistair MacLean novel, starred Richard Burton and Clint Eastwood and was a big hit in America. Goodwin's theme is a masterpiece of sustained tension via counterpoint.

Green, Johnny (1908–1989)

A legendary figure in Hollywood, dapper Johnny Green was musical director at MGM from August 1949 to March 1958, the era of its greatest movie musicals. Nominated for 14 Academy Awards, he won five: for his musical direction of *Easter Parade* (1948), *An American in Paris* (1951), *West Side Story* (1961), and *Oliver!* (1968) and for producing the *MGM Concert Hall* short subject *The Merry Wives of Windsor Overture* (1953).

His fame actually preceded his California career. With lyricist Edward Heyman in New York, he wrote the classic torch song "Body and Soul" for Gertrude Lawrence and such other standards as "Out of Nowhere," "I Cover the Waterfront," "Easy Come, Easy Go," and "I Wanna Be Loved." He also enjoyed popularity as conductor of a dance band that was prominently featured on radio in the '30s.

Green went to Hollywood in 1942, working for MGM as a staff composer, arranger, and conductor for the next four years; he returned there as general music director in 1949, overseeing such musicals as *Summer Stock*, *Brigadoon*, and *High Society*. He often conducted at the Hollywood Bowl, and conducted and/or produced nine of the Academy Awards ceremonies.

Green was particularly proud of his original score for *Raintree County* and of his contributions (both original and adapting music of others) to *Oliver!* and 1969's Oscar-nominated *They Shoot Horses, Don't They?* (which used many of Green's old songs). His original scores also included such '60s dramas as *Twilight of Honor* (1963) and *Alvarez Kelly* (1966).

RAINTREE COUNTY

Preamble 2-PRCD 1781

Green's magnum opus was for MGM's three-hour Civil War melodrama starring Elizabeth Taylor as a spoiled Southern belle who woos and wins Montgomery Clift. He received a 1957 Oscar nomination for his folk-influenced score written for orchestra and choir. The memorable Green–Paul Francis Webster title song is just one of more than a dozen motifs that identify characters, locales, or emotional elements. The 1989 2-CD set preserves nearly 90 minutes of the original score.

PHOTO COURTESY OF GRP RECORDS

Grusin, Dave (1934–)

Born in Colorado, Grusin was a piano major who had planned a career in music education when he was offered a job as music director on Andy Williams's variety show in the early '60s. He began writing TV scores a few years later (including such memorable themes as *The Name of the Game*, *Baretta*, and *St. Elsewhere*) and soon became a sought-after film composer.

One of his first film assignments was the now-classic *The Graduate* (1967), which netted him a Grammy along with song composer Paul Simon ("Mrs. Robinson," etc.)—even though all of his tunes on the album were essentially lounge-style source music, not dramatic cues. He has won eight Grammys since, mostly for his arrangements on jazz albums.

His most consistent professional relationship has been with director Sydney Pollack, with whom he has done eight films, including the Robert Redford hits *Three Days of the Condor* (1975) and *The Electric Horseman* (1979), the Dustin Hoffman comedy *Tootsie* (1982), and the Tom Cruise legal thriller *The Firm* (1993).

Nominated eight times for Academy Awards, Grusin won for his Mexican-flavored music for Redford's *The Milagro Beanfield War* (1988); it also won a Grammy. Well known both as a jazz artist and longtime proprietor of his own record label, Grusin is as adept at jazz scores (such as *The Fabulous Baker Boys*, 1989) as orchestral ones (*Reds*, 1981; *Havana*, 1990).

CINEMAGIC
GRP GRD-9547

This 1987 "greatest movie hits" collection includes much of the best of Grusin, notably themes from his Oscar-nominated scores for *Heaven Can Wait* (1978), *The Champ* (1979), *On Golden Pond* (1981), and *Tootsie* (1982) as well as his evocative theme for *The Heart Is a Lonely Hunter* (1968), his baroque-style chase from *The Goonies* (1985), and themes from his more dramatic *Three Days of the Condor* (1975) and *The Little Drummer Girl* (1984). Grusin conducts the London Symphony Orchestra.

ON GOLDEN POND
MCA 6106 (LP)

Few scores in recent years have captured the emotional center of their films as sensitively or memorably as Grusin's thoughtful, solo-piano-dominated music for *On Golden Pond*, which won 1981 Oscars for Katharine Hepburn and Henry Fonda

and should have for Grusin (who was nominated but lost to Vangelis, for *Chariots of Fire*). Grusin, who has often been inspired throughout 30 years of writing movie scores, was never more so than here. His upbeat "New Hampshire Hornpipe" receives an extended treatment on the LP, which also interpolates dialogue from Ernest Thompson's script. The album spent 11 weeks on the *Billboard* chart.

TOOTSIE
Warner Bros. 23781-2

Grusin's score for the funny and touching 1982 tour de force for Dustin Hoffman (as a desperate actor who dresses up as a woman and becomes a soap-opera star) is alternately jazzy and romantic. It also generated one of the '80s' best movie songs in "It Might Be You" (an Oscar nominee for Grusin and lyricists Alan and Marilyn Bergman). Grusin himself plays keyboards; vocals are by Stephen Bishop, who enjoyed a top-25 hit with the tune.

MIGRATION
GRP GRD-9592

This 1989 album on Grusin's jazz label contains a suite from his Oscar-winning music for Robert Redford's film *The Milagro Beanfield War* (1988). Just 11 minutes long, it suggests the Southwestern flavor; the light, just-this-side-of-fantasy nature of the tale; and the essentially Mexican colors of the music that characters were playing and hearing. No soundtrack was released, so Grusin's re-recording is the only available version. It won a 1989 Grammy for Grusin's arrangement.

THE FABULOUS BAKER BOYS
GRP GRD-2002

Grusin's score for this underrated movie about two lounge-piano–playing brothers (Jeff and Beau Bridges) and their girl singer (Michelle Pfeiffer) received a 1989 Oscar nomination. A highly enjoyable collection of songs (including Pfeiffer's renditions of "Makin' Whoopee" and "My Funny Valentine") and Grusin's spot-on, jazzy underscore, this album won a 1989 Grammy as the year's outstanding film score.

HAVANA
GRP GRD-2003

Few Latin scores for American movies could claim to be as authentic-sounding as Grusin's for Sydney Pollack's 1990 historical epic *Havana,* starring Robert Redford and Lena Olin. The story concerns a gambler caught up in the Cuban Revolution, and Grusin's contribution caught both the dramatic thrust of the tale and the Latin flavor of the music of the period (aided by the trumpet of Arturo Sandoval and vocalist Dori Caymmi). Grusin was rewarded with Oscar and Golden Globe nominations for the score, and with three 1991 Grammy nominations for the album (for composition, performance and engineering).

THE FIRM
MCA/GRP MGD-2007

Sydney Pollack had an offbeat idea for scoring his 1993 film of John Grisham's thriller *The Firm* starring Tom Cruise: solo piano, all written and performed by the composer. It's only been tried a few times (notably by David Shire in *The Conversation*) and it's a tough one to pull off (the same musical sound for over two hours). But Grusin rose to the challenge, and received an Oscar nomination for his creative approach: a stomp worthy of the Memphis setting, a memorable love theme, plenty of blues, and a now-much-imitated chase sequence for "prepared" piano. Interspersed throughout are songs by Jimmy Buffett, Lyle Lovett, Nanci Griffith, and others.

PHOTO COURTESY OF WBGH

Hamlisch, Marvin (1944–)

The winner of three Academy Awards—two for *The Way We Were* and one for *The Sting*—Marvin Hamlisch was hardly an overnight success. He just happened to become a household name after the April 2, 1974, Oscarcast. (Addressing the audience after accepting his third statuette that evening, he quipped, "I think we can talk as friends.")

Hamlisch, a former rehearsal pianist on Broadway, had scored several films before those victories, including Woody Allen's first two movies as a director (*Take the Money and Run*, 1969, and *Bananas*, 1971). He became much sought after, and not just for movie music: Hamlisch's song score for Broadway's *A Chorus Line* won the 1975 Tony and a Pulitzer Prize; a few years later he wrote the tunes for *They're Playing Our Song* (based loosely on his real-life relationship with lyricist Carole Bayer Sager).

Hamlisch and Sager wrote hilarious songs for *Starting Over* (1979). Hamlisch wrote the music for a James Bond film, *The Spy Who Loved Me* (1977), receiving Oscar nominations for Best Song ("Nobody Does It Better" with Sager) and Best Score; adapted Pachelbel for Robert Redford's

Oscar-winning *Ordinary People* (1980); and scored a searing drama based on William Styron's *Sophie's Choice* (1982), winning another Oscar nomination.

He has received six other Best Song nominations, including tunes from *Kotch* (1971), *Ice Castles* (1978), *Same Time, Next Year* (1979), the movie version of *A Chorus Line* (1985), *Shirley Valentine* (1989), and the Barbra Streisand film *The Mirror Has Two Faces* (1996). He also has two Emmys for his work on Streisand's highly rated 1995 "The Concert" TV special.

THE WAY WE WERE

Columbia CK 57381

Hamlisch's Oscar wins for 1973's Best Song and Best Original Score were popular ones in Hollywood; the melody, combined with its bittersweet Alan and Marilyn Bergman lyrics, became an instant standard, going to number 1 as a single (with the soundtrack reaching number 20 in early 1974). The score, with its nostalgic flavor, period tunes, and lush sound, perfectly suited the Barbra Streisand–Robert Redford love story directed by Sydney Pollack. It later won 1974 Grammys as Song of the Year and Best Original Score for a film or TV special (and another Grammy to Hamlisch as Best New Artist).

THE STING

MCA MCAD-11836

Somewhat more controversial was Hamlisch's Oscar win for Best Adaptation Score for 1973's Best Picture winner, the Paul Newman–Robert Redford con-artist caper. Following the instructions of director George Roy Hill, Hamlisch adapted Scott Joplin's turn-of-the-century ragtime into a fun score (even though the period was the mid-1930s and thus a bit off). Some music insiders complained that Hamlisch hadn't given

enought credit to arranger Gunther Schuller (who was credited on the album). Nonetheless, the score was full of high-spirited fun, the album spent five weeks at number 1, and Hamlisch's single of Joplin's "The Entertainer" won a Grammy for Pop Instrumental Performance.

THE SPY WHO LOVED ME

EMI CDP-7-96211-2

Hamlisch's music for the third Roger Moore 007 movie received Best Song and Best Score Oscar nominations for 1977. One of the better Moore entries, this one sports a terrific song ("Nobody Does It Better," with lyrics by Carole Bayer Sager and a Carly Simon vocal) that went to number 2 on the *Billboard* charts. The music for the pre-title sequence—a stunning ski jump off a mountain—was an updated, high-energy arrangement of the "James Bond Theme," and there's a good deal of pseudo-Middle Eastern music for the locale.

SOPHIE'S CHOICE

Laserlight 21 099

Hamlisch's finest hour as a film composer came with this moving Alan J. Pakula film about a Polish woman's nightmarish existence after suffering in the concentration camp at Auschwitz; Meryl Streep won a 1982 Oscar for her performance. Hamlisch received a Best Score nomination for his haunting and unusually restrained music, which lent both atmosphere and support to an extremely difficult subject.

Hancock, Herbie (1940–)

Chicago-born keyboardist-composer Herbie Hancock has dabbled in movies off and on since the mid-1960s, when Michelangelo Antonioni asked him to score the now-classic *Blowup* (1966) with David Hemmings as a photographer in mod, swinging London.

Hancock, a sideman for Miles Davis before becoming one of the leading exponents of jazz-rock in the '70s (with such groundbreaking albums as *Headhunters*), has always been choosy about his film assignments. He had a film hit (if not a record hit) with his jazzy score for the controversial Charles Bronson film *Death Wish* (1974) and later composed the highly acclaimed *A Soldier's Story* (1984).

He won a Best Original Score Oscar for 1986's *Round Midnight*, which was widely viewed more as an award for his supervision of all the live-on-set jazz recordings than for his sparse original music. His few films since then have included the L.A.-gang movie *Colors* (1988) and the Eddie Murphy–Richard Pryor period nightclub drama *Harlem Nights* (1989).

DEATH WISH

One Way A 26659

Michael Winner's 1974 film starred Charles Bronson as an architect who turns vigilante after his wife and daughter are raped (one is left dead, the other comatose). Hugely controversial at the time—some critics felt that it glorified and incited further violence—it was nonetheless effective film-making. Hancock's score ("composed, conducted and performed" by the keyboard player) is jazz-based but contains several dramatic and attractively reflective cues; the rape sequence is disturbingly percussive and savagely dissonant.

ROUND MIDNIGHT

Columbia CK 40464

Hancock won an Academy Award for his scoring of Bernard Tavernier's 1986 exploration of the jazz scene in 1950s Paris. What was unique about *Round Midnight* was Tavernier's insistence that all

of the music be recorded live on the set. The musicians included Hancock, Wayne Shorter, Tony Williams, Ron Carter, Bobby Hutcherson, Chet Baker, and, of course, saxophonist Dexter Gordon, who played bebop jazzman Dale Turner. The album, produced by Hancock, has several classics including the title tune, "Body and Soul," and "How Long Has This Been Going On?" but also includes three of Hancock's originals.

Hayes, Isaac (1942–)

"Hot buttered soul" singer-songwriter Isaac Hayes may have seemed an unlikely Oscar winner to the old-guard music community of Hollywood. But by 1972, with an Oscar, two Grammys, and a number-1 album to his credit, Hayes was one of the most bankable composers in the business. (In fact, ABC wasted no time in signing him to compose the theme for one of its fall TV shows.)

Director Gordon Parks made a shrewd call in signing Hayes to score his 1971 action flick *Shaft* for MGM (which was a colossal hit with black and white audiences alike). The album helped to sell the movie and vice versa, and today the score is better remembered than the film that inspired it. (The singer-songwriter's appearance on the 1972 Oscar show is still talked about, with Hayes arriving on stage dressed entirely in gold chains.)

The film also launched an acting career for Hayes, who not only scored but starred in *Three Tough Guys* (1974) and *Truck Turner* (1974) and later made memorable appearances in films like *Escape From New York* (1981) and *I'm Gonna Git You Sucka* (1988). He also had a recurring role with James Garner on *The Rockford Files*.

SHAFT

Stax SCD-88002-2

SHAFT-Music from the Soundtrack
Composed and Performed by **ISAAC HAYES**

MGM's
SHAFT

© 1971, COURTESY OF FANTASY RECORDS

set; both are collected on this 2-CD set. Highlights are "Hung Up on My Baby" from the first and the nine-minute "Pursuit of the Pimpmobile" from the second.

PHOTO COURTESY OF STEVEN C. SMITH

Herrmann, Bernard (1911–1975)

The brilliant but volatile Bernard Herrmann is probably best known for his 11-year collaboration with director Alfred Hitchcock, which produced several suspense classics including *Vertigo* and *Psycho*. As a musical dramatist, he had few peers, often creating fresh orchestral combinations geared specifically to the nature of the film at hand.

Herrmann came to Hollywood at the request of Orson Welles, for whom he had scored a vast number of CBS radio programs in New York during the 1930s (including the infamous "War of the Worlds" broadcast in 1938). His first assignment was 1941's *Citizen Kane*, which many critics still consider the finest American film ever made; he then made *The Magnificent Ambersons* with Welles and won a 1941 Oscar for *All That Money Can Buy* (*The Devil and Daniel Webster*).

As the '40s and '50s wore on, Herrmann

First-time movie scorer Hayes won a Best Song Oscar and was nominated for Best Original Dramatic Score for his 1971 music for Richard Roundtree as a tough Harlem detective. The album went to number 1 (as did the single), winning Grammys as Best Original Score and Best Instrumental Arrangement. Most of the album (originally a two-LP set) consists of Hayes's bouncy, R&B-inflected source music, but tunes like the title theme, "Ellie's Love Theme," "Cafe Regio's," and "Soulsville" are now Hayes classics. (Hayes contributed a song, "Type Thang," to the sequel, 1972's *Shaft's Big Score!*, which featured a Hayes-style score by writer-director-composer Gordon Parks.)

TRUCK TURNER / TOUGH GUYS
Stax 2SCD-88014-2

After *Shaft*, Hayes combined music with an acting career. In *Three Tough Guys* (1974) he played an ex-cop who teamed up with a priest; in *Truck Turner* (also 1974) he was a bounty hunter. Both were routine blaxploitation films that are thoroughly unmemorable save for Hayes's music. *Tough Guys* was a single LP, *Truck Turner* a 2-LP became known as a specialist in the offbeat, particularly in films made at 20th Century–Fox: a dark piano concerto for *Hangover Square*, weird instrumental combinations for films like *The Day the Earth Stood Still* and *White Witch Doctor*. The '50s and '60s saw a period of colorful scores for fantasy films featuring the creations of Ray Harryhausen: *7th Voyage of Sinbad*, *Three Worlds of Gulliver*, and others.

Herrmann's high artistic standards, his increasingly ill-tempered manner, and his insistence on wide musical latitude antagonized many directors and producers. After a falling out with Hitchcock on *Torn Curtain*, he moved to London, where he spent time recording his concert music, notably an opera based on *Wuthering Heights*. Only near the end of his life did he return to favor in Hollywood, particularly among a new generation of filmmakers such as Brian DePalma and Martin Scorsese; he died just hours after completing the final recording session for Scorsese's *Taxi Driver*.

CITIZEN KANE: THE CLASSIC FILM SCORES OF BERNARD HERRMANN
RCA 0707-2-RG

One of the indispensable releases in the RCA Classic Film Scores series, this 1974 recording contains music from five movies released during Herrmann's first 12 years in Hollywood. Included are nearly 14 minutes of *Citizen Kane* (1941), the first definitive recording of that seminal score; the piano concerto from *Hangover Square* (1945); the rousing "Death Hunt" sequence from *On Dangerous Ground* (1952); and colorful suites from the ocean adventure *Beneath the 12 Mile Reef* (1953) and the African tale *White Witch Doctor* (1953). Charles Gerhardt conducts London's National Philharmonic Orchestra; Kiri Te Kanawa

COURTESY OF UNIVERSAL MUSIC GROUP

sings the aria from *Citizen Kane*; Joaquin Achucarro is pianist in the concerto.

MUSIC FROM THE GREAT HITCHCOCK MOVIE THRILLERS
London 443 895-2

When London Phase 4 issued this on LP in 1969, it was the beginning of a renaissance for Herrmann and the first time that most of these classic scores had been made available. The recording is superb and the suites are definitive: Herrmann's 14-minute "narrative for orchestra" from his all-strings *Psycho* (1960), an expanded overture from *North by Northwest* (1959), 10-minute suites from *Vertigo* (1958) and *Marnie* (1964), and a whimsical, eight-minute "Portrait of Hitch" adapted from *The Trouble with Harry* (1955). Herrmann conducts the London Philharmonic.

BERNARD HERRMANN: GREAT FILM CLASSICS
London 448 948-2

This was the second of the London Phase 4 recordings to feature classic Herrmann from classic films. It contains four of the five movements of "Welles

Raises Kane," a suite drawn from the gay '90s episodes within Welles's *Citizen Kane* (1941) and *The Magnificent Ambersons* (1942); a suite from his dark-hued score for *Jane Eyre* (1944); music from *The Snows of Kilimanjaro* (1952); and excerpts from his Oscar-winning score for *The Devil and Daniel Webster* (1941). Augmenting these are suites from the Ray Harryhausen fantasy films *Mysterious Island* (1961) and *Jason and the Argonauts* (1963). Herrmann conducts the London Philharmonic.

BERNARD HERRMANN: GREAT FILM MUSIC
London 443 899-2

Herrmann recorded two other albums for London Phase 4 in the early 1970s: "The Fantasy Film World of Bernard Herrmann" and "The Mysterious Film World of Bernard Herrmann," which extracted generous suites from seven of his best scores for fantasy and sci-fi movies of the '50s and '60s. Five are reproduced here, with Herrmann conducting the National Philharmonic Orchestra in brilliant sound: music from *The Day the Earth Stood Still* (1951), *The 7th Voyage of Sinbad* (1958), *Journey to the Center of the Earth* (1959), *The Three Worlds of Gulliver* (1960), and *Fahrenheit 451* (1966).

THE GHOST AND MRS. MUIR
Varèse Sarabande VSD-5850

Herrmann considered his music for this 1947 romantic fantasy his finest effort for movies. Certainly it's his most romantic, offering a dreamlike backdrop for the story of a sea captain's ghost (Rex Harrison) who falls in love with the living widow (Gene Tierney) now occupying his seaside cottage in turn-of-the-century England. Herrmann's original soundtrack recording was restored for release in 1997.

THE DAY THE EARTH STOOD STILL
Fox Records 11010-2

Herrmann's landmark score for the science-fiction classic—which included two theremins, electronic violin, electronic bass, and electronic guitar, an unheard-of combination for 1951—was restored for this 1993 release. Eerie without being gimmicky, it anticipated the spate of electronic-music scores that would dominate sci-fi movies later in the '50s and '60s. Michael Rennie and Patricia Neal starred in the film, about an emissary from space who arrives to warn Earth its warlike ways are a threat to other planets.

THE KENTUCKIAN
Preamble PRCD 1777

A 19-minute suite from Herrmann's lively, folk-influenced score for the 1955 Burt Lancaster frontier tale is the highlight of this 1977 re-recording by composer and musicologist Fred Steiner with the National Philharmonic Orchestra and the Ambrosian Singers. Rounding out this Americana-themed CD: brief suites from Alfred Newman's *Down to the Sea in Ships* (1949), Hugo Friedhofer's *In Love and War* (1958), and Franz Waxman's *Sunrise at Campobello* (1960).

VERTIGO
Varèse Sarabande VSD-5600
Varèse Sarabande VSD-5759

Herrmann's score for Alfred Hitchcock's 1958 drama about a detective (James Stewart) who falls for a client's mysterious wife (Kim Novak) and the complications that ensue, is another film-music masterpiece. Within a year, the same label issued two different versions of the score. First, in 1995 (no. 5600), came a re-recording by Joel McNeely and the Royal Scottish National Orchestra, which was widely acclaimed by reviewers. The following year, Varèse restored nearly all of the original soundtrack (no. 5759), recorded in London and Vienna by conductor Muir Mathieson.

NORTH BY NORTHWEST
Rhino R2 72101

Herrmann's thrilling, fandango-based score for Hitchcock's 1959 romp starring Cary Grant as a salesman mistaken for an international spy and Eva Marie Saint as his companion in flight, was restored for this 1995 release (at 65 minutes, its most complete yet, containing all the music and several outtakes). This is the original soundtrack, recorded at MGM with the composer conducting.

JOURNEY TO THE CENTER OF THE EARTH
Varèse Sarabande VSD-5849

The 1959 favorite of fantasy-film buffs, rescued from the 20th Century–Fox vaults, contains some of the strangest sounds ever to emerge from the Fox scoring stage. James Mason and Pat Boone starred in this Jules Verne descent into the bowels of the planet. Herrmann's orchestration choices included woodwinds and brass—often playing in their lowest registers—plus a large percussion section, several harps, no fewer than five organs, and the medieval serpent.

PSYCHO
Unicorn-Kanchana UKCD 2021
Varèse Sarabande VSD-5765

Herrmann's own re-recording of the complete score, made in 1975 with London's National Philharmonic Orchestra (on Unicorn), offers a surprising contrast with the 1996 re-recording by Joel McNeely with the Royal Scottish National Orchestra. The Unicorn album was widely criticized as lethargic, Herrmann's own tempi too slow; McNeely's are closer to those of the 1960 film. Herrmann's creative and original

music—his all-strings ensemble being a "black-and-white sound" for Hitchcock's black-and-white horror film—may be the most widely imitated in the history of film music.

TAXI DRIVER
Arista 07822-19005-2

Arista's 1976 LP outraged Herrmann purists because much of the album consisted of pop re-arrangements of the score to Martin Scorsese's disturbing psychodrama with Robert DeNiro and Jodie Foster. The label atoned in 1998 with Herrmann's original 39-minute score (along with the jazz interpretations, grouped together at the end of the album), elaborately documented (down to the numbers of each "take") with new notes by Scorsese.

Hirschfelder, David (1959–)

Australian composer David Hirschfelder burst onto the international scoring scene with his music for *Shine* (1996), based on the true story of pianist David Helfgott. Hirschfelder's score combined the piano music of Helfgott's repertoire with original music that complemented the traditional classical selections and won an Oscar nomination in the process.

In fact, Hirschfelder has been a fixture on the Australian music scene for many years. Formerly a performer in the jazz group Pyramid and musical director for John Farnham, he first won accolades as a television composer for the internationally acclaimed AIDS documentary *Suzi's Story* (1987). By the '90s, he was scoring films, notably Baz Luhrmann's popular musical *Strictly Ballroom* (1992), which won a British Film and Television Academy Award for its score.

Hirschfelder's *Shine* score also received Golden Globe and BAFTA nominations. He went on to score Gwyneth Paltrow's romantic comedy *Sliding Doors* (1998) and the widely acclaimed historical drama *Elizabeth*, which received a 1998 Oscar nomination and BAFTA's Anthony Asquith Award for his effective period music combined with appropriate classical excerpts.

ELIZABETH
London 289 460 796-2

Hirschfelder's rich choral-and-orchestral score for Shekhar Kapur's 1998 chronicle of the rise of Queen Elizabeth I (played so brilliantly by Cate Blanchett) was deemed one of the year's best by many critics. Nominated for the American Oscar, it won the British Academy's Anthony Asquith Award. He employs clever early-Renaissance pastiche, a more contemporary symphonic sound for the film's many dark moments, and bits of William Byrd, the Mozart Requiem, and Elgar's "Enigma Variations" throughout.

Holdridge, Lee (1944–)

One of the most underrated of contemporary film composers, Haitian-born, Costa Rica–raised Lee Holdridge has spent much of the past two decades writing music for television—including some of the best music the medium has ever had. His theme for *Moonlighting* was a hit for Al Jarreau; his music for the cult favorite *Beauty and the Beast* won two Emmys and inspired a best-selling 1989 album of music and poetry narrated by star Ron Perlman.

Holdridge began his Hollywood career working with Neil Diamond on arrangements and orchestral scoring for the film and album of *Jonathan Livingston Seagull* (1973). He has scored a number of comedic hits, including *Mr. Mom* (1983), *Splash* (1984), and *Micki & Maude* (1984), as well as more dramatic fare like the Gregory Peck–Jane Fonda film *Old Gringo* (1989).

Sometimes, however, the strangest work becomes unexpectedly popular: Holdridge scored *The Beastmaster* (1982), a low-budget sword-and-sorcery affair with Marc Singer that has become one of the most popular, and frequently repeated, films on cable.

The composer's concert music has been widely performed, including his "Jefferson Tribute," his Violin Concerto No. 2, and his orchestral suite "Scenes of Summer," to which Tara Lipinski skated to a gold medal in the 1998 Winter Olympics.

THE FILM MUSIC OF LEE HOLDRIDGE
Citadel STC 77103

This 1985 collection of Holdridge's film and TV scores would be worth having for one track alone: his exquisitely lyrical theme for Ron Howard's amusing romantic comedy *Splash* (1984) with a pre-Oscar Tom Hanks and Daryl Hannah as a mermaid. A suite from his tremendously popular music for *The Beastmaster* (1982) leads off the album, which also has music from *Jonathan Livingston Seagull* (1973) and several of Holdridge's television projects including the swashbuckling *Wizards and Warriors*. Charles Gerhardt conducts the London Symphony Orchestra.

Honegger, Arthur (1892–1955)

French composer Arthur Honegger (some sources call him Swiss, because he maintained Swiss citizenship even though he was born in France and remained there most of his life) was briefly a member of Les Six during the 1920s. Even though he was an active composer of music for the concert hall, with five symphonies, operas, and chamber music to his credit, he often returned to films as a source of both inspiration and income.

Honegger wrote an estimated 40 film scores, mostly for French films that are unknown in America. A handful, however, are famous: the score for Abel Gance's 1927 epic *Napoleon,* which gained fame when restored in 1981 and presented by Francis Ford Coppola; the original 1936 version of *Mayerling*; and MGM's 1938 *Pygmalion* with Leslie Howard and Wendy Hiller.

ARTHUR HONEGGER: FILM MUSIC
Marco Polo 8.223134
This first in a series of four collections of Honegger film music contains an eight-movement suite from the original score of Abel Gance's silent epic *Napoleon* and excerpts from three other French films (including a 1934 version of *Les Misérables*). *Napoleon* is interesting because the 1979 restoration is better known for having two newly composed scores (one in London by Carl Davis; the other in America by Carmine Coppola). The 21 minutes of Honegger's score here recorded offers a tantalizing hint of what the entire four-hour score might have been like. Adriano conducts the Czecho-Slovak Radio Symphony Orchestra in this 1987 re-recording.

ARTHUR HONEGGER: MAYERLING
Marco Polo 8.223467
This collection contains suites from three French films of the '30s, one of which became internationally famous: Anatole Litvak's 1936 *Mayerling,* about the ill-fated 19th-century romance between Austria's Archduke Rudolph (Charles Boyer) and his mistress, the young baroness Marie Vetsera (Danielle Darrieux). Honegger's score—as presented here in an 11-minute suite—suggests the warmth and the tragedy that surrounded their true story. Adriano conducts the Slovak Radio Symphony Orchestra in this 1993 re-recording.

FROM THE AUTHOR'S COLLECTION

Horner, James (1953–)
Talented, prolific, and sometimes controversial, James Horner made film-music history in 1998 with the amazing success of his score for James Cameron's blockbuster film *Titanic,* which sold more than 25 million albums worldwide.

Critics were divided about the score: Some liked the Irish-flavored motifs and Enya-like vocalise over synthesizers, while others felt the approach was anachronistic. In any case, it was a tremendous popular hit, driven in part by Horner's commercially shrewd notion to ask (without Cameron's advance knowledge) Celine Dion to "demo" a song based on his love theme. "My Heart Will Go On," with a lyric by Will Jennings, won the 1997 Best Song Oscar, and Horner's music won the Oscar for Original Dramatic Score. The tune also won Record of the Year, Song of the Year, and Best Movie Song honors at the 1998 Grammys.

The son of famed production designer Harry Horner, the composer studied at London's Royal Academy of Music, USC, and UCLA and had planned a concert-hall career until the movies called. An apprenticeship at Roger Corman's low-budget film factory led to A-level assignments and popular success in the '80s on such films as *Star Trek II: The Wrath of Khan* and *48 HRS.* (both 1982), *Gorky Park* (1983), and *Cocoon* (1985), plus Oscar nominations for *Aliens* (1986) and *Field of Dreams* (1989) and a Grammy for *Glory* (1989). The '90s saw ongoing commercial success with such films as *Patriot Games* (1992), *Legends of the Fall* (1994), dual Oscar nominations for 1995's *Apollo 13* and *Braveheart*, and the worldwide phenomenon of *Titanic* (1997).

Like many composers, Horner has his fans and his detractors, both in the Hollywood music community and in the relatively small fandom devoted to film music. Occasional accusations (notably voiced in a 1998, post-*Titanic New Yorker* article) that he borrows from classical works is a charge that, Horner partisans point out, can apply to many contemporary Hollywood composers.

STAR TREK II: THE WRATH OF KHAN
STAR TREK III: THE SEARCH FOR SPOCK
GNP Crescendo GNPD 8022, 8023
Horner's dynamic scores for the second (1982) and third (1984) movies in the *Star Trek* movie franchise propelled him into the major leagues of film composers. They are also particular favorites among the *Trek* crowd: the sweeping nautical-adventure qualities and the moving orchestral setting of Alexander Courage's TV theme for the death of Spock in *II* are highlights. *III* contains a techno version of the theme "produced by James Horner and Group 87" that appeared as a 12-inch single accompanying the original LP.

KRULL
Southern Cross SCSE CD-4
This big-budget 1983 fantasy with Ken Marshall and Lysette Anthony inspired one of Horner's

most popular early works, particularly for fans of melodic and richly orchestrated symphonic music. The film, with its muddled sword-and-sorcery elements, was a failure, but Horner's swashbuckling, partially choral score is among his most compelling and original work.

AN AMERICAN TAIL
MCA MCAD-39096
Horner's magic touch with animation first became apparent in this Steven Spielberg–produced 1986 film about a little Russian mouse who becomes separated from his family as they emigrate to America in the late 19th century. Charming, sometimes Russian-flavored, it also features several songs (on which Horner collaborated with veterans Barry Mann and Cynthia Weil). It was an Oscar nominee and double Grammy winner for the now-standard "Somewhere Out There" (sung by Linda Ronstadt and James Ingram).

ALIENS
Varèse Sarabande VCD 47263
This 1986 sequel to the frightening science fiction-horror tale starring Sigourney Weaver brought Horner his first Oscar nomination as well as a Grammy nod. While the film also contains excerpts from Khachaturian's "Gayane" ballet suite and Jerry Goldsmith's original *Alien* score, the military motifs and furious action material are entirely Horner's own and have proven popular—to the point of endless recycling by imitators—over the years.

FIELD OF DREAMS
Novus 3060-2-N
Horner received a 1989 Oscar nomination for this gentle, dreamy score that was largely performed by the composer himself on synthesizers. His delicate, mystical touch was a key element in

sustaining credibility in the Kevin Costner film about mysterious voices telling a farmer to build a baseball diamond in the middle of nowhere. Small-ensemble rock and big-band elements (the latter, orchestrated by veteran Billy May) add spice to the work, which culminates in a memorable orchestral treatment.

GLORY

Virgin 91329-2

An original-score Grammy winner, Horner's score for Edward Zwick's 1989 film about the first black soldiers in the Civil War was, to the surprise of many, ignored by the Oscars (despite the film's popularity and its three Oscar wins). Observers felt at the time that its passing resemblance to elements of Prokofiev's *Ivan the Terrible* and Orff's *Carmina Burana* may have cost it a nomination. Horner effectively uses the Boys Choir of Harlem throughout a score that suggests the nobility of the men and the futility of their cause.

LEGENDS OF THE FALL

Epic EK 66462

Horner's second collaboration with director Ed Zwick (1994) is an excursion into musical Americana, perhaps inspired more by John Toll's Oscar-winning cinematography than by the acting by top-billed Brad Pitt that made the movie a hit with smitten Pitt fans. "Brooding and lush, redolent of both love and loss," is how Zwick describes it in his thoughtful notes. Horner conducts the London Symphony Orchestra with fiddle solos by Jay Ungar (from TV's *The Civil War*).

BRAVEHEART

London 448 295-2

Mel Gibson's Oscar-winning epic of 14th-century Scotland was accompanied by one of Horner's finest scores—itself an Oscar nominee for its long melodic lines, the effective use of exotic instruments (kena, uilleann pipes, bodhran drums, whistles), hints of Scottish flavor, and one of the composer's most heartbreaking love themes. Horner conducts the London Symphony Orchestra; the choristers of Westminster Abbey are also featured.

APOLLO 13

MCA MCAD-11241

Horner's Oscar-nominated score for Ron Howard's 1995 chronicle of the ill-fated and nearly tragic moon flight is alternately heroic and dramatic. Quiet choral passages accompany launch and re-entry sequences, and pop's Annie Lennox lends her distinctive vocalise to the end-credits music. Period songs by artists including Jefferson Airplane, The Who, and Jimi Hendrix are interspersed, along with dialogue, with the Horner score. Tom Hanks, Bill Paxton, and Kevin Bacon, as the crew of Apollo 13, are among the voices heard.

TITANIC

Sony Classical SK 63213

BACK TO TITANIC

Sony Classical SK 60691

The biggest-selling orchestral score album of all time, the 73-minute original soundtrack of the Best Picture Oscar-winning 1997 film contains much of the key melodic material that moviegoers loved: the Irish-flavored material (which some observers felt signified *Titanic*'s Dublin origins, others the many steerage passengers who died), the wordless vocals by Norwegian artist Sissel, the synthesizer textures (which some felt were anachronistic for a film set in 1912), and, of course, the love theme, "My Heart Will Go On," sung by Celine Dion. Regardless of one's opinions about the film or the score, it became a worldwide hit because it was tuneful, uplifting, and memorable. The following year Sony Classical released a sequel, *Back to Titanic*, which included a 19-minute suite based on the various themes from the score; additional score excerpts, some of the period source music, and dialogue from the soundtrack.

Howard, James Newton (1951–)

James Newton Howard is part of the new generation of film-music specialists who emerged from the pop world. His rich orchestral scores—often liberally spiced with electronic sounds—have made him one of a handful of A-list composers in Hollywood.

A five-time Oscar nominee (for original score for 1991's *The Prince of Tides*, 1993's *The Fugitive*, and 1997's *My Best Friend's Wedding*; original song for 1994's *Junior* and 1996's *One Fine Day*), Howard has written diverse and impressive music for such other films as the political comedy *Dave* (1993), the epic western *Wyatt Earp* (1994), the critically acclaimed *Glengarry Glen Ross* (1992), the period drama *Restoration* (1996), the wildly popular *Pretty Woman* (1990), and the thriller *The Sixth Sense* (1999). He also created the memorable theme for television's top-rated *ER*, which earned him an Emmy nomination.

Initially trained as a classical pianist, Howard became a session musician in the 1970s for pop and rock artists ranging from Elton John to Carly Simon. He went on to become a sought-after arranger, orchestrator, and record producer, working with such artists as Bob Seger, Randy Newman, Rickie Lee Jones, and Rod Stewart. In 1985, he turned his talents to film and quickly formed lasting relationships with such directors as Lawrence Kasdan, Joel Schumacher, and Michael Hoffman, to name a few.

THE PRINCE OF TIDES
Columbia CK 48627

Howard's first Academy Award nomination came for Barbra Streisand's 1991 movie of Pat Conroy's novel about a South Carolina football coach (Nick Nolte) and the New York psychiatrist (Streisand) who falls for him. Howard's score is just right: a lovely theme, a nuanced score, heavy on the strings, with a Streisand vocal (music by Howard, lyrics by Alan and Marilyn Bergman) at the end.

GLENGARRY GLEN ROSS
Elektra 9 61384-2

How to score a dialogue-heavy David Mamet play about real estate salesmen where the focus is on stellar performances by such greats as Al Pacino, Jack Lemmon, Alec Baldwin, Ed Harris, Alan Arkin, Kevin Spacey, and Jonathan Pryce? Howard's answer was edgy original jazz played by a top L.A. sextet: Wayne Shorter on sax, Mike Lang on piano, John Patitucci on bass, Jeff Porcaro on drums, Lenny Castro on percussion, and Larry Bunker on vibes. Several newly recorded jazz standards round out the 1992 album.

THE FUGITIVE

Elektra 9 61592-2

While TV buffs may have missed Pete Rugolo's original theme for the '60s series, few could deny that Howard provided this 1993 big-screen version (starring Harrison Ford in the David Janssen role) with a relentless, percussive, and driving score that worked superbly (and won an Oscar nomination). Wayne Shorter's contributions on soprano sax lent a distinctive and jazzy touch even in the suspenseful sequences.

WYATT EARP

Warner Bros. 9 45660-2

If Lawrence Kasdan's three-hour Kevin Costner movie had been a commercial success, Howard's music certainly would have been a 1994 Oscar nominee; it might even have won. His richly orchestrated, sweeping Americana not only suited the subject, it ranks with some of the finest western scores ever written for film: big and broad, with memorable themes that evoke the Old West but also provide the necessary emotional beats that every good score must manage (and that resonate without the picture).

WATERWORLD

MCA MCACD-11282

Howard had just six weeks to write two hours of music for Kevin Costner's futuristic 1995 action-adventure, played by a 100-piece orchestra plus the Los Angeles Master Chorale—plus synthesizers, plus ethnic instruments, plus wordless vocals, plus an endless variety of percussion. ("Anything that made noise was in the score," Howard later said.) For all the bad press this $100-million movie got for its story, acting, and direction, no one could criticize its rousing and brassy score.

SNOW FALLING ON CEDARS

Decca 289 466 818-2

Beautifully photographed and richly scored, this 1999 film about murder and racial prejudice in the post-war Northwest starred Ethan Hawke and Max von Sydow. Howard, in one of his most ambitious and successful efforts, combined traditional orchestra, choir, and ethnic Asian instruments (including shakuhachi) to evoke both the place and the atmosphere. The Los Angeles Master Chorale is featured, as is solo cellist Ron Leonard.

Ibert, Jacques (1890–1962)

The well-known French composer was always attracted to the use of music in dramatic and comedic contexts. He wrote six operas, seven ballets, a dramatic cantata, and music for theater and radio. Prior to his fame as a composer, however, he played the piano for silent films and wrote popular songs under a pseudonym.

Ibert worked on more than two dozen films beginning with the French silent *The Italian Straw Hat* in 1927. Most of his film writing was done in the 1930s, including a series of chansons for the primary characters of *Don Quixote* (1935) and a dramatic score for a retelling of the Christ tale in *Golgotha* (1933).

Ibert's best-known dramatic score is probably the music for the Republic version of *Macbeth* directed by Orson Welles (1948), although his delightful "Circus" ballet, composed for Gene Kelly in MGM's *Invitation to the Dance* (1956), was probably heard by far more moviegoers.

JACQUES IBERT: FILM MUSIC

Marco Polo 8.223287

Half an hour of Ibert's music for Orson Welles's 1948 adaptation of Shakespeare's *Macbeth* is preserved in this 1989 re-recording. Colorful and dramatic, it shifts in mood from buoyant martial music to eerie moments for the witches (featuring a choir moaning) and even out-of-tune bagpipes. Also on the disc: suites from the French films *Don Quixote* (1933) and *Golgotha* (1935). Adriano conducts the Slovak Radio Symphony Orchestra of Bratislava.

Isham, Mark (1951–)

New York–born Mark Isham has carved out a niche for himself in film music. A jazz trumpeter and Grammy-winning creator of New Age music, he has contributed unique sounds to more than five dozen movies since starting with Disney's *Never Cry Wolf* in 1983.

Isham seems most comfortable in the small-combo arena: several of his best scores, such as those for director Alan Rudolph (*Trouble in Mind*, *The Moderns*, *Afterglow*), are for small jazz ensembles. But the Americana folk colors of such films as *A River Runs Through It* and *Of Mice and Men* (both 1992) also appeal to him.

A former trumpet player in California's Oakland and San Francisco Symphony Orchestras, Isham went on to play in jazz and rock bands and can be heard on albums by everyone from Bruce Springsteen to Willie Nelson. As adept at synthesizers as he is with a horn, Isham won a 1990 Grammy for Best New Age Performance for his eponymous album.

He has worked on several prestige projects over the years, including *Reversal of Fortune* (1990), Jodie Foster's *Little Man Tate* (1991) and *Nell* (1994), and Redford's *Quiz Show* (1994). He won the Los Angeles Film Critics' music award for *The Moderns* (1988) and won an Emmy for his Irish-tinged theme for the short-lived *EZ Streets* (1996).

THE MODERNS
Virgin 7 90922-2

Alan Rudolph's stunningly mounted 1988 film set in the art world of Paris in the late '20s (with Keith Carradine, Linda Fiorentino, and John Lone) not only looks like Paris but, thanks to Isham's score, sounds like it too. It only took eight players, but the use of solo violin and piano combined with the tempi and style of writing conveys the mood of the piece. French singer-songwriter Charlie Couture contributes two songs that add to the unique atmosphere.

A RIVER RUNS THROUGH IT
Milan 73138 35631-2

Isham received his first Oscar nomination, and a Grammy nomination, for his folk-flavored Americana score for Robert Redford's 1992 film about the very different paths taken by the sons (Brad Pitt, Craig Sheffer) of a fly-fishing Montana minister (Tom Skerritt). One can't help but wonder about the Elmer Bernstein score that Redford discarded, but the subtle, haunted, and occasionally Irish-tinged nature of Isham's music—coupled with the period-appropriate source music arranged by Lennie Niehaus—made this a winner in its time.

NELL
Fox 11023-R

Isham's music for the 1994 drama about a girl raised entirely apart from civilization is pleasant, country-flavored, rural Americana. It is one of the composer's most atmospheric works, accompanying an Oscar-nominated performance by Jodie Foster as the title character along with those of Liam Neeson and Natasha Richardson as the doctor and psychologist, respectively, who discover and study her.

AFTERGLOW
Columbia CK 67929

Julie Christie's performance as a B-movie actress with a philandering husband (Nick Nolte) won wide praise and a 1997 Best Actress Oscar nomination. Alan Rudolph's film about their odd relationship, intertwined with that of another couple, spawned a great jazz album, so surprising that it doesn't seem like a film score. Mellow, bittersweet tunes—reflecting the tone of the movie—feature a septet led by Isham on trumpet and Charles Lloyd on sax.

Jarre, Maurice (1924–)

French composer Maurice Jarre is best known for his sweeping musical canvases for the epic films of director David Lean: *Lawrence of Arabia* (1962), *Doctor Zhivago* (1965), *Ryan's Daughter* (1970), and *A Passage to India* (1984). His "Lara's Theme" from *Zhivago* became one of the most popular film tunes of the 1960s.

For 12 years the musical director of the French National Theatre, Jarre began writing film scores in the early 1950s, several directed by the great Georges Franju.

His Oscar-winning triumphs with *Lawrence* and *Zhivago* led to collaborations with several other great directors in the ensuing years, including René Clément (*Is Paris Burning?*, 1966), John Frankenheimer (*Grand Prix*, 1966), Alfred Hitchcock (*Topaz*, 1969), Luchino Visconti (*The Damned*, 1969), John Huston (*The Man Who Would Be King*, 1975), Elia Kazan (*The Last Tycoon*, 1976), and others.

Jarre's fascination with the instruments and sounds of other cultures has been audible in such scores as *Villa Rides!* (Mexico), television's *Jesus of Nazareth* (ancient Israel) and *Shogun* (Japan), and the Oscar-nominated *Mohammed, Messenger of God* (Arabia). Many of his more recent scores have reflected his interest in electronic music, notably his dramatic music for *Witness* (1984), majestic music for the gentle creatures of *Gorillas in the Mist* (1988), and the mystical moods of *Ghost* (1990)—all Oscar nominees. He has enjoyed major commercial success with such other films as *Mad Max Beyond Thunderdome* (1985), *Fatal Attraction* (1987), and *Dead Poets Society* (1989).

JARRE BY JARRE: FILM THEMES OF MAURICE JARRE
Columbia MK 42307

This collection of classic Jarre themes, recorded in 1986 by Jarre with London's Royal Philharmonic Orchestra, contains the four David Lean classics—three pieces from *Lawrence of Arabia*, one each from *Doctor Zhivago*, *Ryan's Daughter*, and *A Passage to India*—plus four themes from other Jarre films: *Is Paris Burning?* (1966), *The Damned* (1969), *Villa Rides!* (1968), and *Mad Max Beyond Thunderdome* (1985). The barn-building sequence from *Witness*, originally realized on synthesizers, was fully orchestrated for the RPO for this album and has often been performed since.

LEAN BY JARRE

Milan 73138-35629-2

Jarre paid tribute to his longtime friend and collaborator David Lean with a concert at London's Barbican Centre in 1992. This live recording includes generous suites from all four of their films together: 13 minutes from *Lawrence of Arabia*, 10 from *Doctor Zhivago*, 9 from *Ryan's Daughter*, and 10 from *A Passage to India*. Rounding out the album are an overture and a piece that Jarre wrote for Lean's wedding. Jarre conducts the Royal Philharmonic Orchestra.

MAURICE JARRE AT ABBEY ROAD

Milan 73138-35607-2

This companion volume to "Lean by Jarre" offers a wide-ranging overview of the composer's other, more recent scores, including orchestral versions of several of his largely synthesizer-based scores of recent years including *Witness*, the Michael Douglas thriller *Fatal Attraction* (1987), his Oscar-nominated *Gorillas in the Mist* (1988), *Dead Poets Society* (1989, with bagpipes), and his Oscar-nominated *Ghost* (1990). Earlier music is represented by a 16-minute suite from his Georges Franju films and *Behold a Pale Horse* (1963). Jarre conducts the Royal Philharmonic Orchestra.

LAWRENCE OF ARABIA

Varèse Sarabande VSD-5263

This was the music that brought Jarre to the world's attention. His sweeping theme for the endless desert vistas captured so stunningly in David Lean's Best Picture–winning epic of the enigmatic T. E. Lawrence (Peter O'Toole), as well as the military cadences required by Lawrence's British army service and the heroism and brutality of warfare suggested by Jarre's music, earned him the 1962 Oscar, a pair of Grammy nomina-

tions, and a soundtrack album that spent 86 weeks on the *Billboard* chart (reaching number 2 in early 1963).

DOCTOR ZHIVAGO

Rhino R2 71957

That "Lara's Theme" is one of the two or three most popular tunes ever to come out of the movies is a given. Its prominent, and frequent, placement in one of the biggest romantic movies of the '60s helped. David Lean's film of Boris Pasternak's novel (which starred Omar Sharif and Julie Christie) captured the public imagination with his epic story of a physician-poet in love with two women and caught up in the Bolshevik Revolution. Jarre's score is actually quite diverse, incorporating several themes and utilizing balalaikas and Russian-singing choirs for local color. In addition to the 1965 Oscar for scoring, Jarre won a 1966 Grammy (along with Album of the Year and Song of the Year nominations) and was rewarded with a number-1 album (one that remained on the *Billboard* charts for 157 weeks). The restored Rhino release contains far more music than the original, as well as extensive notes and a long reminiscence by Jarre.

GHOST

Milan 73138-35733-2

Varèse Sarabande VSD-5276

Jarre's score for this surprise 1990 hit (starring Patrick Swayze as a murder victim, Demi Moore as the woman he left behind, and Whoopi Goldberg as a spiritualist) combines both orchestral and electronic music. It was Jarre's task to link the romantic, dramatic, and eerie elements of the movie via music. Audiences responded immediately to the use of the Righteous Brothers' rendition of "Unchained Melody" as the Swayze-Moore love song (particularly in the famous "wet clay" sequence), but the score occupied most of the album's playing time. The album went platinum (the first in Varèse Sarabande's history), it hit the top 10 in late 1990, and the score was an Oscar nominee. ("Unchained Melody," incidentally, was written by Alex North for the forgotten 1955 prison drama *Unchained*.)

WITNESS

Varèse Sarabande VCD-47227

The music for *Witness* was one of the most unusual aspects of Peter Weir's 1985 movie about a Philadelphia cop (Harrison Ford) hiding out in an Amish community. Weir insisted on a score played entirely by synthesizers—an odd aesthetic choice considering the Amish people's well-known aversion to modern devices, although somewhat understandable given their antipathy toward traditional musical instruments as well. Jarre complied with a moody, frequently compelling score that Hollywood observers felt merited an Oscar nomination. Jarre's five-minute "Building the Barn" sequence is justly celebrated

(and even more effective in an orchestral setting, available elsewhere).

PHOTO BY GREG GORMAN, COURTESY OF ROGERS & COWAN

Jones, Quincy (1933–)

Writing music for films had been, with rare exceptions, a closed, whites-only shop until Quincy Jones came along. Other black composers had written for films—notably Benny Carter and Duke Ellington—but Jones was the first to work regularly in movies and ultimately achieve celebrity status.

By the time he scored his first American film (*The Pawnbroker*, 1965), he had already broken barriers in several different arenas of the music business: as a top arranger in New York and Paris before the age of 25, writing charts for the likes of Count Basie and Frank Sinatra; leading his own big band; and as the first black vice president of a major record company (Mercury).

Jones was very active in films for a relatively short period (1965 to 1972) but, during that time, scored several classics, received three Oscar nominations—notably for his chilling music for *In Cold Blood* (1967)—and found creative ways to use both jazz soloists and unusual vocal sounds. He demanded screen credit for the performers on his jazzy score for *The Hot Rock* (1972), prominently featured harmonica player Toots Thielemans in *The Getaway* (1972), and utilized vocalist Don Elliott in effective, often outrageous ways throughout all of his later scores, notably *$* (1971). He has since gone on to a far broader career as a producer in music, TV, and films.

Jones co-produced 1985's *The Color Purple* with Steven Spielberg and received three Oscar nominations that year (for Best Picture, Best Original Song, and, with 11 other co-writers, Best Original Score). In 1995, he received the Motion Picture Academy's Jean Hersholt Humanitarian Award.

THE PAWNBROKER / THE DEADLY AFFAIR
Verve 314 531 233-2

Jones's first American movie score, for Sidney Lumet's *The Pawnbroker*, is melodic, inventive, and jazzy—just what you would expect from one of the top arrangers in the field in 1965, but a surprise considering the subject (a Jewish shopkeeper tormented by memories of his concentration-camp past). The CD couples it with the next Lumet-Jones collaboration: *The Deadly Affair* (1967), a James Mason thriller based on a John Le Carré novel. Bossa-nova queen Astrud Gilberto sings the great main-title song "Who Needs Forever."

IN THE HEAT OF THE NIGHT /
THEY CALL ME MR. TIBBS
Rykodisc RCD 10712

One of Jones's most popular scores—for one of the '60s best films—*In the Heat of the Night* (1967) is paired with its 1970 sequel *They Call Me Mister Tibbs!* for this 1997 reissue. The Southern blues, funk, and gospel rock of *Heat* contrasts neatly with the more urban, streetwise

feel of *Tibbs*. (In the first film, Sidney Poitier as Tibbs is in the Deep South; in the second, it's San Francisco.) The first score includes Ray Charles's soulful rendition of the main theme (which made the top 40 in 1967) and such soloists as Rahsaan Roland Kirk on flute, Glen Campbell on banjo, and Ray Brown on bass.

IN COLD BLOOD
Colgems COS-107 (LP)

Quincy Jones received his first two Oscar nominations for 1967 films. Nobody remembers *Banning*, the movie that spawned the song "The Eyes of Love," but everyone remembers *In Cold Blood*, Richard Brooks's harrowing adaptation of the Truman Capote book about a pair of thrill-killers (Scott Wilson, Robert Blake) and their murder of a Kansas family. Jones's highly original score probes the character of the two misfits as it heightens the terror of the real-life events, utilizing both jazz and unsettling orchestral elements.

THE HOT ROCK
Prophesy SD 6055 (LP)
$
Reprise MS 2051 (LP)

Two of Jones's last movie scores, both caper films, are arguably his most fun: *The Hot Rock* (1972), an amusing diamond-heist movie with Robert Redford and George Segal, and *$* (1971), an equally light-hearted Berlin bank-robbery film with Warren Beatty and Goldie Hawn. In both, Jones utilizes jazz soloists and surprising vocal effects by Don Elliott. Both also feature songs, but the one people remember is Little Richard's "Money Is" from *$*; the instrumental, "Money Runner," made *Billboard*'s top-100 chart as a single.

Jones, Trevor (1949–)

Trevor Jones was born in South Africa but moved to London at age 17. In rapid succession he attended the Royal Academy of Music, became a classical music reviewer at the BBC, obtained a graduate degree in film at the National Film School, and started its film-music program.

Jones's first major feature credit was John Boorman's 1981 *Excalibur*, for which he provided period source music and some underscore (much of the film utilized classical music). Just two years later he created the lush score for Jim Henson's fantasy *The Dark Crystal* (still a favorite score among aficionados) and still later the rock score for Henson's *Labyrinth* (1986).

He collaborated with Andrei Konchalovsky on *Runaway Train* (1985), with Alan Parker on *Angel Heart* (1987) and *Mississippi Burning* (1988), Renny Harlin on *Cliffhanger* (1993), and Ridley Scott on *G.I. Jane* (1997). He scored Ian McKellen's performance in *Richard III* (1995) and shifted into television for the miniseries *Gulliver's Travels* (1996) and *Cleopatra* (1999). With Sting, he co-wrote the delightful, Irish-flavored title song for *The Mighty* (1998).

THE LAST OF THE MOHICANS
Morgan Creek 2959-20015-2

Michael Mann's lavish and hugely popular 1992 epic based on the James Fenimore Cooper novel (with Daniel Day-Lewis as Hawkeye) had at least two composers: Trevor Jones and Randy Edelman. While the circumstances have never been clear, Jones appears to have started the project and scored most of the film; Edelman, brought in late, rescored sections. But the music as a whole was so popular that the album—a last-minute decision after the film was released—quickly went platinum, and both composers

wound up with Golden Globe and British Academy Award nominations. Three-fifths of the music on the album is Jones, including the powerful and hypnotic main theme. Edelman's contribution, equally compelling, includes a theme for Cora (Madeline Stowe); both are orchestra-synth combinations.

CLIFFHANGER
Scotti Bros. 72392 75417-2

Jones supplied this 1993 action film with one of his most inspiring themes (performed by the great brass of the London Philharmonic). Renny Harlin directed this scary-stunt-filled comeback movie for Sylvester Stallone as a rescue climber in the Rocky Mountains; Janine Turner and John Lithgow also starred. Jones punctuates the action and underlines, often darkly, the suspense.

PHOTO COURTESY OF CHASEN & COMPANY

Kamen, Michael (1948–)

One of the most successful composers in films today, Michael Kamen counts among his successes the number-1 hit song from *Robin Hood: Prince of Thieves*, "Everything I Do (I Do It for You)" and the music for such successful action franchises as the *Die Hard* and *Lethal Weapon* films.

Kamen's ability to straddle the line between rock 'n' roll and classical music has served him well in an era when the two sensibilities are so frequently merged. Kamen comes from both: he studied oboe at Juilliard while co-founding the New York Rock and Roll Ensemble; he did the orchestral arrangements for Pink Floyd's *The Wall* but has also written 10 ballet scores.

In addition to his two Best Song nominations, for the *Robin Hood* tune (1991) and "Have You Ever Really Loved a Woman?" from *Don Juan DeMarco* (1995), Kamen scored hits with "All for Love," sung by Bryan Adams in *The Three Musketeers* (1993) and "It's Probably Me," sung by Sting in *Lethal Weapon 3* (1992). After scoring *Mr. Holland's Opus* (1995), star Richard Dreyfuss and Kamen co-founded the Mr. Holland's Opus Foundation, which provides musical instruments to schools around the country.

Kamen's more subtle musical touch has been apparent in films like *Mona Lisa* (1986), *Circle of Friends* (1995), and *The Winter Guest* (1997). For Terry Gilliam, he scored *Brazil* (1985) and *The Adventures of Baron Munchausen* (1989). He has eight Grammy nominations and three wins: two for *Robin Hood* and one for *Mr. Holland's Opus*.

MICHAEL KAMEN'S OPUS
London 289 458 912-2

This 1998 collection contains most of Kamen's great themes: the main theme and love theme from *Robin Hood*, the song from *Don Juan DeMarco*, Kate Bush singing the title tune from *Brazil*, an exciting sequence from *Highlander* (1986), touching moments from *Circle of Friends* and *The Winter Guest*, and the moving "Rowena" from *Mr. Holland's Opus* (with Kamen himself on English

horn). Kamen conducts the Seattle Symphony and London Metropolitan Orchestras.

THE ADVENTURES OF BARON MUNCHAUSEN
Warner Bros. 25826-2

One of Kamen's grandest symphonic stews, this royal accompaniment to Terry Gilliam's outrageous 1989 fantasy (which starred John Neville, Eric Idle, and a host of guest stars, including Robin Williams) is a fun mix of faux-classical and wacky writing. Kamen co-wrote, with Idle, three very funny songs including "The Torturer's Apprentice" and "A Eunuch's Life Is Hard." The various cues are episodic, to be sure, but the score as a whole is so rich and varied that it's never a bore.

ROBIN HOOD: PRINCE OF THIEVES
Morgan Creek 2959-20004-2

Critics may have hooted at Kevin Costner's performance in the 1991 version of the legendary Sherwood Forest outlaw, but Kamen's score ranks among his finest work, from his exciting overture (which hints at the early-English period) to his love theme for Maid Marian (Mary Elizabeth Mastrantonio) which became the Oscar-nominated "(Everything I Do) I Do It for You." Bryan Adams, who co-wrote the tune with Kamen, enjoyed a number-1 single with the song, making the album one of the most successful film soundtracks of the '90s, a number-5 ranking on the *Billboard* charts, a 45-week run in all, and platinum status. The popularity of this music with record-buyers was indicated by its five Grammy nominations; Kamen won two, for best movie song and best pop instrumental performance.

LETHAL WEAPON 3
Reprise 9 26989-2

Practically unique among contemporary film

scores is the ongoing collaboration among composer Kamen, guitarist Eric Clapton, and saxophonist David Sanborn on the *Lethal Weapon* series of high-octane, buddy-cop films starring Mel Gibson and Danny Glover. Clapton's guitar is Gibson's musical voice, and Sanborn's sax speaks for Glover. Each score contains variations on the themes Kamen created in the original. The third installment (1992) is notable for Sting's vocal "It's Probably Me," based on the film's love theme, which became a minor hit and received a Grammy nomination for best movie song.

MR. HOLLAND'S OPUS
London 452 065-2

Two creative individuals shone in this 1995 movie: Richard Dreyfuss, Oscar-nominated as the would-be symphony composer who wound up a high-school music teacher; and Kamen, who applied memories of his own musical education to create a score that contains classical influences but is very much his own. Kamen wrote Dreyfuss's dramatic, eight-minute, orchestra-with-rock-band "American Symphony" prior to shooting; he won a Grammy for best instrumental arrangement for the track.

PHOTO FROM THE TONY THOMAS COLLECTION

Kaper, Bronislau (1902–1983)

Bronislau Kaper wrote more than 100 film scores, mostly for MGM movies, but is best known for his songs: the title tune for *San Francisco* (1936); *Green Dolphin Street* (1947), which became a jazz standard; and perhaps his most popular, the title theme for the musical *Lili* (1953) with Leslie Caron.

Kaper was an accomplished pianist who spent the 1920s and early 1930s working in the German theater and film industry. As with many of his colleagues, the rise of Nazism forced him to leave the country. MGM head Louis B. Mayer discovered him in Paris and signed him to a contract as a songwriter. Eventually he began writing orchestral scores for MGM films as well.

Kaper's other notable films included *Gaslight* (1944), *Invitation* (1952), *The Brothers Karamazov* (1958), *Butterfield 8* (1960), and *Lord Jim* (1965). For his grand-scale music for the Marlon Brando–Trevor Howard remake of *Mutiny on the Bounty* (1962), he was accorded Oscar nominations for both the score and its popular song "Follow Me."

Kaper served some 15 years on the board of the Los Angeles Philharmonic (its Kaper award, given annually to outstanding young musicians, was named in his honor). To the younger generation, his theme for the long-running police series *The FBI*, written in 1965, is probably his most familiar work.

THE FILM MUSIC OF BRONISLAU KAPER
Delos FACET 8101

At the behest of producer Tony Thomas, the veteran MGM composer recorded many of his greatest film themes at the piano in 1975. Included are his Oscar-winning *Lili* (1953); the Oscar-nominated *The Chocolate Soldier* (1941) and *Mutiny on the Bounty* (1962); and two of his most popular standards, the title songs from *San Francisco* (1936) and *Green Dolphin Street* (1947). Also included: music from *Invitation* (1952), *The Glass Slipper* (1955), *The Swan* (1956), *Auntie Mame* (1958), *The Brothers Karamazov* (1958), *Butterfield 8* (1960), and *Lord Jim* (1965).

MONSTROUS MOVIE MUSIC
MMM-1950

Kaper's only contribution to the science-fiction genre happened to be for one of the few '50s sci-fi movies that was not only credible but often terrifying. *Them!* (1954) concerned giant ants created by nuclear testing in the Southwestern desert. Ominous and atmospheric, with two very closely miked pianos used prominently within the orchestra, it also features a fascinating fugue for the ants. Masatoshi Mitsumoto conducts the Radio Symphony Orchestra of Cracow in this 1995 re-recording, which also includes suites from *The Mole People* (1956, Herman Stein and Heinz Roemheld), *It Came From Outer Space* (1953, Stein, Irving Gertz, Henry Mancini), and

It Came From Beneath the Sea (1955, Mischa Bakaleinikoff).

MUTINY ON THE BOUNTY
MGM S1E4 (LP)

The closest to a truly symphonic work of all of his scores, Kaper's massive and powerful music for the 1962 version of the classic was arguably its finest element. Marlon Brando and Trevor Howard starred as Fletcher Christian and Captain Bligh in the three-hour epic. Kaper's on-location research into the indigenous music of the South Seas for the Tahitian portions of the film lent an authentic ring to the sound and resulted in Oscar nominations for Best Song ("Follow Me") and Best Original Score. The film's popularity sent the album to number 14 on the *Billboard* charts in early 1963; it remained on the charts for nearly five months.

LORD JIM
Colpix SCP-521 (LP)

Joseph Conrad's novel of honor and redemption was filmed in epic style by Richard Brooks, with Peter O'Toole in the starring role, in 1965. Kaper, newly freed from his long MGM contract, undertook this assignment and—like his previous stint on *Mutiny on the Bounty*—studied gamelan music in an effort to create an authentic sound for the primary location, the Malay archipelago at the turn of the century. Britisher Muir Mathieson conducted the score, which charted briefly, perhaps because of its gorgeous love theme ("The Color of Love").

Karas, Anton (1906–1985)

Before *The Third Man* (1949), nobody had ever heard of Viennese performer Anton Karas. In fact, the average American hadn't even heard of the instrument he played: the zither. By the middle of 1950, Anton Karas was a household name and a single of his "Third Man Theme" had been number 1 for 11 weeks on the pop charts.

The Third Man, directed by Carol Reed from a Graham Greene script, starred Joseph Cotten as an American writer, Orson Welles as his mysterious old friend Harry Lime, and Alida Valli as the woman who loved Harry. Absorbing, fascinating, ultimately bittersweet, its reputation as one of the finest post-war films is fully deserved. A key factor is the music—played from start to finish on a single instrument.

Karas's zither (a fingered and plucked string instrument that is popular in central and eastern European countries) added color and atmosphere. Director Reed reportedly discovered Karas playing in a Vienna tavern while shooting on location and asked him to compose and play for his movie. Most of the score is built on the "Harry Lime" theme, although Karas wrote other tunes, notably the "Cafe Mozart Waltz" that is heard elsewhere in the score.

The popularity of the *Third Man* music led Karas to record an album for Decca. He appeared in one movie (the forgotten 1950 British film *Come Dance With Me*) and, with the proceeds from his hit record, bought a wine bar in Grinzing, named it "The Third Man," and played for patrons.

THE THIRD MAN

London LL-1560 (LP)

Karas' famous zither music from Carol Reed's 1949 thriller is preserved on this 1956 album (reissued in 1959 to coincide with Michael Rennie's TV series of the same name). The familiar "Harry Lime" theme is paired with Karas's "Cafe Mozart Waltz" and other variations.

Karlin, Fred (1936–)

Songwriter, orchestral composer, American-music expert, author: Few film composers have enjoyed the diversity of career that Fred Karlin has.

Chicago-born and a graduate of Amherst College, he was a trumpet player whose early success writing for big bands led to a move to New York and an eclectic musical career composing, arranging, and recording a variety of music. His first film assignment was *Up the Down Staircase* (1967).

It was followed by a series of successful films including the Gregory Peck western *The Stalking Moon* (1969) and Liza Minnelli's *The Sterile Cuckoo* (1969), which yielded a song hit in "Come Saturday Morning" (written with Dory Previn). The very next year, Karlin's "For All We Know" for the comedy *Lovers and Other Strangers* was not only a colossal hit for the Carpenters but also won the Oscar as Best Song.

The Karlins (Fred and his lyricist-wife Meg, writing under the name Tylwyth Kymry) were nominated for their song score for *The Baby Maker* (1970); another Best Song nomination followed, for "Come Follow, Follow Me" from the family film *The Little Ark* (1972). Karlin's career segued into television, where he won an Emmy for his score for Cicely Tyson's landmark TV-movie *The Autobiography of Miss Jane Pittman* (1974), an NAACP Image Award for his score for the musical TV-film *Minstrel Man* (1977), and additional honors. He has written two books on film music: *On the Track* (1990), now the standard text on film scoring for professionals, and *Listening to Movies* (1994), a layman's guide to appreciating movie music.

THE STERILE CUCKOO

Paramount PAS 5009 (LP)

This 1969 film, Alan J. Pakula's directorial debut,

received two well-deserved Oscar nominations: for Liza Minnelli's funny and touching performance, and for Karlin and Previn's "Come Saturday Morning" (which The Sandpipers turned into a top-20 hit). Karlin's quietly contemporary style pervades the entire score (largely based on the song) as it did in *Up the Down Staircase* and *Lovers and Other Strangers*.

WESTWORLD
MGM 1SE-47 (LP)

Karlin's fun score for this cult sci-fi film from 1973, writer Michael Crichton's debut as a feature director, combines traditional western scoring with synthesizers entirely appropriate to the futuristic setting: a Tomorrowland-style theme park where you play out your western fantasies—then, of course, things start to go wrong. Yul Brynner's role as a robot gunslinger is famous; Karlin's electronic work is suspenseful, especially for the chase scenes.

Khachaturian, Aram (1903–1978)

The Armenian composer whose "Sabre Dance" is well-known (in part because Ed Sullivan usually played it for plate-spinners on his variety show), and whose "Gayane" ballet suite became familiar as part of the score of *2001: A Space Odyssey*, actually composed more than two dozen film scores himself.

Few of them are known in the West, because Soviet films of that era rarely crossed the border. But his song from *Pepo* (1935), his first score, and his march from *Zanzegur* (1936) became so popular in their time that they are thought of as part of Armenian folk tradition.

Among the others, *The Battle of Stalingrad* (1949) and *Othello* (1956) have been recorded and, while these works will never eclipse the fame of "Sabre Dance" or the ballet suites, they are signifi-

cant contributions to the art and worthy of attention simply because they are Khachaturian's music.

Stalingrad was a two-part epic lasting nearly four hours and was largely a glorification of Stalin himself. *Othello* has the distinction of casting the great Soviet actor Sergei Bondarchuk in the title role. Interestingly, Khachaturian composed for theatrical productions of two other Shakespeare plays: *Macbeth* and *King Lear*.

THE BATTLE OF STALINGRAD / OTHELLO
Marco Polo 8.223314

Khachaturian arranged an eight-movement suite from his lengthy score for *The Battle of Stalingrad* (1949) that roughly chronicles the 1942–43 battle that was a turning point in World War II. Even though the composer had been publicly denounced just two years before, he won a Stalin Prize for this score in 1950. The *Othello* suite is in 11 movements, including a lyrical solo-violin motif for the title character and a memorable vocalise for Desdemona. Adriano conducts the Slovak Radio Symphony Orchestra of Bratislava in these 1989 and 1992 re-recordings.

Kilar, Wojciech (1932–)

Wojciech Kilar is one of Poland's leading symphonic composers. Only with the 1992 release of *Bram Stoker's Dracula*, however, did he become known to American moviegoers and become a sought-after composer for Hollywood films.

Kilar studied in Katowice and Krakow, and with Nadia Boulanger in Paris. He received numerous composition prizes in both America and Poland in the '60s, '70s, and '80s and has been active as a concert-hall composer throughout his career; his works have been performed by symphony orchestras in New York, Cleveland, and Philadelphia.

Dracula was hardly his introduction to film music, however: He has been writing for Polish movies since the early 1960s, notably the work of directors Andrzej Wajda and Krzystof Zanussi. Kilar's admiration for John Cage is apparent in his tendency towards minimalism. (As he points out in the notes for *Portrait*: "I think the best film music repeats its basic themes, each time with small variations.")

Following the Coppola film, Kilar scored *Death and the Maiden* (1994) for Roman Polanski and *The Portrait of a Lady* (1996) for Jane Campion.

BRAM STOKER'S DRACULA
Columbia CK 53165

Francis Ford Coppola's choice of Kilar to score his splashy, reconceptualized 1992 vampire film with Gary Oldman and Anthony Hopkins was both geographically and dramatically astute. After all the English and American composers who have musicalized the bloodthirsty count, Coppola engaged a composer who knew the Eastern European region personally. Kilar's massive score for orchestra, choir, and solo female voice established an often powerful Gothic atmosphere of darkness and oppression that is relieved only by an occasional tender moment.

THE PORTRAIT OF A LADY
London 455 011-2

Jane Campion's post–*The Piano* film was this 1996 film based on Henry James's 1881 novel of manipulation. Nicole Kidman starred as an independent-minded American woman who becomes trapped in a troubled and constraining marriage; Barbara Hershey received an Oscar nomination for her complex role as Madame Merle, and John Malkovich was the villain. Kilar's score, which

incorporates healthy doses of Schubert, is often exquisitely romantic.

Knopfler, Mark (1949–)

The co-founder, lead guitarist, and vocalist of England's Dire Straits has contributed his signature guitar sounds to half a dozen movies over the past 15 years.

In the wake of Dire Straits' enormous success in both Britain and the U.S. (especially with the band's eponymous album, a number-1 hit in 1979, and the "Sultans of Swing," which went to number 4), Knopfler was invited to score Bill Forsyth's whimsical 1983 film *Local Hero*. His first film score netted him a British Academy Award nomination.

Knopfler scored Forsyth's next film, the less successful *Comfort and Joy* (1984) and Rob Reiner's hugely popular *The Princess Bride* (1987), as well as Uli Edel's bleak '50s story *Last Exit to Brooklyn* (1989). After these synthesizer-oriented efforts, he returned to fine acoustic form with the pleasant, Nashville-recorded guitars of Barry Levinson's prescient political film *Wag the Dog* (1998), starring Dustin Hoffman and Robert DeNiro.

SCREENPLAYING
Warner Bros. 9 45457-2

This 1993 collection contains excerpts from four Knopfler projects: his Scottish-tinged score for *Local Hero* (1983)—on which he plays not only guitars but synthesizers, percussion, and Linn drums—plus his Irish-flavored music for *Cal* (1984), the synthesizer-dominated music for Rob Reiner's fairy tale *The Princess Bride* (1987), and the melancholy, synth-with-violin music for *Last Exit to Brooklyn* (1989).

PHOTO COURTESY OF RUDY BEHLMER

Korngold, Erich Wolfgang (1897–1957)

He composed original scores for just 18 films—but Erich Wolfgang Korngold forever changed the sound of Hollywood movies with his rich symphonic sound and unabashed romanticism.

When Korngold arrived in Hollywood in 1934 to adapt Mendelssohn's music for Warner Bros.' all-star *A Midsummer Night's Dream*, the groundwork had already been laid by such pioneers as Max Steiner at RKO and Alfred Newman at Samuel Goldwyn. But unlike those composers, both of whom came from backgrounds as Broadway conductors, Korngold had major credentials as a composer in the concert world. Acclaimed as a child prodigy in his native Austria by the likes of Mahler, Puccini, and Strauss, he was just 16 when the Vienna Philharmonic played his "Sinfonietta" and 18 when Bruno Walter conducted the debut of his first opera in Munich.

Korngold thought of film music as opera without singing, creating rapturous melodies, writing recurring themes for characters, and supporting the on-screen action with surging orchestral accompaniment.

Nearly all of his films were at Warners, which so respected his contributions that he was highly paid, allowed to choose the films on which he would work, and given prominent title-card placement in the credits. A key contributor to the studio's handsome costume dramas and historical epics, he wrote swashbuckling music for Errol Flynn's *Captain Blood* (1935), *The Adventures of Robin Hood* (1938, an Oscar winner), and *The Sea Hawk* (1940); romantic scores for Bette Davis in *Juarez* (1939), *The Private Lives of Elizabeth and Essex* (1939), and *Deception* (1946); and grand-scale themes and variations for *Anthony Adverse* (1936, another Oscar winner) and *Kings Row* (1942). A revival of interest in his operas and other concert music followed the release of his film music on records in the early 1970s.

MUSIC BY ERICH WOLFGANG KORNGOLD
Stanyan STZ-117

This album, recorded in Germany by Lionel Newman in August 1961 and produced by the composer's son George Korngold, was the first collection of Korngold's film work—as the old Warner Bros. LP cover put it, "music of the foremost composer of the Golden Age of Motion Pictures." Still a favorite of many Korngold enthusiasts, it contains suites and themes from the Oscar-winning *Anthony Adverse* (1936) and *The Adventures of Robin Hood* (1938); the Oscar-nominated *Private Lives of Elizabeth and Essex* (1939) and *The Sea Hawk* (1940); plus *Kings Row* (1942), *The Prince and the Pauper* (1937), and *The Constant Nymph* (1943).

ERICH WOLFGANG KORNGOLD: THE WARNER BROS. YEARS
Rhino R2 72243

This long-awaited two-CD set contains nearly two

hours of excerpts from Korngold's original scores, rescued many years ago by George Korngold and restored for CD release in 1996. Sixteen of Korngold's Warner films are represented, covering the period from 1935 to 1946; all are conducted by the composer. A 44-page booklet containing a long Tony Thomas essay about Korngold's career is included, and lots of colorful movie-poster art adorns the box.

THE SEA HAWK: THE CLASSIC FILM SCORES OF ERICH WOLFGANG KORNGOLD
RCA 60863-2-RG

This 1972 collection, the first in RCA's "Classic Film Scores" series, not only launched a reappraisal of great film music of the '30s and '40s but is also thought to have begun a fresh appreciation of Korngold throughout the world. Included are the swashbucklers (*The Sea Hawk*, 1940; *The Adventures of Robin Hood*, 1938; *Captain Blood*, 1935), the period epics (*Anthony Adverse*, 1936, *Juarez*, 1939, *Kings Row*, 1942), the love stories (*The Constant Nymph*, 1943; *Of Human Bondage*, 1945; *Devotion*, 1946), a fantasy (*Between Two Worlds*, 1944), and the films about composers (*Deception*, 1946, *Escape Me Never*, 1947). Charles Gerhardt conducts London's National Philharmonic Orchestra.

ELIZABETH AND ESSEX: THE CLASSIC FILM SCORES OF ERICH WOLFGANG KORNGOLD
RCA 0185-2-RG

The 1973 sequel contains more evidence of Korngold as one of the greatest composers of Hollywood's golden era: seven minutes of fanfares and romantic scenes from *The Private Lives of Elizabeth and Essex*, five minutes of fun from *The Prince and the Pauper*, more of *Anthony Adverse* and *Of Human Bondage*, more than seven minutes from the grim, complex *The Sea Wolf* (1941), excerpts from the love story *Another Dawn*

(1937), and the single-movement cello concerto from *Deception* (1946). Charles Gerhardt conducts the National Philharmonic.

TRIBUTE TO ERICH WOLFGANG KORNGOLD
Koch 3-7302-2 H1

Extended suites (nearly a half-hour each) from two of Korngold's lesser-known scores for Warner Bros. films make up the bulk of this disc, recorded in 1997: the Mexican-flavored *Juarez* (1939), from the film starring Paul Muni, Bette Davis, and Claude Rains; and the eerie, turmoil-filled *The Sea Wolf* (1941), which starred Edward G. Robinson in Jack London's tale of a psychotic captain. Accompanying these are six minutes of excerpts from Korngold's Oscar-nominated *The Private Lives of Elizabeth and Essex* (1939), with Errol Flynn and Bette Davis. James Sedares conducts the New Zealand Symphony Orchestra.

ANTHONY ADVERSE
Varèse Sarabande VSD 5285

Korngold's operatic style is immediately apparent in his Oscar-winning music for the 1936 epic starring Fredric March and Olivia deHavilland. As annotator Tony Thomas says, Korngold "wrote long lines of continuous music, great chunks that contained the ebb and flow of the film's mood and action." This multi-thematic score chronicled Anthony's adventures throughout the 19th-century world. John Scott conducts the Berlin Radio Symphony Orchestra.

THE ADVENTURES OF ROBIN HOOD
Varèse Sarabande VCD-47202

Korngold's 1938 Oscar winner, what many film fans consider the definitive Robin Hood tale, was a Technicolor Warner Bros. film with Errol Flynn as the bandit of Sherwood Forest, Olivia deHavilland as Maid Marian, and Claude Rains and Basil Rathbone as the bad guys. Korngold's classic score contains a jaunty march for the Merry Men, plenty of exciting orchestral leaps for the action, and a memorable love theme for Robin and Marian. Varujan Kojian conducts the Utah Symphony Orchestra.

THE PRIVATE LIVES OF ELIZABETH AND ESSEX
Varèse Sarabande VSD-5696
Sixty-five minutes of Korngold's lavish score for Warners' 1939 costume drama starring Errol Flynn and Bette Davis was re-recorded in 1991 by Carl Davis and the Munich Symphony Orchestra. Davis was Queen Elizabeth I, Flynn the Earl of Essex in this fanciful pseudo-history based on a Maxwell Anderson play. One of Korngold's most beautiful love themes graces this score, which like the other Flynn films is filled with the musical pomp and ceremony attendant to these historical dramas.

THE SEA HAWK
Varèse Sarabande VCD-47304
Korngold's definitive swashbuckler, this 1940 Warner Bros. film was his sixth with Errol Flynn and contained some of his most exciting writing: fanfares for the throne room of 16th-century England, nautical music for Flynn's pirate ship *Albatross,* a passionate love theme for Flynn and Brenda Marshall, even percussion-filled exotica for Flynn and crew on a gold raid in Panama. Varujan Kojian conducts the Utah Symphony Orchestra and Chorus.

KINGS ROW
Varèse Sarabande VCD-47269
The first substantial recording of this seminal score for Warners' 1942 drama of a Middle American town contains 48 minutes of the 67-minute score. The film is best remembered as a grand soap opera that stars Robert Cummings, Ann Sheridan, and (in his finest performance) Ronald Reagan. Korngold's score exemplifies his leitmotivic approach, brimming with recurring themes for characters and situations. Charles Gerhardt conducts the National Philharmonic Orchestra.

ANOTHER DAWN / ESCAPE ME NEVER
Marco Polo 8.223871
One of Errol Flynn's lesser films, this 1937 movie about a British soldier serving in Africa and falling for his commander's wife (Kay Francis) got a first-rate score from Korngold. The 1995 restoration and re-recording preserves nearly an hour of music from the original score. Also included: an eight-minute ballet sequence from *Escape Me Never* (1947), which cast Flynn in the unlikely role of composer. William T. Stromberg conducts the Moscow Symphony Orchestra.

BETWEEN TWO WORLDS
London 444 170-2
Conductor John Mauceri assembled a 30-minute suite from Korngold's score for Warners' 1944 remake of *Outward Bound,* about a fog-bound ship carrying dead passengers to their final destination: heaven or hell. John Garfield, Eleanor Parker, Faye Emerson, and Paul Henreid are in the cast, but it's Korngold's mystical music and his piano rhapsody that are best remembered. Mauceri conducts the Rundfunk-Sinfonieorchester Berlin.

Lai, Francis (1932–)
When director Claude Lelouch made his romantic *Un Homme et Une femme (A Man and a Woman,* 1966), his decision to engage Francis Lai as com-

poser altered both their lives. The French filmmaker's stunningly photographed love story, as well as its simple but infectious Lai theme, were giant international hits and both were immediately established in movies.

Since then, the Nice-born composer has scored nearly every Lelouch film, including *Vivre pour vivre* (*Live for Life*, 1967), *Toute une vie* (*And Now My Love*, 1974), *Les uns et les autres* (*Bolero*, 1981), and the two *Man and a Woman* sequels—*Another Man, Another Chance* (1977) and *A Man and a Woman: 20 Years Later* (1986).

Ironically, Lai's biggest hit was for an American film, *Love Story* (1970), for which he won his only Academy Award. *Love Story's* soundtrack was on the *Billboard* top-100 charts for 39 weeks, and its theme, with a lyric added later, was a vocal hit ("Where Do I Begin?") for several singers.

Lai had written for Yves Montand and Juliette Greco, and was legendary chanteuse Edith Piaf's accompanist (usually on accordion) in the early 1960s. But it was in movies that he found a niche, and he has now scored more than 80 films, only a handful known in America: *Mayerling* (1968), *Hannibal Brooks* (1969), *Rider on the Rain* (1970), and *International Velvet* (1978). Occasionally he aspires to larger forms, as in his "Concerto for a Love's Ending" for *Un Homme qui me plait* (*Love Is a Funny Thing*, 1969) and "Adagio for Organ, Choir, and Strings" from *La Louve solitaire* (1968).

A MAN AND A WOMAN / LIVE FOR LIFE
DRG 12612

Moviegoers swooned to the love story of Anouk Aimee and Jean-Louis Trintignant in Claude Lelouch's lushly photographed film, which won the Palme d'or at Cannes and went on to Best Screenplay and Best Foreign Film honors at the 1966 Oscars. Lai's accordion- and choir-dominat-

ed score was an equal hit with record-buyers, going as high as number 10 and remaining on the charts for an astounding 93 weeks. Lelouch and Lai's 1967 follow-up, known in America as *Live for Life*, also charted briefly. This 1996 CD combines both scores and includes the songs from *A Man and a Woman* that also contributed so much to its popularity.

LOVE STORY
MCA MCAD-19157

Few film themes have captured the public's heart as immediately or as thoroughly as Lai's piano signature for *Love Story*, the Ryan O'Neal–Ali MacGraw tragic romance based on Erich Segal's enormously popular novella. Lai, hired after a Jimmy Webb score was discarded, won the 1970 Oscar for Best Original Score and the album—Grammy-nominated for both score and the theme as "instrumental composition"—went to number 2 on the *Billboard* charts.

Legrand, Michel (1932–)

Few movie composers can claim quite this many

genuine accomplishments: classically trained composer, arranger for the great singers of our time, talented jazz pianist and vocalist, writer of at least half a dozen standards, internationally recognized concert conductor. Michel Legrand, in fact, may be the only one.

A child prodigy, he entered the Paris Conservatory at 11; at 22 he had a best-selling album in the U.S. ("I Love Paris"); at 26 he was recording a classic jazz LP with Miles Davis, John Coltrane, and Bill Evans. He actually scored his first film at 21 but didn't gain lasting fame until his remarkable collaboration with Jacques Demy on the all-sung romantic musical *The Umbrellas of Cherbourg* in 1964. Subsequent Demy musicals were equally impressive, including *The Young Girls of Rochefort* (1967) and *Donkey Skin* (1971).

One of few composers to have won Oscars for a song, a dramatic score, and an original song score—"The Windmills of Your Mind" (1968), *Summer of '42* (1971), and *Yentl* (1983)—he has 10 other nominations including three for *Umbrellas* alone and for such popular movie songs as "What Are You Doing the Rest of Your Life?," "Pieces of Dreams," and "How Do You Keep the Music Playing?"

Legrand's other dramatic scores include such classically styled works as *The Thomas Crown Affair* (1968) and *The Go-Between* (1970), thrillers like *Ice Station Zebra* (1968), the period pieces *Wuthering Heights* (1970) and *The Three Musketeers* (1974), and such significant television films as *Brian's Song* (1971). He continues to record jazz albums, arrange and conduct for a variety of vocalists, and make concert appearances.

BRIAN'S SONG: THEMES AND VARIATIONS
Bell 6071 (LP)
Highlighted by Legrand's rich orchestrations and

his own jazz piano playing, this 1972 album opens with his theme from the Emmy-winning 1971 TV-movie *Brian's Song* but consists, for the most part, of the best of his late '60s and early '70s film work: the Oscar-winning "The Windmills of Your Mind" (from *The Thomas Crown Affair*, 1968) and theme from *Summer of '42* (1971); and the Oscar-nominated "What Are You Doing the Rest of Your Life?" (from *The Happy Ending*, 1969) and title song from *Pieces of Dreams* (1970). The other classics include "Summer Me, Winter Me" from *Picasso Summer* (1969) as well as themes from *The Go-Between* (1971) and *Wuthering Heights* (1970).

THE UMBRELLAS OF CHERBOURG
Sony SM2K 62678 (Fr.)
THE YOUNG GIRLS OF ROCHEFORT
Philips 558 408-2 (Fr.)
Jacques Demy's one-of-a-kind screen musicals were Oscar nominees in their day and remain quite stunning examples of the union of music, lyrics, cinematography, and production design. In each, all the dialogue is sung. The 1964 *Umbrellas*, the bittersweet love story of a shopgirl and a garage mechanic, gave us the Oscar-nominated "I Will Wait for You" and the equally famous "Watch What Happens." Legrand and Demy were nominated (in 1965) for their musical score and the song; Legrand, for his dramatic score. They also received a pair of Grammy nominations. The 1967 *Rochefort*, about twin sisters and members of a traveling carnival, was not quite as successful either artistically or commercially. Still, it managed an Oscar nomination for its musical score and gave us "You Must Believe in Spring." Catherine Deneuve starred in both films.

THE THOMAS CROWN AFFAIR

Rykodisc RCD 10719

Legrand received two 1968 Academy Award nominations for his music for this classic caper film starring Steve McQueen as a rich corporate magnate who plans elaborate robberies and Faye Dunaway as the insurance investigator out to prove he's responsible. Legrand, and lyricists Alan and Marilyn Bergman, won the Best Song Oscar for "The Windmills of Your Mind," sung on the soundtrack by Noel Harrison and covered by dozens of artists since. Legrand's clever score incorporated both jazz and classical influences; the film's provocative chess-game sequence, completely without dialogue, is a minor classic.

SUMMER OF '42

Warner Bros. WPCR-725 (Japan)

Legrand won his second Academy Award for this 1971 film, a nostalgic coming-of-age story about a teenager (Gary Grimes) whose crush on a young war bride (Jennifer O'Neill) becomes something much more. Legrand's lush, romantic theme also won a Grammy for Best Instrumental Composition (and was nominated twice more in the Pop Instrumental category, once for Legrand and once for Peter Nero's version). Because there was so little music in the film, the album's two versions of the theme are accompanied by Legrand's lavish orchestral score for the unreleased *Picasso Summer* (1969), the source for the now-standard "Summer Me, Winter Me." The album was on the charts for a surprising 34 weeks.

THE GO-BETWEEN

CBS M35175 (LP)

Legrand's "Theme and Variations for Two Pianos and Orchestra" was written for Joseph Losey's remarkable 1971 film with its Harold Pinter screenplay. The film cast Julie Christie and Alan Bates as lovers who secretly defy turn-of-the-century class barriers and engage a 12-year-old boy to deliver their love notes. Legrand wrote a 22-minute, neo-classical score whose dramatic construction works so well that he often plays it in concert. This 1979 re-recording is coupled with Legrand's symphonic suite from *The Umbrellas of Cherbourg*.

THE THREE MUSKETEERS

Bay Cities BCD 3013

Legrand's score for Richard Lester's 1974 retelling of the Alexandre Dumas tale of D'Artagnan joining Athos, Porthos, and Aramis is exuberant, full of Baroque period flavor, and contains one of the composer's most exquisite love themes ("To Love a Queen," for strings and harp). Oliver Reed, Richard Chamberlain, Michael York, Faye Dunaway, and Charlton Heston were just a few of the stars who toplined this colorful swashbuckler. The score received a Grammy nomination.

Mancina, Mark (1957–)

One of the hottest of the current crop of film composers to emerge from the pop ranks, Mark Mancina combines an appreciation for the classics with an understanding of comtemporary sounds that has made him sought-after as a composer of summertime action thrillers.

His best-known scores, for *Speed* (1994), *Twister* (1996), and *Con Air* (1997, a collaboration with Trevor Rabin), had to compete with massive sound-effects budgets. They managed, occasionally, to be heard above the din, propelling the action and helping to convince audiences that the proceedings were more credible than they acutally were.

The Southern California native studied classical composition, formed a band at the age of 18, and eventually joined the rock band Yes, then fronted by guitarist Rabin. He worked with producer Trevor Horn and such artists as Billy Joel, Seal, Prince, and the group Emerson, Lake and Palmer, before joining composer Hans Zimmer as a collaborator on films like *Days of Thunder* (1990) and *True Romance* (1993).

Mancina produced three of Elton John's songs for Disney's *The Lion King* (1994), winning a Grammy and then shifting to Broadway as a writer, producer, and arranger on the Tony-winning theatrical version of the film. Also for Disney, he composed the African-flavored score for *Tarzan* (1999); controversy ensued when it was revealed that Academy music-branch rules left him ineligible for an Oscar. Another notable Mancina score was the 18th-century Daniel Defoe tale *Moll Flanders* (1996).

SPEED

Fox 112020-2

Mancina's breakthrough opportunity came when cinematographer-turned-director Jan De Bont chose him to score the 1994 runaway-bus thriller *Speed*, starring Keanu Reeves and Sandra Bullock. Although the official "soundtrack" consists largely of songs that aren't even in the film, Mancina's heroic, percussion-dominated orchestra-with-synths score received a belated release form the studio's own, short-lived label.

TWISTER

Atlantic 82954-2

Director Jan De Bont's 1996 summer tornado thriller (starring Helen Hunt and Bill Paxton) was long on visual effects but, many critics felt, short on story. Mancina contributed an ambitious score that combined orchestra with choir. An Americana

theme, and alternating moods of wonder and terror, make this one of Mancina's best efforts. Eddie and Alex Van Halen's rock-guitar piece "Respect the Wind," the film's end title, is also included.

Mancini, Henry (1924–1994)

One of the first composers to break into films from the jazz world, ex-big-band pianist-arranger Henry Mancini first found success with his music for television's *Peter Gunn* and almost immediately became a sought-after film composer, winning a pair of Oscars for the *Breakfast at Tiffany's* (1961) score and its song "Moon River."

Mancini's boundless gift for melody resulted in memorable theme songs for such films as *Days of Wine and Roses* (1962), *Charade* (1964), and *Two for the Road* (1967), all of which have become popular outside of their original movie contexts. His shrewd understanding of the record business also enabled him to achieve success with nearly two dozen soundtrack and popular-music albums throughout the 1960s and 1970s.

Mancini's long professional association with director Blake Edwards (which began with *Peter*

Gunn) became the longest-running composer-director collaboration in Hollywood, spanning more than two dozen pictures over three decades, including the seven *Pink Panther* movies (starting in 1964) and such popular successes as *10* (1979) and the Oscar-winning *Victor/Victoria* (1982, which later became a Broadway musical).

His success in the light-comedy and romantic realms belied his abilities as a dramatic composer, evidenced by his suspenseful music for *Experiment in Terror* (1962) and *Wait Until Dark* (1967), the melancholy Irish colors of *The Molly Maguires* (1970), the whaling music of *The White Dawn* (1974), and the grimly powerful score for the sci-fi picture *Lifeforce* (1985). Well known in the Hollywood community as both a tremendously talented composer and a genuinely nice man, Mancini won 20 Grammy awards (out of 70 nominations) before his untimely death due to cancer.

HENRY MANCINI:
THE DAYS OF WINE AND ROSES
RCA Victor 66603-2

This three-CD "greatest hits" collection (drawn from the many albums released during Mancini's 20-year contract as an RCA recording artist) contains more than two and a half hours of vintage Mancini. Included are nearly all the hits from 1959 to 1979 and a 72-page book featuring a long career essay by Gene Lees. Among the tracks are many film themes that didn't have an entire soundtrack, such as *The Days of Wine and Roses* (1962), *Dear Heart* (1964), *A Shot in the Dark* (1964), *Moment to Moment* (1965), *Wait Until Dark* (1967), and *Silver Streak* (1977). Also here are the hard-to-find *Two for the Road* (1967) and several of the TV themes.

MORE MONSTROUS MOVIE MUSIC
MMM-1951

Mancini's contributions to Universal's monster movies of the '50s are remembered on this collection of newly recorded, surprisingly effective scores. Featured is music by Mancini and Herman Stein for *Tarantula* (1955), the giant-spider movie with John Agar. Also on the disc: David Buttolph's music from *The Beast From 20,000 Fathoms* (1953), Irving Gertz's theme from *The Monolith Monsters* (1957), and Angelo Francesco Lavagnino's music from *Gorgo* (1961). Reconstructions were by Kathleen Mayne; Masatoshi Mitsumoto conducts the Radio Symphony Orchestra of Cracow.

TOUCH OF EVIL
Varèse Sarabande VSD-5414

After toiling for several years on Universal "B" pictures, Mancini landed one that has gone down as a cinema classic: Orson Welles's 1958 film about a Mexican detective and a corrupt cop who clash over a murder investigation. Charlton Heston, Welles, Janet Leigh, and Marlene Dietrich are in the cast, and the three-minute opening tracking shot is justly famous. Mancini's score consists almost entirely of Latin-flavored jazz and rock, much of it emanating from the bars and hotels of the film's border-town setting, and he always said it was one of the scores of which he was proudest.

BREAKFAST AT TIFFANY'S
RCA Victor 2362-2-R

The film opens with a plaintive harmonica, a vaguely country-style tune, and a shot of Audrey Hepburn munching on a cruller and sipping coffee while gazing at a Manhattan window display just after dawn. Blake Edwards's 1961 movie turned "Moon River" into a hit, won two Oscars (Best Song, Best Score) for Mancini, and helped make

him the best-known movie composer of the '60s. The soundtrack's lush melodies and big-band charts sent the album to number 1 for 12 weeks (96 weeks on the chart in all) and won five 1961 Grammys including Record of the Year and Song of the Year.

CHARADE
RCA Victor 2755-2-R

Cary Grant and Audrey Hepburn, directed by Stanley Donen, with music by Henry Mancini: How else to describe this combination of talents except "stylish"? Set in Paris, the 1964 Hitchcock-style comedy-mystery benefits greatly from the composer's lightly suspenseful, slightly exotic, and often amusing score. As was the practice in those days, however, Mancini's dramatic music was omitted from the soundtrack in favor of middle-of-the-road instrumental music more likely to receive radio play.

THE PINK PANTHER
RCA Victor 2795-2-R

After "Moon River," Mancini's best-known theme originated as the stealthy motif for a cat burglar in

Blake Edwards's 1964 caper film starring David Niven. The Panther, immortalized in the animated titles that later spawned a cartoon series, was the name of the celebrated diamond whose theft calls for the intervention of bumbling French Inspector Clouseau (Peter Sellers). Mancini wrote the tune specifically with saxophonist Plas Johnson in mind. Much of the rest of the record is light, often pleasantly romantic, and vaguely European back-ground music (including the whimsical vocal "It Had Better Be Tonight"). An Oscar nominee, the soundtrack won three Grammys (Best Instru-mental Composition, Best Arrangement, and Best Performance), went gold, spent 88 weeks on the charts, and hit the top 10 in the spring of 1964 (the single climbed briefly into the top 40). Mancini scored seven sequels beginning with *A Shot in the Dark* (1964).

HATARI!
RCA Victor 2559-2-R

Mancini may have seemed an offbeat choice for Howard Hawks's African-safari adventure film star-ring John Wayne, but the 1962 score turned out to be one of the composer's best early efforts. The amusing boogie-woogie "Baby Elephant Walk" was an unexpected hit, helping to drive the soundtrack to number 4 on the *Billboard* charts. It includes an ominous title theme, an expanded percussion sec-tion, and a seven-minute rhythm piece scored with many of the exotic instruments Hawks brought back with him from the African shoot.

THE MOLLY MAGUIRES
Bay Cities BCD 3029

This 1970 Martin Ritt film with Sean Connery, Richard Harris, and Samantha Eggar was among the first to conclusively demonstrate that Mancini was a first-rate dramatic composer and not just a writer of light romantic-comedy music. The dark Irish motifs, bittersweet title theme, and gentle love theme ("The Hills of Yesterday") reflect the grim setting and subject: strife among the coal miners of late-19th-century Pennsylvania. The "Pennywhistle Jig" from this score is regularly performed in concert by James Galway.

THE GODFATHER & OTHER MOVIE THEMES
RCA Victor 61478-2

This 1993 reissue is notable for its inclusion of Mancini's symphonic suite from *The White Dawn* (1974), a dramatic score of which he was justifiably proud but which—due to the box office failure of the Philip Kaufman film about turn-of-the-century whalers stranded in the Arctic—didn't get its own soundtrack album. This 12-minute suite is played by the London Symphony Orchestra. Also included: his nostalgic "Beaver Valley Suite" recorded in 1969 with the Philadelphia Orchestra Pops.

10
Warner Bros. WPCR 785

Mancini received dual Oscar nominations for his tuneful score for Blake Edwards's 1979 hit about a middle-aged songwriter (Dudley Moore) who runs out on his wife (Julie Andrews) in pursuit of a free-spirited young beauty (Bo Derek): Best Score and Best Song ("It's Easy to Say," lyrics by Robert Wells). Andrews and Moore duet on the tune, one of several written for the movie. Mancini also conducts an abridged version of Ravel's *Bolero*, which figured prominently in the storyline.

COURTESY OF THE COMPOSER

Mandel, Johnny (1925–)

Best known as one of the finest arrangers of our time, Johnny Mandel made a very big splash as a cinema songwriter and score composer in the '60s and '70s. Although he now eschews the movie grind, preferring to work in the more comfortable medium of records, his impact is still felt.

He was an arranger for TV's classic variety series *Your Show of Shows* in the early '50s before moving to Los Angeles and finding work in the record arena. His first movie, *I Want to Live!* (1958), was groundbreaking for its extensive use of jazz in the score—the boldest yet, after Alex North and Elmer Bernstein's earlier experiments with jazz styles in *A Streetcar Named Desire* and *The Man With the Golden Arm*, respectively.

Mandel had an amazing run of great songs from movies. He wrote "Emily" for *The Americanization of Emily* (1964), "The Shadow of Your Smile" for *The Sandpiper* (1965), "A Time for Love" for *An American Dream* (1966), and "Suicide Is Painless" for *M*A*S*H* (1970), which became the theme for the long-running TV series. He won a Best Song Oscar for "The Shadow of Your Smile," now a standard.

A master of musical colors and textures, he provided memorable orchestral accompaniment to some of the best-remembered films of the past 40 years: *The Russians Are Coming, The Russians Are Coming* (1966), *Harper* (1966), *Point Blank* (1967), *Being There* (1979), *Deathtrap* (1982), and *The Verdict* (1982).

I WANT TO LIVE!

Rykodisc RCD 10743

Robert Wise's gritty and hard-hitting 1958 profile of convicted murderess Barbara Graham earned Susan Hayward a Best Actress Oscar. The film earned five other Oscar nominations, but curiously not one for Mandel—his driving jazz score was probably too daring for Academy voters. Mandel wrote the score along with a separate jazz album for saxophone great Gerry Mulligan (who appeared in the film), and both are contained on this 1999 CD. Playing Mandel's music are some of the top West Coast jazz players of the time.

THE SANDPIPER

Verve 314 531 229-2

Mandel's enchanting score, most critics agreed, was the sole redeeming facet of this Elizabeth Taylor–Richard Burton love story (she was a nonconformist painter, he an Episcopal minister) set against the beauty of the California coastline. As Mandel explained in his liner notes, "I have attempted to capture the sounds of the surf, the grandeur of the mountains, the beauty of the land." Mandel's main theme became, with Paul Francis Webster's lyric, the song "The Shadow of Your Smile." It won the 1965 Best Song Oscar; the album won two Grammys including Song of the Year and Best Original Score. Trumpet solos are by Jack Sheldon.

Moroder, Giorgio (1940–)

Italian-born Giorgio Moroder was one of the architects of the disco sound of the '70s and a top record producer whose synthesizer-driven pop was much in demand for movies in the 1980s and won him three Oscars.

As the producer of such mid-1970s Donna Summer records as the sexy, breathy "Love to Love You Baby" and "I Feel Love," the Munich-based Moroder helped to establish disco as a major force in world music. Director Alan Parker heard these records and asked him to score his fact-based Turkish-prison thriller *Midnight Express*.

The success of *Midnight Express*, which won Moroder his first Oscar, influenced other commercial-minded directors searching for a hip sound: Paul Schrader with *American Gigolo* (1980, which spawned Blondie's number-1 hit "Call Me"); Adrian Lyne with *Foxes* (1980, Summer's number-5 hit "On the Radio"); Schrader's remake of *Cat People* (1982, with David Bowie's song "Putting Out Fire"); and Brian DePalma for *Scarface* (1983).

Most of his later efforts focus more on songs than underscore, including two which won him Best Song Oscars: 1983's *Flashdance*, for Irene Cara's number-1 hit "Flashdance . . . What a Feeling" and 1986's *Top Gun*, for Berlin's number-1 hit "Take My Breath Away." He won Grammys for the *Flashdance* score and love theme; then, in 1984, courted controversy with his color-tinted, rock 'n' roll version of the silent classic *Metropolis* (featuring songs by a range of artists including Freddie Mercury, Pat Benatar, and Loverboy).

MIDNIGHT EXPRESS

Casablanca 824 206-2

Traditional orchestral composers were horrified when Moroder walked off with the 1978 Academy Award for Best Original Score for his catchy, synthesizer-driven score for Alan Parker's gripping tale of an American (Brad Davis) trying to escape from an Istanbul prison. But when his "Chase" (an eight-minute instrumental on the soundtrack album) made *Billboard*'s top 40, and the album was a subsequent Grammy nominee, it was clear that Moroder had connected with moviegoers and record-buyers alike.

AMERICAN GIGOLO
Carousel 561103-3 (U.K.)

Blondie's number-1 hit "Call Me" powered Moroder's soundtrack for Paul Schrader's 1980 film starring Richard Gere and Lauren Hutton. Moroder had already scored the film with his patented brand of synthesizer pop when Blondie lead singer Deborah Harry was signed to write the lyrics and sing the main theme. "Call Me" remained at the top of the charts for six weeks and Blondie received a Grammy nomination for the song.

PHOTO COURTESY OF SUSANNA MOROSS TARJAN

Moross, Jerome (1913–1983)
Brooklyn native Jerome Moross was a boyhood chum of Bernard Herrmann and a member of Aaron Copland's Young Composers Group. As a pianist, he debuted Charles Ives's First Sonata, and his groundbreaking 1938 ballet *Frankie & Johnny* (along with its suggestive choreography) caused a scandal during its run in Paris.

Copland brought Moross to Hollywood to help orchestrate *Our Town* in 1940, and he stayed on, orchestrating such scores as Hugo Friedhofer's Oscar-winning *The Best Years of Our Lives* (1946) and eventually being hired to score films on his own. His quintessential Americana style was heard to best advantage in the sprawling western *The Big Country*, which has inspired dozens of stylistically similar scores for the genre ever since.

Moross himself composed other scores in the same vein, including *The Proud Rebel* (1958), *The Jayhawkers* (1959), and his familiar theme for TV's *Wagon Train*. But he could adapt his style to machinations in the Vatican (*The Cardinal*, 1963) or medieval France (*The War Lord*, 1965), to wartime Cuba (*The Sharkfighters*, 1956) or a lost-world dinosaur tale (*The Valley of Gwangi*, 1969).

He scored fewer than 20 films, preferring musical theater—specifically his groundbreaking musical *The Golden Apple* in 1954—and writing for the concert hall (a symphony, a ballet, and a number of chamber pieces). But it is his film music for which Moross is primarily remembered today.

THE BIG COUNTRY
United Artists UAS 5004 (LP)

Moross's score for William Wyler's sprawling 19th-century saga may be the most famous western music ever written: rich, robust, unforgettable, an anthem to the American West. Much imitated but never equalled, it was Moross's magnum opus and a 1958 Oscar nominee for Best Original Score. Gregory Peck, Charlton Heston, Jean Simmons, and Carroll Baker starred in the film, but it's the grandeur and sweep of Moross's symphonic score that people remember. Rhythmically alive, harmonically simple, and rooted in the language of American folk song, the Moross score is *The Big Country's* outstanding, lasting contribution to American culture.

THE VALLEY OF GWANGI: THE CLASSIC FILM MUSIC OF JEROME MOROSS
Silva SSD 1049

This collection features suites from several unsung Moross scores, including his lighthearted theme and langorous motif for the Mississippi River from *The Adventures of Huckleberry Finn* (1960); the jazz-inflected "Romanza" from *Five Finger Exercise* (1962); his powerful score for *The War Lord* (1965); the Latin-influenced music for the Victor Mature, set-in-Cuba adventure *The Sharkfighters* (1956); his touching "Americana Miniature" from *Rachel, Rachel* (1968); the expansive *The Mountain Road* (1960); and a 19-minute suite from *The Valley of Gwangi* (1969), a strange cowboys-and-dinosaurs film with Ray Harryhausen monsters that's a favorite among fantasy fans. Paul Bateman conducts the City of Prague Philharmonic.

THE CARDINAL
Preamble PRCD 1778

Otto Preminger made this 1963 epic with Tom Tryon as a Boston priest who rises through the Church hierarchy to the College of Cardinals. Moross provided one of his most impressive scores, employing modal chord progressions suggestive of the Church as well as deeply emotional music reflecting the conflicts of the central character. A Viennese-style waltz represents Tryon's love interest, whom he meets in the Austrian capital.

THE WAR LORD
Varèse Sarabande VSD-5536

Director Franklin J. Schaffner sought to make an intimate epic of Leslie Stevens's play *The Lovers*, about an 11th-century knight (Charlton Heston) who takes a village girl (Rosemary Forsyth) as his mate and the unhappy consequences. A noble main theme, a tender love theme, and clever suggestions of the medieval period throughout distinguish this 1965 score (augmented by music composed by Hans J. Salter when time ran out during a truncated scoring period).

FROM AUTHOR'S COLLECTION

Morricone, Ennio (1928–)

Prolific Italian composer Ennio Morricone first came to worldwide prominence as a result of his collaboration with director Sergio Leone on a trilogy of Clint Eastwood movies in the mid-1960s: *A Fistful of Dollars*, *For a Few Dollars More*, and *The Good, the Bad, and the Ugly*. His unique approach to those now-classic westerns—including offbeat vocal effects and orchestrations that ranged from the traditionally symphonic to the bizarre—launched a career that has few, if any, parallels in the history of movie music.

Classically trained and one of the rare film composers to insist upon orchestrating all of his own music, he began writing for films in 1961 and quickly gained the attention of other notable European filmmakers, including Elio Petri (*Investigation of a Citizen Above Suspicion*, 1969); Gillo Pontecorvo (*The Battle of Algiers*, 1965); Henri Verneuil (*The Burglars*, 1971); and Bernardo Bertolucci (*1900*, 1976). Many of his scores, particularly those written in the '60s and '70s, were remarkable for their inventiveness and color.

Morricone became a favorite of soundtrack aficionados long before he began to be fully appreciated by American filmmakers for his melodic and dramatic gifts. It's also difficult to understand his paucity of Oscar nominations—just four to date, for Terrence Malick's *Days of Heaven* (1978), Roland Joffe's *The Mission* (1986), Brian DePalma's *The Untouchables* (1987), and Warren Beatty's *Bugsy* (1991). By comparison, he has won five British Academy Awards for *Days of Heaven*, *Once Upon a Time in America* (1984), *The Mission*, *The Untouchables*, and *Cinema Paradiso* (1988), and Golden Globes for *The Mission* and *The Legend of 1900* (1999).

In addition to his estimated 350 motion picture scores, he has written equally memorable music for such acclaimed TV miniseries as *Moses the Lawgiver* and *Marco Polo* and continues to write and perform music for the concert hall.

THE ENNIO MORRICONE ANTHOLOGY:
A FISTFUL OF FILM MUSIC
Rhino R2 71858 / DRC2-1237

This two-CD set is an ideal introduction to more than a quarter-century of Morricone scores. Beginning with the spaghetti westerns of the '60s and running through his Oscar-nominated theme for Warren Beatty's *Bugsy* (1991), this 147-minute

collection of themes and cues is a nice sampler. Among its hard-to-find highlights: the main title from *Uccellacci e Uccellini* (1965, in which all the film's credits are sung); the war march from *The Battle of Algiers* (1965); the strange chimes and nursery-rhyme vocalise of *The Bird With the Crystal Plumage* (1969); Joan Baez's evocative vocals from *Sacco & Vanzetti* (1971); Morricone's reverent, choral theme for Burt Lancaster as *Moses* (1974), and the rock-oriented "Magic and Ecstasy" from *Exorcist II: The Heretic* (1977).

ENNIO MORRICONE: MAIN TITLES;
THE SINGLES COLLECTION
DRG 32920, 32921

Because Morricone has been so prolific, even diehard soundtrack collectors face an impossible task trying to track down every old LP and 45 the maestro released over the years. For this pair of two two-CD sets, DRG collected dozens of themes that offer a kaleidoscopic view of Morricone music from three decades of European movies, many of which never made it to America.

"Main Titles" collects themes from 1965 to 1995, including some of his most haunting melodies: *La Califfa* (1970), *Gott Mit Uns* (1970), the elegant "Chi Mai" from *Maddalena* (1971), *Questa Specie D'Amore* (1972), *La Banchiera* (1980), "Le vent, le cri" from *Joss, Il Professionista* (1981), *Le Marginal* (1982), and *La Venexiana* (1986).

"The Singles Collection," drawn from 1969 to 1981, contains even harder to find music because many of these were released only on 45 rpm discs; in all, there are 47 pieces from 25 movies, again mostly unfamiliar titles distinguished by their Morricone scores. The most memorable include *L'Assoluto Naturale* (1969), the sensuous *Metti Una Sera a Cena* (1969), *Forza G* (1971), four cuts from the bizarre *Four Flies on Grey Velvet* (1971), *La Cosa*

Buffa (1973), the exquisite *La Grande Bourgeoisie* (1974), "Francesca's Theme" from *La Moglie Piu Bella* (1978), *Cosi Come Sei* (1978), and *Il Giocattolo* (1979).

ENNIO MORRICONE: THE LEGENDARY ITALIAN WESTERNS
RCA Victor 9974-2-R

Morricone's music for the first two films of Sergio Leone's "Dollars" trilogy—*A Fistful of Dollars* (1964) and *For a Few Dollars More* (1965)—are the main focus of this single-disc collection of music from nine of the composer's '60s westerns. Also included are four key tracks from a subsequent Leone film, *Once Upon a Time in the West* (1969) and samplings from six other, far more obscure, Italian westerns (with titles like *Guns Don't Argue* and *Death Rides a Horse*). This is the music that first attracted millions of Morricone fans: warm melodies, inventive orchestrations, wordless vocals, strong rhythmic content. The *Dollars* trilogy catapulted Clint Eastwood—then a laconic, second-billed actor in an American TV series—into international stardom, but the intensely visual style of Leone's filmmaking coupled with Morricone's indelible musical contributions can't be discounted as crucial factors in that leap.

AN ENNIO MORRICONE WESTERN QUINTET
DRG 32907

This two-CD collection of obscure but tuneful Italian westerns includes a certified Morricone masterpiece, Sergio Leone's 1971 *Duck, You Sucker* (also known as *A Fistful of Dynamite*), the moving tale of a Mexican peasant (Rod Steiger) and an Irish terrorist (James Coburn) who team up during the Mexican Revolution; and the fun music for the Leone-produced *My Name Is Nobody* (1973), which starred Henry Fonda and Terence Hill. Also

included: *Tepepa* (*Blood and Guns*, 1968), *Vamos a Matar Companeros* (1970), and *Occhio alla penna* (*A Fist Goes West*, 1981).

THE GOOD, THE BAD AND THE UGLY
EMI-Manhattan CDP 7-48408-2

Hugo Montenegro's homogenized version of this title theme went to number 2 on the *Billboard* charts, but Morricone's original soundtrack from Sergio Leone's 1966 western classic is far more compelling. Eastwood (in his third outing as The Man With No Name), Lee Van Cleef, and Eli Wallach starred in this epic treasure hunt set against a Civil War backdrop. Morricone's music, for full orchestra, choir, and various instrumental soloists, was a revelation for its boldness and thematic content.

ONCE UPON A TIME IN THE WEST
RCA Victor 4736-2-R

Morricone's fourth collaboration with Leone (1969) was for, some believe, the filmmaker's masterpiece: an operatic tale of mystery, revenge, and struggle for power set against the coming of the railroad to a small town in the American west, with Henry Fonda, Charles Bronson, Claudia Cardinale, and Jason Robards. As he had done on *The Good, the Bad and the Ugly*, Morricone composed most of his essential material prior to shooting: the lush, beautiful title theme (again featuring soprano Edda Dell'Orso and choir), the strangely off-key harmonica (on which the entire Bronson plot turns), the savage sound of electric guitar for Fonda's sadistic killer, and more.

ONCE UPON A TIME IN AMERICA
Restless 74321619762

Long unavailable in America, this final score in the legendary Leone-Morricone collaboration was as rich and dramatic as ever. The film, a complex exploration of (in Leone's words) "friendship, time, memory, hate and love," moves back and forth between the '20s, '30s, and '60s in the lives of a gang of Jewish toughs from Brooklyn (among them Robert DeNiro and James Woods). Morricone's melancholy main theme, his evocative "Poverty" and gentle motif for Deborah (Elizabeth McGovern) should have guaranteed him a 1984 Oscar nomination—but someone at the studio forgot to enter him in the competition. He did, however, win a British Academy Award and Best Score honors from the Los Angeles Film Critics Association. Famed pan-flutist Gheorghe Zamfir performs; vocals are by Edda Dell'Orso.

THE MISSION
Virgin 90567-2

Morricone's failure to win the 1986 Oscar for this widely praised orchestral and choral work stunned the Hollywood film-music community (although he won a Golden Globe and a British Academy Award for the score). Roland Joffe's sumptuously photographed historical drama written by Robert Bolt, about an 18th-century mission in South America, elicited one of the composer's finest works, combining European religious influences; indigenous flutes, drums, and chants from the region; and woodwind solos inspired by one character's on-screen oboe playing. Robert DeNiro and Jeremy Irons starred in the film.

THE UNTOUCHABLES
A&M CD 3909/DX 1678

Morricone's music for Brian DePalma's 1987 feature version of the old TV series (this one starring Kevin Costner, as Eliot Ness, and Sean Connery, who won an Oscar) features a heroic brass fanfare for the G-men, a sassy '20s-style motif for Al Capone (Robert DeNiro), a lyrical piece for Ness's family, and a com-plex, staccato-rhythm main theme that is reminiscent of Morricone's Italian crime dramas of the '70s. An Oscar nominee, this score won both the Grammy and a British Film Academy Award.

CINEMA PARADISO
DRG CDSLB 12598

Few films have illuminated a passion for movies and moviemaking quite as lovingly as Giuseppe Tornatore's *Nuovo Cinema Paradiso*, which won the 1989 Best Foreign Film Oscar. It's become a favorite of filmgoers worldwide, as has Morricone's nostalgic and moving score, played by a chamber-sized ensemble. The composer's son Andrea wrote the film's love theme, which achieved equal fame with the elder Morricone's primary melody. Ennio and Andrea Morricone shared a British Academy Award for this score.

Morris, John (1926–)

Composer John Morris and director Mel Brooks met in 1956 when both were called in to help save a Broadway show. Eleven years later, Brooks called Morris to arrange a dance number based on a bizarre tune he had written for his first film, *The Producers*.

The song was the satirical "Springtime for Hitler," and that call began a 20-year collaboration that produced several comic masterpieces, including *Blazing Saddles* (1973)—Brooks's western sendup, featuring an Oscar-nominated title song with Morris music and Brooks lyrics, sung by western veteran Frankie Laine—and *Young Frankenstein* (1974), in which Morris successfully parodied the sound of the classic Universal horror films of the 1930s, coupled with his own exquisite, heartbreaking theme for the monster.

For *Silent Movie* (1976), Morris was presented

with a unique challenge: wall-to-wall music for a contemporary film without dialogue. And on *High Anxiety* (1977), Brooks's Hitchcock sendup, Morris provided appropriately Bernard Herrmann-esque music. A notable dramatic composer apart from Brooks, Morris received a second Oscar nomination for his sensitive music for *The Elephant Man* (1980) and has scored such diverse fare as *Ironweed* (1987) and the eight-hour TV miniseries *Scarlett* (1994).

YOUNG FRANKENSTEIN

One Way MCAD-22192

Possibly Morris's single greatest score for Mel Brooks, this 1974 work is also his best remembered. From his beautiful solo-violin lullaby for the monster to Marty Feldman's on-screen French horn solo, it works brilliantly on two levels: first as a parody of the old Universal horror-film scores, second as perfectly effective dramatic scoring on its own. The album mixes Morris's score with dialogue and the top-hat-and-tails "Puttin' on the Ritz" number performed by Gene Wilder and Peter Boyle.

THE ELEPHANT MAN

Milan 35665-2

David Lynch's 1980 film about John Merrick, the so-called "Elephant Man" of Victorian England, and Frederick Treves, the surgeon who found and cared for him, benefits from Morris's Oscar-and Grammy-nominated score. By turns dramatic and moving, it helps to establish both the anguish suffered by the deformed man and the compassion felt for him by Treves, and creates the carnival atmosphere via a bizarrely orchestrated waltz theme. Lynch utilized Barber's *Adagio for Strings*, which is also on the album in a performance by André Previn and the London Symphony Orchestra.

PHOTO COURTESY OF THE USC CINEMA-TELEVISION LIBRARY

Newman, Alfred (1900–1970)

Alfred Newman came to Hollywood in 1930 from a stellar career as a musical director on Broadway, where he befriended such talents as Richard Rodgers, George Gershwin, and Jerome Kern. His first original score, for *Street Scene* (1931), contained an urban-jazz theme that went on to be used in many subsequent films. In 1933 he wrote the 20th Century–Fox fanfare (then, for 20th Century Pictures) which has become the most famous of all studio musical signatures. He spent most of the '30s working for Samuel Goldwyn; in late 1939 he began a 20-year stint as musical director for Fox under Darryl F. Zanuck.

Widely considered the finest conductor in the history of American films, Newman accumulated 45 Academy Award nominations—second only to Walt Disney in number—and won nine Oscars, mostly for musicals that he arranged and supervised, such as *Tin Pan Alley* (1940), *The King and I* (1956), and *Camelot* (1967). The Oscar-winning *The Song of Bernadette* (1943) was one of several inspiring Newman scores on religious themes; others included *The Robe* (1953) and the all-star *Greatest Story Ever Told* (1965).

Newman ranks with Max Steiner and Erich Wolfgang Korngold as one of the three great pioneers of American film music, albeit the only one who was actually born in the U.S. He wrote more than 250 scores, including masterpieces in every genre: adventure (*The Prisoner of Zenda*, 1937; *Gunga Din*, 1939), romance (*Wuthering Heights*, 1939), historical drama (*The Hunchback of Notre Dame*, 1939; *Captain From Castile*, 1947), western (*How the West Was Won*, 1962), contemporary drama (*All About Eve*, 1950; *Airport*, 1970).

Newman founded an entire dynasty of film composers. His brothers Emil and Lionel were top studio conductors and sometime composers; Alfred's sons David and Thomas, and nephew Randy, all followed him into the film-scoring profession.

CAPTAIN FROM CASTILE: THE CLASSIC FILM SCORES OF ALFRED NEWMAN
RCA Victor 0184-2-RG

Originally released on LP in 1973, this album was part of the "Classic Film Scores" series that introduced thousands of record buyers to the best of American movie music. Many Newman classics are here, including suites from *Captain From Castile* (1947), the Oscar-winning *Song of Bernadette* (1943), and *The Robe* (1953). The Fox fanfare and the concert version of "Street Scene" (from *How to Marry a Millionaire*, 1953) open the album. Also in this collection: *Wuthering Heights* (1939), *Down to the Sea in Ships* (1949), *The Bravados* (1958), *Anastasia* (1956), *The Best of Everything* (1959), and *Airport* (1970). Charles Gerhardt conducts the National Philharmonic Orchestra.

THE CLASSIC FILM MUSIC OF ALFRED NEWMAN
Marco Polo 8.223570

Veteran film-score reconstructionists John W.

Morgan and William Stromberg mounted their first all-Newman album in 1997, highlighted by nearly 39 minutes of *The Hunchback of Notre Dame* (1939) with its haunting string passages and powerful choral work. Also featured: more than 20 minutes of the heroic *Beau Geste* (1939) plus a brief suite from Newman's film classic *All About Eve* (1950). Stromberg conducts the Moscow Symphony Orchestra and Chorus.

WUTHERING HEIGHTS: A TRIBUTE TO ALFRED NEWMAN
Koch 3-7376-2 H1

The resurgence of interest in Newman led to this 1997 collection of themes and suites from six films, led by the lushly romantic *Wuthering Heights* (1939) and the swashbuckling *Prisoner of Zenda* (1937). Music from three of his most colorful period films for 20th Century–Fox—*Prince of Foxes* (1949), *David and Bathsheba* (1951), and *Dragonwyck* (1946)—plus the march from *Brigham Young* (1940) round out the album. Richard Kaufman conducts the New Zealand Symphony Orchestra and New Zealand Youth Choir.

HOW GREEN WAS MY VALLEY
Fox 11008-2

Life in the Welsh coal mines of the late 19th century was the subject of this acclaimed, Oscar-winning 1941 film from director John Ford. Walter Pidgeon, Maureen O'Hara, and Donald Crisp starred in this warm family story, and it was Newman's music—filled with authentic Welsh melodies and brimming with male-choir gusto—that provided an appropriate sentimental touch. These are the original film tracks, restored for release in 1993.

THE SONG OF BERNADETTE

Varèse Sarabande VSD-2-6025

Of Newman's nine Academy Awards, the only one earned for a score he conceived and wrote from beginning to end was the Oscar for this 1943 Fox film. (The others were for his work on musicals, and one, *Love Is a Many-Splendored Thing*, is partially based on a title song he didn't write.) *Bernadette* told the story of the 19th-century origins of Lourdes as a Catholic shrine; Newman's reverent and powerful orchestral-and-choral score invested it with an undeniable spirituality that even Oscar-winning Jennifer Jones, in the title role, couldn't convey. This two-CD set restores the entire original score.

ALL ABOUT EVE / LEAVE HER TO HEAVEN

FSM Vol. 2, No. 7

Two of Newman's most dynamic scores are coupled on this newly issued disc. *All About Eve* won six 1950 Academy Awards including Best Picture; Joseph L. Mankiewicz's crisply written story of backstage backstabbing starred Bette Davis, Anne Baxter, George Sanders, and Celeste Holm.

Newman's score features a memorable fanfare and thoughtful thematic material for each of the three female leads. *Leave Her to Heaven* won Gene Tierney a 1945 Best Actress nomination for her performance as a disturbed woman driven to murder. Newman's score was among his darkest and most dramatic.

THE ROBE

Fox 11011-2

Newman's magnificent choral and orchestral score for this, the first Cinemascope film, ranks with *The Song of Bernadette* and *The Greatest Story Ever Told* as one of his finest scores of a religious nature. Richard Burton and Jean Simmons starred in the 1953 tale of a tormented Roman tribune who supervised the crucifixion of Jesus. Newman's failure even to be nominated for a Oscar caused a scandal in the Academy's music branch at the time; this 1993 disc marked the initial release of Newman's actual film tracks.

ANASTASIA

Varèse Sarabande VSD-5422

Ingrid Bergman won her second Academy Award for her portrayal of a woman who may be the last surviving daughter of Czar Nicholas II. Newman's Oscar-nominated score for the 1956 film was one of his last great efforts at 20th Century–Fox, from the passionate, Russian-flavored theme—mirroring, in his words, the "moody uneasiness" of Bergman's performance—to his colorful locale pieces suggesting Paris and Russian Easter services.

HOW THE WEST WAS WON

Rhino R2 72458

One of the last of the Cinerama epics, this sprawling 1962 western sported a rousing Newman score that interpolates many traditional folk tunes including

"Shenandoah" and "When Johnny Comes Marching Home." This two-CD set not only features all of Newman's Oscar-nominated score and the many choral tunes adapted by Newman's longtime associate Ken Darby but also a number of cues that were cut from the final version of the film.

THE GREATEST STORY EVER TOLD

Rykodisc RCD 10734

For his grandiose retelling of the life of Christ, director George Stevens elicited from Newman a reverent orchestral score incorporating choral elements. Unfortunately, Stevens's 1965 film was a turgid, all-star bore (with Max von Sydow as Jesus), and the director tortured the composer for two years, demanding endless score rewrites and ultimately discarding Newman's original choruses in favor of the overexposed Handel *Messiah*. This three-CD set includes the original 1965 LP re-recording as well as the complete, Oscar-nominated film score (including the previously unheard "Alleluias").

AIRPORT

Varèse Sarabande VSD-5436

Newman's score for the first of the '70s disaster films (based on the Arthur Hailey novel) was his last, receiving a posthumous Oscar nomination. Burt Lancaster and Dean Martin headed the all-star cast, propelled by a main theme as powerful as any in Newman's long career. The love theme features a fine, old-fashioned trombone solo. Because Newman was quite ill at the time, this 1970 re-recording was produced by Newman's longtime associate Ken Darby and conducted primarily by Universal music chief Stanley Wilson.

Newman, David (1953–)

Two of Alfred Newman's sons became film com-

posers. Both are superb and much in demand, and their styles are completely different. David Newman, educated at the University of Southern California and a talented violinist as well as a first-rate conductor, seems to prefer traditional orchestral writing.

Starting in low-budget pictures like *Critters* (1985), David Newman quickly linked up with actor-director Danny DeVito for *Throw Momma From the Train* (1987) and became his primary composer, writing such subsequent scores as the darkly comic *The War of the Roses* (1989), the quietly powerful *Hoffa* (1992), and the gamboling *Matilda* (1996).

Newman has found himself much in demand for comedy. He wrote a raucous score for *The Flintstones* (1994), a triumphant one for *The Mighty Ducks* (1992), an unexpectedly charming one for *The Nutty Professor* (1996), and a surprisingly dramatic one for *Bill & Ted's Excellent Adventure* (1989).

Beginning in 1987, Newman also spent four years as music director for Robert Redford's Sundance Institute, conducting film-music concerts around the world. He was the first composer commissioned by the Los Angeles Philharmonic's Filmharmonic program to create an original concert piece; his "1,001 Arabian Nights" debuted in 1998.

HOFFA

Fox 11001-2

One of Newman's most difficult assignments, Danny DeVito's 1992 biopic of the complex, controversial labor leader demanded a score that balanced the heroic with the darker side of the life of Jimmy Hoffa (played by Jack Nicholson). Newman found a sound of restrained heroism, offering a human element to the familiar and mostly grim facts of Hoffa's life. Interestingly, Newman's music for the film's trailer has turned up in an estimated 200 trailers for other movies in recent years.

THE PHANTOM

Milan 73138 35756-2

One of Newman's finest scores, this exciting orchestral romp, with occasional choral elements, propelled a 1996 superhero adventure that no one wanted to see: Billy Zane as Lee Falk's legendary masked, Africa-based "ghost who walks." A hero's fanfare, solid action music, a love theme for piano and orchestra, this is best described as a strong score for a weak film.

ANASTASIA

Atlantic 83053-2

David Newman's long-overdue first Oscar nomination came for this animated Fox film released in 1997. (His father scored the original Ingrid Bergman *Anastasia* some 40 years earlier at the same studio.) The new score captures the flavor of the film's turn-of-the-century St. Petersburg setting, with Russian choir, cold-weather sleighbells, and similar colors; the finale is as joyous and evocative as any animated musical in years. Lynn Ahrens and Stephen Flaherty wrote the songs.

Newman, Randy (1943–)

The average pop-music fan who admires the witty songs and offbeat voice of Randy Newman may not realize that this oldest of the Newman composers—and there are now several of that generation active in Hollywood—is an accomplished writer of symphonic music with strong Americana leanings.

Renowned for his brilliance as a songwriter and musical satirist, Randy Newman came to prominence in that realm in the late 1960s and early '70s. The son of a Beverly Hills physician, he often hung around the 20th Century–Fox stage where his uncles Alfred, Lionel, and Emil Newman were working as composers and conductors. His unique abilities in the pop field resulted in such song classics as "I Think It's Going to Rain Today," "Davy the Fat Boy," "Short People," and "I Love L.A."

He scored his first film (the comedy *Cold Turkey*) in 1971, and by the end of 1999 he had scored just 14 movies—but received 13 Academy Award nominations (for Best Score, Best Song, or both). Among them: an evocative turn-of-the-century score for *Ragtime* (1981), the heroic Americana of *The Natural* (1984), the nostalgic reverie of *Avalon* (1990), the emotional resonance of *Pleasantville* (1998), and a song so popular that it's already ingrained in the American consciousness: "I Love to See You Smile" from *Parenthood* (1989).

Newman established a proficiency with music for animation in his Oscar-nominated *Toy Story* (1995) that led to further assignments including *James and the Giant Peach* (1996) and *A Bug's Life* (1998)—light, amusing confections for youngsters that display a very different musical side of the normally acid-tongued, cynical songwriter.

THE NATURAL

Warner Bros. 25116-2

With only his third feature-film score, Newman crafted an instant classic and a highly influential score. He provided an Americana ambiance to Barry Levinson's 1984 film about a legendary baseball player (Robert Redford); his music for the climactic game made the whole movie work. With orchestrations by veteran Jack Hayes (who orchestrated for Randy's uncle, Alfred Newman), this score was nominated for an Oscar. It lost at the Academy Awards, but Newman picked up a Grammy for Best Instrumental Composition.

PARENTHOOD
Reprise 26001-2

Ron Howard's 1989 comedy-drama about child-rearing and family starred Steve Martin and Mary Steenburgen. Newman's easygoing song "I Love to See You Smile" not only summed up the movie but received Oscar and Grammy nominations and became, he later admitted, "the most lucrative song I ever wrote." The score is consistently light and fun, with occasional classical leanings and a good deal of Newman's patented Americana sound.

AVALON
Reprise 26437-2

One of Newman's most restrained, lilting, and melancholy scores, this Oscar-nominated music ranks with his best work. Written for Barry Levinson's 1990 chronicle of the assimilation of a family of Eastern European Jews into life in early 20th-century Baltimore, it features a recurring use of solo piano (some played by Newman himself) and solo violin.

MAVERICK
Reprise 45816-2

Newman's music for the lighthearted 1994 Mel Gibson–Jodie Foster western (based on the classic James Garner TV series) holds the movie together and punctuates many of its comic moments. Despite Newman's public complaints about director Richard Donner, he managed to write a bold score with a rambunctious western sound, a lovely theme for Annabelle, wild chase music, funny saloon tunes (with Newman vocals), and very little subtlety.

TOY STORY
A BUG'S LIFE
Walt Disney Records 60883-7, 60634-7

Two of Newman's most lively and fun scores accompanied these wildly popular, computer-animated Pixar productions. Both were Oscar-nominated: *Toy Story* (1995), for Best Comedy Score and Best Song ("You've Got a Friend in Me," one of three songs that Newman wrote and sang for the adventures of Woody and Buzz Lightyear), and *A Bug's Life* (1998), for Best Comedy Score. Both orchestral scores are big and brassy, with *Bug's Life* having a slight edge as a listening experience because of its broad Americana outlines.

Newman, Thomas (1955–)

Thomas Newman didn't start out to be a film composer. The youngest son of the legendary Alfred Newman, he studied music at Yale but played in a rock band and dabbled in musical theater. A call from a friend to work on the alienated-youth film *Reckless* (1984) led to scoring the picture and inadvertently launching a career.

Every Newman has an individual sound. Thomas Newman's hallmark is experimentation with unusual sonorities, often integrating electronic music with traditional acoustic instruments. Classically trained, he can and often does write stunningly for the orchestra—but scores like his Oscar-nominated *Unstrung Heroes* (1995) and parts of his *Horse Whisperer* (1998) demonstrate his nontraditional thinking.

In the business for just 15 years, he has already amassed credits on approximately 50 films. Many of his '80s movies are forgettable youth-oriented films (*Revenge of the Nerds*, *Real Genius*, etc.), but in the '90s he became much in demand for his more mature style.

Already a multiple Oscar nominee (including two in one year, for 1994's very different *The Shawshank Redemption* and *Little Women*), Newman's music also accompanied such talked-about films as Al Pacino's Oscar-winning turn in *Scent of a Woman* (1992), the Robert Redford–Michelle Pfeiffer romance *Up Close and Personal* (1996), and the three-hour Tom Hanks prison tale *The Green Mile* (1999).

FRIED GREEN TOMATOES
MCA MCAD-10634

Newman's music for this gentle 1991 comedy-drama based on Fannie Flagg's novel about the unlikely friendship between two very different women (Mary Stuart Masterson, Mary-Louise Parker) is both supportive and evocative. He suggests a gospel flavor with wordless vocals by Marion Williams, adds some delightful down-home pickin' on guitars and mandolins, and supports it all with warm orchestral sounds often featuring solo work from the woodwind section (notably flute, clarinet, and oboe).

THE PLAYER
Varèse Sarabande VSD-5366

Robert Altman's exceedingly clever 1992 exposé of the cutthroat nature of the movie business brought out Newman's experimental side. This strange and magical score—which often seems improvised but isn't—includes offbeat percussion, wild jazz, elec-

tronic textures, cocktail piano, and lots of truly weird sampled sounds. It's one of Newman's most creative scores and, in a nod to old-fashioned Hollywood, ends with everything the rest of the score is not: a big, traditional orchestral finish.

THE SHAWSHANK REDEMPTION
Epic EK 66621
LITTLE WOMEN
Sony Classical SK 66922

Newman received his first two Oscar nominations in the same year (1994), for these two fine, very different, films. The downbeat nature of the Tim Robbins–Morgan Freeman prison drama *Shawshank Redemption* demanded a frequently dark approach for orchestra, piano with synths, and subtle combinations of both. The Robin Colcord–Gillian Anderson adaptation of *Little Women* with Winona Ryder and Claire Danes called for a brighter, often pastoral and intimate sound suggesting 19th-century America.

THE HORSE WHISPERER
Hollywood HR-62137-2

Robert Redford's 1998 film of this popular Nicholas Evans novel didn't please many critics, but its romantic sensibility and wide-open-sky vistas inspired one of Newman's best scores. A blend of country sounds (guitar, mandolin, dulcimer, fiddle, steel guitar) and big orchestral Americana, this music was fully supportive of the drama in an often subtle, textural way. It is a beautiful, memorable score—some say the finest Americana score in years—that should have won an Oscar but was not even nominated.

AMERICAN BEAUTY
DreamWorks 0044-50233-2

Speaking about the unusual, largely percussion-based score of the Oscar-winning Best Picture of 1999, Newman said that director Sam Mendes "wanted things that hammered and thwacked a bit. . . . He was interested in percussion and mallet instruments," and the propulsive nature of that music helped move along this darkly comic tale of suburbia and one man's midlife crisis. The composer's haunting piano motif (the "American Beauty" theme) stayed with viewers long after they left the theater. Newman received his fourth Oscar nomination for this film and won the British Academy Award.

PHOTO FROM THE TONY THOMAS COLLECTION

North, Alex (1910–1991)

One of the most respected voices in modern film music, Alex North came to Hollywood from a background that included friendship with Aaron Copland, ballet commissions from Martha Graham and Agnes de Mille, Broadway scores, and music studies in both New York and Moscow.

Elia Kazan, who had worked with North in the New York theater, was responsible for his first feature-film assignment, an adaptation of Tennessee Williams's play *A Streetcar Named Desire* (1951); it caused a stir as the first major score to rely heavily on jazz influences. The same year, he scored the film version of *Death of a Salesman*. Within a few months, he had two of the five Academy Award nominations for Best Dramatic Score. North was an immediate success in his new field.

His scores for historical epics—*Spartacus* (1960), *Cleopatra* (1963), *The Agony and the Ecstasy* (1965)—demonstrate remarkable depth and complexity compared to similar efforts by other composers in the same era. He scored five films for John Huston, including *The Misfits* (1961) and a clever use of Italian opera in *Prizzi's Honor* (1985).

Fifteen of North's scores were nominated for Oscars, including such memorable work as the Italian folk themes of *The Rose Tattoo* (1955), the quasi-baroque approach to *Who's Afraid of Virginia Woolf?* (1966), and the compelling dissonance of *Dragonslayer* (1981). None won. The Academy of Motion Picture Arts & Sciences rectified its oversight in 1986 by awarding him an honorary Oscar (the first ever given to a composer) "in recognition of his brilliant artistry in the creation of memorable music for a host of distinguished motion pictures."

A STREETCAR NAMED DESIRE
Capitol CDP 95597 2 5
Varèse Sarabande VSD-5500

North's 1951 *Streetcar* was a landmark in American film music for its original use of jazz in a traditional symphonic context—sometimes simmering, sometimes bluesy, sometimes screaming, for the Elia Kazan film of Tennessee Williams's play, with Vivien Leigh as the neurotic Blanche Dubois and Marlon Brando as the brutish Stanley Kowalski. The New Orleans setting suggested the concept, and North received an Oscar nomination for his very first Hollywood score (along with a second, for his *Death of a Salesman*, also 1951 and also based on a popular New York play). Ray Heindorf, who conducted the original score, conducts 29 minutes of the music on the Capitol album (a reissue of an early 1950s recording); Jerry Goldsmith conducts the National Philharmonic Orchestra in the 47-minute re-recording of 1995.

VIVA ZAPATA!
Varèse Sarabande VSD-5900

Talk about impeccable credentials: John Steinbeck writes, Elia Kazan directs, and Marlon Brando plays Mexican revolutionary Emiliano Zapata. Kazan again insisted upon North as his composer for the 1952 film. A resident of Mexico in the 1930s and a visitor to Kazan's Texas shooting locations, North interpolated traditional Mexican folk tunes and rhythms throughout the score, creating what may be the most authentically Mexican film score ever written by an American. Jerry Goldsmith conducts the Royal Scottish National Orchestra in this 1997 re-recording.

THE FILM MUSIC OF ALEX NORTH
Nonesuch 79446-2

Five of North's greatest scores are excerpted on this 1997 collection of new recordings: suites from his jazzy score for *A Streetcar Named Desire* (1951), his ancient-Roman epic *Spartacus* (1960), and the alternately touching and terrifying *The Bad Seed* (1956); and single themes each from *The Misfits* (1961) and *Viva Zapata!* (1952). Eric Stern conducts the London Symphony Orchestra.

SPARTACUS
MCA MCAD-10256

One of the all-time great epics—as much for its thoughtful Dalton Trumbo script as for its grand cinematic scope courtesy of director Stanley

Kubrick—this 1960 film also boasts one of North's finest scores. From its martial, barbaric opening through its melodic love theme for Spartacus and Varinia (Kirk Douglas, Jean Simmons) and his balletic army-training sequence, this music suggests the oppressive atmosphere and human needs that fired the slave rebellion of 73–71 B.C. North worked on this score for 13 months and received another Oscar nomination.

THE MISFITS
Rykodisc RCD 10735

This 1961 film, written by Arthur Miller and directed by John Huston, marked the final film appearances of both Clark Gable and Marilyn Monroe and one of the last of Montgomery Clift. The story of contemporary cowboys and the woman who enthralls them called for a score that combined classical, jazz, and dance-band influences. A highlight is his 15-minute "round-up suite," a modernistic ballet for the pursuit and capture of wild mustangs in the film's climax.

CLEOPATRA
20ᵗʰ Century–Fox SXG-5008 (LP)

North visited Rome during the shooting of Joseph L. Mankiewicz's trouble-plagued, $40-million production and researched music of ancient times. Even his thoughtful, surprisingly intimate music for Cleopatra (Elizabeth Taylor), Marc Antony (Richard Burton), and Caesar (Rex Harrison) couldn't save the four-hour film, but North was rewarded with 1963 Oscar and Grammy nominations. His soundtrack not only spent half a year on the charts but was also the country's number-2 album for three weeks.

CHEYENNE AUTUMN
Label X LXCD 4

Certainly the most introspective music ever written for a John Ford western, this elegiac 1964 score was sadly unappreciated and unreleased at the time of the film; it was released in a limited edition nearly 20 years later. Ford's film, stunningly photographed in his beloved Monument Valley, tells the tragic story of a Cheyenne Indian tribe's attempt to return to its Dakota homeland. North subtly interpolates hints of Native American music without resorting to old-fashioned cowboy-and-Indian musical clichés.

THE AGONY AND THE ECSTASY

Varèse Sarabande VSD-5901

Michelangelo versus Pope Julius II over the 16th-century painting of the Sistine Chapel ceiling: Irving Stone's book was ripe for epic film treatment, and Charlton Heston and Rex Harrison obliged under the direction of Carol Reed. North provided a modal score of richness and grandeur, suggestive of the Renaissance but also accessible to modern movie audiences. He received a 1965 Oscar nomination. Jerry Goldsmith conducts the Royal Scottish National Orchestra in this 1997 re-recording.

WHO'S AFRAID OF VIRGINIA WOOLF?

Varèse Sarabande VSD-5800

Mike Nichols's 1966 film of Edward Albee's shattering play, a landmark film for its adult language and themes, received five Oscars and eight more nominations including Best Picture and Best Original Score. Initially stymied as to a musical approach for the verbal battles of two couples (Richard Burton and Elizabeth Taylor, George Segal and Sandy Dennis), North decided on a "quasi-baroque feeling" that played against the vitriol: sometimes gentle, sometimes dissonant. Jerry Goldsmith conducts the National Philharmonic Orchestra in a 1997 re-recording.

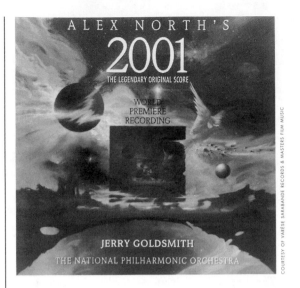

2001: A SPACE ODYSSEY

Varèse Sarabande VSD-5400

It's probably the most famous score that nobody ever heard (until this 1993 re-recording; in fact, the album is called "Alex North's 2001: The Legendary Original Score"). Stanley Kubrick hired North to score his 1968 science-fiction film, then decided to use his own "temporary" score consisting entirely of classical excerpts. The highly respected North constructed a complex, often powerful score that later found its way, in part, into the composer's music for *Africa* and *Dragonslayer*. But, as a score that aficionados had wondered about for decades, it's a fascinating listen. Jerry Goldsmith conducts the National Philharmonic Orchestra.

Nyman, Michael (1944–)

The composer of *The Piano* is something of a controversial figure in Hollywood—his failure to be nominated for the popular music that was such a crucial component of Jane Campion's 1993 film was a cause célèbre among music fans.

The London-born composer spent much of the '60s and '70s writing about music, coining the term "minimalism" and penning a widely read 1974 book, *Experimental Music: Cage and Beyond*. His own music began receiving public performances two years later, and film commissions came almost immediately.

Nyman's celebrated collaboration with director Peter Greenaway spanned some 14 years, including *The Draughtsman's Contract* (1982, based on music of Henry Purcell); *Drowning by Numbers* (1987, a deconstruction of Mozart's "Sinfonia concertante" for violin and viola); *The Cook, The Thief, His Wife & Her Lover* (1989); and *Prospero's Books* (1991, utilizing female voices).

The Campion film brought Nyman his greatest fame to date, along with British Film Academy and Golden Globe nominations, and led him to redesign the score into a piano concerto (just one of many works he has written, and continues to write, for the concert hall).

THE PIANO
Virgin 88274-2

Fans of Jane Campion's period drama, which won three 1993 Oscars (for actors Holly Hunter and young Anna Paquin, and Campion as writer), were outraged that Nyman wasn't even nominated for his unusual and sometimes compelling romantic score. (Industry insiders said they felt his approach was inappropriate for the era being evoked.) Nyman's music for mute pianist Hunter was based on 19th-century Scottish folk tunes, refracted through his very 20th-century vision. Nyman is the pianist.

CARRINGTON
Argo 444 873-2

Acclaimed playwright and screenwriter Christopher Hampton's 1995 directing debut was this ambitious study of a painter (Emma Thompson) and her obsessive relationship with a homosexual writer (Jonathan Pryce). Nyman's score, written for strings, bass guitar, two saxophones, horn, and piano, is largely based on his String Quartet No. 3 (which was, in turn, based on a choral work he wrote for a BBC documentary about the Armenian earthquake).

GATTACA
Virgin 45018-2

In writer-director Andrew Niccol's view, Nyman's music for his 1997 science-fiction film (with Ethan Hawke and Uma Thurman) conveyed "both hope and sorrow," and he may be right. Whatever sense of warmth and musical optimism one senses in Nyman's music is certainly tempered with melancholia—accurately reflecting Niccol's unusual extrapolation of current genetic-experimentation trends. This was one of Nyman's best-liked scores and won over many skeptical, anti-*Piano* listeners.

THE END OF THE AFFAIR
Sony Classical SK 51354

Nyman's cooly romantic music for Ralph Fiennes and Julianne Moore contributed mightily to the impact of Neil Jordan's 1999 adaptation of the Graham Greene novel. The writer's "diary of hate" about his wartime lover is evoked entirely with strings and woodwinds in a theme-and-variations form that is richly recorded and arguably Nyman's most evocative work for films. It was a Golden Globe nominee, although it failed to muster an Oscar nomination.

Poledouris, Basil (1945–)

Missouri-born, California-raised Basil Poledouris was headed for a career as a concert pianist when he decided to shift his attention to filmmaking, joining some of his late '60s University of Southern California classmates—among them future directors John Milius, Randal Kleiser, and George Lucas.

Music ultimately won out, and before long those USC relationships became professional ones: five films for Milius including the surfing movie *Big Wednesday* (1978), the sword-and-sorcery epic *Conan the Barbarian* (1982), and the Soviet-invasion fantasy *Red Dawn* (1984); four for Kleiser including the castaway love story *The Blue Lagoon* (1980) and the AIDS drama *It's My Party* (1996).

Among the most lyrical of contemporary composers, he wrote a warm theme for the trapped-orca tale *Free Willy* (1993) and a moving and powerful score for the recent Liam Neeson version of *Les Miserables* (1998). But because of the success of the films of director Paul Verhoeven—for whom he scored *Robocop* (1987) and *Starship Troopers* (1997)—Poledouris is often thought of in terms of his abilities as an action-adventure composer.

The versatile Poledouris incorporated a choir singing Russian in *The Hunt for Red October* (1990); drew on folk inspirations for his Emmy-winning music for the western miniseries *Lonesome Dove* (1989); and provided an appropriately exotic sound for Disney's *The Jungle Book* (1994).

CONAN THE BARBARIAN
Varèse Sarabande VSD-5390

Perhaps the single most underrated score of its decade, this stunning evocation of the world of 10,000 years ago—blaring brass, pounding percussion, choral invocations of pagan rites—was the perfect accompaniment to macho filmmaker John Milius's 1982 creation of sword-and-sorcery author Robert E. Howard's hero (Arnold Schwarzen-

egger). Poledouris also scored the sequel, *Conan the Destroyer* (1984).

THE HUNT FOR RED OCTOBER
MCA MCAD-6428

The first Tom Clancy techno-thriller to reach the screen (1990) had Alec Baldwin as the American agent investigating Soviet sub commander Sean Connery's odd and potentially dangerous moves. Poledouris's suspense-generating score balances orchestra, choir (singing Russian lyrics), and synthesizers in ways that would anticipate what many other composers would do with similar action thrillers in the next few years.

FREE WILLY
Epic EK 57280

This popular 1993 family film was based on the true story of a captive whale whose 12-year-old human friend arranges for him to escape to the ocean. From the opening whale ballet to the trapped orca's final triumphant leap to freedom, Poledouris's score charms and touches the listener. Several songs also appear on the disc, notably a Michael Jackson tune ("Will You Be There?") that helped to drive this album into *Billboard*'s top 50 and go gold.

LES MISERABLES
Mandalay/Hollywood HR-62147-2

This powerful 1998 version of the Victor Hugo classic (starring Liam Neeson, Geoffrey Rush, and Uma Thurman) inspired one of Poledouris's richest scores. Several critics cited this as one of the year's finest scores, but the film's box-office failure probably cost the composer the Oscar nomination that many predicted. The music is divided into four suites for the album, dramatically underscoring Valjean's journey and Javert's ruthless pursuit.

STARSHIP TROOPERS

Varèse Sarabande VSD-5877

Paul Verhoeven's 1997 sci-fi epic about Earth's war with giant bugs on far-off worlds drew more praise for Poledouris's thrilling music than it did for the plot or special effects. The composer worked for several months on this film, crafting a multilayered action score that works overtime to inject excitement into a movie with thinly drawn characters and a problematic story.

PHOTO BY JOFRE MASCENO, COURTESY OF KRAFT-BENJAMIN-ENGEL

Portman, Rachel (1960–)

On March 24, 1997, Rachel Portman made Oscar history by becoming the first woman composer to win an Academy Award for an original score. The English-born Portman won for her charming period music for *Emma*, which was based on the Jane Austen novel and starred Gwyneth Paltrow.

Oxford-educated and classically trained, Portman began in television and independent films, including Jim Henson's acclaimed *The Storyteller* series for TV and features by Mike Leigh (*Life Is Sweet*, 1991) and Beeban Kidron (*Antonia & Jane*, 1991).

Kidron directed Portman's American-film debut, the offbeat *Used People* (1992). Portman has since gone on to several high-profile projects, including Wayne Wang's touching family saga *The Joy Luck Club* and Jeremiah Chechik's quirky comedy *Benny & Joon* (both 1993).

Her pastoral score for the Hugh Grant comedy *Sirens* (1994) and her emotionally charged music for the Meryl Streep–Diane Keaton drama *Marvin's Room* (1996) were widely acclaimed. The Oscar for Doug McGrath's *Emma* led to a variety of offers, notably the Oprah Winfrey production of Toni Morrison's searing *Beloved* (1998) and *The Cider House Rules* (1999), a much-deserved Oscar nominee and a key element in the emotional resonance of that acclaimed film.

BENNY & JOON

Milan 73138 35644-2

This charming, offbeat 1993 romantic comedy starred Aidan Quinn and Mary Stuart Masterson as big brother and mentally ill sister, respectively, with Johnny Depp as a young would-be Chaplin-Keaton combination who comes into their lives. Portman's music not only captured this delicate balance but provided a circus-like motif for Depp's clever routines.

THE JOY LUCK CLUB

Hollywood HR-61561-2

Not authentically Chinese but lovely on its own terms, this dramatic and beautiful music seemed just right for its 1993 film: an adaptation of Amy Tan's book about four Chinese women, their survival against the odds in the old country, and their American daughters' assimilation issues. Portman's use of Chinese instruments (including bamboo flute and Chinese violin) and solo voice provided appropriate colors.

EMMA

Miramax/Hollywood MH-62069-2

Delicate, sensitively written and classically orchestrated, Portman's music for the 1996 adaptation of
Jane Austen's comedy of manners won an Academy
Award—the first ever given to a female composer.
By turns elegant and wistful, it mirrored and
enhanced Gwyneth Paltrow's performance as the
well-intentioned but error-prone matchmaker of
19th-century England.

BELOVED

Epic/Sony EK 69636

Oprah Winfrey's 1998 production of Toni Morrison's acclaimed best-seller about the post–Civil War
saga of a troubled, haunted woman named Sethe
elicited a complex, underrated Portman score.
Director Jonathan Demme's offbeat ideas about
music led Portman to eschew an orchestral score in
favor of unusual ethnic instruments (mostly
stringed and wind instruments), percussion, and a
variety of wordless vocals, either by soloist Oumou
Sangare or the African Children's Choir.

THE CIDER HOUSE RULES

Sony Classical SK 89031

One of Portman's most affecting scores, the music
of Lasse Hallstrom's film of the John Irving novel
was a 1999 Oscar nominee. Her warm and lyrical
main theme, often voiced by solo piano, embodies
both sadness and hope for the orphans whose story
bookends the movie. Subtle and delicate writing
for strings gently supports the emotions already
present on screen in this story of a young man
(Tobey Maguire) who leaves his Maine home for
adventures in the "outside world," only to return
to fullfill his life's destiny as predicted by his mentor (Oscar winner Michael Caine).

PHOTO COURTESY OF PHOTOFEST

Previn, André (1929–)

André Previn is unique among American composers. He may be the only one to launch a musical career in Hollywood and become highly successful in films, only to leave it behind and become
an accepted and fully credentialed member of the
classical-music community.

Born in Germany, he fled with his family in
1938 to the United States. As a teenager he worked
as a pianist and arranger at MGM; by the time he
was 20 he was scoring films there.

Previn alternated between composing dramatic scores and adapting musicals. Three of his
four Academy Awards—*Gigi* (1958), *Porgy and
Bess* (1959), and *My Fair Lady* (1964)—were for
supervising and conducting song scores for the
screen. Other musicals included *Three Little
Words* (1950), *Kiss Me Kate* (1953), and *Bells Are
Ringing* (1960).

By the 1960s, when he left MGM to pursue
freelance composing opportunities, he had come
into his own as a composer. He had already written
a stark score for the western *Bad Day at Black Rock*
(1954); his jazz chops came in handy on *The Subterraneans* (1960); he scored four comedies for

Billy Wilder, winning an Oscar for *Irma La Douce* (1963); and he wrote intense dramatic scores for *Elmer Gantry* (1960) and *The Four Horsemen of the Apocalypse* (1962). He continued to enjoy success as a songwriter, especially with wife Dory Previn: Their 1967 title song for *Valley of the Dolls* was a million-seller for Dionne Warwick.

In 1969 Previn became principal conductor of the London Symphony Orchestra and rarely worked in film thereafter (conducting *Jesus Christ Superstar* in 1973 and *Rollerball* in 1975).

ELMER GANTRY
Rykodisc RCD 10732

Richard Brooks's 1960 film of Sinclair Lewis's controversial novel about a charlatan preacher (Burt Lancaster) was a Best Picture nominee and won Oscars for Lancaster, Brooks as writer, and Shirley Jones as a blackmailing prostitute. Previn's intelligent and impressive orchestral score not only defines each of the three characters, it offers shading and nuance in its choices—powerful, brusque, romantic, jazzy, depending on the moment. Previn also adapted many of the hymns, bordello tunes, and Prohibition-era speakeasy music; he received his first Oscar nomination for original scoring for this film.

FOUR HORSEMEN OF THE APOCALYPSE
MGM SE-3993 (LP)

This was one of Previn's finest dramatic scores, one of many instances in which a top composer had to work overtime to make a lackluster picture seem more dramatic and compelling than it really was. The 1962 film starred Glenn Ford and Ingrid Thulin in a story of a divided family in German-occupied Paris suring World War II. As *Variety* put it: "Previn has composed a tearing, soaring, emotionally affecting score to take up some of the slack."

Complex and powerful for its wartime scenes, poignant in its romantic moments, Previn's music was the best thing about this Vincente Minnelli film.

IRMA LA DOUCE
Rykodisc RCD 10729

Previn won his third Academy Award for his lively, boisterous score from Billy Wilder's 1963 screen adaptation of the French musical about a prostitute (Shirley MacLaine) and the cop (Jack Lemmon) who falls for her. Wilder's version isn't a musical, but he asked Previn to retain two of the stage tunes ("Dis Donc," "Our Language of Love") and add his own original music. Previn successfully re-creates the sound of Paris with accordion and solo violin.

Prokofiev, Sergei (1891–1953)

Russian-born Prokofiev musically bridged the gap between 19th-century romanticism and 20th-century modernism. One of the leading Soviet composers of this century, he composed several works that are now part of every symphony's basic repertoire: the ballet *Romeo and Juliet*, the Symphony No. 5, and the delightful children's entertainment *Peter and the Wolf*.

He scored only a handful of films, but his collaboration with the brilliant Soviet filmmaker Sergei Eisenstein on the landmark *Alexander Nevsky* changed the way many people thought about the relationship between music and image.

Nevsky—about the 13th-century Russian hero who defended his homeland against Teutonic invaders—was unique in films of the late 1930s because it was a true partnership between director and composer. "Eisenstein's respect for music was so great," Prokofiev later wrote, "that at times he was prepared to cut or add to his sequences so as not to upset the balance of a musical episode."

He reworked his *Nevsky* score into a cantata that has become a concert-hall staple and later worked with Eisenstein on the two-part *Ivan the Terrible*. A suite from his first film, the charming and satirical *Lieutenant Kijé*, has become a classical favorite. He worked on a film of Pushkin's, *The Queen of Spades*, that went unproduced, and created scores for four other 1940s Soviet films that are now forgotten (*Lermontov, Tonya, Kotovsky, Partisans in the Ukrainian Steppes*) and would be fascinating to unearth.

PROKOFIEV: THE FILM MUSIC
VoxBox CDX 5021

This two-CD set contains the major film works of the composer: the familiar concert suite from the delightfully whimsical *Lieutenant Kijé* (op. 60, 1934), the dramatic cantata drawn from *Alexander Nevsky* (op. 78, 1938), and the impressive oratorio (assembled after the composer's death) from the scores for *Ivan the Terrible* (op. 116, 1942–1945). Leonard Slatkin conducts the Saint Louis Symphony Orchestra & Chorus.

ALEXANDER NEVSKY
RCA 09026 61926 2

In 1986, producer John Goberman commissioned orchestrator William Brohn to reconstruct the original *Nevsky* score for live-concert performance with the film; it was recorded in 1993 and, at 51 minutes, is a very different experience from the 39-minute cantata. The highlight, "The Battle on the Ice," here totals 18 minutes in five cues instead of 12 minutes in one stretch. Yuri Temirkanov conducts the St. Petersburg Philharmonic Orchestra and choruses.

IVAN THE TERRIBLE
Chandos CHAN 8977

Eisenstein's projected trilogy of films about the 16th-century tsar in the end produced only two films and a considerable amount of music by Prokofiev, which, like the films themselves, is larger than life and operatic in nature. Abram Stasevich, who conducted the original soundtracks, assembled an oratorio from the scores in 1962. In 1991, orchestrator and film-music scholar Christopher Palmer went back to the original scores and assembled a one-hour "concert scenario" that appears to adhere more closely to Prokofiev's original, including a restoration of the assassination sequence from Part II. Neeme Järvi conducts the Philharmonia Orchestra and Chorus.

Raksin, David (1912–)

David Raksin discovered the marriage of music and motion pictures while watching his father conduct the orchestra that accompanied silent movies in Philadelphia's Metropolitan Opera House. He came to Hollywood in 1935 as a collaborator on *Modern Times* with Charles Chaplin (who hummed and whistled tunes for Raksin to adapt into a score). Within a week and a half, Chaplin fired him for insubordination, but Alfred Newman negotiated a truce, and Raksin and Chaplin finished the job as friends.

Nine years later, Raksin would compose a misty melody for the 1944 Otto Preminger detective mystery *Laura*. The piece met with immediate acclaim by thousands of fans, who demanded a commercial recording. Within months, no fewer than five different artists would enjoy top-10 hits with the vocal version of "Laura"—now one of the most widely recorded songs in history.

Much of Raksin's work in the '40s was at 20th Century–Fox, where he wrote the stunning, Oscar-nominated 17th-century English score for *Forever Amber* (1947). But he composed memorable scores for several different studios including the film noir *Force of Evil* (1948) and the backstage Hollywood story *The Bad and the Beautiful* (1952) for MGM; the all-star romantic drama *Separate Tables* (1958), also Oscar-nominated, for United Artists; the jazz score for John Cassavettes's *Too Late Blues* (1962) and the elegiac Charlton Heston western *Will Penny* (1968) for Paramount.

Raksin wrote the theme for *Ben Casey*, one of the '60s best television dramas, and the music for several telefilms including the acclaimed nuclear-war drama *The Day After* (1983). Now the dean of Hollywood composers, the active, erudite, and witty Raksin continues to teach, write concert music, and mentor younger composers.

DAVID RAKSIN CONDUCTS
HIS GREAT FILM SCORES
RCA 1490-2-RG

Raksin conducted London's New Philharmonia Orchestra in this 1975 recording of suites from his three most famous scores: *Laura* (1944), *Forever Amber* (1947), and *The Bad and the Beautiful* (1952). The six-minute passage from *Laura* is the arrangement that Raksin has conducted with orchestras for many years, while *Forever Amber* gets a 25-minute, five-movement suite; 16 minutes of *The Bad and the Beautiful* round out the album. The booklet contains a long essay by Raksin filled with anecdotes and his trademark dry wit.

LAURA
Fox 11006-2

Although "Laura" has been recorded an estimated 400 times as a song (with a Johnny Mercer lyric), this 1993 CD marked the first release of the original music tracks from the film, conducted by Fox music chief Alfred Newman. Gene Tierney, Dana Andrews, Vincent Price, and Clifton Webb starred in Otto Preminger's 1944 classic. The tune was a

an actress (Lana Turner), a director (Barry Sullivan), and a writer (Dick Powell)—received a classic score from Raksin, who by 1952 was considered one of Hollywood's most talented and thoughtful composers. This 1996 premiere release of the completely restored, hour-long score also features a booklet with detailed reminiscences by the composer.

Revell, Graeme (1955–)

Graeme Revell's experiments with strange sonorities has made him a sought-after composer, especially for directors seeking cutting-edge sounds. His own background is offbeat enough: born in New Zealand, degree in political economics, work as a regional planner, orderly in an Australian mental hospital, founder of the groundbreaking industrial-rock band SPK. His recording career included *The Insect Musicians*, an album based on Revell's recordings of insect sounds from around the world.

His entree into the film world came about on Philip Noyce's Australian thriller *Dead Calm* (1989), for which he utilized synthesizers, opera singers, and the sounds of heavy breathing. Noyce returned to Revell for the high-profile Val Kilmer adventure *The Saint* (1997).

Revell's combination of synthesizer textures, traditional orchestral ensembles, and ethnic instruments has enlivened such thrillers as John Woo's *Hard Target* (1993), Kathryn Bigelow's *Strange Days* (1995), and Ed Zwick's *The Siege* (1998). He has also worked with Wim Wenders (*Until the End of the World*, 1991) and Wayne Wang (*Chinese Box*, 1998).

14-week favorite on radio's *Your Hit Parade* in mid-1945 (generating five top-10 hits by artists ranging from Dick Haymes to Woody Herman within a three-month period). Paired with *Laura* is another classic Fox score from 1944: Bernard Herrmann's *Jane Eyre*.

FOREVER AMBER

Varèse Sarabande VSD-5857

One of the greatest scores of the Golden Age of Hollywood, this rich, multi-layered portrait of romance and tragedy in 17th-century England may be Raksin's magnum opus (despite his far greater fame as the composer of *Laura*). Sixty-five minutes of original tracks (over 100 cues assembled into four musically coherent suites) received their original release in this 1998 CD. Otto Preminger directed the movie, which starred Linda Darnell as the heroine.

THE BAD AND THE BEAUTIFUL

Rhino R2 72400

The quintessential backstage Hollywood story—unscrupulous producer (Kirk Douglas) who exploits

THE CROW

Varèse Sarabande VSD-5499

Alex Proyas's 1994 film, based on James O'Barr's comic strip about an aspiring rock star who returns from the grave to avenge his own murder, generated considerable interest because star Brandon Lee (son of Bruce Lee) was accidentally killed during production. An eclectic mix of voices, Armenian duduk, Japanese shakuhachi, rock guitars, percussion, and orchestra, Revell's eerie music captured the dark soul of the movie a good deal more than the songs that litter the soundtrack. Revell also scored the 1996 sequel.

THE SAINT
Angel 56446 2
Revell's second collaboration with director Philip Noyce was on the big-budget 1997 adaptation of Leslie Charteris's contemporary knight-errant Simon Templar. Again using his trademark voices, synthesizers, and samples in conjunction with full orchestra and plenty of percussion, Revell's score not only drove the action but referred regularly to Edwin Astley's TV theme (which was Roger Moore's aural signature in the '60s).

Rosenman, Leonard (1924–)
Leonard Rosenman's entree to Hollywood film-

scoring came about when one of his piano students—who happened to be James Dean—introduced him to director Elia Kazan. Kazan, who had earlier championed another American composer without film experience (Alex North, on *A Streetcar Named Desire*), invited Rosenman to score *East of Eden* (1955).

A former student of Arnold Schoenberg and Roger Sessions, Rosenman introduced a modern-music sensibility to commercial films, first in *East of Eden* (written in part while the composer was on location with the film) and then immediately thereafter in *The Cobweb* (also 1955), which startled MGM executives as the first 12-tone score for a major motion picture. Rosenman's music was complex, often dissonant, and exactly right for a film set in a psychiatric clinic.

Other films followed, notably Dean's next movie, *Rebel Without a Cause* (1955), and a handful of hard-hitting, low-budget dramas for which Rosenman's avant-garde style was suited: the grim drama *Edge of the City* (1957), and the documentary-style *The Savage Eye* (1960), for example.

He experimented with tone colors and musical textures in *Fantastic Voyage* (1966), adapted the music of the Sioux for *A Man Called Horse* (1970), and created a bizarre Mass for *Beneath the Planet of the Apes* (1970). A lavish, multi-thematic score for the animated version of J.R.R. Tolkien's *The Lord of the Rings* (1978) and a gentle, Oscar-nominated one for *Cross Creek* (1983) are among his more appreciated works of recent times. He won Oscars for adapting classical music in *Barry Lyndon* (1975) and the tunes of Woody Guthrie in *Bound for Glory* (1976). While his music for TV's *The Defenders, Combat!,* and *Marcus Welby, M.D.* is probably better known, he continues to write for the concert hall.

THE FILM MUSIC OF LEONARD ROSENMAN
Nonesuch 79402-2

It took only 42 years for someone to finally do justice to a pair of seminal scores for James Dean films: *East of Eden* and *Rebel Without a Cause*, both 1955 releases and both scored by Rosenman. John Adams conducts the London Sinfonietta in 26 minutes of the often moving music for *East of Eden*—the John Steinbeck adaptation directed by Elia Kazan, starring Dean, Julie Harris, and Raymond Massey—and 23 minutes of the sometimes symphonic, sometimes jazzy *Rebel*, the definitive disenfranchised-youth story with Dean, Natalie Wood, and Sal Mineo.

FANTASTIC VOYAGE
FSM Vol. 1, No. 3

Rosenman's complex, revolutionary music for the 1966 science-fiction film about a team of scientists who are miniaturized for surgery inside a human body wasn't commercially released until 1998. His strange colors and textures in this almost entirely atonal score (which doesn't even begin until the film's fifth reel) made the film far more compelling. Stephen Boyd, Raquel Welch, and Donald Pleasence starred in the film.

BENEATH THE PLANET OF THE APES
FSM Vol. 3, No. 3

With Jerry Goldsmith (an Oscar nominee for the original film) off scoring *Patton*, it fell to Rosenman to score the 1970 sequel about an astronaut (James Franciscus) out to rescue the missing Charlton Heston and finding Heston's mute girlfriend (Linda Harrison) instead. Rosenman's audacious score was one of the film's most original elements: complex rhythmic figures, a primitive-sounding march for the ape army, even a bizarre choral mini-Mass for the bomb-worshipping mutants of the planet's underground society.

THE LORD OF THE RINGS
Intrada FMT 8003D

"When a film fails, it pulls everything connected with it down to oblivion," Rosenman writes in the liner notes for Ralph Bakshi's 1978 animated film of the first half of the classic J.R.R. Tolkien fantasy trilogy. "Unfortunately, in this case, it includes a film score of great complexity and sophistication." With more than 100 musicians and a choir, Rosenman breathed life into the adventures of Frodo, Gandolf, and the hobbits with, in his words, "eerie marches, strange chases, and wild battle scenes." The original two-LP set reached number 39 and remained on the *Billboard* charts for three months; the resequenced, remixed CD adds 12 minutes of music.

STAR TREK IV: THE VOYAGE HOME
MCA MCAD-6195

Rosenman received a 1986 Oscar nomination for his score in the fourth big-screen adventure of the *Enterprise* crew (one of only two music nods the series has received). Taking a more classical approach than his predecessors, the composer wrote a joyous, Bach-style fugue for the endangered whales that Kirk and Spock must save; parodied Tchaikovsky for a chase involving the Russian-born Chekhov; and interpolated jazz (featuring The Yellowjackets) for scenes in San Francisco.

Rosenthal, Laurence (1926–)

Highly respected among his colleagues in the film-composing community but little known to outsiders, Laurence Rosenthal came to movies from a background of studies with Howard Hanson and

Nadia Boulanger and extensive work in the New York theater including both ballets and incidental music for plays.

Rosenthal's blues- and jazz-influenced music for the Sidney Poitier drama *A Raisin in the Sun* (1961) brought him to Hollywood's attention, but it was the Helen Keller story *The Miracle Worker* (1962) that put him on the map. Sensitive and poignant, mirroring a child's confusion while suggesting a teacher's compassion, it was a powerful musical statement within a powerful film.

Three Peter Glenville films—the Oscar-nominated *Becket* (1964), *Hotel Paradiso* (1966), and *The Comedians* (1967)—offered vastly different challenges: medieval cadences and plainsong for the first; turn-of-the-century Parisian colors for the second; and Haitian rhythms for the third. *The Return of a Man Called Horse* (1976) called for the adaptation of Lakota chants and dances, and in *The Island of Dr. Moreau* (1977) he created a bizarre and primitive musical environment for H. G. Wells's half-man, half-animal creatures.

Rosenthal has recently been much in demand for television projects, winning several Emmys for his richly detailed period scores in such miniseries as *Peter the Great* and *Anastasia: The Mystery of Anna*, and George Lucas's critically acclaimed, colorfully scored *Young Indiana Jones Chronicles*.

BECKET
Decca DL-79117 *(LP)*

Rosenthal scored Peter Glenville's adaptation of the Jean Anouilh play with Richard Burton (as Henry II) and Peter O'Toole (as Thomas Becket), receiving a 1964 Oscar nomination for his authentic-sounding music of 12th-century England. The use of Gregorian chant, orchestrational choices including period instruments and choir, and the deft dramatic use of more modern compositional devices

made this score a favorite of composers in the '60s; it even charted briefly. Muir Mathieson conducted a London ensemble.

THE COMEDIANS
MGM SE-4494 *(LP)*

Graham Greene's novel of politics and love affairs in dictator "Papa Doc" Duvalier's Haiti, as translated into a movie by Greene and director Peter Glenville, was a box-office failure in 1967 despite a brilliant cast including Richard Burton, Elizabeth Taylor, Alec Guinness, and Peter Ustinov. Rosenthal's score utilizes authentic Caribbean rhythms and adds a melancholy love theme, an interesting choral element (a children's choir chanting the praises of Duvalier), and plenty of percussion-laced drama.

THE RETURN OF A MAN CALLED HORSE
United Artists UA-LA692-G *(LP)*

The 1976 sequel to Richard Harris's 1970 triumph *A Man Called Horse* benefited from Rosenthal's sensitivity to time and place. The composer researched the music of the Lakota Sioux and combined actual Native American dances and chants with his own original music for the Great Plains locale. Critic Leonard Maltin singled out this score as "magnificent."

CLASH OF THE TITANS
Pendulum PEG 014/A28693

This 1981 fantasy, based on Greek mythology, had a lot going for it: an all-star cast (including Laurence Olivier as Zeus), Ray Harryhausen special effects (including the winged horse Pegasus and the snake-haired Medusa), and a rousing symphonic score by Rosenthal conducting the London Symphony Orchestra. The music mirrors the heroism, romance, and tragedy of the film's various episodes.

PHOTO COURTESY OF NINA ROTA

Rota, Nino (1911–1979)

Although Italian composer Nino Rota worked with many directors, including Luchino Visconti, Franco Zeffirelli, and Francis Ford Coppola, it was for his magical music in Federico Fellini's films that he was justly renowned. Rota was Fellini's music director for nearly 30 years, and their collaboration produced at least half a dozen masterpieces of sight and sound, including *La Strada* (1954), *La Dolce Vita* (1960), *8 1/2* (1963), *Juliet of the Spirits* (1965), *Fellini's Roma* (1972), and *Amarcord* (1974).

Rota, although classically trained and a contributor of works to the concert hall throughout his film career, was quick to incorporate lighter musical forms from jazz to pop to (especially in Fellini movies) carnival music and circus marches.

He also had ongoing relationships with directors Luchino Visconti, for whom he scored *Rocco and His Brothers* (1960) and *The Leopard* (1963); and Franco Zeffirelli, for whom he scored two Shakespearean adaptations: the Richard Burton–Elizabeth Taylor vehicle *The Taming of the Shrew* (1967) and the universally popular *Romeo and Juliet* (1968). He could write in grand sym-

phonic style, as witness the British classical-music film *The Glass Mountain* (1950) and the Tolstoy epic *War and Peace* (1956).

Francis Ford Coppola recruited him for *The Godfather* (1972), and Rota shared an Oscar with Coppola's father, Carmine (who supplied most of the source music in both movies), for *The Godfather Part II* (1974). These two movies made him a Paramount favorite, and two of his final scores were written for that studio: the all-star Agatha Christie mystery *Death on the Nile* (1978) and the disaster film *Hurricane* (1979).

TUTTO FELLINI
CAM CSE 001 (Italy)

This two-CD set, assembled in 1991, contains themes and/or suites from nearly two dozen films by Federico Fellini, 16 of which featured scores by Rota. It's the definitive Fellini/Rota collection, ranging from the jazz-inflected (*I Vitelloni*, 1953; *Nights of Cabiria*, 1957) to the mysterious (*La Dolce Vita*, 1960), from the fun marches (*8 1/2*, 1963; *The Clowns*, 1971) to the seductive (*Juliet of the Spirits*, 1965). Aspects of Rome are conjured in the melancholy *Satyricon* (1970) and *Roma* (1972); Rota's quirky *Amarcord* (1974) and period-colorful *Casanova* (1976) are equally memorable. Carlo Savina conducts the Rota selections; other music is by composers including Mario Nascimbene, Luis Bacalov, and Nicola Piovani. The 64-page booklet is filled with colorful Fellini drawings and poster art.

NINO ROTA: MUSIC FOR FILM
Sony Classical SK 633

The maestro's collaborations with directors Federico Fellini, Luchino Visconti, and Francis Ford Coppola are memorialized in this 1997 recording of suites and themes by Riccardo Muti and the Filarmonica Della Scala in Milan. A 20-minute suite drawn from his scores for *The Godfather* (1972) and its sequel (1974) and a 24-minute suite from Visconti's *The Leopard* (1963) make up the bulk of the album; shorter suites from *Orchestra Rehearsal* (1979) and Visconti's *Rocco and His Brothers* (1960), and themes from *La Dolce Vita* (1960) and *8½* (1963) round it out.

ROMEO AND JULIET
Capitol CDP 7 9205-7 2

Rota's music for Franco Zeffirelli's 1968 version of the Shakespearean classic (which starred Olivia Hussey and Leonard Whiting) is an instance where the dramatic underscore took on a life of its own and became equally famous. The movie was a sensation among young people who found the film a wondrous romantic experience. Capitol released a soundtrack album combining dialogue with music that reached number 2, went platinum, and spent 74 weeks on the *Billboard* charts all told. A four-LP boxed set followed, containing the entire audio track of the movie. Finally, an LP containing just the Rota score was issued. In the meantime, the "Love Theme From *Romeo and Juliet*" became a number-1 single for Henry Mancini and a popular vocal hit (as "A Time for Us," with lyrics added after the film) by Johnny Mathis. The score itself is one of Rota's most effective, intertwining multiple motifs and period orchestrational touches. Mancini and Percy Faith won 1969 Grammys for their performance of the theme; Rota, at least, received a nomination for Song of the Year.

THE GODFATHER
MCA MCAD-10231
THE GODFATHER PART II
MCA MCAD-10232

Rota shifted into Sicilian-gangster mode for this well-liked and beautifully crafted pair of scores for the first two installments of Francis Ford Coppola's organized-crime–family trilogy. The "Godfather waltz," with its lonely solo trumpet, and the expansive, mandolin-flavored love theme, are indelibly linked with the film. They initially earned Rota a 1972 Oscar nomination, which was withdrawn when complaints arose that Rota had actually written the love theme for an obscure movie some years before. Nonetheless, the love theme hit the *Billboard* charts as a single, and the album reached number 21, winning a Grammy. For the sequel—which won a 1974 Oscar for Rota and source-music composer Carmine Coppola, the director's father—Rota augmented the original material with an almost operatic theme for Robert DeNiro as the young Don Corleone.

PHOTO FROM THE TONY THOMAS COLLECTION

Rózsa, Miklós (1907–1995)

To many movie buffs, the name Miklós Rózsa conjures up the sounds of trumpet fanfares, glorious marches, and ancient Roman spectacles; to others, the music of paranoia and schizophrenia, laced with weird theremin tonalities; to still others, the

DRAMATIC UNDERSCORES, BY COMPOSER

exotic sounds of India or the jagged rhythms of urban violence.

They are all correct. Over 40 years, 100 scores, and 17 Oscar nominations (including three wins), the Hungarian-born composer produced music for historical epics, psychological dramas, fantasies based on children's classics, and dark police procedurals—all while maintaining a separate career (to which the title of his 1982 autobiography, *Double Life*, alludes) as a composer of music for the concert hall.

Rózsa came to Hollywood in 1940 while working for producer Alexander Korda, who made *The Thief of Bagdad* (1940) and *The Jungle Book* (1942), the latter spawning one of the earliest albums of orchestral film music (on RCA Victor, with narration by Sabu). As the '40s progressed, he worked for Billy Wilder (*The Lost Weekend*, 1945), Alfred Hitchcock (*Spellbound*, also 1945 and Rózsa's first Oscar winner) and Mark Hellinger (*The Killers*, 1946).

The '50s and '60s saw Rózsa in great demand as a composer of historical dramas, including *Quo Vadis?* (1951), *Ivanhoe* (1952), *Julius Caesar* (1953), the impressive and Oscar-winning *Ben-Hur* (1959), the Spanish-flavored *El Cid* (1961) and the Christ story *King of Kings* (1961). Much of Rózsa's concert music, which includes a violin concerto for Jascha Heifetz, was influenced by the Hungarian folk songs of his youth.

FILM SCORES OF MIKLOS ROZSA
Angel 65993 2

There could be no better introduction to the music of Miklós Rózsa than this 75-minute compilation from long-out-of-print LPs. The most famous of his historical epics are represented by suites from *Ben-Hur* (1959), *El Cid* (1961), *King of Kings* (1961), and *Quo Vadis?* (1951). An early

melodrama, *The Red House* (1947), and the 10-minute concerto drawn from his Oscar-winning *Spellbound* score, round out the album. Rózsa conducts ensembles in America (1952, mono) and Europe (1967, stereo) on this 1996 reissue.

SPELLBOUND: THE CLASSIC FILM SCORES OF MIKLÓS RÓZSA
RCA 0911-2-RG

This 1976 entry in Charles Gerhardt's "Classic Film Scores" series features excerpts from his earlier, rarely recorded scores, notably generous suites from *The Red House* (1947), *The Lost Weekend* (1945)—both of which feature the electronic theremin—and *The Four Feathers* (1939). Themes from *The Thief of Bagdad* (1940), *Double Indemnity* (1944), *Knights of the Round Table* (1953), *The Jungle Book* (1942), and *Ivanhoe* (1952) and two crucial sequences from *Spellbound* (1945) are also included. Gerhardt conducts the National Philharmonic.

MIKLÓS RÓZSA AT MGM
Rhino R2 75723

This two-CD set, issued in late 1999, collects the original tracks of 13 scores that the composer wrote while he was under contract to MGM. Most were historical dramas. Generous suites (most in the 10-to-13-minute range) convey the essence of several Rózsa classics, including the grand waltz of *Madame Bovary* (1949), the medieval pomp of *Ivanhoe* (1952) and *Knights of the Round Table* (1953), the mystery of ancient Egypt in *Valley of the Kings* (1954), and the English colors of *Moonfleet* (1955). Highlights of the second disc are the swashbuckling *The King's Thief* (1955), the western idiom of *Tribute to a Bad Man* (1956), the baroque feel of *Diane* (1955), a French-impressionist suggestion for the Van Gogh biography *Lust for Life* (1956), and the alternately reverent and triumphant sounds of the Christ tale *King of Kings* (1961).

THE THIEF OF BAGDAD/THE JUNGLE BOOK
Varèse Sarabande VCD 47258

Alexander Korda's two classic films starring Sabu—the Arabian Nights tale *The Thief of Bagdad* (1940) and Rudyard Kipling's *The Jungle Book* (1942)—boasted delightful and very descriptive Rózsa scores, each filled with the color and exotic flavor of their respective locales (Persia and India). This disc includes 18 minutes of *Bagdad*, conducted by the composer; and 29 minutes of *Jungle Book*, conducted by Klauspeter Seibel, both played by the Nurnberger Symphoniker.

SPELLBOUND
Stanyan STZ116-2

One of Rózsa's most recognized and popular works, his Oscar-winning score for this 1945 Alfred Hitchcock film was a crucial element in aurally illuminating both Gregory Peck's psychosis (via the then-unusual use of the electronic theremin) and his love for psychiatrist Ingrid Bergman. The film is equally famous for its

Salvador Dali dream sequence. Nearly 40 minutes of the score, as re-recorded in the '50s by conductor Ray Heindorf with the Warner Bros. studio orchestra, is preserved here.

DOUBLE INDEMNITY
Koch International 3-7375-2-H1

Three great Rózsa scores from his film noir period of the mid-1940s were reconstructed (by orchestrator Patrick Russ) and re-recorded in 1996 by James Sedares with the New Zealand Symphony Orchestra. Thirty-three minutes of his music for Billy Wilder's nightmarish 1945 alcoholism thriller *The Lost Weekend*, together with 26 minutes of the James M. Cain–Raymond Chandler tale *Double Indemnity* and 11 minutes of the Ernest Hemingway crime story *The Killers*, demonstrate Rózsa's ability to musically illustrate the darker side of human behavior.

QUO VADIS
London 820 200-2

In 1977, Rózsa re-recorded *Quo Vadis?* (1951), one of his most powerful scores and, despite the popularity of his Oscar-winning *Ben-Hur*, arguably his finest effort among the several historical epics that were to come his way in the 1950s and '60s. Rózsa served as the film's musical supervisor, overseeing the construction of instruments depicted in the film, and adapting existing ancient material into early-Christian hymns and pseudo-ancient-Roman music. At the end of the process, Rózsa composed the dramatic underscore, illustrating everything from Nero's burning of Rome to chariot-racing gladiators. The composer received one of the film's eight Academy Award nominations. The Royal Philharmonic Orchestra performs.

IVANHOE
JULIUS CAESAR
Intrada MAF 7055D, 7056D

These early Rózsa historical-epic scores for MGM —from 1952 and 1953, respectively, and both Oscar nominees—have been reconstructed by Rózsa authority Daniel Robbins and conducted by Bruce Broughton with the Sinfonia of London. Set in medieval England, the heroic *Ivanhoe* (which starred Robert Taylor and Elizabeth Taylor) contains especially ambitious battle music. The all-star *Julius Caesar* (with Marlon Brando, James Mason, and John Gielgud), based on Shakespeare's version of events in ancient Rome, is appropriately brooding and tragic.

BEN-HUR
Rhino R2 72197

Widely considered Rózsa's magnum opus, this 1959 masterpiece has been recorded many times by many conductors, including two "original" score LPs (actually re-recordings done in Europe). The first album, issued in early 1960, spent 98 weeks on the charts, reaching number 6, and received a Grammy nomination. This 1996 two-

COURTESY OF TURNER ENTERTAINMENT GROUP INC.

CD set marks the first release of the music actually used in the film. All 148 minutes of the Rózsa score, plus outtakes, have been fully restored and packaged with a lavish, 52-page booklet detailing the history of the production and Rózsa's celebrated music—the majestic fanfares and marches, passionate love themes, delicate choral work, and undeniably inspirational music that accompanies the Charlton Heston epic of a Jew whose boyhood friendship with a Roman nearly destroys his life and those of his family. Rózsa's score earned one of the film's record 11 Oscars.

KING OF KINGS
Sony AK 52424

Rózsa, under contract to MGM at the time, was distressed to find that he had to compose the score for this 1961 Biblical epic on the heels of his monumental *Ben-Hur*—and on practically the same subject (the coming of Christ). Still, most observers agree, the composer rose to the challenge with yet another memorable score for orchestra and choir, including a setting of "The Lord's Prayer," his only 12-tone music (for the temptation of Jesus in the desert), and themes based on Hebraic modes.

EL CID
Koch 3-7340-2 H1

The last of Rózsa's great historical epics (1963's *Sodom and Gomorrah* is pretty much forgotten), this 1961 chronicle of Spain's 11th-century hero starred Charlton Heston with Sophia Loren as his longtime love. James Sedares conducted the New Zealand Symphony Orchestra in 66 minutes of the newly recorded score released in 1996. Like *Ben-Hur*, this is music (Oscar-nominated for song and score) filled with richness, color, and power.

Sakamoto, Ryuichi (1952–)

Classically educated Japanese composer-performer Ryuichi Sakamoto has dabbled in virtually every field of music, from the traditionally orchestral to the most contemporary techno styles, and is an outspoken advocate of what has popularly become known as world music (or as he calls it, "neo geo," a musical map of the globe).

Sakamoto is widely recognized as both an actor and a composer. He had a major role in Nagisa Oshima's 1983 film *Merry Christmas, Mr. Lawrence*, also his first film as composer; and his music for *The Last Emperor*, supplemented by that of pop star David Byrne and Chinese composer Cong Su, won a 1987 Academy Award.

He collaborated again with *Emperor* director Bernardo Bertolucci on *The Sheltering Sky* (1990) and *Little Buddha* (1993), with Volker Schlondorff on *The Handmaid's Tale* (1990), with Oliver Stone on the groundbreaking miniseries *Wild Palms* (1993), and with Brian DePalma on *Snake Eyes* (1998).

THE LAST EMPEROR
Virgin 86029-2

Bernardo Bertolucci's epic story of the last emperor of China—a god at the age of 3, a gardener at the end of his life—won nine Academy Awards including Best Picture of 1987. Sakamoto (who also had a supporting role in the film) shared the Original Score Oscar with Talking Heads songwriter David Byrne and traditional Chinese music composer Cong Su. Sakamoto wrote the lion's share of the score, a lyrical orchestral work with occasional choral and electronic moments and an often quite specific Chinese flavor. Byrne's opening title music and his several ambient cues utilize mostly ethnic instruments and are for smaller musical moments; Cong Su's traditional Chinese sounds provide the most authenticity. Hans Zimmer was Sakamoto's "musical associate" and producer.

THE SHELTERING SKY
Virgin 2-91597

Bernardo Bertolucci's film of Paul Bowles's 1949 novel of an American couple (Debra Winger, John Malkovich) and their gradually disintegrating marriage as they travel through post-war North Africa drew mixed reviews but elicited a rich score from Sakamoto. For this, his second collaboration with Bertolucci, Sakamoto created a haunting main theme that recurs throughout the score; traditional sounds of Burundi, Morocco, and Tunisia add authenticity.

PHOTO FROM THE TONY THOMAS COLLECTION

Salter, Hans J. (1896–1994)

The music of Hans Salter—perhaps more than any other single element—scared us into believing that the ghouls of Universal's horror films of the 1930s and 1940s were real. His scores accompanied the Frankenstein, Wolf Man, and Mummy pictures of that era, and he performed similar musical magic on the genre films of the 1950s, including such sci-fi classics as *This Island Earth* and *The Incredible Shrinking Man*.

Although many of his films were regarded as program pictures, usually playing as the bottom half of a double bill at the local Bijou, Salter's accomplishments (often managed with little time and on minuscule musical budgets) were well known to his peers, who accorded him six Academy Award nominations (including three for Deanna Durbin musicals) between 1942 and 1945.

Born in Vienna, Salter conducted in opera houses, studied composition (with Alban Berg, among others), and eventually moved to Berlin, where he became organist at a silent-film palace and eventually began conducting the orchestra. He wrote music for early talkies at Berlin's famous UFA studios until the rise of Hitler brought him to America in 1937.

He joined Universal in 1938 and worked on literally hundreds of films there through the late 1950s, with occasionally work at other studios starting in the late 1940s. In a late '70s interview, Salter recalled: "Do you know what they used to call me in those days? The master of terror and suspense! Pretty good. They couldn't understand how a nice, mild-mannered fellow from Vienna could develop such a sense of horror and mayhem."

THE MONSTER MUSIC OF HANS J. SALTER & FRANK SKINNER
Marco Polo 8.223747

Three thrilling scores composed for Universal horror classics: Frank Skinner's *Son of Frankenstein* (1939), orchestrated by Salter, and two scores composed jointly by Skinner and Salter: *The Invisible Man Returns* (1940) and *The Wolf Man* (1941). As reconstructionist-orchestrator John W. Morgan points out, "this music became the thematic basis for reuse and further development in

dozens of the studio's films over the next 20 years." Certainly it will be familiar to every monster-movie fan. William T. Stromberg conducts the Moscow Symphony Orchestra.

HOUSE OF FRANKENSTEIN
Marco Polo 8.223748

Nearly an hour of romantic, melodramatic, and terror-inducing music accompanied the 1944 Universal monster picture that starred Boris Karloff as a mad scientist, John Carradine as Dracula, Lon Chaney, Jr., as the Wolf Man, and Glenn Strange as the Frankenstein monster. It wasn't much of a movie but it contained one of Salter's most memorable horror scores (composed in collaboration with Paul Dessau). William Stromberg conducts the Moscow Symphony Orchestra in this John Morgan restoration.

LEGENDARY HOLLYWOOD: MUSIC BY HANS J. SALTER
Citadel STC 77115

Salter's 1941 "Horror Rhapsody" was drawn from original scores for four Universal monster movies: *Son of Frankenstein* (1939) with Basil Rathbone, Boris Karloff, and Bela Lugosi; *The Mummy's Hand* (1940) with Dick Foran and Peggy Moran; *Black Friday* (1940) with Karloff and Lugosi; and *Man Made Monster* (1941) with Lionel Atwill and Lon Chaney, Jr. A highlight of this 25-minute suite is the "Chorus of Egyptian Priests" from the Mummy picture. Also included is Salter's exotic Indian score for the TV series *Maya*.

A SYMPHONY OF FILM MUSIC
BY HANS J. SALTER
Intrada MAF 7054D

Lengthy suites from four of Salter's later films comprise this 1994 collection, all drawn from original session tapes. Jack Arnold's *The Creature From the Black Lagoon* (1954) and *The Incredible Shrinking Man* (1957), both classics of the horror and fantasy genre, benefited enormously from Salter's mixture of romance and shock music. The lesser-known swashbuckler *The Black Shield of Falworth* (1954), with Tony Curtis and Janet Leigh, contains musical suggestions of its 15th-century English setting, and *Hitler* (1962), which starred Richard Basehart, contains frightening musical reminders of the Third Reich.

Sarde, Philippe (1945–)

Paris-born Philippe Sarde was France's most prolific screen composer in the '70s, providing music for literally dozens of films, including a number that became art-house hits in America. His directors included Claude Sautet (*César and Rosalie*, 1972; *Vincent, Francois, Paul and the Others*, 1974; *A Simple Story*, 1978) and Bertrand Tavernier (*Coup de Torchon*, 1981; *A Sunday in the Country*, 1984).

Sarde achieved fame in America for his Oscar-nominated score to Roman Polanski's *Tess* (1979) and followed it with a classically styled horror-film score for *Ghost Story* (1981) and music for two of director Jean-Jacques Annaud's ambitious epics: *Quest for Fire* (1981) and *The Bear* (1989). He was briefly in demand in Hollywood, scoring such films as the Dudley Moore comedy *Lovesick* (1983), *The Manhattan Project* (1986), and Costa-Gavras's war-crimes story *Music Box* (1989).

Also for Polanski, Sarde scored the cult favorite *The Tenant* (1976) and the little-seen comic adventure *Pirates* (1986).

TESS
MCA MCAD-5193

Sarde's romantic, often moving music for Roman Polanski's mesmerizing adaptation of Thomas Hardy's *Tess of the D'Urbervilles* received a 1979 nomination for Best Original Score. (It also received a Best Picture nomination and Oscars for cinematography, costume design, and art direction.) Sarde composed a heartbreaking theme for the tragic heroine (Nastassia Kinski) and employs it in theme-and-variations form throughout.

QUEST FOR FIRE
Milan CDFMC 1

Music was particularly crucial for director Jean-Jacques Annaud's unusual, ambitious, and fascinating exploration of mankind's Stone Age origins. Much of the story (about cavemen in search of fire) is told largely in visual terms. Sarde's symphonic score (played by the London Symphony Orchestra) employs complex harmonic schemes, unusual percussion patterns, pan and bass flutes, and surprising a capella choral moments (the Ambrosian Singers). The LP charted briefly in early 1982.

Schifrin, Lalo (1932–)

Lalo Schifrin combines an eclectic musical background with a love for movies that began during his boyhood in Argentina. His father was concertmaster of the Buenos Aires Symphony, and he studied at the Paris Conservatory. But his discovery of American jazz, keyboard prowess, and talent as an arranger led to a stint with jazz great Dizzy Gillespie in the late 1950s and early 1960s.

Schifrin composed a series of highly original jazz works, including the combo-plus-orchestra *Gillespiana* and *The New Continent*, the classically styled *Marquis de Sade*, and the Grammy-winning *Jazz Suite on the Mass Texts*. He found great success in television, creating such classic themes as *Mission: Impossible*, *Mannix*, and *Medical Center*, inevitably leading to big-screen assignments starting in the mid-1960s.

The composer's penchant for musical research led to authentic-sounding musical backgrounds for such diverse pictures as *Cool Hand Luke* (1967, Southern bluegrass), the kung-fu movie *Enter the Dragon* (1973, Chinese scales), and *The Four Musketeers* (1975, late-Renaissance period music). His Oscar-nominated scores for *The Amityville*

Horror (1979) and *The Competition* (1980) featured, respectively, eerie children's voices and a classical-music backdrop.

Long a specialist in action movies, Schifrin scored the classic chase film *Bullitt* (1968) and four of the five *Dirty Harry* movies, beginning with the controversial 1971 original. In recent years, he has reduced his output of film scores in order to concentrate on his concert-hall career, both as a composer and conductor. His series of "Jazz Meets the Symphony" recordings has been acclaimed, and he continues to be in demand as an arranger for The Three Tenors (Pavarotti, Domingo, Carreras).

THE REEL LALO SCHIFRIN
Hip-O *HIPD-40127*

This 1998 collection offers a nice overview of Schifrin's film output, including themes from his Oscar-nominated scores for *Cool Hand Luke* (1967, gentle and guitar-dominated), *The Fox* (1968, classically styled, chamber ensemble), *Voyage of the Damned* (1976, Latin source), and *The Sting II* (1983, big-band). His jazz roots are also apparent in selections from *The Cincinnati Kid* (1965) and *Rollercoaster* (1977). *Kelly's Heroes* (1970) has a country flavor, and the Schifrin themes for TV's *Mission: Impossible* and *Mannix* are also included.

COOL HAND LUKE
MCA *MVCM-22048 (Japan)*

Schifrin accurately captured the sound of the contemporary South with his bluegrass score for this 1967 classic starring Paul Newman as the quintessential nonconforming chain-gang prisoner (and George Kennedy in an Oscar-winning performance as a fellow inmate). Guitar, banjo, harmonica, and similar folk and jazz flavors set the mood. This brought Schifrin his first Oscar nomination;

one cue was later adopted by ABC television stations for its "Eyewitness News" theme.

THE FOX
Aleph 017

Schifrin scored his second Oscar nomination for this delicately handled 1968 drama, an adaptation of the D. H. Lawrence novel with Sandy Dennis, Anne Heywood, and Keir Dullea. The bleak Canadian woods setting inspired the composer to adopt a semi-classical style, beginning with a string quartet and woodwind quintet and occasionally adding guitar, percussion, and keyboard sounds. Schifrin received Grammy nominations for Best Instrumental Theme and Best Original Score. Schifrin's 1999 re-recording, with the Sinfonia of London, adds considerable dramatic music that was not available on the original 1968 LP.

BULLITT
SLC SCC-1015 (Japan)

Steve McQueen's seminal action thriller of 1968 sports one of Schifrin's best jazz scores. Coming off successful jazz albums for Verve (notably his Grammy-nominated *Marquis de Sade*) and the popular jazz albums for TV's *Mission: Impossible* and *Mannix*, the composer supplied a succession of very hip source pieces and mesmerizingly suspenseful cues for McQueen as a San Francisco cop. The famous chase sequence, however, is largely unscored.

DIRTY HARRY ANTHOLOGY
Aleph 003

Although Schifrin has written music in every genre, his most famous scores may be those for the *Dirty Harry* movies. A longtime associate of Clint Eastwood and director Don Siegel (who helmed the original), Schifrin created music for four of the five in the series. This disc contains tracks from the three most successful: *Dirty Harry* (1971), *Magnum Force* (1973), and *Sudden Impact* (1983), which range from jazz-rock to eerie, breathy solo voice for the killers, to serial techniques for the more violent moments of each.

ENTER THE DRAGON
Warner Bros. 15923-00-CD

This disc contains nearly an hour of music, a classic Schifrin score for a classic Bruce Lee movie and probably the best kung-fu picture ever made. Lee's last completed movie, released in 1973, demanded an action score with Asian elements: Schifrin applied Chinese scales and deployed Oriental-sounding instruments in a large-scale action-adventure framework. (Twenty-five years later, this score inspired director Brett Ratner to make the Chris Tucker–Jackie Chan action-comedy *Rush Hour*—and to hire Lalo Schifrin to supply the score, a Grammy nominee.)

THE FOUR MUSKETEERS/ VOYAGE OF THE DAMNED
Label X LXCD 5

This 1987 disc contains excerpts from three Schifrin scores of the mid-1970s: 26 minutes from *The Four Musketeers* (the 1975 conclusion of the rollicking Oliver Reed–Richard Chamberlain–Faye Dunaway retelling of the Dumas classic), and 18 minutes each from 1977's Michael Caine wartime adventure *The Eagle Has Landed* and 1976's all-star *Voyage of the Damned* (about a boatload of German-Jewish refugees searching for asylum at the start of World War II). *Musketeers* is one of Schifrin's best scores, displaying his love for Renaissance music; and *Damned* was Oscar-nominated.

THE COMPETITION

MCA 5185 (LP)

Richard Dreyfuss and Amy Irving starred in this romantic drama about classical pianists who meet at a competition and fall in love. Schifrin rose to the challenge of creating a score that interpolates the classics (notably Prokofiev's third piano concerto and the Beethoven "Emperor" concerto) with dramatic music that carefully underlines the emotional aspects of the story. Schifrin's love theme, "People Alone," received a 1980 Best Song Oscar nomination.

TANGO

Deutsche Grammophon 459 145-2

Writer-director Carlos Saura's Oscar-nominated examination of the lure and passion of Argentina's favorite dance was a 1998 Oscar nominee. Schifrin, a creative partner with Saura and cinematographer Vittorio Storaro, acted as overall musical director, incorporating several tango classics into the score. He also wrote several new tangos as well as the film's climactic setpiece—the dramatic "La represión," performed by members of the Buenos Aires Philharmonic Orchestra and Chorus.

Scott, John (1930–)

John Scott, today one of England's finest composers for film and television, got his start as a musician in the British armed forces and later with the big bands of the '50s. He became an arranger for Ted Heath's band and, during the '60s, arranged and conducted recording sessions for many successful artists of the day, including Tom Jones, Cilla Black, and The Hollies.

Scott led his own jazz quintet and was a top session player (flute and saxophone) for many film composers, including Henry Mancini and John Barry. He composed his first film score for the Sherlock Holmes film *A Study in Terror* in 1965, and became much in demand in the '70s and '80s. His symphonic score for Charlton Heston's widely panned *Antony & Cleopatra* (1973) has long outlived the film.

Attesting to his versatility are his contemporary jazz score for the football film *North Dallas Forty* (1979); the opening fanfare and theme for the science-fiction suspense drama *The Final Countdown* (1980); and the alternately pastoral and percussive moments throughout *Greystoke: The Legend of Tarzan, Lord of the Apes* (1984).

Scott composed rich symphonic scores for several of Jacques Cousteau's television documentaries (notably a five-part series on the Amazon), and has written a number of concert works, including a pair of string quartets and a symphony.

ANTONY & CLEOPATRA

JOS JSCD-114

Charlton Heston's 1973 film of the Shakespearean tragedy of the Egyptian queen and the Roman soldier didn't fare well either critically or at the box office, but it inspired one of the great romantic scores of the 1970s. Scott's memorable love theme performed by full orchestra and chorus, his theme for Cleopatra delicately scored for strings, oboe, harp, and exotic percussion, and his more dramatic sequences have enjoyed an afterlife on records.

Shaiman, Marc (1959–)

From a Greenwich Village piano bar to scoring some of Hollywood's biggest movies: that's been Marc Shaiman's route, accompanied by a quick wit, a mind like a song encyclopedia, and a little help from such friends as Bette Midler (for whom he was pianist and arranger) and Billy Crystal (whom he met on TV's *Saturday Night Live*).

Crystal's pal Rob Reiner hired Shaiman to supervise the songs for *When Harry Met Sally . . .* (1989) and gave him his dramatic break scoring the Stephen King thriller *Misery* (1990). Shaiman's development as a dramatic composer has gone hand-in-hand with Reiner's own directorial career, Shaiman scored Reiner's *A Few Good Men* (1992), the Oscar-nominated *An American President* (1995), and the Medgar Evers historical drama *Ghosts of Mississippi* (1996).

Shaiman remains in demand for his deft touch with comedies, including two *City Slickers* films (1991, 1994), two *Addams Family* movies (1991, 1993), and pictures ranging from the wacky *George of the Jungle* (1997) to *The First Wives Club* (1996), for which he received an Oscar nomination.

Shaiman's long professional relationships with Midler and Crystal, and by extension Crystal's friend Whoopi Goldberg, have led to creative musical-supervision jobs on Midler's *Beaches* (1988) and *For the Boys* (1991) and Goldberg's two *Sister Act* movies (1992, 1993) as well as gigs writing specialty material (notably Crystal's funny Oscar-night songs). He is especially proud of his work on the raucous animated musical *South Park: Bigger, Larger & Uncut*, for which he received a 1999 Oscar nomination for Best Song.

CITY SLICKERS
Varèse Sarabande VSD-5321

Shaiman's score played a crucial role in sustaining the comic timing and tension of this popular Billy Crystal comedy about three hopeless "cowboys" on a two-week cattle drive (which won Jack Palance a 1991 supporting-actor Oscar). Shaiman wrote a wide-open-spaces theme à la Elmer Bernstein and incorporated everything from traditional guitar-and-harmonica to blues, raucous jazz, and a wild soul number for a cattle-stampede sequence.

THE ADDAMS FAMILY
Capitol CDP 7-98172 2

Vic Mizzy's unforgettable TV theme launches the movie and this score, but most of Shaiman's music for the 1991 feature-film version of the 1960s sitcom (starring Anjelica Huston, Raul Julia, and Christopher Lloyd) is original. By turns charming, grandly romantic, and slyly demonic, this score mirrors the darkly comic moods of the movie and includes "Mamushka," a song written with legendary lyricists Adolph Green and Betty Comden. Shaiman also scored the 1993 sequel, *Addams Family Values*.

THE AMERICAN PRESIDENT

MCA MCAD-11380

Shaiman's finest hour, and his first Oscar nomination for Best Original Score, came with Rob Reiner's popular 1995 film on Washington politics, starring Michael Douglas as the chief executive and Annette Bening as the lobbyist who wins his heart. It's worth seeing for the main title sequence alone, which beautifully weds images of the White House and past presidents with Shaiman's sweeping, romantic anthem. Although it was nominated in the "comedy or musical" category, this is really Shaiman's best dramatic score.

GEORGE OF THE JUNGLE

Walt Disney 60806-7

Disney's silly 1997 adaptation of the cult-favorite cartoon character was accompanied by one of Shaiman's most creative scores, incorporating an often wild Spike Jones style (throw in everything including the kitchen sink). There's a heroic theme for George (apart from the fun cartoon song by Sheldon Allman and Stan Worth) and a hilarious, vaudeville-style swing-band number for George's jungle antics. Unfortunately the album contains only seven minutes of Shaiman and several pointless songs.

Shire, David (1937–)

A compelling musical voice during the 1970s, the last truly creative era of American filmmaking, David Shire scored some of the decade's most important films: *The Conversation* (1974) and *All the President's Men* (1976) on the artistic side, *Saturday Night Fever* (1977) on the commercial side.

Shire came to films from the theater, where he wrote off-Broadway musicals with his partner Richard Maltby, and from television, where he had achieved success with such shows as *McCloud* and *Lucas Tanner*. At Francis Ford Coppola's request, he scored *The Conversation* for solo piano and played it himself with a restrained jazz feel. For director Alan J. Pakula, he very sparsely scored the Watergate film *All the President's Men* with a quietly suspenseful theme that only occasionally creeps into the film.

Although Shire has returned to the theater (writing, among other shows, the off-Broadway revue *Closer Than Ever* and the Broadway musical *Big*) and TV (scoring such miniseries as *The Kennedys of Massachusetts* and cable films like *Last Stand at Saber River*), some of his '70s scores are still strikingly original: the '40s period feel of *Farewell, My Lovely* (1975), the 12-tone-mixed-with-jazz-rock approach of *The Taking of Pelham One-Two-Three* (1974), the soaring beauty of his music for *The Hindenburg* (1975).

He won the 1979 Best Song Oscar for "It Goes Like It Goes," the theme for *Norma Rae*, and a 1977 Grammy for his contributions to the *Saturday Night Fever* soundtrack. His effective electronic score for *2010* (1984) charted briefly.

DAVID SHIRE AT THE MOVIES

Bay Cities BCD 3021

Reduced-scale renditions of some of Shire's most memorable music are featured on this 1991 collection, with the composer himself playing piano on such gems as the '40s-style *Farewell, My Lovely* (1975), the haunting *The Conversation* (1974), and the lighthearted *Max Dugan Returns* (1983). Shire's original, rejected, concept for *The Hindenburg* theme (1975), for soprano voice and trumpet, makes its first appearance here. Maureen McGovern sings Shire's Oscar-winning "It Goes Like It Goes" from *Norma Rae* (1979), the Oscar-nominated "I'll Never Say Goodbye" from *The Promise* (1979), "Halfway Home" from *The Earthling* (1980), and the title song from *Only When I Laugh* (1981).

THE TAKING OF PELHAM ONE-TWO-THREE

Retrograde FSM-DS-123

Faced with the problem of musically depicting New York City for this 1974 action film about terrorists who hijack a subway train, Shire decided on music that was "jazz-oriented, hard-edged [with a] wisecracking subtext . . . a feeling of organized chaos." The result was this highly original 12-tone work for big-band ensemble plus strings, an aggressive and energetic score. Walter Matthau and Robert Shaw starred in the film.

THEMES BY HOLLYWOOD'S GREAT COMPOSERS

Sony AK 47019

This 1991 collection contains Shire's great big-band theme for *Farewell, My Lovely* (1975) starring Robert Mitchum in a fine, world-weary portrayal of Raymond Chandler's detective Philip Marlowe. Other notable themes, largely unavailable elsewhere, include Jerry Goldsmith's *The Great Train Robbery* (1979), Richard Rodney Bennett's concerto-style *Billion Dollar Brain* (1967), and Percy Faith's arrangement of Max Steiner's *A Summer Place* (1959). The Faith record lasted nine weeks at number 1, making it the most successful instrumental single of the rock era.

RETURN TO OZ

Bay Cities BCD-3001

The ill-fated 1985 sequel to *The Wizard of Oz*, with Fairuza Balk and Nicol Williamson, sported stunning special effects and a rich symphonic score by Shire. He intertwined nine themes of various rhythms and colors: a turn-of-the-century waltz for Jack Pumpkinhead, a rag march for Dorothy's return to Oz, a brass quintet for the mechanical Tik Tok, a mandolin for Mombi, and more. Expansive, romantic, and lush, performed by the London Symphony Orchestra, it unfortunately sank with the movie.

COURTESY CHASEN & COMPANY

Shore, Howard (1946–)

Canadian-born Howard Shore first came to prominence as the original bandleader on NBC's *Saturday Night Live*—the result of a call from old friend Lorne Michaels. He attended Boston's Berklee School of Music and gained an appreciation of a wide range of composers from Ornette Coleman to Toru Takemitsu.

Shore is best known for his long and productive relationship with director David Cronenberg: nine films so far, including box-office hits like *Scanners* (1981) and *The Fly* (1986) and such controversial films as *Naked Lunch* (1991) and *Crash* (1997). While Shore is as adept as anyone at writing for orchestra, in the strange accident-as-sensuality film *Crash* he relied on a metallic sound involving electric guitars, harps, woodwinds, and percussionists.

Shore has been associated with several hit films throughout the '80s and '90s, though he has never been nominated for an Oscar—not even for the multiple-Oscar-winning *The Silence of the Lambs* (1991), perhaps his most widely heard work. He wrote music for Robert Benton's *Places in the Heart* (1984), Martin Scorsese's *After Hours* (1985), Penny Marshall's *Big* (1988), and Chris Columbus's *Mrs. Doubtfire* (1993).

Shore is one of a handful of top "Hollywood" composers who lives and works in New York.

THE FLY
Varèse Sarabande VCD-47272
David Cronenberg's most mainstream film was this 1986 remake of the classic 1958 horror flick about a scientist (Jeff Goldblum) whose experimentation results in his accidental transformation into a grotesque creature. Shore's music is perfectly attuned to Cronenberg's disturbing and extremely graphic nightmare—tonal but modern, frightening and even shocking.

THE SILENCE OF THE LAMBS
MCA MCAD-10194
Jonathan Demme's thriller about an FBI trainee who matches wits with one serial killer in an effort to capture another won five 1991 Oscars: Best Picture, Best Director, Best Actor (Anthony Hopkins), Best Actress (Jodie Foster), and Best Adapted Screenplay. Shore's score wasn't nominated—probably because it was effective without being obtrusive. More than anything else he had written to date, this music demonstrated his mastery of the symphonic ensemble, sometimes gently foreboding, sometimes grandly dramatic.

ED WOOD
Hollywood HR-62002-2
Tim Burton's only movie without composer Danny Elfman was this hilarious and touching 1994 story of the Z-film auteur that starred

Johnny Depp in the title role and won an Oscar for Martin Landau as the tragic figure Bela Lugosi in his last days. Shore captured the era and the Hollywood craziness with his pastiche of '50s-specific bongo drums, pipe organ, and that sci-fi-movie favorite, the theremin. His horror-film riffs and exotic Latin beats, notably the tango and mambo, add to the fun.

SEVEN
TVT 6510-2
Director David Fincher's 1995 descent into hell, courtesy of Morgan Freeman and Brad Pitt as detectives on the trail of a particularly sick serial killer, was scored by Shore in one of his most unsettling orchestral moods. The title refers to the seven deadly sins being illustrated via sadistic murders, and Shore's music is not so much suspenseful or frightening as it is stark, cold, and relentlessly grim. The album contains 20 minutes of the score; songs complete the package.

Shostakovich, Dmitri (1906–1975)
One of the century's greatest composers—some say the greatest—this Russian artist wrote enduring

music despite a lifelong rollercoaster of in-favor/out-of-favor status with Soviet authorities.

Shostakovich began his musical career in Leningrad as a pianist for silent films, and the dramatic and powerful nature of his own music made him an ideal specialist in the new medium. He wrote his first film score for the silent *The New Babylon* (1929) and continued (particularly when Stalin demanded it) to write for the cinema in every decade that followed.

Reports differ as to whether Shostakovich enjoyed writing for the cinema. He was much in demand, and it was relatively lucrative work, particularly during times when his concert music was banned. In his few public comments on the subject, he said that film-scoring helped keep his musical reflexes sharp. The sheer variety and volume of music he created for Soviet films seems to indicate that it was, at the very least, a stimulating creative challenge and a workshop for musical experimentation.

In all, Shostakovich composed 36 film scores, and while the movies are all but unknown outside Russia, the opening of doors to the West has made possible the re-recording of many. Some, like his powerful 1964 *Hamlet*, have been recorded by a number of orchestras. But several others are masterpieces, too, notably *Zoya* (1944), *Pirogov* (1947), *Michurin* (1949), *The Gadfly* (1955), and *A Year Is Like a Lifetime* (1965).

THE NEW BABYLON / FIVE DAYS AND FIVE NIGHTS
Capriccio 10 341/42

This two-CD set contains the first recording of the entire 85-minute score of the 1929 film by Grigori Kozintsev and Leonid Trauberg, which chronicled the events of the Paris Commune in 1870–71 and launched Shostakovich's long career as composer

for all of Kozintsev's films. This score (op. 18) is accompanied by half an hour of music from Shostakovich's *Five Days and Five Nights* (op. 11, 1960), the German-Soviet film about the post-war salvation of the treasures of the Dresden Art Gallery. James Judd conducts the Berlin Radio Symphony Orchestra.

SHOSTAKOVICH: THE FILM ALBUM
London 289 460 792-2

Excerpts from nine Shostakovich film scores are included here, including 20 minutes of *Alone* (1930) and a 12-minute version of the recently unearthed *Tale of the Silly Little Mouse* (1939). What's unusual is the 17-minute suite from *Hamlet* (1964) that includes three short, rarely heard movements (music for the palace, the ball, and the military) among the otherwise familiar sections of this film-music masterpiece. Riccardo Chailly conducts the Royal Concertgebouw Orchestra.

ZOYA / THE FALL OF BERLIN
Capriccio 10 405

One of Shostakovich's most dramatic and beautiful scores, *Zoya* (op. 64, 1944) was written for a Socialist fairy tale about a peasant girl, a film made by his close friend Lev Oskarevich Arnstam (for whom he also scored *Five Days and Five Nights* and two other films). On the same disc is *The Fall of Berlin* (op. 82, 1949), depicting Stalin as a hero of World War II and which the composer was obliged to write "in order to survive." Michail Jurowski conducts Deutsches Symphonie-Orchester Berlin.

THE GADFLY / PIROGOV
RCA 6603-2-RC

Nearly 46 minutes long, *The Gadfly* (op. 97, 1955) was written for a film about Austrian-occupied

Italy in 1840. Its memorable "Romance" was later used as the theme for the popular PBS series *Reilly, Ace of Spies*, starring Sam Neill. The more subdued *Pirogov* (op. 76, 1947) profiled a Russian doctor who helped to defend Sebastopol during the Crimean War. José Serebrier conducts the Belgian Radio Symphony Orchestra.

MICHURIN / THE FALL OF BERLIN / THE GOLDEN MOUNTAINS
RCA 602262-RC

Shostakovich's *Michurin* (op. 78a, 1949), written for a film about a Soviet agronomist, contains one of his most inspiring film themes. Its 30 minutes is paired with 24 minutes of the inspiring and powerful *The Fall of Berlin* (op. 82a, 1950) and 12 minutes of excerpts from Shostakovich's third film score, *The Golden Mountains* (op. 30a, 1931). José Serebrier conducts the Belgian Radio Symphony Orchestra.

HAMLET / KING LEAR
RCA 7763-2-RC

Shostakovich's most famous film score for Grigori Kozintsev's *Hamlet* (op. 116, 1964) is also among his most arresting and memorable; its eight movements, over 30 minutes—not all used in the film—is striking in its sheer boldness and energy. This is coupled with 20 minutes of *King Lear* (op. 137, 1970), also for Kozintsev, and three excerpts of the *Five Days and Five Nights* score totalling another 20 minutes. José Serebrier conducts the Belgian Radio Symphony Orchestra.

PHOTO COURTESY OF ROGERS & COWAN

Silvestri, Alan (1950–)

Alan Silvestri is one of those composers who was at the right place at the right time, not once but twice. A lyricist friend, mistakenly called about music for a low-budget feature, suggested the desperate, out-of-work Silvestri for *The Doberman Gang* (1972). Then, after several seasons of scoring TV's *CHiPs*, its music editor recommended Silvestri for an action-adventure called *Romancing the Stone* (1984).

The latter cemented a relationship with director Robert Zemeckis, and Silvestri has scored all of his films since, including the *Back to the Future* trilogy (1985–90), the groundbreaking animated *Who Framed Roger Rabbit?* (1988), the wicked comedy *Death Becomes Her* (1992), and the multiple-Oscar-winning *Forrest Gump* (1994).

Silvestri, who attended Boston's Berklee College of Music for two years but is largely self-taught, has been much in demand for comedies from Bette Midler in *Outrageous Fortune* (1986) to Steve Martin in *Father of the Bride* (1991) to Lemmon and Matthau in *Grumpy Old Men* (1993). Yet he has also demonstrated his abilities in other genres, including horror (*Predator*, 1987), science-fiction (*The Abyss*, 1989), thrillers (*Blown Away*, 1994), and westerns (*The Quick and the Dead*, 1994).

Although *The Bodyguard* (1992) was essentially a song score, Silvestri was fortunate once more: his melancholy theme from the Kevin Costner–Whitney Houston romance was included on the album. It's now among the top-selling soundtracks of all time.

VOYAGES: THE FILM MUSIC JOURNEYS OF ALAN SILVESTRI
Varèse Sarabande VSD-5641

Twelve of the 14 tracks on this 1995 disc are original-soundtrack recordings conducted by the composer, so this is as definitive a collection as one is likely to find. Included are most of the early favorites, including the theme from Silvestri's first hit, *Romancing the Stone* (1984), and such oddities as his Morricone-style theme for *The Quick and the Dead* (1994), and his cha-cha from *Soapdish* (1991).

BACK TO THE FUTURE I, II, III
MCA MCAD-6144
MCA MCAD-6361
Varèse Sarabande VSD-5272

Robert Zemeckis's 1985 time-travel story starring then-popular TV actor Michael J. Fox was so successful that it spawned two sequels. Silvestri scored them all with a big, broad brush in the John Williams mode, with a heroic theme and rapid-fire orchestral pyrotechnics. The first album contains mostly songs (including Huey Lewis's Oscar-nominated "The Power of Love"); subsequent albums are all score, with the third in western-parody mode.

WHO FRAMED ROGER RABBIT?
Touchstone CD-013

Zemeckis's 1988 groundbreaking mixture of live action and animation cast Bob Hoskins as a private eye investigating dark doings in the all-animation Toontown. Silvestri delivered a score that was wild and wacky, with music that ranges from saloon jazz (where Jessica Rabbit worked) to darkly suspenseful (for detective Eddie Valiant's dangerous work) to purely manic (for the many cartoon characters that fly in and out of the picture). Traditional cartoon themes, including "The Merry-Go-Round Broke Down" and "Merrily We Roll Along," are appropriately featured.

THE ABYSS
Varèse Sarabande VSD-5235

Silvestri's sole assignment for director James Cameron was this 1989 sci-fi love story with Ed Harris and Mary Elizabeth Mastrantonio. He composed a mixture of muscular action music, low-key suspense, and awe-inspiring choral-and-orchestral scoring for the alien lifeforms that ultimately appear in the film. The finale, with its partially a capella choir, is a highlight.

FORREST GUMP
Epic EK 66430

This Eric Roth–written, Robert Zemeckis–directed epic of one slightly slow-witted but big-hearted Southern boy (Tom Hanks) and his journeys through post-war America won six 1994 Oscars including Best Picture. Silvestri's score, while nominated, did not win, and that's a shame considering its depth and its effectiveness within the film. Multi-thematic, gentle, and subtle—where the many period songs in this movie are not—this is Silvestri's finest work.

COURTESY WARNER BROS. ANIMATION

Stalling, Carl W. (1888–1974)

The most celebrated of cartoon composers, Carl Stalling was a key collaborator with some of the century's great film artists—notably Walt Disney and Chuck Jones—and one whose innovations are just now being widely recognized and appreciated.

Stalling, who originally conducted an orchestra and improvised at the organ to silent pictures in Kansas City, scored the famous Mickey Mouse cartoon *Steamboat Willie* (1928) and conceived the idea for Disney's first *Silly Symphony* the same year. In 1936, he joined Warner Bros., where he became musical director for the animation department and scored more than 600 cartoons over the next 22 years.

Stalling's penchant for interpolating songs from the Warner Bros. music catalog ("The Lady in Red" for any woman wearing a red dress, "A Cup of Coffee, a Sandwich and You" for a scene involving food, "How Dry I Am" for drunks) and the novelty tunes of Raymond Scott ("Powerhouse" for machinery and spaceships, "Dinner Music for a Pack of Hungry Cannibals" for jungle scenes) became running gags of their own.

Chuck Jones and Stalling collaborated on sev-eral cartoons based on concert music, especially *Long-Haired Hare* (1949), in which Bugs Bunny torments an arrogant tenor at the Hollywood Bowl, and *The Rabbit of Seville* (1950), a sendup of the Rossini opera.

THE CARL STALLING PROJECT, VOLS. 1 & 2
Warner Bros. 9 26027-2, 45730-2
These two collections of musical madness demonstrate Stalling's remarkable wit and inventive capacity for any crazy situation the Warner Bros. animators could concoct for their *Merrie Melodies* and *Looney Tunes* series. Medleys of music for Bugs Bunny, Porky Pig, the Road Runner, Daffy Duck, Sylvester and Tweety, Speedy Gonzales, and more are included, covering the years 1936–1958.

FROM THE AUTHOR'S COLLECTION

Steiner, Max (1888–1971)

One of the first composers for sound films, Max Steiner also became the most prolific, writing music for more than 250 movies over nearly four decades. Born in Vienna, he emigrated to the U.S. during World War I and became music director for the famed Ziegfeld Follies. In 1929, he was invited to Hollywood to conduct a score at RKO and subsequently became the studio's music director.

Steiner's landmark score for 1933's *King Kong* marked the first time that a dramatic underscore played a vital role in the filmmaking process, helping to define characters and create atmosphere in ways that only music can. He also pioneered the use of the click-track, a device that enabled precise synchronization of music to film during recording and one that is still in use to this day.

Steiner left RKO in 1936 and, in 1937, began a long association with Warner Bros. (although he scored several pictures for David O. Selznick and, on rare occasions, worked for other studios). Nominated for 25 Academy Awards, he won three: for John Ford's *The Informer* (1935), the Bette Davis romance *Now, Voyager* (1942), and the wartime drama *Since You Went Away* (1944).

His most famous work, however, is his sweeping, multi-faceted score for MGM's beloved 1939 classic *Gone With the Wind*, whose "Tara" theme became one of the most often recorded in movie-music history. At Warners, he was Bette Davis's favorite composer, scoring 20 of her films. He also scored several Humphrey Bogart classics including *Casablanca* (1943), *The Big Sleep* (1946), and *The Treasure of the Sierra Madre* (1948), as well as several Errol Flynn pictures, including *They Died With Their Boots On* (1941) and *Adventures of Don Juan* (1948).

Steiner surprised everyone by writing a pop hit at the age of 71: the theme for *A Summer Place* (1959), which in Percy Faith's recording spent nine weeks at number 1 in 1960 and won a Grammy as Record of the Year.

KING KONG

Southern Cross SCCD 901
Marco Polo 8.223763
Rhino R2 75597

Steiner's 1933 score for the giant-ape fantasy demonstrated the viability of original music for movies as a conveyor of excitement, emotion, and atmosphere. The strange plot and its unusual visual effects demanded dynamic, colorful music for much of its running time, and Steiner obliged with this masterwork. Fred Steiner's (no relation) 1976 re-recording with the National Philharmonic for Southern Cross offers 48 minutes of highlights. John W. Morgan meticulously reconstructed the entire 72-minute Steiner original for the 1997 re-recording by William J. Stromberg and the Moscow Symphony Orchestra. Twenty-five minutes of Steiner's original tracks were restored for a beautifully packaged Rhino sic in 1999.

GONE WITH THE WIND

Rhino R2 72269
RCA 0452-2-RG

Steiner's magnum opus, his 1939 masterpiece for David O. Selznick's multiple-Oscar-winning epic of the South, contains—according to Selznick expert and film historian Rudy Behlmer—11 primary motifs, 16 additional melodies, and any

number of adaptations of folk and patriotic material, 99 separate pieces in all. Steiner's score (which, astoundingly, did not win an Oscar) is a well-crafted blend of traditional American melodies (Stephen Foster, "Dixie," etc.) and his own original themes, notably the memorable "Tara." This two-CD set, issued in 1996, contains virtually all of the Steiner-conducted original (along with a comprehensive, colorfully illustrated 48-page book written by Behlmer). RCA's stereo CD is the 44-minute distillation of the score produced for the "Classic Film Scores" series of the '70s, featuring Charles Gerhardt and the National Philharmonic Orchestra, and is probably the most authentic of the several re-recordings available.

NOW, VOYAGER:
CLASSIC FILM SCORES OF MAX STEINER
RCA 0136-2-RG

This 1973 installment in RCA's "Classic Film Scores" series skips the obvious (*Gone With the Wind, Casablanca*) in favor of other great, but more obscure, examples of the composer's talent: Seven- to eight-minute suites from *King Kong*

(1933), *The Big Sleep* (1946), and *The Fountainhead* (1949), plus the "Symphonie Moderne" from *Four Wives* (1939) played by pianist Earl Wild. Shorter suites from the Oscar-winning *Now, Voyager* (1942) and *The Informer* (1935), and single themes from *Since You Went Away* (1944), *Saratoga Trunk* (1946), and *The Charge of the Light Brigade* (1936) are also included. Charles Gerhardt conducts the National Philharmonic.

CASABLANCA: CLASSIC FILM SCORES
FOR HUMPHREY BOGART
RCA 0422-2-RG

Seven of the 12 score excerpts on this 1974 entry in the "Classic Film Scores" series are Steiner's: strong, colorful suites from *Casablanca* (1943), *The Treasure of the Sierra Madre* (1948), and *Key Largo* (1948), plus single themes or short suites from *Passage to Marseille* (1944), *The Big Sleep* (1946), *The Caine Mutiny* (1954), and *Virginia City* (1940). Also included: music from *To Have and Have Not* and *The Two Mrs. Carrolls* (Franz Waxman), *Sabrina* (Frederick Hollander), *The Left Hand of God* (Victor Young), and *Sahara* (Miklós Rózsa). Charles Gerhardt conducts the National Philharmonic.

CLASSIC FILM SCORES FOR BETTE DAVIS
RCA 0183-2-RG

Bette Davis, speaking of the composer, once said, "Max knew more about drama than any of us." Because Steiner and Davis were both associated with Warner Bros. for much of their careers, eight of the many romantic cuts on this album are Steiner compositions: long suites from *Dark Victory* (1939), *Beyond the Forest* (1949), and *All This and Heaven Too* (1940), and shorter bits from *Now, Voyager* (1942), *A Stolen Life* (1946), *In This Our Life* (1942), *Jezebel* (1938), and *The Letter* (1940). Also included: music from *The Private Lives of Elizabeth and Essex* and *Juarez* (Korngold), *Mr. Skeffington* (Waxman), and *All About Eve* (Newman). Charles Gerhardt conducts the National Philharmonic.

CAPTAIN BLOOD: CLASSIC FILM SCORES FOR ERROL FLYNN
RCA 0912-2-RG

Although the title might imply a heavy dose of Erich Wolfgang Korngold—and much of the disc contains excerpts from his *Sea Hawk*, *Captain Blood*, and *Adventures of Robin Hood*—in reality more than half its content is Steiner: long suites from the romantic, Spanish-flavored *Adventures of Don Juan* (1948) and the Flynn westerns *They Died With Their Boots On* (1941) and *Dodge City* (1939). Also included: bits of Waxman's *Objective, Burma!* and Friedhofer's *The Sun Also Rises*. Charles Gerhardt conducts the National Philharmonic.

MUSIC BY MAX STEINER
Capitol CDP 95597 2 5

This CD edition of a much sought after Capitol LP contains Steiner's own suites from his three Oscar-winning scores: His heartfelt music for *Since You Went Away* (1944), David O. Selznick's three-hour look at life on the homefront during World War II with Claudette Colbert and Jennifer Jones; *Now, Voyager* (1942), the classic Bette Davis–Paul Henreid romance; and *The Informer* (1935), the John Ford film about betrayal during the Irish Rebellion. These are coupled with Alex North's music for *A Streetcar Named Desire*.

HISTORICAL ROMANCES
Marco Polo 8.223608

Nearly a half-hour of Steiner's music for the 1936 adaptation of the Tennyson poem *The Charge of the Light Brigade* has been reconstructed here by John W. Morgan and conducted by Richard Kaufman with the Brandenburg Philharmonic Orchestra. Warner Bros. turned the Crimean War story into an action vehicle for Errol Flynn, with Olivia deHavilland as the romantic interest, and Steiner's first score for the Warner studio turned out to be one of his most exciting.

THE LOST PATROL / VIRGINIA CITY
Marco Polo 8.223870

This 1995 re-recording contains half an hour apiece of Steiner's exciting *The Lost Patrol* (1934), for director John Ford, and his sprawling western *Virginia City* (1940), which starred Errol Flynn. Also included: 16 minutes of Steiner's sinister music for *The Beast With Five Fingers* (1946), which incorporates Bach's "D minor Chaconne." William T. Stromberg conducts the Moscow Symphony Orchestra in these John Morgan restorations.

THEY DIED WITH THEIR BOOTS ON
Marco Polo 8.225079

Errol Flynn's portrayal of George Armstrong Custer leading up to the events at the Little Big Horn was immeasurably enhanced by one of Max Steiner's greatest western scores. Steiner incorporates such traditional cavalry-related tunes as "Garry Owen," "Boots and Saddles," and others throughout the score, restored to 70 minutes by John W. Morgan and performed by conductor William Stromberg and the Moscow Symphony Orchestra. As Morgan points out in his notes, Steiner's "Indian music" was original in 1941 but, as adopted by other film composers, quickly became a cliché.

THE ADVENTURES OF MARK TWAIN / THE PRINCE AND THE PAUPER
BMG/RCA 09026 62660 2 (Germany)

Fredric March played Samuel Langhorne Clemens in Warner Bros.' 1944 film *The Adventures of Mark Twain*, featuring a delightful Americana underscore from Steiner (who received an Oscar nomination for his work). Tuneful and folk-oriented (interpolating such favorites as "Oh Susanna" and "My Darling Clementine"), Steiner's music illustrated the action of the film, as did Erich Wolfgang Korngold's richly orchestrated score for *The Prince and the Pauper* (1937). The latter was based on a Twain novel and starred Errol Flynn and the Mauch Twins. John W. Morgan reconstructed the scores; William T. Stromberg conducted the Brandenburg Philharmonic.

Stothart, Herbert (1885–1949)

One of the unsung pioneers of film scoring, Wisconsin-born Herbert Stothart was the primary musical director at MGM from 1930 until his death in 1949, scoring more than 100 films and winning a Best Original Score Oscar for the 1939 classic *The Wizard of Oz*. (While the songs are the work of Harold Arlen and E. Y. Harburg, much of the underscore is original Stothart music.)

Stothart was musical director on the Jeanette MacDonald–Nelson Eddy film operettas of the 1930s and scored many of MGM's adaptations of classic literature, including *Treasure Island* (1934), *David Copperfield*, *Mutiny on the Bounty*, and *A Tale of Two Cities* (all 1935), *Romeo and Juliet* (1936), and *Pride and Prejudice* (1940).

A respected musicologist, he often drew on classical and folk traditions to provide an immediate musical identification with time and place, including Mexican folk songs in *Viva Villa!* (1934), Russian colors in *Anna Karenina* (1935), Chinese scales in *The Good Earth* (1937), and 18th-century French music for *Marie Antoinette* (1938). Parts of the score for *The Yearling* (1947) were based on Delius themes, *The Three Musketeers* (1948) on Tchaikovsky.

Stothart's music accompanied several wartime classics, including Greer Garson's Oscar-winning *Mrs. Miniver* and Ronald Colman's *Random Harvest* (both 1942), Elizabeth Taylor's *National Velvet* and Spencer Tracy's *Thirty Seconds Over Tokyo* (both 1944). Several of the tunes he wrote—often with famous collaborators from George Gershwin to Oscar Hammerstein II—are familiar even today, from "I Wanna Be Loved by You" to "The Donkey Serenade." Little of his music was ever made commercially available.

THE LION'S ROAR: CLASSIC MGM FILM SCORES 1935–1965
Rhino R2 75701

Short suites from four Stothart classics are included on this two-CD retrospective of MGM film music. His energetic music for the mutinous sailors of *Mutiny on the Bounty* (1935), the authentic sounds of the Far East for *The Good Earth* (1937), his powerful and mysterious opening for the Ronald Colman film *Random Harvest* (1942), and the soaring, Delius-derived melodies for orchestra and chorus of *The Yearling* (1946) are included. Other unreleased or hard-to-find music: Bronislau Kaper's *Invitation* (1952), *Lili* (1953), and the remake of *Mutiny on the Bounty* (1962); André Previn's *Bad Day at Black Rock* (1955), *Designing Woman* (1957), and *The Subterraneans* (1960); Elmer Bernstein's *Some Came Running* (1958); David Raksin's *Two Weeks in Another Town* (1962); and Jerry Goldsmith's *The Prize* (1963).

Takemitsu, Toru (1930–1996)

Toru Takemitsu was perhaps the most internationally recognized of Japanese composers. Renowned for his unique sounds and avant-garde style, his many orchestral works included a *Requiem* for strings (1957) and *November Steps* for biwa, shakuhachi, and orchestra (1967).

Born in Tokyo, Takemitsu was as acclaimed for his movie scores as for his concert music. He was identified with Japan's New Wave Cinema of the '60s and '70s, and he wrote music for many of his country's greatest film directors.

The best known of his more than 90 films included *Woman in the Dunes* (1964) and *Rikyu* (1989), both directed by Hiroshi Teshigahara; *Dodes'ka-den* (1970) and *Ran* (1985), directed by Akira Kurosawa; *Kwaidan* (1964), *Samurai Rebellion* (1967), and *Tokyo Trials* (1983), all directed by Masaki Kobayashi; *The Ceremony* (1971) and *Empire of Passion* (1978), directed by Nagisa Oshima; *Pale Flower* (1964), *Double Suicide* (1969), and *Ballad of Orin* (1977), directed by Masahiro Shinoda; and *Black Rain* (1989) directed by Shohei Imamura. His sole American film was Philip Kaufman's *Rising Sun* (1993); the experience was so unpleasant that he never did another one.

Stylistically, he was eclectic and original. "I want to give sound the freedom to breathe," Takemitsu once wrote. "In the world in which we live, silence and unlimited sound exist. I wish to carve that sound with my own hands." In freeing his sounds from what he called "the trite rules of music," Takemitsu offered a unique aural signature to every movie he scored.

THE FILM MUSIC OF TORU TAKEMITSU
Nonesuch 79404-2

This 1997 collection contains music from ten of Takemitsu's films, including *Woman in the Dunes*, *Dodes'ka-den*, *Empire of Passion*, and *Black Rain*. The longest suite, 15 minutes of spare and often arresting sounds, is devoted to *Rikyu*. Strings alone are featured in the boxing documentary *José Torres* (1959), the grim Hiroshima bombing film *Black Rain*, and the waltz of *The Face of Another* (1966). The biwa of *Harakiri* (1963), the eerie female voice of *Banished Orin* (1978), the plaintive guitar of *Kaseki* (1975), and the stark orchestral landscape of *Empire of Passion* are also included. Suites from the uncharacteristically bright *Dodes'ka-den* and the strange, shifting-sand musical textures of *Woman in the Dunes* conclude the set.

Tangerine Dream

A German techno-pop group (before there was such a term) formed in 1967, when synthesizers were just emerging as a significant new element of music-making, Tangerine Dream was already a popular recording entity by the time director William Friedkin discovered them on a trip to Munich while promoting *The Exorcist*.

Edgar Froese, Chris Franke, and Peter Baumann played various synthesizers and electric guitars on Friedkin's next movie, *Sorcerer* (1977)—

Friedkin actually "scoring" the film based on a 90-minute tape of "musical impressions" he received from the group during shooting. Michael Mann's *Thief* (1981) followed, along with two dozen other films over the next 15 years, notably the Tom Cruise smash *Risky Business* (1983), the Stephen King thriller *Firestarter* (1984), and Andrei Konchalovsky's *Shy People* (1987).

Tangerine Dream unwittingly incurred the wrath of thousands of film-music fans when the group was hired to replace Jerry Goldsmith's music for Ridley Scott's 1986 fantasy *Legend*. While Goldsmith's music remained in the European version, the Dream's vastly different synth score appeared in the U.S. cut.

The group's personnel has changed over the years, notably with the departure of Franke in 1988 to pursue his own composing career. While maintaining a separate studio in Berlin, he opened a second studio in Los Angeles, where he has since scored such films as *Universal Soldier* (1992) and TV series, including the five years of *Babylon 5*.

SORCERER
MCA MCAD-10842

Tangerine Dream's first movie score consisted of improvisations based on a reading of the script for William Friedkin's taut 1977 remake of the French classic *The Wages of Fear*. Some critics thought it was a wildly inappropriate score, with electronic noises playing against the rain-soaked Central American jungles where Roy Scheider and company were driving trucks of highly volatile nitroglycerine 200 miles across rough roads. But several tracks, regardless of their effectiveness in the film, are surprisingly compelling.

Theodorakis, Mikis (1925–)

Greek composer Mikis Theodorakis is probably best known for his popular score for *Zorba the Greek* (1964), but he is also one of Greece's most important and widely respected composers of concert music. His output includes several symphonies, oratorios, ballets, and song cycles.

Born on Chios, he was educated at the Paris Conservatory and, upon his return to Greece in 1959, issued a manifesto condemning elements of the Greek artistic community. He was imprisoned and his music banned from public performance in 1967, but world pressure led to his release and exile.

His two dozen film scores include some of the most critically acclaimed movies of the '60s and '70s: *Phaedra* (1962); *Zorba*, which he adapted into a ballet in 1988; two politically charged thrillers from director Costa-Gavras, the Oscar-winning *Z* (1969) and *State of Siege* (1973); the police corruption film *Serpico* (1973); and the Eurpides adaptation *Iphigenia* (1977).

It's a shock to realize that Theodorakis was never acknowledged at the Academy Awards, even with a nomination, for his memorable music. A Grammy nominee for *Zorba* and later for *Serpico*, he even lost for *Z*—Henry Mancini won a Grammy for his arrangement of the theme but the composer wasn't nominated for his original version.

MIKIS THEODORAKIS ON THE SCREEN
DRG 32901

This two-CD set contains four complete scores from Theodorakis's films of the '60s and '70s. *Z*, written while the composer was in exile, was the landmark Costa-Gavras film about political oppression, scored with traditional bouzoukis as well as full orchestra. *State of Siege* offers the Latin American group Los Calchakis intepreting the composer's music for Costa-Gavras's bracing tract about political assassination in Uruguay with guitars, wooden flutes, and indigenous percussion instruments. Jazz great Bob James arranged Theodorakis's music for *Serpico* but remained true to the composer's colors and emotional intent. *Phaedra*, the earliest of these movies, is the most symphonic of the four and also includes a vocal by actress Melina Mercouri.

Thomson, Virgil (1896–1989)

Kansas City–born, Harvard-educated, a witty writer and highly influential New York music critic, Thomson wrote three operas, two ballets, and a host of orchestral music, songs, and chamber music. Yet his most famous works are a trio of film scores, all written for rarely seen documentaries of the '30s and '40s.

The Plow That Broke the Plains (1936) and *The River* (1937) were the work of Pare Lorentz, a filmmaker working under the auspices of the federal Farm Services Administration. The first examined the Dust Bowl of the 1930s and the efforts that the government had undertaken to ease the plight of suffering Midwestern residents; the second concerned the mighty Mississippi.

Louisiana Story (1948) was the work of legendary documentary filmmaker Robert Flaherty (*Nanook of the North*), who received an Oscar nomination. Thomson was ignored by the Oscars but won a Pulitzer Prize for his score. This much more widely distributed "industrial" film (financed by the Standard Oil Company) was in essence a docudrama about a Cajun family in the Louisiana bayou country and the impact of oil technology on their daily lives.

Thomson scored five other films (including one studio picture, Columbia's *The Goddess* with Kim Stanley, in 1958) but none achieved the musical popularity of these three.

THE RIVER / THE PLOW THAT BROKE THE PLAINS
ESS.A.Y CD 1005

Richard Kapp conducts the Philharmonia Virtuosi in the complete scores for the first two Thomson documentaries. Both films contain about 24 minutes of music each, and both are rich in the harmonies traditionally thought of as "American": *The Plow That Broke the Plains* is filled with quotations from such cowboy tunes as "I Ride an Old Paint" and "Streets of Laredo," while much of *The River* derives from what the composer termed "white spirituals," the Christian hymns he remembered from his youth.

LOUISIANA STORY
Hyperion CDA 66576

Thomson prepared two concert suites from his score for Flaherty's 1948 semi-documentary about the arrival of an oil-well crew to an unspoiled part of Louisiana bayou country. "I wrote original music for scenes dominated by landscape and used folk tunes with the people," Thomson later wrote. His *Louisiana Story* suite contains the former; "Acadian Songs and Dances," based on Louisiana French folk tunes he discovered, contains the latter. This music, to date the only film music to win the Pulitzer Prize, is both dramatic and lyrical. Also included: *The Plow That Broke the Plains* suite and "Fugues and Cantilenas" from the 1958 documentary *Power Among Men*. Ronald Corp conducts The New London Orchestra.

Tiomkin, Dimitri (1894–1979)

Ukrainian-born Dimitri Tiomkin studied with Alexander Glazounov before leaving Russia in 1919. He embarked on a career as a concert pianist, notably in Berlin and Paris, where he gave the European premiere of Gershwin's piano concerto in 1928.

His marriage to Austrian-born choreographer Albertina Rasch eventually brought both to Hollywood—she to oversee short ballet sequences in films, he as a fledgling film composer. His grand orchestral-and-choral score for *Lost Horizon* (1937) marked the first of five pictures with director Frank Capra, including such classics as *It's a Wonderful Life* (1946).

Tiomkin's use of the song "Do Not Forsake Me, Oh My Darling" as a narrative device throughout *High Noon* (1952) not only brought him two Oscars (for Best Song, with lyricist Ned Washington, and Best Score) but launched a new trend: the use of a title song as a commercially released record for promotional purposes. *High Noon* was just one of his many western scores; others included *Duel in the Sun* (1946), *Red River* (1948), *Gunfight at the O.K. Corral* (1957), *Rio*

Bravo (1959), *The Alamo* (1960), and others.

A shrewd businessman and tireless self-promoter, Tiomkin was extremely savvy about the commercial exploitation of music for films, often lobbying for singles and albums, aggressively pursuing music-publishing rights for himself, and even campaigning for Academy Awards. He won two more, for *The High and the Mighty* (1954) and *The Old Man and the Sea* (1958).

When he accepted his Academy Award for *The High and the Mighty*, he proceeded to thank a litany of classical composers, including Brahms, Strauss, Wagner, Beethoven, and Rimsky Korsakov. The crowd laughed, and many thought Tiomkin was acknowledging a popular misconception that film music was largely appropriated by hacks from masters; Tiomkin later claimed that he was simply expressing "a musician's homage to the heroes of the musical past."

LOST HORIZON: THE CLASSIC FILM SCORES OF DIMITRI TIOMKIN
RCA 1669-2-RG

This 1976 collection contains a stunning 23-minute re-creation of Tiomkin's ambitious, Oscar-nominated score for Capra's memorable 1937 film of the James Hilton classic starring Ronald Colman. One of Tiomkin's seminal works, its mystery and serenity reflects the atmosphere of Shangri-La itself. A suite from *The Big Sky* (1952) and themes from *The Fourposter* (1952), *Friendly Persuasion* (1956), *Search for Paradise* (1958), and *The Guns of Navarone* (1961) are also included. Charles Gerhardt conducts the National Philharmonic Orchestra.

THE FILM MUSIC OF DIMITRI TIOMKIN
Columbia CK 44370

This 1988 compilation of music from a variety of '50s and '60s scores that Columbia released as singles or LPs showcases the composer's versatility. A highlight is Frankie Laine's powerful vocal renditions of some of Tiomkin's classic film and TV songs: themes from *High Noon* (1952), *Blowing Wild* (1953), *Gunfight at the OK Corral* (1957), and *Rawhide* (1960). Short suites from Tiomkin's Oscar-nominated music for *Giant* (1956), *The Alamo* (1960), *The Guns of Navarone* (1961), *55 Days at Peking* (1963), and *The Fall of the Roman Empire* (1964), plus his Oscar-winning music for *The Old Man and the Sea* (1958), are included, along with music for *Wild Is the Wind* (1957).

LOST HORIZON
BYU Film Archives FMA-DT103
Tiomkin's original soundtrack for the 1937 adaptation of James Hilton's novel of Shangri-La made its debut in this 1999 compact disc, drawn from a collection of old 78 rpm discs discovered in Canada (and probably made for private use either by Tiomkin or conductor Max Steiner). Ronald Colman starred in Frank Capra's Best Picture-nominated film, a grand fantasy made even more grand by Tiomkin's Oscar-nominated, romantic score (his first important work in Hollywood).

IT'S A WONDERFUL LIFE
Telarc CD-88801
The only disc to emerge from conductor David Newman's brief stint as musical director at Robert Redford's Sundance Institute, this Christmas-themed collection has as its centerpiece a 39-minute suite from Tiomkin's most-heard score: Frank Capra's 1946 classic *It's a Wonderful Life*. Suites from Richard Addinsell's 1951 *A Christmas Carol* and Cyril J. Mockridge's 1947 *Miracle on 34th Street* are also included. Newman conducts the Royal Philharmonic Orchestra.

HIGH NOON:
THE MUSIC OF DIMITRI TIOMKIN
BMG/RCA 09026 62658 2 (Germany)
Generous suites from four Tiomkin classics, all arranged by frequent Tiomkin collaborator Christopher Palmer, are included in this 1994 re-recording. Eighteen minutes of Tiomkin's lively score for José Ferrer's Oscar-winning portrayal of *Cyrano de Bergerac* (1950), including the moving "Requiem"; 10 suspenseful minutes from *High Noon*, the seminal western score that won Tiomkin 1952 Oscars for Best Score and Best Song ("Do Not Forsake Me, Oh My Darling"); nearly half an hour from the John Wayne epic *The Alamo*, 1960 nominees for Best Song ("The Green Leaves of Summer") and Best Score; and more than 22 minutes from his choral-and-orchestral epic *55 Days at Peking*, a 1963 Best Score nominee. Lawrence Foster conducts Berlin's Rundfunk Symphony Orchestra and Choir.

THE WESTERN FILM WORLD
OF DIMITRI TIOMKIN
Unicorn-Kanchana UKCD 2011
Orchestrator Christopher Palmer (whose 1984 biography, *Dimitri Tiomkin: A Portrait*, is a nice complement to Tiomkin's 1959 autobiography, *Please Don't Hate Me*) assembled scores from six of the composer's many westerns for this 1981 collection: themes from *Giant* (1956) and *Night Passage* (1957) and longer suites from *Red River* (1948), *Duel in the Sun* (1946), *High Noon* (1952), and *Rio Bravo* (1959). Laurie Johnson conducts the London Studio Symphony Orchestra with the John McCarthy singers.

MUSIC FROM ALFRED HITCHCOCK FILMS
Varèse Sarabande VCD-47225
Tiomkin scored four films for the Master of Suspense, and 16 minutes of his *Strangers on a*

Train (1951, starring Farley Granger and Robert Walker) are preserved on this 1985 re-recording by Charles Ketcham and the Utah Symphony Orchestra. Also included: 12 minutes of Franz Waxman's *Suspicion* (1941, with Cary Grant and Joan Fontaine) and snippets of Roy Webb's *Notorious* (1946, with Grant and Ingrid Bergman) and John Williams's *Family Plot* (1976, Hitchcock's last film, with Barbara Harris and Bruce Dern).

GIANT

Capitol CDP 7 92056 2

Tiomkin wrote one of the longest scores of his career (two and a quarter hours) for George Stevens's sprawling adaptation of the Edna Ferber novel about two generations of Texans—and he also made the highest fee ever paid to a Hollywood composer up to that time ($35,000). In addition to his themes for the land and the main characters (played by Rock Hudson, Elizabeth Taylor, and, in his last performance, James Dean), Tiomkin interpolates several traditional folk tunes ("Yellow Rose of Texas," "The Eyes of Texas"). He won a 1956 Oscar nomination and the album was a top-20 hit.

THE ALAMO

Varèse Sarabande VSD-5224

John Wayne's epic 1960 production was based on the story of Davy Crockett, Jim Bowie, Sam Houston, William Travis, and company defending the military fort in 1836 Texas. Tiomkin supplied one of his best scores, filled with (as the original liner notes quaintly put it) "rustic simplicity and crude vigor." It was a double Oscar nominee for Tiomkin's score and for the song "Green Leaves of Summer," with lyrics by Paul Francis Webster (one of several songs they wrote for the film). Commercially speaking, it was a hit: the album went to number 7, Marty Robbins's "Ballad of the Alamo" into the top 40.

THE FALL OF THE ROMAN EMPIRE

Pendulum PEG-029

Tiomkin conducted a 110-piece orchestra in England for producer Samuel Bronston's three-hour, all-star epic of ancient Rome. Five themes intertwine throughout the album's 15 tracks (40 minutes chosen from two and a half hours of music), many of them dark, moody, and powerful. Sophia Loren, James Mason, Alec Guinness, and Anthony Quayle were among the stars; Tiomkin's 1964 Oscar nomination was the only one the film received.

Vangelis (1943–)

Praised in some quarters as a one-man symphony, damned in others as a pop star who got lucky with a few machines, Evangelos Papathanassiou was born in Greece and began playing the piano at the age of 4. He played in rock bands before moving to Paris and then London, where he built a state-of-the-art synthesizer laboratory in the mid-1970s.

Documentary scores for French television, best-selling LPs like *Heaven and Hell* and *Beaubourg*, and collaborations with ex-Yes vocalist Jon Anderson, led to calls from adventurous filmmakers interested in his romantic sensibility and then-popular synthesized sounds. A 1981 Oscar for *Chariots of Fire* led to collaborations with director Ridley Scott (*Blade Runner*, 1982; *1492: Conquest of Paradise*, 1992), Costa-Gavras (*Missing*, 1982), Roger Donaldson (*The Bounty*, 1984) and others. French filmmaker Frederic Rossif (*L'Apocalypse des Animaux*, 1970) was a favorite.

Even projects he did not score benefited from the Vangelis touch. Two tracks from *Opera Sauvage* (1979) became popular—one as a recurring theme in Peter Weir's 1983 *The Year of Living Dangerously*, the other in an American wine commercial.

Music from his 1975 album *Heaven and Hell* became the main theme of Carl Sagan's PBS astronomy series *Cosmos*.

CHARIOTS OF FIRE

Polydor 800 020-2

Vangelis's hypnotic synthesizers—a seemingly strange choice for a movie about two runners preparing for the 1924 Olympics—propelled this music into a Best Original Score Oscar for the 1981 film (which also won Best Picture). Critics are still divided over the merits of this score: Some thought it was a brilliant choice; others, an impossibly anachronistic one. Ben Cross and Ian Charleson starred in the movie, but it was Vangelis who reaped the biggest rewards: a career in film scoring and a best-selling album (number 1 on *Billboard*'s charts for four weeks).

BLADE RUNNER

Atlantic 82623-2

If ever an all-electronic score was right for its film, it was Vangelis's moody, often bittersweet synthesizer music for Ridley Scott's 1982 sci-fi-noir tale with Harrison Ford, Rutger Hauer, and Sean Young. Atmospheric in the extreme, it set just the right tone—downbeat—for this dark exploration of the near future. Dick Morrissey's bluesy saxophone on the love theme and vocals by Mary Hopkin and Don Percival add diversity to the mix; dialogue and sound effects detract from it.

THEMES

Polydor 839 518-2

This 1989 compilation, a kind of "Vangelis's greatest hits," includes themes from the then-unreleased soundtracks of *Blade Runner* (1982), Costa-Gavras's Oscar-winning political film *Missing* (1982), and the Mel Gibson–Anthony Hopkins mutiny-on-the-high-seas tale *The Bounty* (1984). Also included: themes from the Japanese film *Antarctica* (1983) and several tracks from his non-film albums.

1492: CONQUEST OF PARADISE

Atlantic 7 82432-2

Ridley Scott turned again to Vangelis for an unconventional score for his 1992 film about Christopher Columbus and his voyage to the New World 500 years earlier (with Gerard Depardieu as Columbus and Sigourney Weaver as Queen Isabel). This time the composer supplemented his usual synthesizers with choir and various acoustic instruments (Spanish guitar, mandolin, violin, flutes), and the effect is sometimes haunting.

Vaughan Williams, Ralph (1872–1958)

Vaughan Williams's music reflected his deep interest in English folk tunes and the music of the English Renaissance. His *Fantasia on a Theme by Thomas Tallis*, *The Lark Ascending*, and *Fantasia* on *Greensleeves* for orchestra are among his most familiar pieces, but he also composed nine symphonies—the seventh of which, the haunting *Sinfonia Antartica*, was based entirely on his music for the 1949 film *Scott of the Antarctic*.

Vaughan Williams scored 11 films during the last 17 years of his life, some of them short wartime documentaries. Already one of England's leading composers by the time he wrote music for *49th Parallel* (1941, known in the U.S. as *The Invaders*), his contribution was so valued that he was billed, along with the actors, before the title ("and the music of Vaughan Williams"). He later turned the film's hymn-like theme into a song, "The New Commonwealth."

Several of the composer's films, like *49th Parallel*, were designed to serve the war effort, including *Coastal Command* (1942) and *The Story of a Flemish Farm* (1943). His score for the 1947 film *The Loves of Joanna Godden* had the rare distinction of being sold on records in England. Most of the other films are forgotten or unavailable, but all of his scores contain Vaughan Williams's unmistakable personal style, and his *Scott of the Antarctic* is unforgettable.

VAUGHAN WILLIAMS: FILM MUSIC
Marco Polo 8.223665

The only collection of purely movie music from the pen of the composer, this unusual 1993 disc contains the stirring prelude from *49th Parallel* (1941), an eight-movement suite from *Coastal Command* (1942), a seven-movement suite from *Story of a Flemish Farm* (1943), and "Three Portraits" from *The England of Elizabeth* (1957). These bits and pieces are alternately inspiring, folk-influenced, and soaringly patriotic. Andrew Penny conducts the RTE Concert Orchestra.

CLASSIC BRITISH FILM MUSIC
Silva Screen FILMCD 072

A 21-minute suite from Vaughan Williams's 1942 *Coastal Command* score is the highlight of this collection (which also includes Brian Easdale's 1948 *The Red Shoes* ballet, a Gerard Schurmann piece, and a suite from Arthur Bliss's 1940 *Conquest of the Air*). *Coastal Command*, a "dramatized documentary" of Royal Air Force fliers who protected shipping lanes, features some of the composer's most thrilling music for films. Kenneth Alwyn conducts the Philharmonia Orchestra in this 1990 re-recording.

THEMES BY HOLLYWOOD'S GREAT COMPOSERS VOL. II
Sony AK 57136

A nine-minute suite from Vaughan Williams's score for the 1947 Ealing film *The Loves of Joanna Godden* contains the composer's pastoral evocations of the Romney Marsh countryside. Googie Withers starred as a headstrong woman who runs a sheep farm; one of its sequences caused the composer to remark that it was the only time in his long career that he had been asked to set hoof-and-mouth disease to music. Ernest Irving conducts the Philharmonia Orchestra in this original recording.

SINFONIA ANTARTICA
EMI CDC 7 47216 2

Sir Adrian Boult, one of the foremost interpreters of Vaughan Williams, conducts the London Philharmonic Orchestra and choir in this definitive version of the composer's seventh symphony, based entirely upon his atmospheric score for the 1948 film *Scott of the Antarctic*. John Mills starred in the Ealing film based on Captain Robert Scott's doomed 1911 expedition to the South Pole. The score itself was written without the composer's actually seeing the film; whole sequences were cut to the music later. In addition to large orchestra, organ, and wind-machine, Vaughan Williams employed wordless women's chorus and soprano soloist to achieve a feeling of bleakness, unimaginable cold, loneliness, and death at the bottom of the world.

Walton, Sir William (1902–1983)

One of the most distinguished composers in English history, Walton wrote in many forms, including vocal music (*Facade*, 1922), orchestral (*Portsmouth Point* overture, 1925), choral works (*Belshazzar's Feast*, 1931), and opera (*Troilus and Cressida*, 1954).

But Walton also wrote some of the finest film music of his time, notably for the three Shakespearean plays directed by, and starring, his friend Laurence Olivier: *Henry V* (1945), *Hamlet* (1948), and *Richard III* (1955), which ranged from Elizabethan period–style source music and court fanfares to highly dramatic and evocative underscore for the timeless scenarios of the Bard.

Walton composed nearly a dozen other scores from 1934 to 1969. His "Spitfire Prelude and Fugue" (from *The First of the Few*, 1942) was among the most famous pieces to come out of wartime films and is often played in concert. Yet Walton's last assignment for a war movie, *The Battle of Britain* (1969), ended in scandal when the producers decided that Walton's mere 20 minutes of music was insufficient for a soundtrack album.

Thus, they summarily dismissed England's most famous composer and discarded his entire score. When Olivier (who played Air Chief Marshal Dowding) learned of this, he threatened to go public with the outrage unless at least some of the music was retained. The five-minute "Battle in the Air" sequence remains in the film; Ron Goodwin rescored the rest.

HENRY V

Chandos CHAN 8892

One in a series of Christopher Palmer reconstructions of Walton film music, this 1990 re-recording contains an hour-long "Shakespeare Scenario" that combines the score with readings by Christopher Plummer, and another seven minutes of period music that Walton utilized as source music. This was Walton's first collaboration with Laurence Olivier and remains one of his most compelling and memorable scores; the glorious choral finale is among the greatest in the history of film. It was a 1946 Oscar nominee. Sir Neville Marriner conducts the orchestra and chorus of the Academy of St. Martin in the Fields.

HAMLET

Chandos CHAN 8842

This first of four 1990–91 volumes of Walton's film music features the first recording of the entire *Hamlet* score (1948) with occasional narration by Sir John Gielgud, and a 12-minute "poem for orchestra" based on Walton's score for *As You Like It* (1936). Previous recordings simply extract Walton's grim funeral march for Hamlet and his dark tone poem "Hamlet and Ophelia." Arrangements by Christopher Palmer; Sir Neville Marriner conducts the Academy of St. Martin in the Fields. The film, incidentally, won the Best Picture Oscar, although Walton lost the scoring Oscar to his fellow countryman Brian Easdale for *The Red Shoes*.

RICHARD III

Chandos CHAN 8841

Walton's third collaboration with Olivier, and his last major film score, was on this 1955 adaptation of Shakespeare's dark tale of the mad king. Christopher Palmer's "Shakespeare scenario" reconstructs the original film score and incorporates a monologue by John Gielgud. Neville Marriner conducts the Academy of St. Martin in the Fields. The album also includes a 10-minute suite from Walton's *Major Barbara* score (1941).

BATTLE OF BRITAIN SUITE
Chandos CHAN 8870

The second volume devoted to Walton's film music includes the stirring "Spitfire Prelude and Fugue" from *The First of the Few* (1942) and suites from the dramatic *Escape Me Never* (1935), Olivier's Chekhov adaptation *The Three Sisters* (1970), and *Battle of Britain* (1969), most of which was discarded by the filmmakers. The 25-minute "A Wartime Sketchbook" (arranged by Christopher Palmer) consists of excerpts from Walton's previously unrecorded scores for three 1942 films: *Went the Day Well, Next of Kin,* and *The Foreman Went to France.* Sir Neville Marriner conducts the Academy of St. Martin in the Fields.

THE BATTLE OF BRITAIN
Rykodisc 10747

Ron Goodwin accepted one of the most difficult assignments of his career when he agreed to replace the producer-rejected score that Walton had written for the epic 1969 film commemorating the Royal Air Force's 1940 defeat of the German Luftwaffe over England in 1940. The cast was a who's who in acting (including Laurence Olivier, Michael Caine, Trevor Howard, and Robert Shaw). Goodwin provided a suitably heroic theme, plenty of battle music, and moments of melancholy. Olivier, however,

appalled that his friend Walton's music had been discarded, threatened to remove his name from the film if at least some was not reinstated; the producers relented, retaining only the five-minute "Battle in the Air" sequence. This disc contains both the Goodwin music and the entire, recently rediscovered, Walton score, conducted by Malcolm Arnold.

MUSIC FROM SHAKESPEAREAN FILMS
Angel S-36198 (LP)

This 1964 re-recording has Walton conducting the Philharmonia Orchestra in his own suites from the three great Olivier films: the five-part, 15-minute suite from *Henry V* (1945); the funeral march from *Hamlet* (1948); and the seven-minute prelude and 10-minute "Shakespeare Suite" from *Richard III* (1955). For many years this was the definitive collection of Walton's Shakespeare scores.

PHOTO COURTESY OF JOHN W. WAXMAN

Waxman, Franz (1906–1967)

Born in Germany, Franz Waxman studied in Berlin, where he began orchestrating and conducting for German films (including the songs for the

1930 Marlene Dietrich movie *The Blue Angel*). By 1933 he had composed his first film score (for a Fritz Lang film) and by 1935 he was on a Hollywood scoring assignment: The Universal sequel *The Bride of Frankenstein*, whose spine-tingling music was so effective that it was used again and again in horror movies for years afterward.

After two years at Universal, Waxman shifted to MGM for the next seven, scoring several Spencer Tracy classics including *Captains Courageous* (1941); while on loan to David O. Selznick, he scored *Rebecca* (1940), the first of his four films for director Alfred Hitchcock (later came *Suspicion*, *The Paradine Case*, and *Rear Window*).

He became the first composer ever to win back-to-back Oscars, for the Paramount films *Sunset Boulevard* and *A Place in the Sun* in 1950 and 1951. He also scored significant films for 20th Century–Fox (*Prince Valiant* in 1954, *Peyton Place* in 1957) and Warner Bros. (*The Spirit of St. Louis* in 1957, *The Nun's Story* in 1959).

Waxman founded the Los Angeles Music Festival in 1947 and was its principal conductor. In this capacity, he introduced to the West Coast such new works as Britten's *War Requiem*, Stravinsky's *Soldier's Tale*, and symphonies by Shostakovich, Walton, and Prokofiev. His own concert music includes the song cycle *Song of Terezin* and his "Carmen" Fantasy originally written for *Humoresque* (1946, with Isaac Stern playing the violin solos).

SUNSET BOULEVARD: THE CLASSIC FILM SCORES OF FRANZ WAXMAN
RCA 0708-2-RG

The Waxman entry in RCA's definitive "Classic Film Scores" series of the early 1970s contains suites and reconstructions from eight of the composer's movie triumphs, including his two Oscar winners: *Sunset Boulevard* (1950) with its demented-tango finale for Norma Desmond, and *A Place in the Sun* (1951), with its memorable alto saxophone part. Also featured are music from *Prince Valiant* (1954), the classic monster-creation scene from *The Bride of Frankenstein* (1935), "Elegy for Strings and Harp" from *Old Acquaintance* (1943), a suite from Hitchcock's *Rebecca* (1940), themes from *The Philadelphia Story* (1940), and the "Ride to Dubno" scene from *Taras Bulba* (1962). Charles Gerhardt conducts the National Philharmonic Orchestra.

THE BRIDE OF FRANKENSTEIN
Silva SSD 1028

Waxman's innovative, sophisticated score for the 1935 sequel to *Frankenstein* was so successful that it was frequently recycled in Universal's less costly product, notably serials and B movies. The five-note "monster" theme is immediately recognizable even today, and the 10-minute "creation" sequence is still a favorite among buffs. Kenneth Alwyn conducts the Westminster Philharmonic Orchestra in this complete re-recording, which also features Waxman's music for *The Invisible Ray* (1936).

LEGENDS OF HOLLYWOOD: FRANZ WAXMAN, VOLUME ONE
Varèse Sarabande VSD-5242

This first in a series of re-recordings presents suites from some of Waxman's best film work. The longest are the martial- and Oriental-flavored *Objective, Burma!* (1945), the "Rhapsody for Piano and Orchestra" from Hitchcock's *The Paradine Case* (1947), and his Roman musical mosaic from *Demetrius and the Gladiators* (1954). Also featured: fanfares from *Task Force* (1949), "Reminiscences for Orchestra" from *Come Back, Little Sheba* (1952), the romantic *Peyton Place* (1957), the

"Overture for Trumpet and Orchestra" from Jack Benny's classic *The Horn Blows at Midnight* (1945), and "Passacaglia for Orchestra" from *Sorry, Wrong Number* (1948). Richard Mills conducts Australia's Queensland Symphony Orchestra with the Jones & Co. Chorale.

LEGENDS OF HOLLYWOOD: FRANZ WAXMAN, VOLUME TWO
Varèse Sarabande VSD-5257

The second volume of the series contains the "Pioneer Suite" drawn from *Red Mountain* (1951), *Cimarron* (1960), and *The Indian Fighter* (1955); a suite from *The Nun's Story* (1958) and another from *Possessed* (1947). Also included: suites from *Anne of the Indies* (1954), *Captains Courageous* (1937), *Botany Bay* (1953), and *Mister Roberts* (1955); an overture from *Huckleberry Finn* (1939); and "Danse Macabre" from *The Bride of Frankenstein* (1935). Richard Mills conducts the Queensland Symphony Orchestra.

LEGENDS OF HOLLYWOOD: FRANZ WAXMAN, VOLUME THREE
Varèse Sarabande VSD-5480

Distinguishing this third volume are 12-minute suites from the Ceylon adventure *Elephant Walk* (1954) and the Biblical saga *The Silver Chalice* (1955, an Oscar nominee). Also featured: "Night-ride for Orchestra" from *Night & the City* (1950), "Dusk: A Setting for Orchestra" from *Night Unto Night* (1949), "Cafe Waltzes" from *Hotel Berlin* (1945), a "Montage for Orchestra" from *Destination Tokyo* (1944), and excerpts from *The Furies* (1950) and *Mr. Skeffington* (1944). Richard Mills conducts the Queensland Symphony Orchestra.

LEGENDS OF HOLLYWOOD: FRANZ WAXMAN, VOLUME FOUR
Varèse Sarabande VSD-5713

This 1996 volume builds on the previous with music from eight more Waxman films: *On Borrowed Time* (1939), *The Story of Ruth* (1960), *Dark City* (1950), and *A Christmas Carol* (1938). Also: *Untamed* (1955), *My Geisha* (1962), *The Devil Doll* (1936), and *My Cousin Rachel* (1952). Richard Mills conducts the Queensland Symphony Orchestra.

PRINCE VALIANT
FSM Vol. 2, No. 3

One of Waxman's most celebrated scores, this music for the 1954 adaptation of the long-running comic strip is as richly detailed and ornate as Hal Foster's famous artwork and stories. Robert Wagner, James Mason, and Janet Leigh starred in the movie, but Waxman's score was the real star, with its grand fanfares, thrilling chase sequences, heartbreaking love theme, and hints of early English music.

THE SPIRIT OF ST. LOUIS
Varèse Sarabande VSD-5212

Billy Wilder's 1957 film about Charles A. Lindbergh's famous solo flight across the Atlantic starred James Stewart but was often kept aloft by Waxman's fine score. Written for a large orchestra including oversized percussion ensemble, four keyboards, and small female choir, it was particularly effective during the Atlantic crossing sequence, musically suggesting Lindbergh's loneliness, exhaustion, and eventual elation at having reached France.

SAYONARA: ORCHESTRAL SUITES
BMG/RCA 09026 62657 2 (Germany)

This 1995 album contains impressively recorded suites from four of Waxman's finest scores of the '50s and '60s. Included are nearly 20 minutes of his colorful, Russian-flavored, Oscar-nominated *Taras Bulba* (1962); the "symphonic scenario" from his Oscar-winning *A Place in the Sun* (1951), which restores the composer's original conceptions (altered in the film by director George Stevens); the lyrical *Hemingway's Adventures of a Young Man* (1962); and over 20 minutes of his rich, Occident-meets-Orient score for *Sayonara* (1957), the Best Picture nominee that starred Marlon Brando and Miyoshi Umeki. Elmer Bernstein conducts Berlin's Rundfunk Symphony Orchestra and Choir.

THE NUN'S STORY

Stanyan STZ-114

This Oscar-nominated score for Fred Zinneman's 1959 film starring Audrey Hepburn was one of Waxman's finest. Because the music was recorded in Rome, the composer had the opportunity to research music in the Vatican's Papal library and base much of the score on Gregorian chant. Nearly 55 minutes long, the CD incorporates a number of tracks not present on the original, much-sought-after LP.

TARAS BULBA

Rykodisc RCD 10736

While the movie was generally derided as terrible, this Yul Brynner–Tony Curtis action picture from 1962—the colorful, action-filled story of a legendary 16th-century Cossack leader and his rebellious son—boasts an equally colorful, Oscar-nominated score. Waxman used his 1962 concert tour of the Soviet Union to visit Kiev and study Ukrainian folk music in preparation for writing the music.

Webb, Roy (1888–1982)

One of the forgotten masters of the American film

score, Roy Webb is seriously underrepresented on records. Only in recent years has his talent begun to be recognized, due largely to the growth in appreciation of the films of RKO, the studio where he spent nearly his entire career.

Like Max Steiner and Alfred Newman, Webb came out of the theater; he taught Richard Rodgers the rudiments of musical notation. When RKO summoned him to Hollywood in 1929, he discovered an opportunity to pursue his compositional interest in "light music," which eventually, and ironically, turned him into the film capital's specialist in dark subjects—namely, RKO's many films noirs.

Webb's sophisticated harmonic sense and ability to achieve subtleties with musical colors and moods made him the perfect collaborator in such shadowy melodramas as *Murder, My Sweet* (1944), *The Spiral Staircase* (1946), *Out of the Past* (1947), and *Crossfire* (1947).

His most famous work is probably the music for Hitchcock's *Notorious* (1946) and his music for the macabre thrillers of Val Lewton, including *Cat People* (1942), *I Walked With a Zombie* (1943), *The Curse of the Cat People* (1944), and *Bedlam* (1946). The last of his seven Oscar nominations was for *The Enchanted Cottage* (1945), which features a miniature piano concerto that was later performed at the Hollywood Bowl.

THE CURSE OF THE CAT PEOPLE: THE FILM MUSIC OF ROY WEBB

Cloud Nine CNS 5008

This 73-minute collection of Roy Webb music for RKO films was drawn directly from the composer's own acetate recordings of the original scores. Seventeen minutes from his Val Lewton masterpiece *The Curse of the Cat People* (1944), nine minutes from Hitchcock's *Notorious*, nine from *Bedlam*, and ten from *The Locket* (all 1946) are the most generous selections; bits and pieces from nine other films are included, all from the 1942–49 period.

CAT PEOPLE: CLASSIC MUSIC BY ROY WEBB FOR THE VAL LEWTON FILMS
Marco Polo 8.225125

Suites from five Lewton-produced chillers for RKO are featured in this new re-recording: *Cat People* (1942), the classic thriller with Simone Simon as a woman who may suffer from an ancient curse; *Bedlam* (1946), with Boris Karloff in charge of a London insane asylum; *The Seventh Victim* (1943), about devil worshippers in New York; *The Body Snatcher* (1945), the final teaming of Karloff and Bela Lugosi; and *I Walked With a Zombie* (1943), about voodoo on a Caribbean island. Webb's modern harmonies and subtly atmospheric music are realized in these reconstructions by John W. Morgan; William T. Stromberg conducts the Slavic Radio Symphony Orchestra.

PHOTO BY BACHRACH, COURTESY OF CHASEN& COMPANY

Williams, John (1932–)

No composer in the past 30 years has achieved the fame and stature of John Williams. From the rela-

tive obscurity of studio pianist and TV musician to A-level film composer and world-renowned conductor, he has enjoyed a career unlike any other American composer; his impressive scores and his association with blockbuster films have made movie music more popular than ever.

Born in New York, he moved to Los Angeles in 1948 and began working in the motion picture studios during the mid-1950s, first as a pianist and later as an orchestrator. He found initial success in television (winning Emmys for *Heidi,* 1968, and *Jane Eyre,* 1970) and gradually moved into music for the big screen. His folk-flavored Americana score for *The Reivers* (1969) was the first to attract attention, which grew with his music for such disaster films as *The Towering Inferno* and *Earthquake* (both 1974).

Williams's scores for the films of Steven Spielberg and George Lucas catapulted him to the top of his profession. He won Oscars for Spielberg's *Jaws* (1975), *E.T., the Extra-Terrestrial* (1982), and *Schindler's List* (1993), and one for Lucas's *Star Wars* (1977). The *Star Wars* soundtrack made history by becoming the first nonpop album to sell four million records.

When the two filmmakers collaborated on *Raiders of the Lost Ark* (1981), Williams joined them; this triumvirate remained intact for all of the Indiana Jones trilogy. For Lucas, Williams created music of even greater depth and complexity for succeeding films in the *Star Wars* saga. Now the single most sought after composer for films, he has also worked for Richard Donner (*Superman,* 1978), Chris Columbus (*Home Alone,* 1990), Ron Howard (*Far and Away,* 1992) and Oliver Stone (three films including *JFK,* 1991).

Williams succeeded the venerable Arthur Fiedler as conductor of the Boston Pops Orchestra, recording many albums during his 1980–93 tenure and becoming (unlike most of his film-composing colleagues) a familiar public face via the orchestra's *Evening at Pops* series on TV. He now balances movies with a burgeoning career in concert music (with two symphonies, several concertos, and a song cycle to his credit) and continues to be artist-in-residence at Tanglewood.

THE REIVERS
Columbia/Legacy CK *66130*
THE COWBOYS
Varèse Sarabande VSD-*5540*

Williams's music for director Mark Rydell's pictures has always had a strong grounding in Americana, from the Stephen Foster ambiance of *The Reivers* (1969) to the modern-country-styled *The River* (1984). *The Reivers*, based on a William Faulkner novel, and starring Steve McQueen, and Williams's bluegrass-flavored, banjos-and-fiddles score netted him his first Oscar nomination for original music. His even more exuberant score for *The Cowboys* incorporates harmonica, acoustic guitar, and country fiddle into his usual full orchestral treatment. The overture to this 1972 John Wayne western has become a staple of Williams's concerts.

JAWS
MCA MCAD-*1660*

"Without that score, to this day I think the film would only have been half as successful," Steven Spielberg has said of Williams's contribution to *Jaws*. Hollywood was aware of the composer before this 1975 thriller, but it was his now-legendary shark motif (that repeated two-note signature for celli and basses signaling the underwater predator's presence) that won him an Oscar and his first Grammy. The score is much more than that, however: fugues and sea chanteys and inventive writing appear throughout.

COURTESY OF UNIVERSAL MUSIC GROUP

STAR WARS
RCA 09026-68746-2
THE EMPIRE STRIKES BACK
RCA 09026-68747-2
RETURN OF THE JEDI
RCA 09026-68748-2
STAR WARS TRILOGY:
ORIGINAL SOUNDTRACK ANTHOLOGY
20ᵗʰ Century–Fox/Arista 07822-11-12-2
THE PHANTOM MENACE
Sony Classical SK *61816*

Not only did the commercial success of George Lucas's 1977 space opera change the way Hollywood made movies (with every film now seeking $100-million blockbuster status), Williams's enormously popular music single-handedly brought about the rebirth of the symphonic film score. His swashbuckling style reminiscent of earlier composers from Holst to Korngold, multi-thematic approach, and meticulously scored space battles made an entire generation sit down and listen to orchestral music for the first time. It won an Oscar and (in its original Fox LP format) three Grammys.

The definitive two-CD set of *Star Wars*, issued

for the film's 20th anniversary in 1997, restored all of the 106-minute score in pristine sound. As for the two sequels, the 125-minute *Empire*, a 1980 Oscar nominee, is highlighted by new themes for Han Solo, Princess Leia, and the wise old Yoda, as well as an "imperial march" for Darth Vader. Williams also won two Grammys (for the complete soundtrack and for Best Instrumental Composition; he received three of the five nominations in that category for *Empire*). The 148-minute *Jedi*, a 1983 Oscar and Grammy nominee, contains nearly an hour of previously unreleased music including Williams's newly composed "Victory Celebration" cue for the finale. The earlier, four-CD box set contains a lavishly illustrated, 64-page book, extensive analysis, and a smattering of music not found on the later discs, including "Lapti Nek."

The *Phantom Menace* score, written for the long-awaited prequel released in the spring of 1999, contains Williams's exciting orchestral-and-choral "Duel of the Fates," from an old Welsh poem translated into Sanskrit.

CLOSE ENCOUNTERS OF THE THIRD KIND
Arista 07822-19004-2

Williams's other instant classic from 1977, for Steven Spielberg's aliens-visit-Earth tale starring Richard Dreyfuss, is poles apart conceptually from the ultra-romantic *Star Wars*. Williams's five-note extraterrestrial "greeting," his often atonal musical language (employing fascinating choral and orchestral effects), and the score's final, joyous burst of tonality, were fully restored in a 77-minute 1998 disc.

SUPERMAN
Rhino RZ 75874

"You'll believe a man can fly," trumpeted the ads for the 1978 adaptation of the comic-book leg-

end, and audiences did—thanks largely to this Oscar-nominated score. The story was fun, and the special effects super, but the heroics were often provided by Williams. His opening fanfare, soaring main title, memorable love theme ("Can You Read My Mind"), and comic march for the villains are played with gusto by Williams and the London Symphony Orchestra. This two-CD set, issued in early 2000, restores the complete original score (previously available only in an abridged form on a single Warner Bros. disc), with several outtakes.

RAIDERS OF THE LOST ARK
DCC DZS-090
INDIANA JONES AND
THE TEMPLE OF DOOM
Polydor 821592-2
INDIANA JONES AND
THE LAST CRUSADE
Warner Bros. 25883-2

It was only a matter of time before Spielberg and Lucas teamed up together, and the result was not only a new film franchise but also a trio of great Williams scores. This trilogy begins with the fun, often wildly melodramatic, Oscar-nominated and Grammy-winning *Raiders* score, restored and reissued in a 74-minute disc in 1995 with a colorfully illustrated 24-page booklet. The sequels (1984 and 1989, both Oscar-nominated) contain darker but no less effective scores. Williams conducts the London Symphony in the first, Los Angeles ensembles in the others.

E.T. THE EXTRA-TERRESTRIAL
MCA MCAD-31073
MCA MCAD-11530

Williams's score for Steven Spielberg's touching 1982 masterpiece about a little boy and an alien visitor left behind by a UFO was originally issued (number 31073) in a 40-minute collection of excerpts and specially recorded-for-the-soundtrack music, then reissued in 1996 in a 71-minute, remastered chronological edition that unfortunately omits the classic "Flying" and "Over the Moon." Williams's magic touch with simple human emotions and his thrilling, no-holds-barred finale made this a very deserving Oscar winner.

HOME ALONE
CBS SK 46595

John Hughes's box-office hit with then-adorable Macaulay Culkin inspired one of Williams's most lighthearted scores, one with considerable Christmas charm (replete with celeste, sleigh bells, and occasional Tchaikovsky inspiration) and an original holiday song ("Somewhere in My Memory," lyrics by Leslie Bricusse). Score and song were 1990 Oscar nominees; Mel Tormé's rendition of "Have Yourself a Merry Little Christmas" is among the featured songs.

JFK
Elektra 9 61293-2

Of Williams's three collaborations with director Oliver Stone—the others being the Vietnam-themed *Born on the Fourth of July* (1989) and *Nixon* (1995)—this 1991 film may be the most musically potent. It was an Oscar nominee for its elegiac solo trumpet for the fallen president, the much-imitated percussive track for the conspiracy, and his touching theme for obsessed prosecutor Jim Garrison's family.

SCHINDLER'S LIST
MCA MCAD-10969

Williams's moving score for Steven Spielberg's Best Picture–winning 1993 film about the Holocaust is,

observers agree, among his finest: Music of "dignity and compassion . . . gentle simplicity," accurately sums up Spielberg in his notes. Itzhak Perlman played the violin solos; the main theme and "Remembrances," both subtly influenced by Hebrew themes, are now concert staples. Williams won the Oscar and a Grammy.

JURASSIC PARK
MCA MCAD-10859
THE LOST WORLD: JURASSIC PARK
MCA MCAD-11628

Williams composed the thrilling action score for *Jurassic Park* in the same year (and for the same director, Spielberg) as his heartfelt score for *Schindler's List*. Williams's choral anthem for the dinosaur theme park, his complex suspense music, and his furious action cues for the raptor chases brought the Michael Crichton–Steven Spielberg conceptions to life. The score to their 1997 sequel, *The Lost World*, seems to tip its hat to the mystical, tribal rhythms of Max Steiner's *King Kong* and is in some ways even more compelling.

Williams, Patrick (1939–)

One of the most respected and honored musicians in Los Angeles, Patrick Williams has managed to keep a foot in every musical arena for over 30 years. He's a jazz composer, arranger, and bandleader with two Grammys and several more nominations; a longtime film composer with an Oscar nomination for his clever adaptations of Mendelssohn and Rossini in *Breaking Away* (1979); a veteran television writer with dozens of credits and three Emmys; and a concert-hall composer who may be the only one in Hollywood with a nomination for the prestigious Pulitzer Prize.

Born in Missouri, raised in Connecticut,

Williams received a degree in history from Duke University but pursued his musical muse in graduate studies at Columbia. Soon he was a busy arranger in New York, started making jazz albums, and turned to film and television scoring as an outlet for orchestral composition that combined both classical and jazz writing.

His Pulitzer-nominated *An American Concerto* (1976) is, in the opinion of many, one of the most successful attempts yet to combine jazz elements with traditional symphonic writing. He is, however, better known for his TV music, which includes *The Mary Tyler Moore Show, The Bob Newhart Show, Lou Grant, The Streets of San Francisco,* and *The Days and Nights of Molly Dodd.*

Williams's films include the family film *Casey's Shadow* (1978), the Sean Connery action-adventure *Cuba* (1979), Robert Zemeckis's cult classic *Used Cars* (1980), the big-band-era Goldie Hawn movie *Swing Shift* (1984), and the Carl Reiner–directed comedies *All of Me* (1984, with Steve Martin and Lily Tomlin) and *That Old Feeling* (1997, with Bette Midler). His acclaimed TV-movie scores include *Jewels, Geronimo,* and *Jesus.*

THE GRASS HARP

Windham Hill 01934 11224-2

This touching 1996 film with Piper Laurie, Sissy Spacek, and Walter Matthau, based on the Truman Capote memoir, was considerably enhanced by Williams's heartfelt orchestral score. Subtle yet emotional, melodic, and dramatically apt, this was among Williams's best work in recent years. Period tracks by Benny Goodman and Ella Fitzgerald augment the score.

Yared, Gabriel (1949–)

Born in Lebanon but a longtime resident of France, Gabriel Yared is a self-taught musician who began scoring films in the 1980s after a successful career as an arranger for pop singers and a composer of commercial jingles.

Yared came to prominence with his Oscar- and Grammy-winning score for *The English Patient* (1996), but in fact he was already well known to art-house audiences for his music from such European films as *Betty Blue* (1986) and *Camille Claudel* (1988), both of which netted him César nominations in his home country.

He also scored *Hanna K.* (1983) for Costa-Gavras, *Vincent & Theo* (1990) for Robert Altman, and *The Lover* (1992) for Jean-Jacques Annaud; the latter won the César in France. His score for the Nicolas Cage–Meg Ryan hit *City of Angels* (1998) was similarly touching and was included on the best-selling (mostly songs) album.

THE ENGLISH PATIENT

Fantasy FCD-16001-2

Yared's score was one of nine 1996 Oscar winners including Best Picture, for Anthony Minghella's sweeping epic of love and war set in Italy and North Africa in the late '30s. Ralph Fiennes, Kristin Scott Thomas, and Juliet Binoche starred. Yared's score, as the notes point out, incorporates "traditional Hungarian folk tunes, spare Baroque themes and dense Romantic orchestrations." The composer visited the set and was involved in the project from the start of shooting, enabling him to create his score while the film itself was being assembled.

THE TALENTED MR. RIPLEY

Sony Classical SK 51337

Minghella again turned to Yared, early in production, for the music for his 1999 thriller starring Matt Damon as Patricia Highsmith's amoral Tom Ripley, whose talent for assuming identities and getting away with murder was uncanny. Yared's Oscar-nominated orchestral score—alternately quizzical and urgent, jazzy and semi-classical—makes up about half of this disc (including a song performed by Sinéad O' Connor). The rest consists of the jazz tunes heard in the movie, with several performed by Guy Barker but a handful by such greats as Charlie Parker, Miles Davis, and Dizzy Gillespie. Minghella's thorough notes explain the musical structure of the film.

PHOTO COURTESY OF COSTA COMMUNICATIONS

Young, Christopher (1957–)

Widely considered one of the finest of the younger generation of film composers, Christopher Young toiled for years in low-budget horror and exploitation films before being admitted to the upper echelon of big-budget studio movies of the '90s, such as *Species* (1995), *Murder at 1600* (1989), and *Entrapment* (1999).

Born in New Jersey, he received his musical education in Massachusetts, Texas, and California, and scored his first studio picture in 1982. He was typecast for years as a suspense-and-terror composer on the basis of films like *Hellraiser* (1987) and

the widely imitated *Jennifer 8* (1992), and is still much in demand in the thriller genre, for films like *Copycat* (1995) and *Hard Rain* (1998).

His resumé also includes the introspective Americana of *Murder in the First* (1995), the dramatic urgency of the Vietnam War film *Bat-21* (1988), and the smoky jazz of his Emmy-nominated score for the HBO film *Norma Jean & Marilyn* (1996).

Young's frequently underutilized lyrical sensibility has more recently been on display in scores such as the mystery-comedy *The Man Who Knew Too Little* (1997) and the jazzy *Rounders* (1998). In an era when so much film music sounds alike, Young has a distinctive and original voice.

HELLBOUND: HELLRAISER II
GNP Crescendo GNPD 8015

One of the grandest and darkest scores ever to emerge from low-budget horror, the music for the 1988 sequel to Clive Barker's grisly original Pinhead movie brims with Gothic romanticism. Full orchestra and choir provide the tension and evil atmosphere that the movie's cheap visuals lack. Had it been written for a mainstream studio film, this score would have instantly catapulted Young onto the "A" list; in reality, that took a few more years to accomplish. This score won the Saturn award from the Academy of Science Fiction, Fantasy, and Horror Films.

JENNIFER 8
RCA Victor 07863 66120-2

Young's music for this so-so suspense picture (starring Uma Thurman as a blind woman targeted for murder and Andy Garcia as the cop who tries to save her) may be his most haunting, incorporating solo piano over strings and the subtle use of softly recorded female voices. It was imitated by other composers for years following its 1992 appearance.

DREAM LOVER
Koch 3-8700-2H 1

James Spader and Madchen Amick starred in Nicholas Kazan's erotic mystery from 1994. The ethereal voices of Young's main-title theme and his partly orchestral, partly synthesized funhouse carousel waltzes lend an alternately eerie and exciting quality to this elegant score. The occasional offbeat touches include strange Japanese colors and bawdyhouse-style Dixie jazz.

ROUNDERS
Varèse Sarabande VSD-5980

Matt Damon, Edward Norton, John Malkovich, and Martin Landau starred in this 1998 film set against the gambling world of Las Vegas. Young's score harks back to the great West Coast–style jazz scores of the late '50s and '60s by the likes of Henry Mancini, Johnny Mandel, and Quincy Jones—filled with jazz, swing, and rock sounds, sometimes musically designed within traditional orchestral structures. Soloists include Brandon Fields on flute and saxophones and Mike Lang on organ.

THE HURRICANE
MCA 088 112 235-2

Denzel Washington's bravura performance as boxer Rubin "Hurricane" Carter battling for exoneration from an unjust murder conviction, was the highlight of Norman Jewison's 1999 dramatization. But Young's score was with him all the way, providing atmosphere and emotional support with jazz-inflected moments for Carter's boxing career and introspective, melancholy touches for the long years in prison. The use of "scatting" vocals adds a nice color.

PHOTO FROM THE TONY THOMAS COLLECTION

Young, Victor (1900–1956)

One of the great melodists of movie history, Victor Young was born in Chicago but studied in Poland, making his debut as solo violinist with the Warsaw Philharmonic at 17. He returned to the U.S. in 1920 and played in silent-movie orchestras in both Chicago and Los Angeles, eventually turning his talents toward arranging and composing.

Young spent most of his movie career at Paramount. A workaholic, he averaged eight scores a year in addition to his work as an arranger and bandleader for radio and records. He wrote more than 160 complete scores in less than 20 years and contributed to dozens more as conductor, arranger, music director, or in some other capacity.

Oscar-nominated 21 times, he won posthumously for his tuneful score for Michael Todd's epic *Around the World in Eighty Days*. No fewer than five other Young scores were released after his death from a heart attack at the age of 56.

At least a dozen of his songs (many derived from his movie scores) became popular standards. Among them are "When I Fall in Love," from *One Minute to Zero* (1952); "Sweet Sue," written in 1928 and used in several films; "Stella by Starlight" from *The Uninvited* (1944); and the title songs from *Love Letters* (1945), *Golden Earrings* (1947), *My Foolish Heart* (1949), and *Around the World in Eighty Days* (1956).

SHANE: A TRIBUTE TO VICTOR YOUNG
Koch 3-7365-2 H1

Five of Young's most significant film scores are excerpted here: his heartbreaking music for the 1953 western classic *Shane*, starring Alan Ladd and set against the mountains of Wyoming; the Spanish-flavored, Oscar-nominated music for *For Whom the Bell Tolls* (1943); the quasi-religious settings for Victor Mature and Hedy Lamarr as *Samson and Delilah* (1950); the Irish folk–laced *The Quiet Man* (1952) for director John Ford and star John Wayne; and the David Niven travelogue *Around the World in Eighty Days* (1956). Also included: Henry Mancini's medley of great Young songs. Richard Kaufman conducts the New Zealand Symphony Orchestra.

FOR WHOM THE BELL TOLLS
Stanyan STZ-112

Ernest Hemingway's novel of the Spanish Civil War, starring Gary Cooper and Ingrid Bergman, received nine 1943 Oscar nominations, including Best Picture and one for Young's flavorful score, rich in Spanish rhythms and containing one of Young's most bittersweet love themes. Ray Heindorf conducted the Warner Bros. Orchestra in this 1958 re-recording.

THE UNINVITED: THE CLASSIC FILM MUSIC OF VICTOR YOUNG
Marco Polo 8.225063

Young, famous as a tunesmith but surprisingly unheralded as a composer of dramatic scores, gets his due in this 1997 collection that features his atmospheric music for the 1944 ghost story that starred Ray Milland and Ruth Hussey (from which Young extracted his famous "Stella by Starlight") and his Old South music for Gary Cooper and Patricia Neal in 1950's *Bright Leaf*. An exuberant march for Cecil B. DeMille's Best Picture–winning *The Greatest Show on Earth* (1952) and a delightful suite from the 1939 animated feature *Gulliver's Travels* (an Oscar nominee for Young) are also included. Reconstructions by John W. Morgan; William T. Stromberg conducts the Moscow Symphony Orchestra and Chorus.

SWASHBUCKLER
Marco Polo 8.223607

This 1994 collection of four classic swashbucklers includes the Korngold classic *Captain Blood*, Max Steiner's *The Three Musketeers* (both 1935), and Miklós Rózsa's *The King's Thief* (1955), but its centerpiece is *Scaramouche* (1952) and nearly 19 minutes of Young's lilting, romantic, and memorable score. William Stromberg reconstructed the score; Richard Kaufman conducts the Brandenburg Philharmonic Orchestra of Potsdam.

SAMSON & DELILAH / THE QUIET MAN
Varèse Sarabande VSD-5497

This disc of two of Young's best-loved scores is a 1994 reissue of two mono Decca LPs: a 23-minute suite from Young's lush, often exotic-flavored score for Cecil B. DeMille's 1950 Biblical epic *Samson and Delilah*, with Victor Mature and Hedy Lamarr in the title roles; and 16 minutes from John Ford's picturesque 1952 Irish romantic drama *The Quiet Man*, with John Wayne and Maureen O'Hara, much of which is adapted from traditional Irish melodies.

AROUND THE WORLD IN EIGHTY DAYS
MCA MCAD-31134

Michael Todd's 1956 extravaganza won five Academy Awards including Best Picture and a posthumous Oscar for composer Young. David Niven starred as Phileas Fogg in the adaptation of Jules Verne's 19th-century fantasy about circling the globe to win a wager. Light, infectious, and with a title song that went on to "standard" status, this score contains some of Young's most colorful writing to suggest the many exotic locales of the picture—France, Spain, India, the American West, etc.—and an amusing motif for Fogg's manservant, Passepartout (played by Mexican comic Cantinflas).

PHOTO BY MATTHEW RALSOTN, COURTESY OF DREAMWORKS

Zimmer, Hans (1957–)

Among the most successful of the current crop of film composers, German-born, British-educated Hans Zimmer combines the background of a rock 'n' roller with the sensibilities (if not the education) of a classical composer.

Zimmer admits that his formal music training consisted of two weeks of piano lessons, but his background ranges from jingle writing to pop producing (like The Buggles' "Video Killed the Radio Star"). He apprenticed, then partnered, with British composer Stanley Myers in the '80s (on such films as *Moonlighting* and *My Beautiful Laundrette*) and moved to Los Angeles, where he composed his first Oscar-nominated score, for *Rain Man* (1988).

Because he was so fluent with the computer technology and electronic keyboards that were his primary tools in England, his early American scores, such as *Rain Man* and *Driving Miss Daisy* (1989), were primarily created on synthesizers in his own studio. By the time he won a 1994 Oscar for Disney's animated *The Lion King*, he was utilizing orchestrators to translate his ideas into music for the traditional Hollywood symphonic ensemble (and sometimes chorus).

Zimmer forged close relationships with directors Ridley Scott (*Black Rain*, 1989; *Thelma & Louise*, 1991), James L. Brooks (*I'll Do Anything*, 1994; *As Good As It Gets*, 1997) and other filmmakers that, together with his friendship with Disney executive-turned-DreamWorks-partner Jeffrey Katzenberg, helped secure his current job as head of music for DreamWorks. His Media Ventures studio complex is a giant Los Angeles think tank serving as home to several composers and other artists working in film.

RAIN MAN
Capitol CDP 7 91866 2

Barry Levinson's decision to hire Zimmer for the affecting Tom Cruise–Dustin Hoffman road movie changed the composer's life. Not only did he receive a 1988 Oscar nomination for his mostly synth-and-percussion score, but the film's Best Picture win made him instantly bankable in Hollywood. Only two of the CD's 10 tracks are his (the "road" cues and hard-rockin' Las Vegas theme with end credits); the others are songs by such artists as the Belle Stars, Johnny Clegg & Savuka, Etta James, and Bananarama.

DRIVING MISS DAISY
Varèse Sarabande VSD-5246

Twenty-three minutes of Zimmer's score are preserved on this disc, along with songs by Louis Armstrong and Eartha Kitt and an excerpt from Dvorak's opera *Rusalka* also heard in the film. The winner of 1989's Best Picture Oscar (as well as Best Actress, for Jessica Tandy, and Best Screenplay, for Alfred Uhry), it was not a nominee for Zimmer, perhaps because Academy music-branch members tend to discount synthesizer-generated music. He received a Grammy nomination instead.

BACKDRAFT
RCA Victor 3141-2-R

One of Zimmer's earliest forays into the use of large-scale orchestra and chorus was written for Ron Howard's dramatic 1991 film about professional fire fighters (Kurt Russell, William Baldwin). Strange synthesizer effects and massive percussion mixed with the orchestra and chorus heighten the tension of the realistic firestorm sequences. Zimmer strikes a heroic, martial tone for the men. The score is bookended by a pair of Bruce Hornsby songs.

CRIMSON TIDE
Hollywood HR-62025-2

One of 1995's most popular films was this battle of wits between naval nuclear-sub commander Gene Hackman and his first officer, Denzel Washington, produced and directed by the *Top Gun* team of Bruckheimer, Simpson, and Scott. Zimmer's mus-

cular score, which combined massive orchestra with male chorus and the now-omnipresent synthesizers, won a Grammy; it incorporates the traditional Navy hymn "Eternal Father Strong to Save."

AS GOOD AS IT GETS
Columbia/Sony CK 69112

Zimmer's music for James L. Brooks's hit (about a misanthropic writer played by Jack Nicholson and a single-mom waitress played by Helen Hunt) received a 1997 Oscar nomination. A warm and gentle score, written for small ensemble (primarily strings, woodwinds, and piano), it solved delicate problems of mood and humor throughout the film. Several songs, including Art Garfunkel's "Always Look on the Bright Side of Life" and Nat King Cole's "For Sentimental Reasons," are also included.

THE THIN RED LINE
RCA Victor 09026-63382-2

For Terrence Malick's Oscar-nominated Guadalcanal epic, Zimmer wrote nearly six hours of music over several months during 1998. A highly unconventional war-movie score, it has no militaristic snare drums, no brass fanfares, no heroic off-to-war marches. Atmospheric in nature, much of Zimmer's music often plays in five- or seven-minute passages, quite long for conventional film music, establishing moods that range from hypnotic to elegiac.

AGAINST ALL ODDS

Atlantic 7 80152-2

Phil Collins's title theme, subtitled (and better known as) "Take a Look at Me Now," anchored this collection of songs and score from Taylor Hackford's 1984 film noir starring Rachel Ward, Jeff Bridges, and James Woods. Collins's tune spent three weeks at number 1 and drove the album to number 12. The scandal came later, after it received an Oscar nomination for Best Song, when the Academy didn't even bother to ask Collins to sing it on the annual Oscarcast. Collins later won a Grammy for Best Male Pop Vocal Performance (the tune was a Song of the Year nominee); the album (which included six score cuts by co-composers Michel Colombier and Larry Carlton) was nominated for best soundtrack.

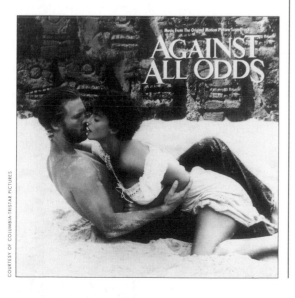

ALADDIN

Walt Disney 60846-2

The third and last of the Broadway-style, Alan Menken–Howard Ashman collaborations on Disney animated musicals won Oscars for Best Original Score (for Menken) and Best Song—although this time the lyric honors went to Ashman's successor, Tim Rice, for the love song "A Whole New World"; Ashman was posthumously nominated for his lyrical contribution to Robin Williams's wild your-wish-is-my-command "Friend Like Me." The score won five 1993 Grammys, including two for the album, two for the song "A Whole New World," and one for the Peabo Bryson–Regina Belle performance of the tune, which went to number 1 on the *Billboard* pop charts.

AMADEUS

Fantasy FCD-900-1791-2

No movie since *Fantasia* had so broadened the appeal of classical music to the masses. Eight 1984 Academy Awards went to director Milos Forman's film of Peter Shaffer's play about composer Antonio Salieri (F. Murray Abraham) tortured with guilt at the thought that he had killed the young musical genius Wolfgang Amadeus Mozart (Tom Hulce). Neville Marriner conducted the Academy of St. Martin-in-the-Fields in a two-record set of well-chosen pieces by Mozart, including excerpts from his *Symphonie Concertante*, *The Marriage of Figaro*, *Don Giovanni*, and the *Requiem*; extensive notes document each piece's use in the film. It won the 1984 Grammy as Best Classical Album, was nominated as Best Classical Orchestral Recording, and was a rare classical entry in *Billboard*'s hot-100 charts, reaching number 56 in the spring of 1985.

AMERICAN GRAFFITI
MCA MCAD-11871

One of the great all-time rock 'n' roll soundtracks accompanied George Lucas's much-loved valentine to high-school graduation in Northern California, 1962. The film was a 1973 Best Picture nominee (enabling Lucas to go on to make *Star Wars* and TV to rip off the concept as *Happy Days*, also starring Ron Howard). The two-LP set was an early and prime example of the all-song compilation score with tracks by a litany of late '50s and early '60s artists, including Bill Haley, Buddy Holly, Chuck Berry, Fats Domino, and the Beach Boys. The album spent over a year on the *Billboard* charts, peaking at number 10.

AN AMERICAN IN PARIS
Rhino R2 71961

This celebrated 1951 cavalcade of the George and Ira Gershwin songbook (with some key Gershwin concert works) won eight Oscars including Best Picture and Best Scoring for Johnny Green and Saul Chaplin. Included are such classics as "Love Is Here to Stay," "I Got Rhythm," and "'S Wonderful"; the two-CD restoration offers about 100 minutes of music (performed by Gene Kelly, Oscar Levant, Benny Carter's band, and others) with underscore, outtakes, and a lengthy transcript of co-musical supervisor Chaplin in conversation with Gershwin expert Michael Feinstein.

ARMAGEDDON
Columbia/Sony CK 69440

Written for the 1998 end-of-the-world thriller starring Bruce Willis, songwriter Diane Warren's

"I Don't Want to Miss a Thing" turned out to be a huge hit for Aerosmith and drove this soundtrack into multi-platinum territory and a number-1 ranking. Three other Aerosmith tunes are on the album, as well as tracks by Jon Bon Jovi, Shawn Colvin, and score composer Trevor Rabin.

AUSTIN POWERS:
THE SPY WHO SHAGGED ME
Maverick 9 47348-2

Madonna won a Grammy for her retro-style "Beautiful Stranger," written for the 1999 sequel to Mike Myers's popular, tongue-in-cheek *Austin Powers: International Man of Mystery* spoof of two years earlier. *The Spy Who Shagged Me* album, one of the year's biggest pop hits, also featured a new version of "I'll Never Fall in Love Again," performed by comeback kid Burt Bacharach and Elvis Costello, and a remix of Quincy Jones's "Soul Bossa Nova," which Myers shrewdly chose as a key theme in the original.

BACK TO THE FUTURE
MCA MCAD-6144

Robert Zemeckis's time-traveling movie with Michael J. Fox, Lea Thompson, and Christopher Lloyd was a big hit in the summer of 1985, and so was "The Power of Love," written and performed by Huey Lewis and the News—it went to number 1 on the *Billboard* pop charts and drove the album to number 12. Lewis also wrote "Back in Time," for the film; it's on the album along with tracks by composer Alan Silvestri, pop artists Eric Clapton, Etta James, and Lindsey Buckingham, and remakes of three old classics—"Night Train," "Earth Angel," and "Johnny B. Goode"—heard in the 1955 time-frame of the movie. "The Power of Love" was a Best Song Oscar nominee, the album a Grammy nominee as best soundtrack.

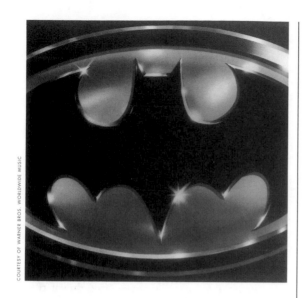

BATMAN

Warner Bros. 9 25936-2

This 1989 album established new norms for synergy between corporate divisions of an entertainment monolith. Warner Bros. executives convinced Prince, the hottest recording star of the '80s, to contribute songs to the company's summer blockbuster movie about the legendary comic-book hero. Prince visited the set and wrote nine songs, which Warner Bros. (the artist's home label) released as a "soundtrack" even though only a few minutes of Prince music are actually in the movie. "Batdance," which isn't in the film at all, went to number 1; "Partyman" hit the top 20, and the album spent six weeks at number 1. Only several weeks later did Warner release the actual soundtrack—that is, Danny Elfman's orchestral score.

BATMAN FOREVER

Atlantic 82759-2

Val Kilmer donned the cowl for the third installment of the Warner Bros. trilogy, with Tommy Lee Jones as Two-Face and Jim Carrey as the Riddler. Elliot Goldenthal's wild orchestral score was released separately, but it was this rock collection that scored big on the charts (number 5, multi-platinum) in large part because of Seal's number-1 hit "Kiss From a Rose" and U2's top-20 track "Hold Me, Thrill Me, Kiss Me, Kill Me." Seal's soulful ballad, which would later win Grammys for Record of the Year and Song of the Year, was in fact written by the British pop star eight years earlier and included on his own album in 1994.

BEACHES

Atlantic 7 81933-2

It was Marc Shaiman's idea for Bette Midler to record a cover of "Wind Beneath My Wings." She thought it was a bit over the top for an already sentimental movie about the 30-year relationship between two girlfriends from opposite sides of the tracks. Shaiman was proven right: The tune gave Midler her first number-1 hit, her first triple platinum album, her highest charting album (number 2), and one that stayed on the charts for over three years. This is all vintage Midler—oldies like "Under the Boardwalk," classics from Cole Porter to Disney, a couple of originals ("Otto Titsling," "Oh Industry"), and more (including composer Georges Delerue's movie theme). "Wind Between My Wings" won both Record and Song of the Year at the 1989 Grammys.

BEAUTY AND THE BEAST

Walt Disney 60618-2

A true Disney classic, this powerful 1991 fable was the studio's only animated Best Picture nominee. Songwriters Alan Menken and Howard Ashman received, and deserved, three Best Song nominations for the title song (which won), "Belle," and the delightful singing-and-dancing-dishes-and-flatware extravaganza "Be Our Guest." Menken won the Original Score Oscar. Angela

Lansbury, Jerry Orbach, Paige O'Hara, and Robby Benson are joined by a full chorus for the film's tunes; Celine Dion and Peabo Bryson sing the pop version of the title song and won a 1992 Grammy for their work. Menken won two Grammys, and Ashman one for the score; Ashman died of AIDS-related illness before he could receive any of these honors. No Disney score since has quite matched the Broadway-style quality of the Menken-Ashman collaborations.

BEVERLY HILLS COP
MCA MCAD-5553

This wildly popular album—a 1985 Grammy winner as the year's best soundtrack—contained a batch of high-energy rock songs that fueled Eddie Murphy's 1984 portrayal of a wisecracking Detroit cop in L.A. Hitting the charts were Patti LaBelle's "New Attitude" (which went to number 17), the Pointer Sisters' "Neutron Dance" (number 6), and Glenn Frey's "The Heat Is On" (number 2). Score composer Harold Faltermeyer's instrumental "Axel F" surprised many by reaching number 3. The album itself spent 62 weeks on the charts (two weeks at number 1).

THE BIG CHILL
Motown 314530953-2

Another of the classic rock compilations, this collection of Motown hits was specifically designed by writer-director Lawrence Kasdan to evoke the sounds and feel of the '60s—the era relived by a close group of college buddies (William Hurt, Glenn Close, Tom Berenger, Jeff Goldblum, Kevin Kline, Mary Kay Place, and JoBeth Williams) who gather for a close friend's funeral. Marvin Gaye's "I Heard It Through the Grapevine" opens the movie (as the group learns of his suicide); everyone dances around the kitchen to the Temptations'

"Ain't Too Proud to Beg"; and tracks by Aretha Franklin, Smokey Robinson and The Miracles, and other artists figure prominently. The film was a 1983 Best Picture nominee and remains a favorite of baby boomers; the album peaked at number 17 and went platinum with its ongoing sales over two years. It spawned a second album with seven songs that are in the film (notably "When a Man Loves a Woman" and "Bad Moon Rising") and four that aren't.

BLUE HAWAII
RCA 67459-2

Elvis Presley's most popular movie soundtrack, this 1961 release (which cast The King as the son of a pineapple mogul) lasted 20 weeks at number 1 on the *Billboard* pop charts. "Can't Help Falling in Love," one of Presley's trademark songs, went to number 2; the album also includes the title tune and the great "Rock-A-Hula Baby," which went to number 23. It was a 1961 Grammy nominee as best movie soundtrack.

THE BODYGUARD
Arista 18699-2

The single best-selling movie soundtrack to date—an estimated 16 million copies in the U.S. alone, 30 million worldwide—was a song score for a movie that the critics hated (tough-guy security expert Kevin Costner falls for his client, singer-actress Whitney Houston). Although two of its romantic ballads were Oscar- and Grammy-nominated ("I Have Nothing" by David Foster and Linda Thompson, "Run to You" by Jud Friedman and Allan Rich), it was Houston's cover of Dolly Parton's old "I Will Always Love You" that was the big hit: number 1 for 14 weeks. Three of Houston's other songs on the record charted: "I Have Nothing," to number

4; "I'm Every Woman," number 4; "Run to You," number 31. The album remained number 1 for five months and on the *Billboard* charts for 141 weeks. Other contributing artists were Kenny G and Aaron Neville, Lisa Stansfield, the S.O.U.L. S.Y.S.T.E.M., Curtis Stigers, Joe Cocker, and Sass Jordan. Alan Silvestri's dramatic orchestral theme was also included. The Grammy tally was impressive: Album of the Year, Record of the Year, and Best Female Pop Vocal Performance (the latter two for "I Will Always Love You"). Eight American Music Awards were added to the honors.

BONNIE AND CLYDE
Warner Bros. 1712 (LP)
One of the seminal films of its time, Arthur Penn's fanciful 1967 look at '30s bank robbers Clyde Barrow and Bonnie Parker ("they're young, they're in love, and they kill people") propelled Warren Beatty and Faye Dunaway to stardom and won a Best Picture nomination for producer Beatty. Charles Strouse wrote an evocative Depression-era score that incorporated guitar-and-banjo greats Lester Flatt and Earl Scruggs performing their classic "Foggy Mountain Breakdown," and the soundtrack album reached number 12. Strouse was nominated for a Grammy, and Flatt and Scruggs won one for Best Country Performance by a Duo or Group.

THE BREAKFAST CLUB
A&M CD 3294
One of the mid-'80s Brat Pack movies, this study in teen angst starred the usual crowd, including Molly Ringwald, Judd Nelson, Emilio Estevez, Ally Sheedy, and Anthony Michael Hall. Simple Minds' "Don't You (Forget About Me)," by composer-producer Keith Forsey and Steve Schiff, shot

to number 1 in May 1985, sending the album into the top 20 and onto the gold-certification list.

THE BRIDGES OF MADISON COUNTY
Malpaso/Warner Bros. 2-46259
Clint Eastwood's romantic 1995 film version of the popular Robert James Waller novel starred Eastwood and Meryl Streep—and the classic song stylings of soulful romantic singer Johnny Hartman and jazz-blues great Dinah Washington, who occupy seven of the eleven slots on the soundtrack album. Reflecting the popularity of the film, the album landed in the *Billboard* top 50. Also included on the album is the movie's theme, "Doe Eyes," composed by Eastwood and arranged by his longtime composer Lennie Niehaus.

BYE BYE BIRDIE
RCA 1081-2-R
The 1963 film version of the Charles Strouse–Lee Adams Broadway hit starred Dick Van Dyke, Janet Leigh, Ann-Margret, and Paul Lynde. With such songs as "Put on a Happy Face," "A Lot of Livin' to Do," and "Kids," the movie soundtrack was enormously successful, reaching number 2 on the charts and nabbing an Oscar nomination for musical director Johnny Green.

CABARET
MCA MCAD-40027
Liza Minnelli and Joel Grey won Oscars for their portrayals of Sally Bowles and the Master of Ceremonies in Bob Fosse's 1972 screen adaptation of the Broadway musical by John Kander and Fred Ebb. Ralph Burns also won an Oscar for his musical adaptation. The film, set in 1920s Berlin, won five other Oscars, including Best Director, and is widely considered the last great musical based (loosely) on a Broadway show. Six of the show

songs were holdovers, including the title tune (now a signature song for Minnelli); tunes added to the movie included "Maybe This Time" (an old Kander-Ebb trunk song) and "Money."

CAMELOT

Warner Bros. 3102-2

The 1967 film adaptation of Lerner & Loewe's musical of King Arthur, Guinevere, Lancelot, and the Knights of the Round Table was a major hit with record-buyers. Richard Harris, Vanessa Redgrave, and Franco Nero (the latter, dubbed by Gene Merlino) performed songs including the title tune, the great "If Ever I Would Leave You," "How to Handle a Woman," and more. Alfred Newman and Ken Darby won Oscars for their musical direction and vocal arrangements—despite being put through their paces by director Joshua Logan—and the album went to number 11 in 1968, platinum eventually.

CAN-CAN

Polydor 814 079

Frank Sinatra's presence in the 1960 film version of the Cole Porter musical helped to sell thousands of soundtrack albums, and Shirley MacLaine, Maurice Chevalier, and Louis Jordan didn't hurt. Nelson Riddle's arrangements of songs such as "I Love Paris," "Let's Do It," and "Just One of Those Things" (some from the original production, others from previous Porter scores) helped him win an Oscar nomination for the Fox film, too. The album went to number 3.

CAR WASH

MCA MCAD-11502

The soundtrack for this 1976 comedy starring Richard Pryor, George Carlin, and other comedians proved far more successful than the movie itself. Norman Whitfield's songs, performed for the most part by the soul group Rose Royce, were heard blaring virtually nonstop from the loudspeakers of the car wash. The title tune hit number 1, "I Wanna Get Next to You" number 10, and the two-LP set itself went to number 14. It beat out such established film-score composers as Jerry Goldsmith, Bernard Herrmann, and Alex North for the 1976 soundtrack Grammy.

CAROUSEL

Angel 64692

A commercial failure upon its release in 1956—losing millions for 20th Century–Fox—this Rodgers & Hammerstein fantasy about a carousel barker (Gordon MacRae), the mill worker (Shirley Jones) he marries, and the tragedy that befalls them is today considered a first-rate adaptation. The score contains some of their most haunting songs: "If I Loved You," "Soliloquy," and "You'll Never Walk Alone." Veteran Fox musical director Alfred Newman, and his vocal arranger Ken Darby, brought their sharp cinema sensibilities to this great Broadway score. The album spent two weeks at number 1 and remained on *Billboard*'s pop chart for over a year. The musical, released in the same year as *The King and I*, didn't score a single Oscar nomination.

CINDERELLA

Walt Disney 60879-7

Walt Disney's 1950 adaptation of the fairy tale about the girl with the wicked stepsisters who becomes a prince's favorite contained one of the era's most tuneful scores. Oscar voters agreed, nominating "Bibbidy-Bobbidi-Boo" (by songwriters Jerry Livingston, Mack David, and Al Hoffman) as Best Song and the Oliver Wallace–Paul J. Smith music for Best Scoring of a Musical Picture. "The

Work Song" and "A Dream Is a Wish Your Heart Makes" have also become standards over the years.

CITY OF ANGELS
Warner Sunset/Reprise 9 46867-2

This soundtrack was a colossal hit for its lineup of top artists and songs (notably Alanis Morissette's "Uninvited" and the Goo Goo Dolls' "Iris"), reaching number 1 in late 1998 and remaining on the *Billboard* charts for over a year. Nicolas Cage starred as an angel who fell in love with Meg Ryan in this four-hanky weeper from 1998. Morissette's tune won Grammys for Best Female Rock Vocal and Best Rock Song. Gabriel Yared's touching orchestral-and-choral score occupies the final 20 minutes of the disc.

A CLOCKWORK ORANGE
Warner Bros. 2573-2

Walter Carlos, whose synthesizer renderings of classical music made *Switched-on Bach* a major seller in the '60s, contributed electronic versions of Beethoven, Rossini, and Purcell for Stanley Kubrick's nightmarish 1971 vision of the future. The album, which also contained more traditionally recorded classical excerpts and Gene Kelly's "Singin' in the Rain," reached number 34 on the pop chart. Years later, Walter Carlos became Wendy Carlos and worked on Kubrick's *The Shining* (1980, featuring an ominous electronic adaptation of the traditional "Dies Irae" chant over the main title) and Disney's *Tron* (1982).

COCKTAIL
Elektra 9 60806-2

Nobody was going to win any awards for the 1988 Tom Cruise–Elisabeth Shue–Bryan Brown movie about a hotshot bartender, but the tavern setting was perfect for a rock soundtrack. This collection not only delivered for the movie, but went to number 2 on the *Billboard* album chart, thanks to the Beach Boys' number-1 hit "Kokomo" along with other new tunes from The Fabulous Thunderbirds and Starship, and licensed material from Bobby McFerrin, Georgia Satellites, John Cougar Mellencamp, Little Richard, and others.

THE COMMITMENTS
MCA MCAD-10286

Alan Parker's well-received 1991 movie about the rise to fame of a Dublin rock band spawned an equally popular album of '60s favorites ("Mustang Sally," "Try a Little Tenderness," "In the Midnight Hour," etc.) performed by the singer-actors who portrayed the group on film. In fact, the band was nominated for a Grammy for Best Performance by a Duo or Group With Vocal. The album was a top-10 hit in late 1991, stayed on the charts for over a year, and spawned a second album that mixed songs from the movie with several new ones.

THE CROW
Miramax/Hollywood MH-62047-2
THE CROW: CITY OF ANGELS
Atlantic 82519-2

The 1994 adaptation of the dark-visioned comic book about an aspiring rock star who is murdered and returns from the dead on a mission of vengeance became a cult hit in part because of the accidental death of its star, Brandon Lee, during filming. The soundtrack, however, went on to be much more than a cult favorite—its mixture of alternative, industrial, and metal rock went all the way to number 1 on *Billboard*'s album charts. Stone Temple Pilots, Violent Femmes, Rage Against the Machine, Nine Inch Nails, Jesus and Mary Chain, and other bands contributed tracks. The soundtrack for the panned 1996 sequel (with Vincent Perez), featuring Hole, Iggy Pop, White Zombie, and other bands, also leaped into the top 10.

DANGEROUS MINDS

MCA MCAD-11228

Michelle Pfeiffer's stint as an inner-city school-teacher was accompanied by a soundtrack of appropriately urban style songs by artists ranging from Rappin' 4-Tay to Immature and Wendy & Lisa. The big hit off this album, however, was Coolio's "Gangsta's Paradise," which went to number 1 as a single and drove the album to the number 1 position as well in the summer of 1995. Coolio won the 1995 Grammy for Best Rap Solo Performance; the track was nominated as Record of the Year.

DELIVERANCE

Warner Bros. 2683-2

A memorable moment in John Boorman's harrowing 1972 adventure of Atlanta businessmen on a wilderness trip in the Appalachians occurs when Ronny Cox and a local boy engage in a friendly down-home pickin' contest—the boy on banjo, Cox on guitar. Mistitled "Dueling Banjos," it went to number 2 as a single and spent three weeks at number 1 as an album. Bluegrass musicians Eric Weissberg and Steve Mandell won a 1973 Grammy for Best Country Instrumental Performance for this classic tune.

DIRTY DANCING

RCA 6408-2-R

Nobody really knew what they had in *Dirty Dancing*—neither Vestron, which produced this unassuming little film about a love affair between dancers at a Catskills resort, nor RCA, which released the soundtrack (a collection of new tunes and old classics circa the 1963 period of the film by the likes of the Ronettes and Maurice Williams). The Patrick Swayze–Jennifer Grey

COURTESY OF RCA RECORDS LABEL, A UNIT OF BMG ENTERTAINMENT

movie went through the roof, and the album became the biggest seller of 1987 (18 weeks at number 1, two years on the chart). The Bill Medley–Jennifer Warnes duet "(I've Had) The Time of My Life" won the Best Song Oscar, and the singers won a Grammy as Best Pop Performance by a Duo or Group with Vocal. Swayze's own "She's Like the Wind" (co-written by Stacy Widelitz) reached number 3. The album spawned a sequel, *More Dirty Dancing*, that did almost as well—number 3 in 1988.

DUMBO

Walt Disney 60949-7

The Disney studio continued its winning streak at the Oscars by taking the 1941 statue for Best Scoring of a Musical Picture. Disney composers Frank Churchill and Oliver Wallace won for their wide-ranging music—from circus marches to tender lullabies—for this heartwarming tale of a little elephant whose giant ears enable him to fly. The sweet "Baby Mine," which Mrs. Jumbo sings to her little Dumbo, was a Best Song nominee for Churchill and lyricist Ned Washington.

EASTER PARADE

Rhino R2 71960

Irving Berlin's perennial tunes highlight this holiday musical, a 1948 Fred Astaire–Judy Garland vehicle. Over a dozen classic Berlin songs are featured, some written for the film ("It Only Happens When I Dance With You," "Steppin' Out With My Baby," "A Couple of Swells") and others from Berlin's chest of Tin Pan Alley treasures ("Shakin' the Blues Away," "I Love a Piano," "Easter Parade"). The 1995 CD, produced from restored production masters, includes all of the songs along with most of Roger Edens and Johnny Green's Oscar-winning underscore.

EASY RIDER

MCA MCLD-19153 (U.K.)

Dennis Hopper and Peter Fonda raided their record collections for the rock 'n' roll score of their Oscar-nominated, low-budget 1969 exploration of disenfranchised bikers on the road to New Orleans. Songs by Steppenwolf (notably their "Born to Be Wild," a big hit the year before), The Byrds, The Band, and the Jimi Hendrix Experience were thoughtfully integrated with Laszlo Kovacs's cinematography to create a portrait of a young America previously unseen in mainstream cinema. Roger McGuinn contributed "The Ballad of Easy Rider" to the soundtrack, which spent 72 weeks on the charts and got as high as number 6. The original LP, on Dunhill, was widely regarded as the first of the rock compilation soundtracks and the father of the entire genre of high-profile, million-selling soundtracks of today.

THE EDDY DUCHIN STORY

Decca DL-8289 (LP)

The 1956 biopic was dismissed by critics as a lugubrious tearjerker, but audiences who remembered the late pianist-bandleader made it a hit and bought the soundtrack in droves. Duchin (played in the movie by Tyrone Power) was a tremendously popular musician, and his 1951 death from leukemia made him even more famous. Carmen Cavallaro recorded the piano tracks and made the soundtrack a number 1 hit, lasting some 99 weeks on the charts.

ENDLESS LOVE

Mercury 422826277-2

Lionel Richie's title song received a 1981 Best Song Oscar nomination, and the duet he sang with Diana Ross not only reached the top of the charts, it sent the album (a few songs and a few of composer Jonathan Tunick's instrumental cues) into the top 10 and gold-record status. Grammy nominations went to Ross and Richie for Record of the Year, to Richie for Song of the Year, and to the album as top movie soundtrack. Nobody much liked Franco Zeffirelli's movie, which starred Brooke Shields and Martin Hewitt as teenage lovers.

EVERY WHICH WAY BUT LOOSE

Elektra 503 (LP)

Clint Eastwood teamed up with an orangutan named Clyde for this first of two action comedies about a trucker and bare-knuckled fighter who falls for a country singer (Sondra Locke). Critics hated it, but audiences made it his most profitable movie up to that time (1978). The soundtrack was all country, from Eddie Rabbitt's title song (which topped the country charts and even made the top-40 pop chart) to tunes by Charlie Rich and Mel Tillis and a couple of songs warbled by Locke herself. Musical director Steve Dorff has a handful of underscore cues on the record; Dorff and co-writers Snuff Garrett and Milton Brown were Grammy-nominated for writing the title tune.

EVITA

Warner Bros. 46346-2

Alan Parker's 1996 adaptation of the Andrew Lloyd Webber–Tim Rice rock opera drew mixed reviews—many critics thought it was stunning looking but strangely distant. Madonna came away surprisingly unscathed, considering her controversial reputation, perhaps because she was so right for the role of the Argentinian actress-turned-politician-turned-cult-figure. The familiar tunes are here: "Don't Cry for Me, Argentina," "Another Suitcase in Another Hall," "The Art of the Possible," along with the new song that Lloyd Webber and Rice wrote, "You Must Love Me," which won the Best Song Oscar.

FM

MCA 12000 (LP)

Cashing in early on the rock-musical trend, this film (about a radio station's disc jockeys and their crusade against corporate greed) contained an amusing performance by comedian Martin Mull but generated far more profits from its two-LP soundtrack album. Steely Dan's title song cracked the top 25, but the set was more like a '70s greatest-hits collection with such artists as Foreigner, Steve Miller, Billy Joel, Boz Skaggs, and Boston. The film contains concert footage of Linda Ronstadt, Jimmy Buffett, Tom Petty, and REO Speedwagon. The album spent half of 1978 on the *Billboard* chart and reached number 5.

FAME

Polydor 800 034

Composer Michael Gore won both 1980's Best Song and Best Original Score Oscars for this popular fictionalized story of New York's High School of the Performing Arts (lyricist Dean Pitchford shared the song Oscar). Irene Cara (who sang the energetic title song to a number-4 position as a single, driving the album to number 7) played one of several gifted young singers, dancers, and actors seeking success in the arts. Gore went on to another Oscar nomination for *Terms of Endearment* (1983) and other popular films including *Pretty in Pink* (1986) and *Defending Your Life* (1991). Cara's "Out Here on My Own" (written by Michael and his sister, Lesley Gore, the '60s singer) also made the top 20.

FANTASIA

Buena Vista 600077

Walt Disney's grand experiment in combining classical music with animation met with mixed critical reaction on its premiere in 1940. Leopold Stokowski conducted the Philadelphia Orchestra in (mostly abridged versions of) Bach, Tchaikovsky (the *Nutcracker* suite), Beethoven (the *Pastoral* symphony), Ponchielli, Stravinsky (*The Rite of Spring*), and others. Dukas's *The Sorcerer's Apprentice* contained the only familiar character in Mickey Mouse, but the finale, which combined Mussorgsky's *Night on Bald Mountain* with Schubert's *Ave Maria* in a grand struggle between the forces of darkness and light, became a favorite. *Fantasia* is equally significant as the first film shown in stereophonic sound ("Fantasound," as it was called).

FIDDLER ON THE ROOF

EMI-USA CDP 7 46091-2

John Williams won his first Academy Award for adapting and conducting the outstanding 1971 film version of the long-running Jerry Bock–Sheldon Harnick Broadway musical. Warm and affecting, Norman Jewison's film starred Topol as Tevye and garnered several other nominations including Best Picture. But it's the songs that people remember: "Tradition," "If I Were a Rich Man," "Matchmaker," and especially "Sunrise, Sunset." Isaac Stern played the violin solos. The album went gold and spent 90 weeks on the charts.

FLASHDANCE

Casablanca 314 558 682-2

Proving once again that he was in touch with the sound of youth, composer-producer Giorgio Moroder scored another Oscar—this time, for Best Song of 1983—for his title tune for Jennifer Beals's welder-by-day, dancer-by-night romantic drama. "Flashdance . . . What a Feeling" also spent six weeks at number 1 and propelled the album to multi-platinum status, keeping it on the charts for 78 weeks. Irene Cara co-wrote (with Moroder and Keith Forsey) the lyrics, sang it, and won a Grammy for Best Female Pop Vocal Performance. Moroder also won Grammys for the album as the year's top soundtrack and for his love theme as Best Instrumental Composition. Michael Sembello's "Maniac" also went to number 1 as a single, was the movie's other Best Song Oscar nominee, and also nabbed a Grammy nomination as Song of the Year.

FOOTLOOSE

Columbia/Legacy CK 65781

The second biggest album of 1984 was this multi-platinum smash that lasted 10 weeks at number 1 and further defined a new style of making movie musicals. Kevin Bacon starred as a city kid who spearheads a movement to bring back dancing to a conservative, religious community. The album yielded six danceable top-40 hits, including two number-1 songs, each of which received a Best Song Oscar nomination: Kenny Loggins's title song (by Loggins and screenwriter Dean Pitchford) and Deniece Williams's "Let's Hear It for the Boy" (by Pitchford and Tom Snow). Shalamar's "Dancing in

the Streets," Loggins's "I'm Free," Mike Reno and Ann Wilson's "Almost Paradise," and Bonnie Tyler's "Holding Out for a Hero" also charted.

FORREST GUMP

Epic E2K 66329

The Oscar-winning Best Picture of 1994 generated a two-CD set of equally popular proportions, reaching number 2 on the pop charts and lasting two years in all. Robert Zemeckis's film, with Tom Hanks as a simple-minded, good-hearted Southern boy who unwittingly took part in some of the '60s and '70s most important political and cultural events, was littered with pop hits from throughout those decades. The 32 tracks include such era-specific songs as "Hound Dog," "Mrs. Robinson, "Aquarius/Let the Sunshine In," "Turn! Turn! Turn!," "California Dreamin'," and "What the World Needs Now." Joel Sill, one of the pioneers in movie music supervision, oversaw this collection.

FUNNY GIRL

Columbia CK 3220

FUNNY LADY

Arista 19006-2

Barbra Streisand won an Oscar for her performance as Fanny Brice in the 1968 musical adaptation of her Broadway hit, *Funny Girl*, and the soundtrack album was her best selling to date, reaching number 12 on the *Billboard* charts and lasting 108 weeks in all. Songs in the Jule Styne–Bob Merrill score included the now-classic "People" and "Don't Rain on My Parade," and the Oscar-nominated title song (written for the film). The 1975 sequel, with Streisand and James Caan, boasted a score by John Kander and Fred Ebb (including the Oscar-nominated "How Lucky Can You Get") and reached number 6 on the *Billboard* charts. Musical directors Walter Scharf and Peter Matz received respective Oscar nominations for their work on the films.

G.I. BLUES

RCA 67460

Elvis Presley's first post-Army movie—a 1960 outing in which he plays a G.I. stationed in West Germany who falls for cabaret singer Juliet Prowse—spawned one of his most successful albums, spending 10 weeks at number 1 and lasting on the *Billboard* charts for over two years. Presley's numbers include the title song, "Tonight Is So Right for Love," "Doin' the Best I Can," and "Wooden Heart"; the album was a double Grammy nominee, both for Presley's vocal performance and as best soundtrack.

GHOSTBUSTERS

Arista ARCD-8246

"Who ya gonna call?" Ray Parker, Jr., wrote and performed the crowd-pleasing title song for the Dan Aykroyd–Bill Murray supernatural comedy, which won an Oscar nomination as Best Song and

was number 1 for three weeks in the summer of 1986, driving the album to a number 3 spot on the LP chart. Parker wound up with a Grammy for Best Pop Instrumental Performance. The Bus Boys' lively "Cleaning Up the Town" also charted briefly, with artists including Laura Branigan and Air Supply also on the record. Score composer Elmer Bernstein contributed two tracks.

GIGI

Rhino R2 71962

Widely considered one of the screen's greatest musicals, MGM's 1958 film won nine Academy Awards, including Best Picture (plus a special Oscar to Maurice Chevalier), Best Song ("Gigi"), and Best Scoring of a Musical Picture. This was Alan Jay Lerner and Frederick Loewe's only original film score, but what a score, with such memorable songs as Chevalier's "Thank Heaven for Little Girls," the Chevalier-Hermione Gingold "I Remember It Well," and Louis Jordan's "Gigi." André Previn did the arrangements (with Conrad Salinger) and music direction, winning not only the Oscar but the first Grammy ever awarded for Best Soundtrack Album. It was one of the biggest-selling records of the decade, staying 10 weeks at number 1 and lasting 172 weeks on the *Billboard* charts altogether; the CD restoration includes the entire score with outtakes.

GOODFELLAS

Atlantic 7 82152-2

Often cited as an example of first-rate music supervision and placement of contemporary songs in dramatic contexts, Martin Scorsese's 1990 seriocomic look at life inside an organized-crime family does not have a conventional score. Rather, Scorsese plays (almost nonstop) carefully chosen songs from the '50s and '60s period of the film. Twelve of the film's

43 songs are on the soundtrack, including cuts by Tony Bennett, The Shangri-Las, Bobby Darin, Cream, and The Moonglows.

THE GRADUATE
Columbia CK 3180

Mike Nichols's Oscar-winning 1967 comedy about a young college graduate who has an affair with an older woman, then falls for her daughter, remains one of the most important films of the '60s—as much for its score as for its importance to American cinema. Nichols decided on contemporary music and settled on a score by pop duo Simon & Garfunkel, who had had a number-1 hit in early 1966 with "The Sounds of Silence." Nichols borrowed that tune, a couple of others (notably "Scarborough Fair" and "April Come She Will") and asked Paul Simon to write "Mrs. Robinson"—the only song specifically created for the movie, and then only a few bars. The success of the film led Simon to flesh out the tune which, in mid-'68, became a huge hit: three weeks at number 1, plus three 1968 Grammys, including Record of the Year and Best Original Score. Dave Grusin, who composed the film's source music and was lucky enough to have several Muzak-style tracks on the album, shared the Grammy. If Hollywood outsiders were left scratching their heads over the film's failure to receive even one music nomination, it was because Academy rules precluded the entry of old tunes in new movies. (They still do.)

GREASE
Polydor 825 095-2

In the wake of the success of *Saturday Night Fever*, John Travolta was teamed with then-hot pop star Olivia Newton-John for the 1978 screen version of the long-running Broadway musical. Supplementing the Jim Jacobs–Warren Casey score

(which produced a number-5 hit in "Summer Nights") were three notable new tunes: "Grease" by Barry Gibb, sung by Frankie Valli, which spent two weeks at number 1; the Travolta–Newton-John duet "You're the One That I Want," also a number 1 hit, and Newton-John's "Hopelessly Devoted to You," number 3, both the work of her producer John Farrar. Only "Hopelessly" wound up with a Best Song Oscar nomination; the 2-LP soundtrack was an Album of the Year Grammy nominee but lost to *Saturday Night Fever*.

GYPSY
Warner Bros. BS 1480 (LP)

Rosalind Russell and Natalie Wood starred in this 1962 version of the Jule Styne–Stephen Sondheim Broadway smash about a domineering stage mother whose lesser-talented daughter stripped her way to stardom as Gypsy Rose Lee. The many familiar tunes include "Everything's Coming Up Roses," "Let Me Entertain You," "Some People," "You Gotta Have a Gimmick," and "Together Wherever We Go" (which was cut from the film but is on the album). Music director Frank Perkins received an Oscar nomination; the album was a top-10 hit.

A HARD DAY'S NIGHT
Parlophone CDP 7 46437 2
HELP!
Parlophone CDP 7 46439 2
YELLOW SUBMARINE
Parlophone CDP 7 46445 2
LET IT BE
Parlophone CDP 7 46447 2

At the height of their popularity, The Beatles made a pair of movies with director Richard Lester: loosely plotted, anarchic affairs that had the Fab Four playing themselves in a visually stylish mix that would anticipate MTV-style videos more than a decade later. The albums were colossal hits: *Hard Day's Night* (including the title tune, "Can't Buy Me Love," and "And I Love Her") spent 14 weeks at number 1 in 1964, *Help!* (title tune, "Ticket to Ride" and "Yesterday") nine weeks at number 1 in '65. Producer George Martin received an Oscar nomination for his music direction on the first film. Half of the album for the animated *Yellow Submarine* (1967, including the title tune and "All You Need Is Love") is actually Martin's underscore. Ironically, the Beatles themselves received an original song score Oscar for *Let It Be* (1970)—even though the film was a documentary and none of the songs were specifically written for the movie.

HARD TO HOLD

Razor & Tie 82056

Singer-songwriter-turned-actor Rick Springfield shifted from daytime soaps to the big screen with this 1984 feature about a spoiled rock star. The soundtrack wound up being more successful than the movie, going platinum and reaching number 6 on the album chart, powered by three top-40 hits: "Love Somebody" (the most successful at number 5), "Don't Walk Away," and "Bop 'Til You Drop."

HELLO, DOLLY!

Philips 810 368-2

The hit Broadway musical about a widow-turned-marriage broker was transformed into a star vehicle for Barbra Streisand in this expensive 1969 film, one of three musical behemoths that nearly bankrupted 20th Century–Fox. The soundtrack album did fairly well, reaching into the top 50 on the strength of such Jerry Herman songs as "Before the Parade Passes By" and Streisand's title-song duet with Louis Armstrong, the movie's show-stopper.

Lionel Newman and Lennie Hayton won the musical-adaptation Oscar.

HEAVY METAL

Full Moon/Elektra 60691-2

The 1981 movie was a collection of animated vignettes based loosely on the sexy, often violent sci-fi graphic-story magazine. The producers assembled a wild collection of head-banging metal bands, not only for the movie but for a two-LP set—groups like Nazareth, Cheap Trick, Black Sabbath, Journey, Grand Funk Railroad, and Blue Oyster Cult. The result was an offbeat soundtrack (that reached number 12 and spent half a year on the charts) but a music-rights-clearance nightmare that kept the film off cable for years and delayed a video release for more than a decade.

HIGH SOCIETY

Polydor 814 079

Cole Porter's sophisticated score for the 1956 musicalization of *The Philadelphia Story* contains a handful of great tunes, including "True Love" (a top-10 hit for Grace Kelly and Bing Crosby), "Now You Has Jazz" (Crosby and Louis Armstrong), "Well Did You Evah?" (Frank Sinatra and Crosby), and "You're Sensational" (Sinatra). "True Love" received an Oscar nomination, as did MGM musical supervisors Johnny Green and Saul Chaplin. The LP peaked at number 5 and went gold.

HONEYSUCKLE ROSE

Columbia CGK 36752

"On the Road Again" won a Grammy as the year's best country song, was nominated for the Best Song Oscar, and managed to make the unusual crossover from the country realm to the pop charts. More than that, it's now universally recognized as one of Willie Nelson's signature tunes. It was written for this 1980 tale of a country star who succumbs to temptation on the road. The simple, easygoing song was number 1 on the country charts (the album went to number 1 too) and was accompanied on the LP by several tunes sung by co-stars Dyan Cannon and Amy Irving.

THE JAZZ SINGER
Columbia CK 67569

Neil Diamond tried his luck at the movies again in 1980 with this second remake of the Al Jolson classic, this time as both songwriter and star, with Laurence Olivier as his father, the cantor who disapproved of his becoming a rock 'n' roller. Three of the 10 original songs he wrote for the 1980 movie wound up as top-10 hits and are now instantly recognizable standards: "Love on the Rocks" (number 2), "Hello Again" (number 6), and "America" (number 8). The album went to number 3 and stayed on the charts for 115 weeks. Diamond's songs—so popular with the public—were ignored by the Motion Picture Academy.

JESUS CHRIST SUPERSTAR
MCA 11000 (LP)

Norman Jewison's 1973 version of the Andrew Lloyd Webber–Tim Rice rock opera received mixed reviews but sent its soundtrack album into the top 25 for a few weeks. Ted Neeley played Jesus; Yvonne Elliman (the original Mary Magdalene, who had hits with "Everything's Alright" and "I Don't Know How to Love Him" off the original concept album) and Carl Anderson were also in the cast. Receiving Oscar nominations for their adaptation were conductor André Previn, orchestrator Herbert Spencer, and original composer Lloyd Webber.

JONATHAN LIVINGSTON SEAGULL
Columbia CK 32550

When filmmaker Hall Bartlett acquired the rights to make Richard Bach's best-selling allegorical novel into a movie, he signed Neil Diamond to write an original song score. The 1973 movie bombed, but Diamond's album spent two weeks in the number-2 spot on *Billboard*'s pop chart (34 weeks all told). The album, which Diamond called "an original musical narrative," included five tunes (notably "Lonely Looking Sky" and "Be") and several lush orchestral numbers arranged and conducted by Diamond's musical director Lee Holdridge (which launched Holdridge's own career as a film composer). Despite its commercial success and a Grammy win for best movie album, Diamond's music was ignored at the Oscars.

THE JUNGLE BOOK
Walt Disney 60950-7

For Disney's 1967 adaptation of Rudyard Kipling's "Mowgli" stories, songwriter Terry Gilkyson was originally hired to create the songs for a serious version. But when Disney decided to lighten the mood, he jettisoned Gilkyson's tunes—except for Baloo the Bear's philosophy-spouting rag "The Bare Necessities," which, as sung by Phil Harris, became the film's Best Song Oscar nominee. New songs by Richard and Robert Sherman were added (including Louis Prima as ape King Louis scatting with Harris on the amusing "I Wan'na Be Like You"); George Bruns wrote the atmospheric score. The original album received a Grammy nomination as best children's record.

THE KING AND I
Angel ZDM 64693 2 4

This classic Rodgers & Hammerstein musical won five 1956 Academy Awards, including Best Actor for Yul Brynner and Best Scoring of a Musical Picture for musical director Alfred Newman and vocal arranger Ken Darby. Brynner's 19th-century King of Siam and Deborah Kerr's English governess (dubbed by Marni Nixon) sing such familiar songs as "Hello, Young Lovers," "Getting to Know You," "I Whistle a Happy Tune," and "Shall We Dance?" The film, a Best Picture nominee, was a huge box-office success and is now widely considered one of the finest adaptations ever made of a Broadway musical. While it spent just one week in the number-1 position on *Billboard*'s album chart, at 274 weeks total it holds the number-2 spot as the movie soundtrack with the greatest longevity. The definitive version of the score is the special-edition CD available with the movie laserdisc package.

L.A. CONFIDENTIAL
Restless 01877-72946-2
Varèse Sarabande VSD-5885

Curtis Hanson's 1997 drama of police corruption in early 1950s Los Angeles spawned two discs: one consisting mostly of the songs he very specifically chose to establish the setting (Johnny Mercer's "Ac-Cent-Tchu-Ate the Positive," Chet Baker's "Look for the Silver Lining," Lee Wiley's "Looking at You," etc.), the other (the Varèse album) focusing on Goldsmith's dark, evocative underscore that won an Oscar nomination.

LA BAMBA
Slash 25605

Lou Diamond Phillips played rock 'n' roll pioneer Ritchie Valens in this 1987 biopic, written by Luis Valdez and produced by Taylor Hackford. It made Phllips a star, just as the movie made the East L.A. rock band Los Lobos a household name. The group's version of the title song—a hit for Valens around the time of his 1959 death in a plane crash—spent three weeks at number 1 in the summer of 1987. Los Lobos's authentic re-creation of Valens's tunes (plus tracks by Marshall Crenshaw, Bo Diddley, and others) sent the album to the top spot too.

LADY SINGS THE BLUES
Motown 3746307582

Diana Ross was Oscar-nominated for her 1972 portrayal of jazz legend and tragic figure Billie Holiday. Gil Askey was also nominated for his adaptation score, filled with classic Holiday tunes, from the title song to "Lover Man" and "God Bless the Child." The arrangements (by Askey, Benny Golson, and Oliver Nelson) were first-rate, helping to send this album to the top of the *Billboard* pop charts, where it stayed for two weeks. Michel Legrand supplied the dramatic underscore.

THE LION KING
Walt Disney 60858-7

Disney's animated success of the summer of 1994—about a lion cub whose family tragedy causes him to leave home—sported a song score by

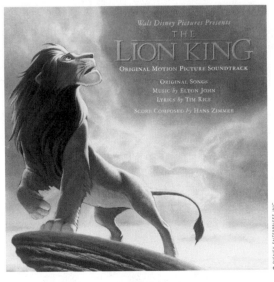

© DISNEY ENTERPRISES INC.

rocker Elton John and pop lyricist Tim Rice. It was a shrewd commercial move, generating Oscars and Grammys for the composers and producers. John's "Can You Feel the Love Tonight?" went to number 4 and won the Best Song Oscar, defeating the film's other nominated songs, the philosophical "Circle of Life" (also a top-20 hit) and the no-worries warble "Hakuna Matata." Hans Zimmer won an Oscar for his orchestral and choral underscore and a Grammy (along with his choral partners Andrae Crouch and Lebo M) for Best Instrumental Arrangement Accompanying Vocals. The CD was a huge success for Disney's records division, spending 10 weeks at number 1 and 88 weeks on the charts altogether.

THE LITTLE MERMAID
Walt Disney 60946-7

This was the movie that brought back Disney animation, and animated musicals, from the dead. Composer Alan Menken and lyricist-librettist Howard Ashman, with their musical-theater sensibilities (*Little Shop of Horrors*), turned the tide with their 1989 score, which won Best Original Score for Menken and Best Song for Menken and Ashman for the delightfully Caribbean "Under the Sea." "Kiss the Girl" was also nominated, and "Part of Your World" (the anthem of a mermaid who wants to be human) has joined the list of Disney standards. The album went triple platinum, and the duo won a 1990 Grammy for Best Movie Song.

LIVE AND LET DIE
EMI-Manhattan CDP 7 90629 2

With composer John Barry unavailable for Roger Moore's screen debut as 007, the producers of the 1973 James Bond film turned to ex-Beatle Paul McCartney for the title song—the first Bond theme to be nominated for an Oscar. Performed by McCartney with his band Wings, the song went to number 2 on the pop charts and drove the album into the top 20. Longtime colleague George Martin wrote a score based on McCartney's theme, his own material, and the traditional "James Bond Theme"—and won a Grammy for Best Arrangement Accompanying Vocalists. McCartney and Martin shared a nomination for Best Soundtrack.

LOVE ME OR LEAVE ME
Columbia/Legacy CK 47503

The very first movie soundtrack to reach number 1 on *Billboard*'s pop album chart came from a dramatic Doris Day musical. Day played popular '20s blues singer Ruth Etting, with James Cagney as the gangster husband who tries to possess her. Day wasn't Oscar-nominated, as many critics thought she should have been, but the Nicholas Brodszky–Sammy Cahn song "I'll Never Stop Loving You" (a top-20 hit) was, as was the musical direction of Percy Faith and George Stoll. At 17 weeks in *Billboard*'s number-1 position, it was by far the biggest album of 1955. The CD contains bonus tracks.

MAGNOLIA
Reprise 9 47583-2

Writer-director Paul Thomas Anderson made no secret of the fact that he wrote his ambitious three-hour drama (a 1999 Oscar nominee for Best Original Screenplay) while listening to the songs of cult folk-pop singer-songwriter Aimee Mann. Nine Mann songs, including her Oscar-nominated "Save Me" and a cover of Harry Nilsson's "One," dominate this widely acclaimed soundtrack. Score composer Jon Brion (Mann's producer) later got his own score album.

MARY POPPINS

Walt Disney 60615-7

It's impossible to overstate the importance of *Mary Poppins* to the Disney studio, or its value in the hearts of those lucky folk who were charmed by its magic in theaters in 1964. The film's 13 Oscar nominations included three in the music categories. Songwriting brothers Richard M. Sherman and Robert B. Sherman took home Music Score and Best Song honors (the latter, for "Chim Chim Cheree"); Irwin Kostal was nominated for his adaptation score. Among its other now-standard tunes are "A Spoonful of Sugar" and "Supercalifragilisticexpialidocious." The Sherman brothers also received a 1964 Grammy for the LP, which spent a remarkable 14 weeks at number 1 on the *Billboard* charts. The last track of the new CD version includes a 16-minute interview with the Shermans, along with demo versions of four of their tunes.

MIDNIGHT COWBOY

EMI-Manhattan CDP 7-48409-2

John Schlesinger's downbeat portrait of two New York City hustlers (Dustin Hoffman, Jon Voight) not only won the 1969 Best Picture Oscar; it was one of the earliest examples of a contemporary song score applied along with a more traditional score. John Barry won a Grammy for his lonely harmonica theme, but the film is equally famous for Harry Nilsson's rendition of Fred Neil's song "Everybody's Talkin'." Barry supervised the selection and recording of most of the tunes, which accurately reflected both the mood and the times. The Nilsson tune went to number 6, the album to number 19, on *Billboard*'s pop chart.

MORTAL KOMBAT

TVT 6110-2

This 1995 action flick knew its audience—kids who played the ultra-violent video game—and tailored its soundtrack accordingly: techno, metal, industrial, and rap from the likes of Gravity Kills, Traci Lords, and Orbital. The result was an album that made *Billboard*'s top 10 and spent nearly a year on the charts. George S. Clinton's score accounted for just three tracks, and his score was released separately somewhat later.

THE MUSIC MAN

Warner Bros. 1459-2

Robert Preston's reprise of his Broadway stage role as Professor Harold Hill was immortalized in the 1962 screen version of Meredith Willson's Broadway hit, about a visiting con man in a small Iowa town circa 1912. Several of the songs had already become standards, notably "Seventy-six Trombones" and "Til There Was You." Shirley Jones and Ron Howard were also in the cast. Ray Heindorf's musical direction won an Oscar, and the album was a big hit, with six weeks in the number-2 spot on *Billboard*'s album charts.

MY BEST FRIEND'S WEDDING

Sony 68166

The tremendously popular Julia Roberts romantic comedy about a woman who tries to sabotage a male pal's nuptials was a key factor in the late '90s resurgence of interest in '60s songs by Burt Bacharach and Hal David. Mary Chapin Carpenter sings "I'll Never Fall in Love Again," Ani DiFranco does "Wishin' and Hopin'," Diana King sings "I Say a Little Prayer," and there's an original of Jackie DeShannon's "What the World Needs Now Is Love." James Newton Howard's score rounds out the album.

MY FAIR LADY

Sony SK 66711

Eight Academy Awards, including Best Picture, went to this 1964 screen adaptation of the Lerner & Loewe musical based on Shaw's *Pygmalion*, with Rex Harrison, Audrey Hepburn (dubbed by Marni Nixon), and Stanley Holloway. The choice of Hepburn was controversial, as many observers felt the role should have gone to Broadway's own Eliza, Julie Andrews. André Previn won his fourth and final Oscar for his adaptation of such famous songs as "I Could Have Danced All Night," "Get Me to the Church on Time," "On the Street Where You Live," "I've Grown Accustomed to Her Face," "The Rain in Spain," "Wouldn't It Be Loverly," and others. The album was a smash, lasting 111 weeks on the *Billboard* charts and reaching number 4 in early 1965.

NASHVILLE

MCA 088 170 133-2

Robert Altman's 1975 satire on politics, country music, and the American people—a Best Picture nominee—remains one of the great films of the era, its Joan Tewkesbury script a brilliant tapestry of 24 different characters whose lives intertwine over a few days in Tennessee. Altman's great conceit, and one that worked surprisingly well, was to ask most of the key actors to write their own simple country songs. Purists were outraged, but Keith Carradine's "I'm Easy" not only cracked the top 20 but won the Best Song Oscar, and all the songs used were perfect reflections of their character: Henry Gibson's "200 Years," Karen Black's "Memphis," Ronee Blakley's "Tapedeck in His Tractor," music supervisor Richard Baskin's "One, I Love You" (sung by Blakley), and others. The album lasted three months on the charts and was finally released on CD in May 2000.

NATURAL BORN KILLERS

Nothing/Interscope INTD-92450

Oliver Stone's movie about America's obsession with outlaws was reviled by much of the mainstream press and continues to be cited in studies of screen violence and its effect on young people. One of the few elements that seemed to work in this 1994 film (from a Quentin Tarantino script) was the rock score produced by Trent Reznor of Nine Inch Nails. A kitchen-sink mixture of everything from Berg's *Wozzeck* to Duane Eddy, Leonard Cohen, and Patti Smith, with a few Nine Inch Nails tunes thrown in, it landed among the top 20 albums in late 1994 and went gold.

NEW JACK CITY

Giant 9 24409-2

Wesley Snipes and Ice T starred in this 1991 crime drama about cops versus drug lords in New York City. The setting inspired a best-selling soundtrack filled with the rap, urban-groove, and contemporary rhythm tracks that urban film audiences— clearly the target for Mario Van Peebles's film— would find hip. Ice T leads off the album, which

COURTESY OF MGM

also features Christopher Williams, Color Me Badd, and Queen Latifah and reached the number 2 position on *Billboard*'s album chart.

OKLAHOMA!
Angel ZDM 64691 2 6

In terms of sheer endurance and ongoing popularity, this remains the single most successful movie soundtrack of all time. The Capitol album of the 1955 film version of Rodgers & Hammerstein's first Broadway hit was on *Billboard*'s album chart for an astounding 305 weeks. (Among soundtracks, only four have exceeded 200 weeks on the chart, and they're all Rodgers & Hammerstein musicals.) It was a testimonial to the power of this score, as realized by Gordon MacRae, Shirley Jones, Gloria Grahame, and the rest of the cast under Fred Zinnemann's direction. Everyone knows tunes like "Oh, What a Beautiful Mornin'," "The Surrey With the Fringe on Top," "People Will Say We're in Love," and the title song. Orchestrator Robert Russell Bennett, musical director Jay Blackton, and underscore composer Adolph Deutsch all won 1955 Oscars for Best Scoring of a Musical Picture.

OLIVER!
RCA 4113-2-RG

The 1968 movie of Lionel Bart's long-running London/Broadway musical version of Charles Dickens's *Oliver Twist* won six Oscars including Best Picture and Best Score Adaptation for Johnny Green. The soundtrack spent 91 weeks on the charts, peaking at number 20; the 1990 CD reissue (with Mark Lester, Jack Wild, Shani Wallis, and Ron Moody in his Oscar-winning performance as Fagin) features "Consider Yourself," "As Long as He Needs Me," "Where Is Love?," and more.

ONE FROM THE HEART
Columbia CK 37703

Tom Waits's great, Oscar-nominated song score was the one salvagable element of Francis Ford Coppola's overproduced, phony–Las Vegas romantic comedy with Frederic Forrest, Teri Garr, Raul Julia, and Nastassia Kinski. It didn't make the charts in 1982, but Waits's evocative tunes ("Is There Any Way Out of This Dream?," "This One's From the Heart," "I Beg Your Pardon"), his raspy whisper, and Bob Alcivar's late-night-jazz arrangements have made this a perennial favorite. Crystal Gayle sings some of the tunes solo and duets on others.

PAT GARRETT & BILLY THE KID
Columbia CK 32460

Director Sam Peckinpah cast scruffy-looking singer-songwriter Bob Dylan in a bit part in his 1973 version of the friendship between the lawman (James Coburn) and the outlaw (Kris Kristofferson), then asked Dylan to contribute an authentic folk sound as its score. He composed a "Billy" theme with several verses used throughout the film, a number of instrumentals used in bits and pieces, and a second tune, "Knockin' on Heaven's Door," that has long outlived the film. Whether Dylan's folk-style, guitars-and-rhythm approach actually worked as dramatic music within the context of the film has long been debated, but the album proved popular. It reached number 16 on the *Billboard* chart; "Knockin' on Heaven's Door" made the top 20 and is now something of a standard.

PHILADELPHIA

Epic EK 57624

It took a lot to convince Bruce Springsteen to write and record a song specifically for a movie, but the performances of Tom Hanks and Denzel Washington in Jonathan Demme's film about an HIV-positive lawyer fighting for his dignity did it. Springsteen's melancholy "Streets of Philadelphia" and Neil Young's tender "Philadelphia," also original to the film, were both nominated for 1993 Academy Awards; Springsteen won. He also took home four 1994 Grammys (Song of the Year, rock song, rock vocal performance, and movie song). "Streets" jumped into the top 10, sending the album into the top 15. Other artists range from Peter Gabriel and Spin Doctors to Indigo Girls and opera star Maria Callas.

PINOCCHIO

Walt Disney 60845-7

Every child knows—or should know—"When You Wish Upon a Star," introduced by Jiminy Cricket (voiced by Cliff Edwards) in this 1940 animated classic about a wooden marionette who wants to be a real little boy. It became the first Disney tune to win a Best Song Oscar (music by Leigh Harline, lyrics by Ned Washington); the charming score, by Harline, Washington, and Paul J. Smith, also won the Original Score Academy Award. "Hi-Diddle-Dee-Dee (An Actor's Life for Me)" has also become a classic.

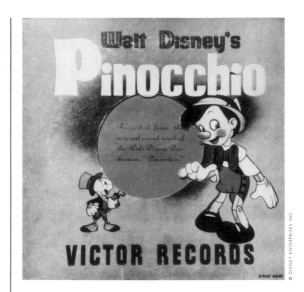

© DISNEY ENTERPRISES INC.

POCAHONTAS

Walt Disney 60874-7

Composer Alan Menken won his seventh and eighth Academy Awards for Best Song and Best Original Score for Disney's 1995 animated story of the love between free-spirited Algonquin Pocahontas and English soldier John Smith (voiced by Judy Kuhn and Mel Gibson, respectively). The song was the poignant Native American nature call "Colors of the Wind," with lyrics by Stephen Schwartz (who shared the Oscar and went on to share a Grammy with Menken for best movie song) and which scored in the top 10 with a cover record by Vanessa Williams. The album, following on the heels of Disney's top-selling *Lion King* disc, ascended to number 1 and went triple platinum.

PORGY AND BESS

Columbia 2016 (LP)

Members of the Gershwin family were so furious with this adaptation of the classic folk opera that they tried to bury it and have never permitted a video version. Otto Preminger directed Sidney Poitier, Dorothy Dandridge, Pearl Bailey, Brock

Peters, and Sammy Davis, Jr., in the moving story of life in a 1930s South Carolina ghetto. André Previn and Ken Darby won 1959 Oscars for their adaptation of the score, which includes such standards as "Summertime," "It Ain't Necessarily So," "I Got Plenty O' Nuthin'," "Bess, You Is My Woman Now," and "I Loves You, Porgy." The Columbia album made the top 10 of *Billboard*'s album charts, remained on the chart for nearly two years, and went gold.

PRETTY IN PINK
A&M CD 3293

Another of the Brat Pack movies to spawn a hit soundtrack, this 1986 film from writer-producer John Hughes (with Molly Ringwald, Jon Cryer, and Andrew McCarthy) had a big hit with "If You Leave" by Orchestral Manoeuvres in the Dark, and the title tune, which Psychedelic Furs released in 1981. The album went to number 5 and spent half a year on the charts.

PRETTY WOMAN
EMI America 93492

Roy Orbison died in 1988. His most famous song, "Oh, Pretty Woman," became the title of a modern Cinderella love story just two years later—you remember, the one with Richard Gere as a millionaire and Julia Roberts as the hooker he falls for. Orbison's 1964 classic was one of several hits on this song compilation that jumped into the top 5 in 1990 and went triple platinum. Roxette's "It Must Have Been Love" went to number 1, and Go West's "King of Wishful Thinking" to number 8.

PULP FICTION
MCA MCAD-11103

Quentin Tarantino's violent crime thriller (a 1994 Oscar winner for Best Original Screenplay) fea-

tured a batch of oldies, notably Dick Dale's "Misirlou," the Statler Brothers' "Flowers on the Wall," Al Green's "Let's Stay Together," Rick Nelson's "Lonesome Town," and Dusty Springfield's "Son of a Preacher Man." Urge Overkill enjoyed a minor hit covering "Girl, You'll Be a Woman Soon," and the album quickly went platinum. Dialogue from the film is also included.

PURPLE RAIN
Warner Bros. 25110-2

Prince—he was still known as that in 1984—was just 24 years old when this film was released, but already a star in the music biz, having recorded such albums as *Dirty Mind* and *1999*, replete with danceable rhythms and sexually explicit lyrics. This semi-autobiographical film (about a self-indulgent rock star from Minneapolis) secured the reclusive artist's fame and temporarily made him a movie star. The movie was successful, but not like the record: the soundtrack was the biggest album of the year, lasting a phenomenal six months at number 1 and generating a slew of top-10 hits including "When Doves Cry" and "Let's Go Crazy" (both number-1 singles),

plus the title tune and "I Would Die 4 U." He won Grammys for Best Rock Performance and Best Original Score, and a few weeks later received the Original Song Score Oscar as well. Prince went on to direct *Under the Cherry Moon* (1986) and *Graffiti Bridge* (1990), both of which were failures as films but generated top-10 albums. Not long thereafter he dispensed with the name Prince and became known by an unpronounceable symbol.

THE ROSE
Atlantic 82778-2

Bette Midler starred as a Janis Joplin–type singer in this critically acclaimed film and won a 1979 Oscar nomination and a double-platinum album for her efforts. Midler's performance of Amanda McBroom's song "The Rose" went to number 3, and her "Stay With Me" and "When a Man Loves a Woman" wowed both moviegoers and listeners. "The Rose" was nominated as Record of the Year and Song of the Year and won Midler a Grammy for Best Female Pop Vocal Performance.

RUNAWAY BRIDE
Columbia/Sony CK 69923

The popular Julia Roberts–Richard Gere romantic comedy sported a hit 1999 soundtrack that mixed up rock, pop, and country in equal measures. New songs by the Dixie Chicks, Eric Clapton ("Blue Eyes Blue," by Hollywood's best-known hit song-writer, Diane Warren), Martina McBride, Marc Anthony, Allure, and Shawn Colvin were featured on this platinum album.

ST. ELMO'S FIRE
Atlantic 7 81261-2

One of several mid-'80s Brat Pack movies, this 1985 installment of yuppies coping with the cold, cruel world had the usual suspects (Emilio Estevez,

Rob Lowe, Andrew McCarthy, Demi Moore, Judd Nelson, Ally Sheedy, Mare Winningham) and a hit soundtrack. John Parr's "St. Elmo's Fire (Man in Motion)" went to number 1, and, interestingly enough, the score by composer David Foster (better known as one of the top producers in the business) yielded a top-20 hit in his instrumental love theme.

SATURDAY NIGHT FEVER
Polydor 42282 5389 2

One of the three or four most influential and commercially successful soundtracks of all time, this 1977 two-LP set broke all kinds of records and made a ton of money for everyone involved. John Badham's movie about a Brooklyn disco-dancing king (John Travolta, the film's sole Oscar nominee) was both trend-setting and hugely popular with audiences. To date it has sold an estimated 27 million copies worldwide. Four of the Bee Gees' songs—"How Deep Is Your Love," "Stayin' Alive," and "Night Fever," which they performed, and "If I Can't Have You" sung by Yvonne Elliman—went to number 1 in late 1977 and early 1978. The album itself spent 24 weeks at number 1 and won four 1978 Grammys including Album of the Year. Score composer David Shire, whose own disco-flavored compositions were forgotten in all the hubbub over the Bee Gees' song score, also received a Grammy. The great mystery, and very public controversy, surrounded the Motion Picture Academy music branch's failure to nominate any of the songs, or the song score, for an Oscar. Producer Robert Stigwood's demand for a revote fell on deaf ears.

SGT. PEPPER'S LONELY HEARTS CLUB BAND
Polydor 31455 7076-2

Nobody much liked this movie, a misguided attempt to weave Beatles songs from the title record and "The White Album" into a plot starring Peter Frampton and the Bee Gees. But the two-record set managed to reach number 5 on the Billboard charts and went platinum anyway, generating three top-40 hits: Aerosmith's "Come Together," Robin Gibbs's "Oh Darling," and Earth, Wind & Fire's "Got to Get You Into My Life."

SHOW BOAT
Rhino R2 71998

Kathryn Grayson, Howard Keel, Ava Gardner (dubbed by Annette Warren), and Marge and Gower Champion led a mammoth MGM cast in the 1951 screen version of the 1927 Jerome Kern–Oscar Hammerstein II Broadway musical based on the acclaimed Edna Ferber novel. MGM released several songs in all three formats common in 1951: 78, LP, and EP. The 1995 CD includes all of the songs ("Make Believe," "You Are Love," "Ol' Man River," "Can't Help Lovin' Dat Man," "Bill," and more) and most of Oscar-nominated Conrad Salinger and Adolph Deutsch's underscore.

SINGIN' IN THE RAIN
Rhino R2 71963

Surprisingly, this 1952 satire of Hollywood and the birth of talking pictures didn't win a single Oscar, but it has grown in critical stature over the years and is now considered one of the movies' best musicals. It was designed by Betty Comden and Adolph Green as a vehicle for the Arthur Freed–Nacio Herb Brown song catalog. Gene Kelly, Debbie Reynolds, and Donald O'Connor performed such musical gems as "Make 'Em Laugh," "You Are My Lucky Star," and the title song. The entire score was restored and released in 1996.

SLEEPLESS IN SEATTLE
Epic EK 53764

The unlikeliest number-1 hit of the '90s was this collection of classic love songs that linked would-be lovers Tom Hanks and Meg Ryan in Nora Ephron's charming movie. Jimmy Durante's renditions of "As Time Goes By" and "Make Someone Happy" bookend the movie, with an attractive, timeless roster of other romantic tunes, including performances by Nat King Cole, Louis Armstrong, Carly Simon, Dr. John, and others. Music supervisor Marc Shaiman's own "A Wink and a Smile," written for the movie with Ramsey McLean and sung by Harry Connick, Jr., won a 1993 Oscar nomination; Celine Dion and Clive Griffin duet on "When I Fall in Love" (a Grammy winner for Jeremy Lubbock's arrangement). The album went triple-platinum.

SNOW WHITE AND THE SEVEN DWARFS
Walt Disney 60850-7

This 1937 classic, still one of the most beloved of all Disney films, was also responsible for the first American movie soundtrack album: RCA Victor issued, in 1938, five songs from the film on 78 rpm records. Disney's first full-length animated feature contains not one but three standards: "Whistle While You Work," "Heigh-Ho," and "Some Day My Prince Will Come," all the work of composer Frank Churchill and lyricist Larry Morey. Composers Leigh Harline and Paul J. Smith also contributed to the background score, which received a 1937 Oscar nomination.

THE SOUND OF MUSIC
RCA 07863 66587-2

An important Broadway show, for its politics as much for its score, Rodgers & Hammerstein's musicalization of the von Trapp family's escape from Nazi persecution in occupied Austria received a worthy 1965 screen adaptation starring Julie

Andrews and Christopher Plummer. The film won five Oscars including Best Picture and Best Scoring, the latter for Irwin Kostal's adaptation, arrangements, and conducting. The score contains such familiar songs as "Sixteen Going on Seventeen," "My Favorite Things," "Climb Ev'ry Mountain," "Do-Re-Mi," "Edelweiss," and the title song (to that famous opening panorama of Andrews twirling in the Alpine meadows). Two weeks at number 1, its 233 weeks total make it the fourth-longest-reigning soundtrack in the history of *Billboard*'s pop chart.

SOUTH PACIFIC
RCA 3681-2-R

Rodgers & Hammerstein's long-running Broadway musical, based on a James Michener book about military life on a small South Seas island during World War II, became a 1958 movie starring Mitzi Gaynor and Rossano Brazzi (the latter, dubbed by Giorgio Tozzi). The album joined the best-selling movie soundtracks of all time, spending most of the year (31 weeks) at number 1 on *Billboard*'s album charts—262 weeks (more than five years!)

on the charts in total. Alfred Newman and Ken Darby were Oscar-nominated for their musical direction and vocal arrangements, but critics were generally downbeat in their appraisal of the movie. The songs, however, are beyond reproach. Among them: "Some Enchanted Evening," "I'm Gonna Wash That Man Right Outa My Hair," "There Is Nothin' Like a Dame," and "Bali Ha'i."

SOUTH PARK: BIGGER, LONGER & UNCUT
Atlantic 83199-2

Matt Stone and Trey Parker's outrageous animated cartoon proved to be even raunchier and funnier on the big screen, a sendup of movie ratings and of movie musicals in general that was a massive hit in 1999. Parker wrote most of the songs, some in collaboration with score composer Marc Shaiman, including the incredibly rude "Uncle Fucka" and the Oscar-nominated "Blame Canada." Better-known performers on the album include Michael McDonald, Isaac Hayes, and RuPaul.

SPACE JAM
Warner Sunset/Atlantic 82961-2

One of the most successful movie soundtracks of the '90s, this collection of rock tunes from (and "inspired by") the Michael Jordan–meets–Bugs Bunny live action–animated movie–cum–soundtrack deal was a triumph of corporate synergy, promotion, and marketing. Four of the tunes jumped into the top 40—R. Kelly's "I Believe I Can Fly" (number 2), Monica's "For You I Will" (number 4), Seal's remake of "Fly Like an Eagle" (number 10), and Quad City DJ's "Space Jam" (number 37)—making the album the nation's biggest seller in the first half of 1997. Other artists included All-4-One, Spin Doctors, and Salt-N-Pepa. R. Kelly was a big winner at the 1997 Grammys, winning Best R&B Song, Best R&B Vocal Performance and Best movie song. Score composer James Newton Howard is represented only by the Bugs Bunny rap "Buggin'."

STAND BY ME
Atlantic 81677

Stephen King's novella "The Body" became the film *Stand by Me* after Ben E. King's 1961 hit was licensed for Rob Reiner's 1986 movie about four boys growing up in the '50s. Its use as a main theme in the popular drama catapulted King's tune back into the top 10 and the album onto the charts for nearly a year, reaching gold status. King even made a video with film stars River Phoenix and Wil Wheaton. More than half a dozen other top-10 hits of the past, including the Coasters' "Yakety Yak," the Silhouettes' "Get a Job," and the Chordettes' "Lollipop," are included.

A STAR IS BORN
Columbia CK 44389

Barbra Streisand and Kris Kristofferson starred in the 1976 rock 'n' roll update of the venerable show-biz love story of a man on his way down and a woman on her way up. It was a colossal hit with audiences—the year's second-highest-grossing movie—and an equal hit with record-buyers, the soundtrack spending six weeks at number 1 and going platinum. Most of the album was a live stadium recording (with Kristofferson on five of the 12 tracks). The potpourri of songs included such writers as Paul Williams, Kenny Ascher, Kenny Loggins, Rupert Holmes, and Leon Russell, but it was the Streisand-Williams love song "Evergreen" that listeners most remember. It won the 1976 Best Song Oscar and three 1977 Grammys including Song of the Year and Best Pop Female Vocal Performance.

STAYING ALIVE
RSO 813269 (LP)

Platinum, but nowhere near the success of its predecessor, this 1983 sequel to *Saturday Night Fever* contained five new Bee Gees songs but generated just one top-10 hit, and that for Frank Stallone (songwriter brother of Sylvester Stallone, who co-wrote and directed): "Far From Over," one of four songs he contributed to the soundtrack. Johnny Mandel produced three of the tunes and wrote the underscore (not on the record) in one of his last big-screen assignments.

SUPERFLY
Rhino R2 72836

Singer-songwriter and former Impressions leader Curtis Mayfield's most famous work was for this 1972 blaxploitation film that starred Ron O'Neal as a Harlem cocaine dealer out to make one last big score. Mayfield's album consisted mostly of songs that were written for, but were not in, the final version of the film; even "Freddie's Dead," its best known and most successful song (number 4 on the pop charts), appears only as an instrumental, notably during the opening credits and as O'Neal's funky driving music. The antidote theme of "Freddie's Dead" struck a chord with radio listeners and record buyers, and the song was a Grammy nominee for Best Rhythm & Blues Song and Best R&B Male Performance. The end-title song, "Superfly," was the second single issued and went to number 8. The LP itself—another Grammy nominee, as Best Soundtrack—lasted four weeks at number 1 and sold nearly two million copies. Critics cried racism, however, when "Superfly" (unlike Isaac Hayes's "Shaft" the year before) failed to receive an Oscar nomination as Best Song. The two-CD set issued in 1997 adds several sequences that were in the film but not on the original single LP on Curtom.

TARZAN

Walt Disney 60645-7

Phil Collins, whose movie career has included hits ("Against All Odds") and misses ("Buster"), came up a winner with Disney's 1999 animated version of the Edgar Rice Burroughs jungle-man character. He wrote five new songs and had a huge adult-contemporary hit with the love theme, "You'll Be in My Heart," which won a Best Song Oscar. Vocals by Glenn Close and Rosie O'Donnell are featured; Mark Mancina's percussion-dominated score makes up the other half of the album.

THANK GOD IT'S FRIDAY

Casablanca/Mercury 534 606

Record companies Motown and Casablanca pooled their fortunes to cash in on the disco-movie craze in the wake of *Saturday Night Fever*, and while critics unanimously hated this 1978 one-night-in-a-disco travesty, the album shot to number 10 and went platinum. It also generated a number-3 single for Casablanca artist and disco queen Donna Summer—who made her film debut as Nicole and sang "Last Dance." Actor-songwriter Paul Jabara, who penned that tune, later collected a Best Song Oscar and the Grammy for Best R&B song, while Summer picked up the Grammy for Best R&B female vocal performance.

THERE'S NO BUSINESS LIKE SHOW BUSINESS

Varèse Sarabande VSD-5912

The final Irving Berlin film musical was 20th Century–Fox's 1954 all-star cavalcade starring Ethel Merman, Donald O'Connor, Marilyn Monroe, Dan Dailey, Johnnie Ray, and Mitzi Gaynor. The songs include some of Berlin's best known: "A Pretty Girl Is Like a Melody," "Alexander's Ragtime Band," "Play a Simple Melody," "Heat Wave," and the classic title tune. Brothers Alfred and Lionel Newman shared an Oscar nomination for musical direction; the Decca LP jumped into the *Billboard* top 10 in early 1955.

THOROUGHLY MODERN MILLIE

MCA 10662

Julie Andrews, Mary Tyler Moore, and Carol Channing starred in this 1968 Universal spoof of the nonconformist Roaring '20s. Andrews (in the title role) was at her vocal peak singing mostly jazz-age pop tunes (and four original songs, including the title tune by James Van Heusen and Sammy Cahn). Elmer Bernstein won an Oscar for his score, although none of it appears on the album; André Previn handled musical direction on the songs.

TO SIR, WITH LOVE

Sindrome Retroactive SD 8935

Looking back, it's hard to believe: The title song for James Clavell's poignant movie—about a teacher (Sidney Poitier) who wins over an unruly class of London high-schoolers—failed to be nominated for a 1967 Best Song Oscar. Lulu, who played one of the students, sang the Marc London–Don Black song to a number-1 berth on the *Billboard* charts for five weeks in October-November 1967. Other tunes by Lulu and by the Mindbenders fill out the album, along with Ron Grainer's score; it made the top 20 and was nominated for a Grammy.

TOMMY

Polydor 841 121-2

Ken Russell's 1975 film of The Who's influential 1969 rock opera featured an all-star cast: Roger Daltrey as the "deaf, dumb and blind boy" who becomes a pinball champion; Ann-Margret as his mother; Jack Nicholson as a doctor; Elton John as the pinball wizard and Tina Turner as the acid queen. Russell's flashy visual interpretations of such rock classics as "See Me, Feel Me," "Pinball Wizard," "Listening to You," and "Acid Queen" met with critical brickbats but sold enough records to drive the soundtrack to number 2 and earn Pete Townshend an Oscar nomination for the adaptation.

TOP GUN

Columbia CK 40323

One of the most popular and commercially successful of the song-driven soundtracks of the '80s, this collection from the action-packed Tom Cruise movie about naval aviators landed atop the *Billboard* charts for five weeks in the summer of 1986, sporting a number-1 hit in Berlin's "Take My Breath Away" (for which composer Giorgio Moroder and lyricist Tom Whitlock won the Best Song Oscar) and a number-2 hit in Kenny Loggins's "Danger Zone" (by the same duo). Loverboy's "Heaven in Your Eyes" also made the top 20.

TROUBLE MAN

Motown 314530884-2

In the wake of Isaac Hayes's *Shaft* and soul sensation Marvin Gaye's gold record for "What's Going On," Gaye was recruited to provide the score for this 1972 blaxploitation film starring Robert Hooks as a private eye in the midst of a gang war. Despite Gaye's photo on the album cover, he contributes only brief vocals to this pleasant collection of instrumentals (mostly arranged by film veterans Leo Shuken, Jack Hayes, Bob Ragland, and J. J. Johnson) but plays piano and Moog synthesizer on several tracks. The album made *Billboard*'s top 20.

TWISTER

Warner Sunset 46254

This album for the 1996 tornado movie was a perfect example of the growing importance of music supervisors to the movie and record business. Joel Sill and Budd Carr commissioned new songs, and licensed old ones, for use in the film and on an album. The unusual aspect of the *Twister* album is that all of the songs are actually in the movie (some, just for a few seconds, and most playing on the radios of the various vehicles chasing the twisters). The styles range from rock (Van Halen, Soul Asylum) to country (Shania Twain, Rusted Root) and everything in between (Lisa Loeb, Tori Amos). Eddie and Alex Van Halen's original rock-guitar ballad "Respect the Wind" served as the film's end title. The album spent four months on the charts and climbed into the top 30.

200 MOTELS
Rykodisc RCD 10513/14

Nobody saw the 1971 movie, a surreal semi-documentary about a rock band's travels, but the soundtrack became famous because it was, after all, a Frank Zappa production featuring the Mothers of Invention. The "soundtrack," a bizarre collection of orchestral pieces featuring London's Royal Philharmonic Orchestra, rock songs, and other Zappa business, made *Billboard*'s album chart but then became a sought-after collector's item. More than 20 years later, Rykodisc made a huge deal for the entire United Artists soundtrack catalog specifically to acquire the Zappa album, which has now been expanded into a two-CD set with a massive illustrated booklet.

2001: A SPACE ODYSSEY
Rhino R2 72562

Stanley Kubrick's temporary music track for his landmark 1968 science-fiction epic wound up in the final picture, even though he had commissioned Alex North to write an original score. Today, the main-title music is far better known as the "Theme from *2001*" than as the opening of Richard Strauss's 1896 tone poem *Also Sprach Zarathustra*, and Gyorgi Ligeti enjoys far more fame than he ever might have if Kubrick had not used his *Requiem* as the recurring theme for the monolith, his *Lux Aeterna* for the moonbus sequence, and *Atmospheres* for Keir Dullea's mind-bending ride through the Stargate. Kubrick's use of Johann Strauss's already-familiar *Blue Danube* waltz remains controversial; Khachaturian's *Gayane* Ballet Suite excerpt, used onboard the Jupiter-bound Discovery ship, served to introduce millions to the Soviet composer. The original *2001* soundtrack (which contained a different *Zarathustra* than that heard in the film) was on *Billboard*'s charts for 120 weeks, reached number 24 at one point, and spawned a second volume—arguably the first of many "inspired by" (euphemism for "most of this music isn't in the movie") soundtrack albums. North's unused music was finally recorded by Jerry Goldsmith and the National Philharmonic Orchestra in 1993.

URBAN COWBOY
Full Moon/Elektra 60690-2

John Travolta as a good ole boy and Debra Winger as a mechanical bull–riding country gal made this 1980 modern-Texas romantic drama a hit. A two-LP set of country tunes—music mostly played at Gilley's, the honky-tonk where much of the action occurs—contained a batch of top country artists including the Charlie Daniels Band ("The Devil Went Down to Georgia"), Bonnie Raitt, Anne Murray, Kenny Rogers, and others. The album reached number 3 on the *Billboard* charts and went platinum, winning a Grammy for Mickey Gilley's performance of "Orange Blossom Special" and receiving a nomination as the year's top soundtrack.

VALLEY OF THE DOLLS
Philips 314 536 876-2

The one saving grace of this 1967 adaptation of the Jacqueline Susann novel about three aspiring actresses (Barbara Parkins, Patty Duke, Sharon Tate) was the song score by André and Dory Previn, arranged and conducted by Johnny (later John) Williams. The Previns' title song—a top-10 hit for Dionne Warwick, not on this album—and tunes like "Come Live With Me" and "Give a Little More" have that indelible '60s sound; the score earned Williams his very first Oscar nomination.

VICTOR / VICTORIA

GNP Crescendo GNPD 8038

Henry Mancini's fourth and final Oscar—shared with lyricist Leslie Bricusse—was for Blake Edwards's last big hit, this 1982 musical that starred his wife Julie Andrews, James Garner, Robert Preston, and Lesley Ann Warren. Mancini's songs, including "Crazy World," "Le Jazz Hot," and "Gay Paree," are among his best late work, and many of them resurfaced in the Broadway version that Edwards mounted with Andrews just after Mancini's death.

WAITING TO EXHALE

Arista 187962

Whitney Houston starred in this 1995 adaptation of the Terry McMillan novel about black women and their troubles with men, but what most people remember about the film is its music: 15 songs written and produced by Kenneth "Babyface" Edmonds, sung by Houston, Brandy, Toni Braxton, Mary J. Blige, and others. Houston's "Exhale (Shoop Shoop)" went to number 1 and the album remained on the pop charts for nearly all of 1996. The soundtrack was an Album of the Year nominee, "Exhale" a Song of the Year nominee and winner of the Best R&B Song Grammy (the album and its performers accounted for another eight nominations, including three of the five nominated movie songs). Once again the Motion Picture Academy generated controversy when neither "Exhale" nor any of the film's other tunes received a Best Song

nomination at the Oscars. The album now ranks as one of the 10 best-selling soundtracks of all time.

WAYNE'S WORLD

Reprise W2 26805

Mike Myers and Dana Carvey took a goofy *Saturday Night Live* sketch and turned it into a big-screen box-office hit in 1992, complete with an offbeat soundtrack that was the best-selling album in the country for two weeks that year. Even more surprising, Wayne and Garth's sing-along to Queen's old "Bohemian Rhapsody" propelled that classic back into the top 10 nearly two decades after its first appearance on the chart. The rest of the album is a wild mix of hard rockers, such as Alice Cooper and Black Sabbath, rockabilly by Eric Clapton, quieter pieces like Gary Wright's "Dream Weaver," and, of course, an extended version of the idiotic "Wayne's World" theme for the boys' cable-access show.

WEST SIDE STORY

Sony SK 48211

With a spectacular 54 weeks in the number-1 position on the *Billboard* album charts, the soundtrack for the movie version of the Leonard Bernstein–Stephen Sondheim Broadway smash is considered the best-selling album of its time. The film won 10 1961 Academy Awards including Best Picture and Best Scoring of a Musical Picture (for orchestrators Sid Ramin and Irwin Kostal, conductor Johnny Green, and associate producer Saul Chaplin). The songs are legendary in musical theater and standards that are well known everywhere: "Somewhere," "Tonight," "Maria," "America," "I Feel Pretty," "Something's Coming," and more. Natalie Wood, Richard Beymer, George Chakiris, and Rita Moreno starred; Robert Wise and choreographer Jerome Robbins directed Ernest Lehman's script of

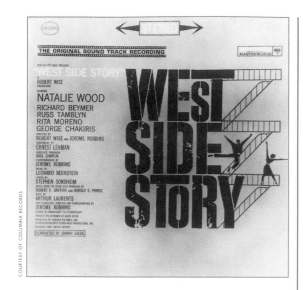

the Romeo-and-Juliet tale set among the gangs of contemporary New York.

WHEN HARRY MET SALLY . . .

Columbia CK 45319

Rob Reiner's winning 1989 romantic comedy, with its Oscar-nominated Nora Ephron script and memorable Billy Crystal and Meg Ryan performances, didn't have a traditional score. Rather, Marc Shaiman supervised a collection of songs, including performances by Harry Connick, Jr., that make up this album, a top-50 hit and long-running (two years) installment on the *Billboard* charts.

WHITE NIGHTS

Atlantic 81273-2

"Separate Lives," which Phil Collins and Marilyn Martin sang to the number-1 spot on the pop charts in November 1985—and which propelled this soundtrack to gold-record status—was Oscar-nominated for its use in the Taylor Hackford film *White Nights.* Only later did Academy voters learn that Stephen Bishop had actually written the song three years earlier. Tracks by Lou Reed, Chaka

Khan, Roberta Flack, and others are featured on the record, which is equally notable for the one *White Nights* song that is missing: "Say You, Say Me," which won the Oscar for singer-songwriter Lionel Richie (and which hit number 1 in December and remained there for four weeks). The film starred Gregory Hines and Mikhail Baryshnikov as defecting dancers (Hines from the U.S. to the Soviet Union, Baryshnikov vice versa).

WHO'S THAT GIRL?

Sire 9 25611-2

Danceable and hummable, Madonna's title song for the forgettable 1987 would-be screwball comedy became a number-1 single on the pop charts. Madonna (who starred in the movie with Griffin Dunne) wrote four tunes for the picture, which had been called *Slammer* until "Who's That Girl?" came in. She and co-writer Patrick Leonard were Grammy-nominated for writing the tune; another one, "Causing a Commotion," went to number 2 three months after "Who's That Girl?" The album (which also included tunes by Kid Creole & the Coconuts, Scritti Politti, and Club Nouveau) shot to a number-7 position on the album charts.

WILD WILD WEST

Overbrook/Interscope INTD-90344

Trashed by almost every critic in the country, the Will Smith–Kevin Kline high-tech western nonetheless generated a number-1 single for Smith and a multi-platinum 1999 album of rock and rap tunes that had little to do with the movie. Joining Smith's "Wild Wild West"—co-written by Stevie Wonder and featuring Smith, Dru Hill, and Kool Mo Dee—was Enrique Iglesias's flavorful "Bailamos" and tracks by Tatyana Ali, MC Lyte, Dr. Dre & Eminem, and others.

THE WIZARD OF OZ
Rhino R2 71964

The most beloved of all family film musicals—maybe of all family films—received one of the first commercial album releases in 1939 (albeit a re-recording with Judy Garland and Ken Darby's singers). When the movie first appeared on TV in 1956, an LP (a true "original soundtrack") was released, but it took until 1995 for a deluxe package that included the entire, fully restored score. The memorable songs by Harold Arlen and E. Y. Harburg include "If I Only Had a Brain," "We're Off to See the Wizard," and the Oscar-winning "Over the Rainbow"; veteran MGM composer Herbert Stothart won an Oscar for his underscore. Also included: rare recordings and a 52-page chronicle by *Oz* expert John Fricke.

THE WOMAN IN RED
Motown 3746361082

Gene Wilder's movie is practically forgotten today (and whatever happened to model/actress Kelly LeBrock?) but his genius was in signing legendary recording artist Stevie Wonder to contribute songs. One of those tunes, "I Just Called to Say I Love You," shot to number 1 in just eight weeks and won the 1984 Best Song Oscar (opposite four other number-1 hits). The album, which featured Wonder and, in duets, Dionne Warwick, received four Grammy nominations including a Song of the Year nod for "I Just Called to Say I Love You."

WORKING GIRL
Arista ARCD-8593

Singer-songwriter Carly Simon won the 1988 Best Song Oscar for "Let the River Run," her anthem from the Mike Nichols film (itself a Best Picture nominee) starring Melanie Griffith as an ambitious secretary, Harrison Ford as her paramour, and Sigourney Weaver as her difficult boss. Simon, whose arranger Rob Mounsey created the score around the tune, has written other film music for Nichols, notably *Heartburn* (1986) and *Postcards From the Edge* (1990).

XANADU
MCA MCAD-11857

The soundtrack to this 1980 music-and-dance extravaganza was half Olivia Newton-John (star of this misbegotten enterprise) and half Electric Light Orchestra. The record generated no fewer than five top-20 singles: Newton-John's "Magic" (four weeks at number 1) and "Xanadu," with Newton-John backed by ELO, went to number 8. Also charting: her duet with Cliff Richard, "Suddenly," and two ELO singles, "I'm Alive" and "All Over the World." The album reached number 4.

YENTL
Columbia CK 39152

Certainly among Barbra Streisand's finest work—star, director, producer, and co-writer—this 1983 screen musical won Original Song Score Oscars for composer Michel Legrand and lyricists Alan and Marilyn Bergman (while the Academy's failure to acknowledge Streisand as star or director caused an uproar, including charges of sexism). Legrand's score, with its roots in ancient Hebraic music and its subtle use of choir and ethnic instruments, was a masterwork. Two of the songs were Oscar-nominated: "Papa, Can You Hear Me?" and "The Way He Makes Me Feel." The album went to number 9 in '84.

YOU LIGHT UP MY LIFE
Arista 4159 (LP)

Songwriter Joe Brooks won the 1977 Oscar for the sentimental title song of his musical drama (which he also wrote, directed, produced, and scored) with the sympathetic and credible Didi Conn as a singer trying to make it in a ruthless business. The album went gold, but Kacey Cisyk's original film version barely cracked the top 100 while 21-year-old Debby Boone's cover spent 10 weeks at number 1—the longest-running number-1 single in more than 20 years. Boone won the 1977 Grammy as Best New Artist and Brooks's album was nominated for the soundtrack Grammy.

ZABRISKIE POINT
Rhino R2 72462

For his failed hippie-culture movie of 1970, acclaimed director Michelangelo Antonioni called on a diverse group of rock artists in an apparently vain attempt to compile an accurate musical portrait of American youth in revolt. Tracks by Pink Floyd (notably "Heart Beat, Pig Meat," and "Come In Number 51, Your Time Is Up"), The Grateful Dead ("Dark Star") and its guitarist Jerry Garcia (who created extensive solo guitar improvisations for the film's infamous sex scene), folk-rock group Kaleidoscope, and others were featured. The expanded two-CD set of this score, issued in 1997, contains much previously unreleased Pink Floyd and Garcia material.

Collections

THAT'S ENTERTAINMENT: THE ULTIMATE ANTHOLOGY OF MGM MUSICALS
Rhino R2 72182

The ultimate sampler of numbers from the studio that specialized in the movie musical, this lavish six-CD box of 128 musical numbers runs from "Aba Daba Honeymoon" to "Zing! Went the Strings of My Heart," from 1929's *Broadway Melody* to 1958's *Gigi*. Released in 1995, it repre-

sents the first original-soundtrack releases of many of these numbers by Judy Garland, Fred Astaire, Gene Kelly, Donald O'Connor, Lena Horne, Frank Sinatra, Kathryn Grayson, Bing Crosby, Jane Powell, Howard Keel, Debbie Reynolds, Ann Miller, and many others. Included is a 100-page history of MGM musicals, filled with original production photos and vintage color artwork.

MICKEY & JUDY: THE JUDY GARLAND & MICKEY ROONEY COLLECTION
Rhino R2 71921

Rooney, Garland, and others in MGM's talent pool made a very popular series of let's-put-on-a-show musicals just before and during the war years. This four-CD collection, released in 1995, marked their initial release as original soundtrack recordings: *Babes in Arms* (1939, with a Rodgers & Hart score featuring "Where or When"); *Strike Up the Band* (1940, joined by Paul Whiteman and his Orchestra, featuring Roger Edens and Arthur Freed's "Our Love Affair"); *Babes on Broadway* (1941, with Burton Lane and Ralph Freed's charming "How About You?"); and *Girl Crazy* (1943, with a George and Ira Gershwin score, including Tommy Dorsey and His Orchestra doing a symphonic jazz rendition of "Fascinating Rhythm").

WARNER BROS.: 75 YEARS OF FILM MUSIC
Rhino R2 75287

This four-CD box, issued in 1998 to commemorate Warner's 75 years in the movie business, includes one disc of score excerpts and three of classic Warner movie songs over the years. The scores include classic bits of Korngold, Steiner, North, Waxman, Rosenman, and others, plus more contemporary film music by the likes of Schifrin, Elfman, Williams, and Vangelis. Songs date back to Al Jolson's classic "My Mammy" from

The Jazz Singer (1927) and Dooley Wilson's complete "As Time Goes By" from *Casablanca* (1942) to Barbra Streisand's "Evergreen" from *A Star Is Born* (1976) and Sting's "It's Probably Me" from *Lethal Weapon 3* (1992). An 80-page book chronicles the history of music at the studio.

LULLABY OF BROADWAY: THE BEST OF BUSBY BERKELEY AT WARNER BROS.
Rhino R2 72169

The classic movie songs of Harry Warren and Al Dubin (among others) from the Busby Berkeley– choreographed Warner films of the '30s are celebrated in this two-CD set. The films include *42nd Street*, *Gold Diggers of 1933*, and *Footlight Parade* (all 1933); *Wonder Bar*, *Fashions of 1934*, and *Dames* (all 1934); *Gold Diggers of 1935* and *In Caliente* (both 1935); *Gold Diggers of 1937* and *Hollywood Hotel* (both 1937). The tunes are among the greatest ever written for American movies, including "We're in the Money," "I Only Have Eyes for You," and "Lullaby of Broadway." A 44-page booklet contains dozens of photos of Berkeley's classic dance routines.

Agel, Jerome, editor. *The Making of Kubrick's 2001*. New York: New American Library, 1970.

Alvarez, Max Joseph. *Index to Motion Pictures Reviewed by Variety*, 1907–1980. Metuchen, N.J.: The Scarecrow Press, 1982.

Balio, Tino. *United Artists: The Company That Changed the Film Industry*. Madison, Wis.: The University of Wisconsin Press, 1987.

Barrios, Richard. *A Song in the Dark: The Birth of the Musical Film*. New York: Oxford University Press, 1995.

Bazelon, Irwin. *Knowing the Score: Notes on Film Music*. New York: Van Nostrand Reinhold, 1975.

Behlmer, Rudy. *Behind the Scenes: The Making of . . .* Hollywood, Calif.: Samuel French, 1990.

Behlmer, Rudy. *Inside Warner Bros. (1935–1951)*. New York: Simon & Schuster, 1987.

Behlmer, Rudy, editor. *Memo From David O. Selznick*. New York: The Viking Press, 1972.

Bergan, Ronald. *The United Artists Story*. New York: Crown Publishers, 1986.

Bond, Jeff. *The Music of Star Trek: Profiles in Style*. Los Angeles: Lone Eagle Publishing, 1999.

Bronson, Fred. *The Billboard Book of Number One Hits*. New York: Billboard Publications, 1988.

Brooks, Elston. *I've Heard Those Songs Before: The Weekly Top Ten Hits of the Past Six Decades*. Fort Worth, Texas: The Summit Group, 1991.

Brown, Royal S. *Overtones and Undertones: Reading Film Music*. Berkeley, Calif.: University of California Press, 1994.

Carroll, Brendan G. *The Last Prodigy: A Biography of Erich Wolfgang Korngold*. Portland, Ore.: Amadeus Press, 1997.

Dearling, Robert and Celia, with Brian Rust. *The Guinness Book of Recorded Sound*. Middlesex, England: Guinness Books, 1984.

DeBoer, Henk J., with Martin van Wouw. *The Ennio Morricone Musicography*. Amsterdam: MSV, 1990.

Deutsch, Didier C., editor. *VideoHound's Soundtracks: Music From the Movies, Broadway and Television*. Detroit: Visible Ink Press, 1998.

Eames, John Douglas. *The MGM Story*. New York: Crown Publishers, 1977.

Eames, John Douglas. *The Paramount Story*. New York: Crown Publishers, 1985.

Erlewine, Michael, Vladimir Bogdanov, Chris Woodstra, Stephen Thomas Erlewine, editors. *All Music Guide*, third edition. San Francisco: Miller Freeman Books, 1997.

Evans, Mark. *Soundtrack: The Music of the Movies*. New York: Hopkinson and Blake, Publishers, 1975.

Fiegel, Eddi. *John Barry: A Sixties Theme*. London: Constable and Company, 1998.

Fordin, Hugh. *The World of Entertainment: Hollywood's Greatest Musicals*. Garden City, N.Y.: Doubleday and Company, 1975.

Francillon, Vincent J., editor. *Film Composers Guide*, fourth edition. Los Angeles: Lone Eagle Press, 1997.

The Grammy Winners Book. Santa Monica, Calif.: National Academy of Recording Arts & Sciences, 1995.

Hardy, Phil, and Dave Laing. *The Faber Companion to 20th-Century Popular Music*. London: Faber and Faber, 1990.

Harris, Steve. *Film and Television Composers: An International Discography, 1920–1989*. Jefferson, N.C.: McFarland & Company, 1992.

Harris, Steve. *Film, Television and Stage Music on Phonograph Records: A Discography*. Jefferson, N.C.: McFarland & Company, 1988.

Hirschhorn, Clive. *The Columbia Story*. New York: Crown Publishers, 1989.

Hirschhorn, Clive. *The Universal Story*. New York: Crown Publishers, 1983.

Hirschhorn, Clive. *The Warner Bros. Story*. New York: Crown Publishers, 1979.

Kaplan, Mike, editor. *Variety's Directory of Major U.S. Show Business Awards*. New York: R.R. Bowker, 1989.

Karlin, Fred. *Listening to Movies: The Film Lover's Guide to Film Music*. New York: Schirmer Books, 1994.

Katz, Ephraim. *The Film Encyclopedia*, second edition. New York: HarperCollins Publishers, 1994.

Kramer, Stanley, with Thomas M. Coffey. *A Mad, Mad, Mad, Mad World: A Life in Hollywood*. New York: Harcourt Brace & Company, 1997.

Larson, Randall D. *Music From the House of Hammer: Music in the Hammer Horror Films, 1950–1980*. Lanham, Md.: Scarecrow Press, 1996.

Limbacher, James L., editor. *Film Music: From Violins to Video*. Metuchen, N.J.: The Scarecrow Press, 1974.

MacDonald, Laurence E. *The Invisible Art of Film Music: A Comprehensive History*. New York: Ardsley House, Publishers, 1998.

Maltin, Leonard, editor. *Leonard Maltin's Movie & Video Guide*, 1999 edition. New York: Penguin Putman, 1998.

Maltin, Leonard. *The Disney Films*. New York: Bonanza Books, 1973.

Marmorstein, Gary. *Hollywood Rhapsody: Movie Music and Its Makers, 1900 to 1975*. New York: Schirmer Books, 1997.

Mancini, Henry, with Gene Lees. *Did They Mention the Music?* Chicago: Contemporary Books, 1989.

Mattfeld, Julius. *Variety Music Cavalcade 1620–1961*. Englewood Cliffs, N.J.: Prentice-Hall, 1962.

McAleer, Dave. *The All Music Book of Hit Albums*. San Francisco: Miller Freeman Books, 1995.

McCarty, Clifford. *Film Composers in America: A Filmography, 1910–1970*. New York: Oxford University Press, 2000.

McGilligan, Patrick. *Jack's Life: A Biography of Jack Nicholson*. New York: W.W. Norton & Company, 1994.

McNally, Keith and Dorie. *McNally's Price Guide for Collectible Soundtrack Records, 1950–1990*. Newhall, Calif.: West Point Records, 1994.

The Movie Guide. New York: Berkley Publishing Group, 1998.

Murray, R. Michael. *The Golden Age of Walt Disney Records, 1933–1988*. Dubuque, Iowa: Antique Trader Books, 1997.

Nash, Jay Robert, and Stanley Ralph Ross. *The Motion Picture Guide, 1927–1983*. Chicago: Cinebooks, 1985.

O'Neil, Thomas. *The Grammys*. New York: Berkley Publishing Group, 1999.

Osborne, Jerry. *The Official Price Guide to Movie/TV Soundtracks & Original Cast Albums*, second edition. New York: House of Collectibles, 1997.

Palmer, Christopher. *The Composer in Hollywood*. London: Marion Boyars Publishers, 1990.

Previn, André. *No Minor Chords: My Days in Hollywood*. New York: Doubleday, 1991.

Rózsa, Miklós. *Double Life*. New York: Wynwood Press, 1989.

Sackett, Susan. *Hollywood Sings! An Inside Look at Sixty Years of Academy Award–Nominated Songs*. New York: Billboard Books, 1995.

Sadie, Stanley, editor. *The Norton/Grove Concise Encyclopedia of Music*. New York: W.W. Norton & Company, 1988.

Sanjek, Russell, and David Sanjek. *American Popular Music Business in the 20th Century*. New York: Oxford University Press, 1991.

Shale, Richard. *Academy Awards*, second edition. New York: Frederick Ungar Publishing Company, 1982.

Shapiro, Nat, and Bruce Pollock, editors. *Popular Music, 1920–1979*. Detroit: Gale Research Company, 1985.

Smith, Jeff. *The Sounds of Commerce: Marketing Popular Film Music*. New York: Columbia University Press, 1998.

Smith, Robert L. *U.S. Soundtracks on Compact Disc: The First Ten Years (1985-1994)*. Vineyard Haven, Mass.: Film Score Monthly, 1995.

Smith, Steven C. *A Heart at Fire's Center: The Life and Music of Bernard Herrmann*. Los Angeles: University of California Press, 1991.

Thomas, Tony. *Film Score: The Art & Craft of Film Music*. Burbank, Calif.: Riverwood Press, 1991.

Thomas, Tony. *Music for the Movies*, second edition. Los Angeles: Silman-James Press, 1997.

Thomas, Tony, and Aubrey Solomon. *The Films of 20th Century-Fox*. Secaucus, N.J.: Citadel Press, 1979.

Tietyen, David. *The Musical World of Disney*. Milwaukee, Wis.: Hal Leonard Publishing Corporation, 1990.

Tiomkin, Dimitri, and Prosper Buranelli. *Please Don't Hate Me*. Garden City, N.Y.: Doubleday & Company, 1959.

Walker, John, editor. *Halliwell's Filmgoer's and Video Viewer's Companion*, 10th edition. New York: HarperCollins Publishers, 1993.

Walker, John, editor. *Halliwell's Film Guide*. New York: HarperCollins Publishers, Inc., 1994.

Walker, Mark, editor. *Gramophone Film Music Good CD Guide*. Harrow, Middlesex, Great Britain: Gramophone Publications, 1997.

Warner, Alan. *Who Sang What on the Screen*. London: Angus & Robertson, Publishers, 1986.

Whitburn, Joel. *Pop Memories 1890-1954: The History of American Popular Music*. Menomonee Falls, Wisc.: Record Research Inc., 1986.

Whitburn, Joel. *The Billboard Book of Top 40 Hits*. New York: Billboard Publications, 1987.

Whitburn, Joel. *Top Pop Albums, 1955–1996*. Menomonee Falls, Wis.: Record Research Inc., 1996.

Wiley, Mason, and Damien Bona. *Inside Oscar: The Unofficial History of the Academy Awards*. New York: Ballantine Books, 1993.

Zinman, David. *Fifty Classic Motion Pictures*. New York: Crown Publishers, 1970.

Zinman, David. *Fifty From the '50s*. New Rochelle, N.Y.: Arlington House, 1979.

Zinman, David. *Fifty Grand Movies of the 1960s and 1970s*. New York: Crown Publishers, 1986.

These indexes are designed to help you find the music you're seeking. If you're interested in the music of a specific individual, the composer/songwriter index will guide you to the listings of recordings that contain music they have written for movies. If you're looking for the music of a specific film, the movie-title index will direct you to those references in the text.

Selected Composers and Songwriters

Index of Film Titles